The Most Valuable Asset of the Reich

The Most Valuable Asset of the Reich

A History of the German National Railway

Volume 2
1933–1945

by
Alfred C. Mierzejewski

The University of North Carolina Press
Chapel Hill and London

© 2000 The University of North Carolina Press
All rights reserved

Set in Minion multiple masters type
by Tseng Information Systems, Inc.
Manufactured in the United States of America

∞ The paper in this book meets the guidelines
for permanence and durability of the Committee
on Production Guidelines for Book Longevity of the
Council on Library Resources.

Library of Congress Cataloging-in-Publication Data
Mierzejewski, Alfred C.
The most valuable asset of the Reich : a history of the
   German National Railway / by Alfred C. Mierzejewski.
      p.   cm.
   Includes bibliographical references and index.
   Contents: v. 1. 1920–1932—
            v. 2. 1933–1945—
   1. Deutsche Reichsbahn (Germany)—History—20th century.
   2. Railroads and state—Germany—History—20th century.
   I. Title.   HE3080.D4M535   1999
   385'.06'543—dc21   98-53440
                        CIP
ISBN 0-8078-2496-8 (v. 1)
ISBN 0-8078-2574-3 (v. 2)

04 03 02 01 00   5 4 3 2 1

Contents

Preface   xi
Acknowledgments   xvii
Abbreviations   xix

1. The Coordination of the Reichsbahn, 1933-1939   1

2. The Reichsbahn in the Period of Rearmament, Job Creation, and Motorization, 1933-1939   25
    A. Passenger Service: The Flying Trains   25
    B. Freight Service and Modal Competition   39
    C. Finances, Raw Materials, and Manpower   57

3. The Reichsbahn in War and Holocaust, 1939-1945   77
    A. The Years of Conquest, 1939-1940   77
    B. The Attack on the Soviet Union and the Winter Crisis, 1941-1942   94
    C. The Nazi Racial Restructuring of Europe, 1941-1944   114
    D. The Years of Retreat, 1942-1944   129
    E. The End of the Third Reich, 1944-1945   158

Conclusions   162
Appendix   165
Notes   169
Bibliography   225
Index   241

Tables

2.1. Summary of Reichsbahn Operating Account, 1933-1939, 26
2.2. Profile of Reichsbahn Passenger Traffic and Operations, 1933-1939, 37
2.3. Trucks Owned by the Deutsche Reichsbahn, 1929-1938, 45
2.4. Tonnage Carried by Reichsbahn Truck Service, 1924-1938, 46
2.5. Reichsbahn Truck Service Net Ton-Kilometers, 1924-1938, 47
2.6. Profile of Reichsbahn Freight Traffic and Operations, 1933-1939, 52
2.7. Reichsbahn Rolling-Stock Acquisition Expenditures, 1933-1939, 71
2.8. Capital Budget of the Deutsche Reichsbahn, 1933-1939, 72
2.9. Reichsbahn Spending for Expansion of Capital Assets, 1933-1939, 73
2.10. Reichsbahn Rolling-Stock Acquisitions, 1930-1939, 74
2.11. Reichsbahn Track Renewal, 1933-1939, 75
3.1. Reichsbahn Vehicle Acquisition Expenditures, 1939-1944, 112
3.2. Reichsbahn Rolling-Stock Acquisitions, 1939-1944, 113
3.3. Profile of Reichsbahn Freight Traffic and Operations, 1939-1944, 144
3.4. Reichsbahn Freight Car Placings, 1937-1944, 145
3.5. Profile of Reichsbahn Passenger Traffic and Operations, 1939-1944, 146
3.6. DRB Personnel Strength, 1937-1944, 147
3.7. Capital Budget of the Deutsche Reichsbahn, 1939-1944, 154
3.8. Reichsbahn Spending for Expansion of Capital Assets, 1939-1944, 155
3.9. Summary of Reichsbahn Operating Account, 1939-1944, 156
3.10. Reichsbahn Track Renewal, 1939-1944, 157
A.1. Basic Characteristics of the Deutsche Reichsbahn, 165
A.2. Basic Operating Statistics of the Deutsche Reichsbahn, 166
A.3. Basic Financial Information Concerning the Deutsche Reichsbahn, 166
A.4. Operating Accidents of the Deutsche Reichsbahn, 167
A.5. Organization of the Deutsche Reichsbahn, 1 September 1937, 167

Maps and Illustrations

MAPS

1. Main Routes of the Deutsche Reichsbahn, 1940, xxii
2. The Reichsbahn Divisions, 1940, xxiii
3. DRB/Ostbahn Routes and Nazi Death Camps, 1942, 118

ILLUSTRATIONS

Julius Dorpmüller, with Adolf Hitler and Wilhelm Ohnesorge, 3
Albert Ganzenmüller, 104

Preface

This second volume of the history of the Deutsche Reichsbahn begins with the Nazi acquisition of power in January 1933 and continues to the end of World War II in May 1945. During this period, not only was the railway heavily involved in the Hitler regime's prosecution of aggressive war, it also formed an essential component of the machinery that made possible the Holocaust. January 1933 is a convenient point at which to begin since it marked a distinct caesura in the history of the Reichsbahn. The semiprivate Deutsche Reichsbahn-Gesellschaft, which responded at least in part to market signals, was transformed into a tool of the dirigiste state.

The Reichsbahn had been created through the amalgamation of the railways owned by Germany's states on 1 April 1920. In the wake of military defeat and the collapse of the imperial regime, the old state railways were unable to meet the transportation demands of the German nation and accumulated massive deficits. To overcome these problems, and to help hold the country together in the face of separatist sentiment in the Rhineland and Bavaria, the fledgling republican government unified Germany's state railways under its newly created Reich Transportation Ministry. The Reichsbahn struggled to overcome the problems of redundant personnel, surplus rolling stock and excess physical plant, the loss of territory, poor morale, and the wide variety of operating procedures and types of equipment inherited from its predecessors. The transportation minister and chief of the railway for most of the period 1920 to 1923, Wilhelm Groener, struggled manfully to overcome these problems. The inflation and political instability that gripped Germany during these years made it impossible for him to implement fully his plans to separate the Reichsbahn from the national budget, introduce new management procedures and personnel policies, and employ new technologies to gain operating efficiencies. Although he made significant progress, the problems of inefficient operations, poor morale, and a bloated capital budget remained when he left office in August 1923.

The collapse of the mark and the end of passive resistance against the French occupation of the Ruhr made possible the beginning of the effective reform of the Reichsbahn. The railway was removed from the general Reich budget and was made responsible for paying its operating and capital expenses from its own revenues. It rid itself of many of its excess employees and drastically reduced rolling-stock purchases and construction programs. The result was that the railway was able to balance its operating budget for the first time since it was created. The reorganization of the Reichsbahn was also an attempt to preempt the Allies in their effort to extract reparations from Germany through its railway. The gambit failed and Germany accepted the Dawes Plan in August 1924. The railway was reorganized again, this time as a state-owned, company-operated enterprise, the Deutsche Reichsbahn-Gesellschaft (DRG). Carl Friedrich von Siemens was appointed chairman of the railway's new board of directors. An experienced and wise businessman, Siemens steered the DRG along a course of financial responsibility, technological innovation, managerial reform, and independence from the government. He dominated the Reichsbahn until the early 1930s, when he was gradually overshadowed by the railway's general director, Julius Dorpmüller. The DRG met its obligations to Germany's commonweal economy by offering tariff discounts to various social groups and industries. However, it resisted spending on rolling-stock and capital projects that were not operationally necessary. The DRG introduced new locomotive and freight car designs as well as modern communications systems. The semiprivate DRG also reformed its financial and cost accounting methods under pressure from the Allied reparations authorities. Ludwig Homberger oversaw the effort, paying particular attention to the improvement of the railway's financial accounting and reporting procedures. Kurt Tecklenburg reformed the Reichsbahn's cost accounting apparatus. The result was that the DRG had one of the most sophisticated railway cost accounting and financial reporting systems in the world by 1930. Measures to streamline management procedures throughout the organization and to devolve authority to the lowest possible level increased operating efficiency and improved service. By limiting government influence on the DRG's activities, especially its capital spending, Siemens was able to overcome the problems remaining from the early 1920s and enable the railway to earn surpluses sufficiently large so that it could meet its reparations obligations without difficulty.

The Great Depression and the withdrawal of direct Allied supervision of the DRG due to implementation of the Young Plan in 1930 allowed the cabinet lead by Chancellor Heinrich Brüning to begin to restore the government's influence over the railway. Brüning used the DRG to fight the Depression by compelling it to employ people that it did not need, pressuring it to purchase rolling stock that was surplus to its requirements, and forcing it to engage in construction projects that were unnecessary. He also compelled the railway to reduce its prices and cut the pay of its employees.

During the Depression, the challenge posed by motor vehicles to the Reichsbahn's land transportation monopoly became more acute than ever before. The DRG responded by purchasing the Schenker company, a large freight forwarder, in 1931. The Reichsbahn organized a cartel around Schenker, called the Bahnspedition, intended to enable it to offer door-to-door service to shippers at competitive prices. Reacting to the outcry from the private truckers, other forwarders, and the motor vehicle industry, the government intervened to modify the Schenker cartel by issuing a regulation, in October 1931, that set maximum and minimum prices and allowed all truckers and forwarders to participate. In effect, the government adhered to its traditional policy of dividing markets and limiting price competition. Neither party was satisfied with this arrangement. Consequently, the issue of the relationship between rail and road in the domestic land freight market remained unresolved at the end of the Weimar period.

When Hitler established his government, the Reichsbahn was a reasonably efficient organization that was able to satisfy all of Germany's demands for rail transportation. It disposed over excess capacity throughout its organization, from personnel, to lines, to rolling stock. It delivered moderately priced, safe, punctual service to shippers and travelers alike. It carried a modest debt burden due to the conservative credit policies of Siemens and its board of directors.

The Reichsbahn was organized around a strong headquarters in Berlin, the Main Administration, which set policy for the entire railway. The operating divisions enjoyed considerable latitude in handling traffic. Each division was responsible for paying its allocated operating and capital expenses. The divisions ran trains and assigned freight cars and locomotives to them. Passenger cars were controlled by the headquarters in Berlin. Cooperation among the divisions was ensured by three Higher Operating Offices, each of which supervised a number of divisions. Maintenance of rolling stock was coordinated by separate but similar groupings of divisions. This combination of centralized policy making and decentralized implementation gave the Reichsbahn the flexibility to use its ample physical and human assets to meet any demand for rail transportation.

Turning to the years 1933 to 1945, this volume confirms the traditional view that rail transportation requirements, and therefore the Reichsbahn, were not adequately anticipated in the Nazi regime's war preparations.[1] However, this should not lead to the specious conclusion that they should have been. The only solution to Germany's transportation problems in September 1939 would have been for it to have abandoned its aggressive plans. Because this would have meant overthrowing Hitler, for which there was no majority in Germany, speculation about what might have happened if the Deutsche Reichsbahn had received more steel or been integrated into the strategic planning mechanism is pointless. It may be painful to German ears, but it was in fact preferable that the Reichsbahn did not take all of the preparatory steps imaginable during the 1930s because that prevented Nazi Germany from conquering even more territory than it did and hastened its defeat. This account shows that in spite of the disadvantages under which it labored, the Reichsbahn delivered a remarkably large volume of transportation service during the war. It was for this reason that it had no trouble moving 3 million Jews to their deaths.

This second volume, however, revises the accepted view of the Reichsbahn in three respects. It demonstrates how the Reichsbahn, rather than being the victim of governmental policy that forced it to subsidize the construction of the competing Autobahn network, attempted to seize control of motorization through the Autobahnen, but lost the political struggle to do so.[2] It also decisively revises the view that the Reichsbahn knew nothing about the Holocaust and was immune to the Nazi message.[3] While the vast majority of German railroaders at all levels focused on their jobs, the Reichsbahn, led by its general director, Julius Dorpmüller, made its peace with the Nazi Party during 1934 and participated fully and knowingly in the implementation of the Holocaust. Yet the examination of the behavior of the Reichsbahn in this darkest chapter of its history also makes clear that the argument made by Daniel Jonah Goldhagen, that all Germans desired the elimination by death of all Jews, is not justified by the evidence. Rather, it supports the contention of Rainer Baum that most Germans were indifferent to the fate of the Jews, concentrating instead on their own personal affairs and the course of the war.[4] It also undermines the traditional view of Julius Dorpmüller as a strong leader. The picture of Dorpmüller that emerges from the record is of a man who sought to retain his position as chief of the Reichsbahn at all costs, who was politically inept, who had only a rudimentary understanding of finances, who was interested primarily in running trains, and who took a paternalistic view of his employees. He adjusted his message to suit the government of the day and cared nothing about the fate of the Jews transported by his railway.[5]

The earlier chapters of this volume also make clear the extent to which the Nazi government abandoned the price mechanism as a means for allocating resources, resorting instead to state planning. The result was a series of mistakes in apportioning resources, notably to the Reichsbahn, the masking of Germany's inherent resource limitations in comparison with its potential opponents, and the steady increase of powerful inflationary pressures. The section on World War II offers detailed information on how the Nazi government sought to exploit the economies of the occupied territories, and how ineffectively it actually did so. It also provides the first comprehensive account in English of the operations of the Ostbahn. Finally, it gives the most complete account yet of the Reichsbahn's involvement in the Holocaust and provides new details about the number of Jews transported to their deaths by rail.

During the early Nazi period, the Reichsbahn introduced technologically innovative high-speed passenger trains that gave it an aura of modernity and reflected positively on the Nazi regime. The description of the gestation of the "Flying Trains" makes clear that they were conceived and developed before the advent of the Hitler government in response to market signals that were abhorred by the Nazis. Credit for this major advance in passenger service, therefore, must be given to the market-oriented DRG, not to the dirigiste Nazi regime. Moreover, Hitler's ambitious rearmament plans prevented the completion of the high-speed passenger train net planned by the Reichsbahn. At the same time that the railway introduced this technological innovation, the Nazis within the Reichsbahn Main Administration gutted one of the most important achievements of the DRG, the operating cost accounting system. The man who supervised the effort to reform the Reichsbahn's accounting practices, Ludwig Homberger, was humiliated and ultimately driven from his post by Nazi racial legislation. This account makes unmistakably clear that the racial laws were implemented by Nazis within the Reichsbahn in collaboration with its general director, Julius Dorpmüller. Nothing better symbolizes the departure from rational market economics, democratic politics, and respect for human rights within the Reichsbahn than the shabby treatment meted out to Homberger, one of the Reichsbahn's most gifted and loyal servants. It was symptomatic of the degeneration of German public morals and a portent of much worse that was to come. It also underscores how the Reichsbahn was at the center of events and reminds us once again just how important its story is to understanding modern German history in general.

This volume incorporates a wealth of new information drawn primarily from archival materials and contemporary industry publications, most of which have never been cited before. The most important sources of that information were, again, the Reichsbahn's own files preserved, at the time that this book was prepared, at the Bundesarchiv, Koblenz, and the Bundesarchiv Abteilung III, Aussenstelle Coswig (Anhalt). These very extensive and extremely revealing records are now housed at the new Bundesarchiv facility at Berlin-Lichterfelde. The documents of the Zentrale Stelle der Landesjustizverwaltungen in Ludwigsburg, the Staatsanwaltschaft in Düsseldorf, and the former Berlin Document Center are essential for setting the record straight concerning the Reichsbahn's participation in the Holocaust. The papers of Carl Friedrich von Siemens kept by the Siemens-Archiv in Munich include new information concerning Siemens's reaction to the attempt by the Nazis to coordinate the DRG and especially its board of directors. The military records held by the Bundesarchiv-Militärarchiv in Freiburg-im-Breisgau provide valuable information on the relationship between the DRG and the military during the Weimar years and on the Reichsbahn's role in supporting the Wehrmacht's field operations during the war. Finally, contemporary industry periodicals, especially the excellent publications produced by the Reichsbahn itself, also provide useful information. Not surprisingly, their value declined with the beginning of the war.

In sum, this second volume, as was the case with the first, is intended to be more than the story of a railway. It provides a record of the major events in the Reichsbahn's history and offers new insights concerning the political and economic affairs of the Third Reich.

Acknowledgments

This second volume of the history of the Reichsbahn, like the first, could not have been written without the extensive use of documentary evidence held in archives. Access to these materials was made possible by the helpful staffs of these institutions. I would like to begin, once again, by thanking the outstanding personnel of the Bundesarchiv, Koblenz, for their excellent support of my efforts during my stays with them. I would especially like to acknowledge the help of Dr. Rest, Herr Scharmann, and Frau Jacobi. At the Bundesarchiv Aussenstelle in Coswig (Anhalt), I received the best help imaginable from that institution's director, Frau Wessling, and her two skilled, energetic, and friendly subordinates, Frau Redlich and Frau Wittkowsky. The latter two made my stay especially pleasant and helped me find documents that I would otherwise have overlooked. In Potsdam, and later in Berlin-Lichterfelde, I was assisted by Herr Roeske and his staff. I was also ably supported by the staff of the Bundesarchiv-Militärarchiv in Freiburg-im-Breisgau. Hans-Liudiger Dienel and Helmuth Trischler provided me with a warm welcome and expert assistance at the Deutsches Museum in Munich. Herr Hartmut Korn provided me with the benefit of his extensive expertise and energetic help during my stay at the Bayerisches Hauptstaatsarchiv. Professor Dr. Wilfried Feldenkirchen and Herr Bien helped me with the Carl Friedrich von Siemens papers at the Siemens-Archiv. Monika Deniffel made my work at the Institut für Zeitgeschichte productive and pleasant. I would like to thank Herr Franz Josef von Kempis for allowing me to see the von Eltz-Rübenach documents in Pulheim. Willi Dressen was especially helpful during my stay at the Zentrale Stelle der Landesjustizverwaltungen in Ludwigsburg. I would like to thank Herr Ernst in the office of the Leitende Oberstaatsanwalt in Düsseldorf for allowing me to see the Ganzenmüller prosecution documents in his possession. I would like to extend my special thanks to Professor Doctor Wolfgang Scheffler for allowing me to quote from his statistical compilations included in this collection.

I profited greatly from the assistance given to me by the staff of the Staatsbibliothek in Berlin, the staff of the Rheinische Landesbibliothek in Koblenz, and the staff of the library of the Universität Dortmund, home of the collection of the Deutsche Gesellschaft für Eisenbahngeschichte. At the archive of the Reichsbahndirektion Berlin, I was assisted by Frau Christa Müller, its chief, and Frau Vera Schmäh. Finally, I would again like to extend my very special thanks to Alfred Gottwaldt of the Deutsches Technikmuseum in Berlin, who not only gave me the benefit of his extensive knowledge of the Reichsbahn but also helped me in many other important ways.

In the United States, I was assisted by George D. Arnold and Robert Forman of the American University Archives. I received especially valuable help from the staff of the library of the University of Illinois at Urbana-Champaign. I would like to thank Henry Mayer and the staff of the United States Holocaust Museum Archive for helping me during my visit there. Finally, but certainly not least, I would like to thank Robert Burkhardt and his staff at the Athens State University library.

Visiting these archives would have been impossible without the help of the Fulbright Commission in Bonn, the German Academic Exchange Service in New York, and the National Endowment for the Humanities in Washington, D.C. I am extremely grateful to all of them.

I would like to thank my wife, Carolann, for her understanding of my long absences, both physical and spiritual.

Abbreviations

The following abbreviations are used in the text. For abbreviations used in the notes, see pages 169–70.

AG	Aktiengesellschaft (joint-stock company)
BBC	Brown, Boveri et Cie
Beko	Betriebskostenrechnung (Operating Cost Account)
DIHT	Deutscher Industrie- und Handelstag (German Chamber of Industry and Commerce)
DRB	Deutsche Reichsbahn, 1937–45 (German National Railway)
DRG	Deutsche Reichsbahn-Gesellschaft, 1924–37 (German National Railway Company)
DVKB	Deutsche Verkehrs-Kredit-Bank (German Transportation Credit Bank)
EBD	Eisenbahndirektion (Railway Division)
ETRA	Eisenbahntransportabteilung (Railway Transport Section)
EVA	Eisenbahn-Verkehrsmittel-AG (Railway Transportation Device Company)
GB	Generalbevollmächtigter (General Plenipotentiary)
Gbl/GBL	Generalbetriebsleitung (General Operating Office)
Gedob	Generaldirektion der Ostbahn (General Directorate of the East Railway)
GV	Gruppenverwaltung (group administration)
GVD	Generalverkehrsdirektion (General Transportation Directorate)
GVT	Gesellschaft für Verkehrstechnik (Transportation Technology Company)
Hafraba	Verein zur Vorbereitung der Autostraße Hansestädte-Frankfurt-Basel (Association for the Preparation of the Highway from the Hansa Cities to Frankfurt and Basel)

HBD	Haupteisenbahndirektion (Main Railway Division)
HTK	Heerestransportkommission (Army Transportation Commission)
HVD	Hauptverkehrsdirektion (Main Transportation Division)
kph	kilometers per hour
LCL	less-than-carload freight (Stückgut)
NS	Nederlandse Spoorwegen (Netherlands National Railways)
NSBO	National Sozialistische Betriebszellenorganisation (National Socialist Factory Cell Organization)
NSDAP	Nationalsozialistische Deutsche Arbeiterpartei (National Socialist German Workers' Party)
ÖBB	Österreichische Bundesbahnen (Austrian Federal Railways)
Obl	Oberbetriebsleitung (Higher Operating Office)
Öffa	Deutsche Gesellschaft für öffentliche Arbeiten (German Company for Public Works)
OKH	Oberkommando des Heeres (High Command of the Army)
OKW	Oberkommando der Wehrmacht (High Command of the Armed Forces)
RAB	Reichsautobahn-Gesellschaft (National Highway Company)
RBD	Reichsbahndirektion (National Railway Division)
RKB	Reichs-Kraftwagen-Betriebsverband (Reich Truck Operating Association)
RM	Reichsmark
RSHA	Reichssicherheitshauptamt (Reich Security Main Office)
RVD	Reichsverkehrsdirektion (Reich Transportation Division)
RVM	Reichsverkehrsministerium (Reich Transportation Ministry)
RWKS	Rheinisch-Westfälisches Kohlen-Syndikat (Rhenish Westphalian Coal Syndicate)
RZA	Reichsbahnzentralamt (Reichsbahn Central Office)
RZM	Reichsbahnzentralamt für Maschinenbau (Reichsbahn Central Office for Mechanical Engineering)
RZR	Reichsbahn-Zentralamt für Rechnungswesen (Reichsbahn Central Office for Accounting)
SA	Sturmabteilung (Storm Troopers)
SNCB	Societé Nationale des Chemins de Fer Belges (Belgian National Railway)
SNCF	Societé Nationale des Chemins de Fer Français (French National Railway)
SPD	Sozialdemokratische Partei Deutschlands (Social Democratic Party of Germany)
SS	Schutzstaffel (Protection Squad)
SSW	Siemens-Schuckert-Werke

SVT	Schnellverbrennungstriebwagen (high-speed internal-combustion motor car)
Transchef	Chef des Transportwesens (chief of military transportation)
Wumag	Waggon- und Maschinenbau AG, Görlitz
WVD	Wehrmachtverkehrsdirektion (Armed Forces Transportation Division)
ZVL	Zentralverkehrsleitstelle (Central Transportation Directorate)

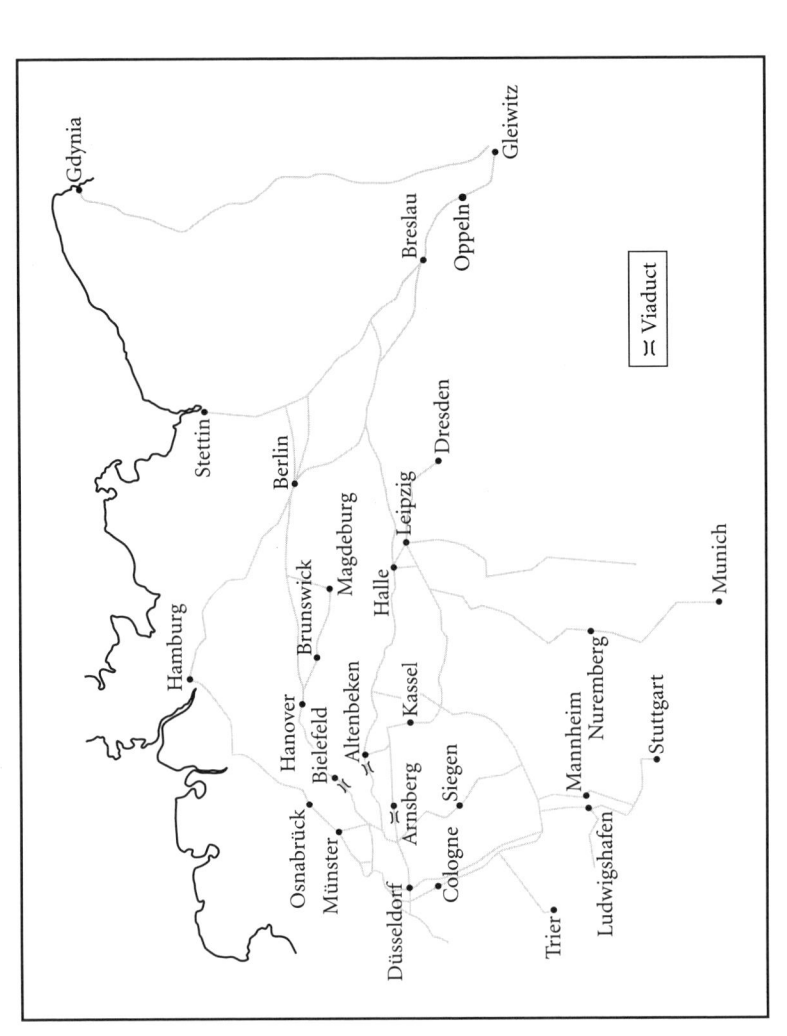

Map 1. Main Routes of the Deutsche Reichsbahn, 1940

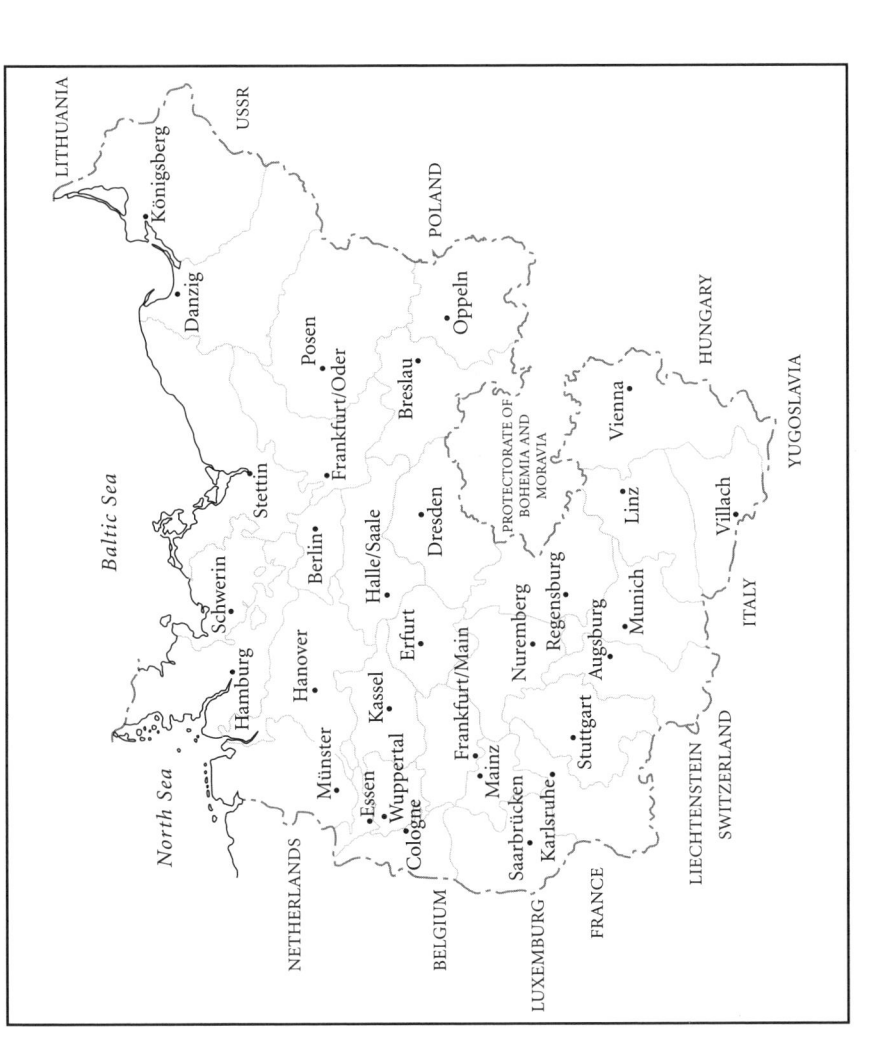

Map 2. The Reichsbahn Divisions, 1940

The Most Valuable Asset of the Reich

Chapter One

The Coordination of the Reichsbahn, 1933–1939

In August 1932 Carl Stieler told Adolf von Batocki, his colleague on the Reichsbahn board of directors, that he expected that Hitler would end the Reichsbahn's autonomy and dramatically change its affairs.[1] With his long experience in government, Stieler was completely correct, yet he was unable to prevent the changes that he feared. The Reichsbahn's relationship with the Nazi Party was ambivalent from the outset. The railway considered itself an apolitical, technical, service-oriented enterprise. Yet its actions were in fact highly charged with political significance. The Reichsbahn's view of itself would lead it to fashion a compromise with the new national leadership that would ensure it a considerable measure of internal autonomy while serving the regime's expansionist and racist ends.

In its general propaganda, the Nazi Party had been scathing in its criticism of the Deutsche Reichsbahn-Gesellschaft (German National Railway Company, or DRG), referring to it as the "Dawes Railway," complaining that Germany's socialized railway was under the control of American banks and stock exchange Jews. That did not stop the party from attempting to gain support from among Reichsbahn employees. Indeed, such propaganda may have been advantageous for it to do so, given the anticapitalist, anti-Western views of many DRG officials. After the abortive Beer Hall Putsch of November 1923, and after Hitler's shift to a strategy of gaining power through electoral means, the party canvassed support among various occupational groups, including railroaders. It won some initial success in Saxony in 1925, when its first regional cell was founded by a Reichsbahn official in the town of Garbolzum. In 1926 the local party branch in Göttingen was led by a locomotive engineer. One of his two secretaries was a fireman. In 1928 the party began a concerted effort to increase its following among union members. To that end, it created the National Socialist Factory Cell Organization (NSBO). By November 1930 the NSBO had cells in 203 Reichsbahn offices and operating facilities, a small number compared with the overall size of the railway. The NSBO won only 3.5 percent of the total vote cast in March 1931 works council elections, though it gained a substantially greater following among the DRG's officials. Twenty percent of the votes cast at Reichsbahndirektion (RBD) headquarters went to Nazi candidates. Clearly, the DRG's tenured officials, frustrated at what they perceived to be the disadvantages that they suffered compared with their colleagues in Reich service, turned to the Nazis more often than the workers. Indeed, at least in Franconia, the party leadership considered DRG officials to be sympathetic to its message.[2]

Officially, the Reichsbahn's leadership forbade subversive political activity on the part of its employees. This position was stated clearly and frequently and was implemented. It applied to all parties, the SPD, Communists, and the Nazis alike. During its meeting on 23 September 1930, the board of directors discussed what stance it should take on the approaching works council elections in light of the intense Nazi propaganda. The general director of the DRG, Julius Dorpmüller, stated that "the Reichsbahn-Gesellschaft, as an unpolitical body, must refuse to take any position concerning legal campaign positions. Of course, no political agitation of any kind will be tolerated during work hours."[3] In line with this policy, the Personnel Section of the Main Administration issued a directive forbidding political activities while on duty. It specifically forbade the distribution of political literature of any kind at any time, even during breaks.[4] Shortly afterward, a case arose concerning agitation for the Nazi Party by a DRG official who was a Nazi county leader. After an initial warning, he was punished by a Reichsbahn disciplinary court with a transfer. He continued his political activities, however, and was fired as a result. The disciplinary court refused his appeal, stating that "activity by an official for the National Socialist German Workers Party is a violation of service regulations, because it seeks to overthrow the existing form of government through the use of force."[5]

The matter of political agitation and the reliability of its employees came up before the board again in March 1931. Mattäus Herrmann, one of the labor representatives on the board, proposed saving money by reducing the budget for the Bahnschutz, implying that it was filled with Nazis. Dorpmüller insisted that the Bahnschutz was necessary, adding that "the Main Administration will act severely against any political agitation on the job."[6] Herrmann returned to the Bahnschutz issue during the board's discussion of the closing of RBD Magdeburg in November 1932. He suggested that political considerations be used to choose who would be allowed to join this voluntary, paramilitary orga-

Julius Dorpmüller, Reich transportation minister, 1937–45, and general director of the Deutsche Reichsbahn, 1926–45 (left), with Adolf Hitler (center) and Reich postal minister Wilhelm Ohnesorge (right) in Berlin on 2 February 1937. Courtesy of Alfred Gottwaldt.

nization. Paul Wolf, chief of the Administrative Section, responded forcefully that the "Main Administration would not tolerate the selection of employees for the Bahnschutz according to party political viewpoints."[7] Herrmann clearly feared that the Bahnschutz would be used by the Nazis to subvert the Reichsbahn. Ironically, the Nazis considered the Bahnschutz to be a bastion of Social Democratic sentiment.

The DRG's relationship with the Nazis arose as a matter of controversy in another connection as well. The Nazi Party hired special trains from the Reichsbahn to transport its members and sympathizers to rallies in various parts of Germany. The Weimar government and many of the state administrations sought to prevent it from doing so. The DRG, however, citing its common-carrier responsibilities, denied that it could refuse the Nazis access to its services. In June 1931 both the Reich and the government of the state of Prussia attempted to stop the Reichsbahn from operating special trains that had been arranged by the Nazis to bring members to a Hitler rally at Cloppenburg. The DRG had granted them the usual 40 percent discount, hoping to keep the traffic away from bus operators. Ultimately, the two governments had to throw up their hands in despair because the Reichsbahn had the final say in the matter.[8]

Clearly, in the years leading up to the Nazi rise to power, the DRG had treated the NSDAP as it had the SPD and other parties that it considered subversive. However, the Reichsbahn's employees had been no more and no less susceptible to the Nazi message than other Germans. Nevertheless, since 1945 a myth about the nature of the Reichsbahn's relationship with the Nazi Party and the government of the Third Reich has been propagated by former Reichsbahner. In a contribution to an abortive official history of the Reichsbahn during World War II that was planned during the 1950s, Günter Kausche, who served in the Reich Transportation Ministry (Reichsverkehrsministerium, or RVM) during the war, contended that until late in the war, the Nazis had little influence on the Reichsbahn. The railroaders had concentrated on their technical responsibilities and avoided politics.[9] Another author who contributed to the same project, Franz Bruckauf, who was assigned to RBD Essen, claimed that the party had usually been unable to influence hiring and firing decisions.[10] As late as 1981, Anton Joachimsthaler, who was fifteen years old when the war ended and was an official with the German Federal Railway, repeated the myth that the Reichsbahn had closed itself to political influences and concentrated on its operational responsibilities.[11] In fact, the Reichsbahn was coordinated (*gleichgeschaltet*) like every other organization in Germany under the Third Reich.

Soon after Hitler became chancellor, Nazi political organizations were created in the Reichsbahn. The Fachschaft (Professional Association) Reichsbahn in the National Federation of German Officials (Reichsbund der Deutschen Beamten) was formed, and the Fachgruppe Reichsbahn was created in the German Labor Front (Deutsche Arbeitsfront) for the workers. In addition, an emissary of the Hitler Youth was assigned to the RVM.[12] The Fachschaft Reichsbahn was especially vehement in its attacks on the Reichsbahn leadership. On 20 March 1933 it made twenty-three demands for changes in the DRG. They centered on removing Jews and leftists from responsible positions and replacing them with Nazis and alleged cases of corruption.[13] The DRG ignored these demands. Consequently, the Fachschaft informed the state secretary in the chancellor's office, Hans Lammers, that the DRG had not conformed to the Nazi revolution. It complained that many democrats and Jews remained in its upper leadership, especially its publicity chief, Hans Baumann, and the head of its financial section, Ludwig Homberger, and demanded a quick rectification of these problems.[14] The government took no action, so the fanatics took matters into their own hands. At 10:30 A.M. on 6 April 1933, twenty SA men broke into the headquarters building of the DRG and approached Alfred Beyer, who headed an office that handled personnel matters relating to the DRG's leading officials. They demanded that the entire board of directors be dismissed, all Jews and Freemasons be removed, and the Social Democrats be cleaned out of the Bahnschutz. They also sought the cancellation of all contracts with Jewish firms and the laying off of employees over sixty-five and all women to make way for young men.[15] On the following day, SA men invaded the offices of the German Transportation Credit Bank (Deutsche Verkehrs-Kredit-Bank, or DVKB) and made similar demands.[16]

The Fachschaft assembled a list of people whom it wanted expelled from the DRG. Among the board members it included Carl Bergmann, because he opposed Hjalmar Schacht, the minister of economics and chief of the Reichsbank; Herrmann and Ernst Kaiser, because they were union leaders; Paul Silverberg, because he was a "half Jew"; and Vitus von Hertel and Franz Honold, because they represented the Catholic Church and particularist interests. The Nazis also demanded that Homberger should go because he was a "baptized Jew"; Beyer, because he was a Freemason; Wolf, because he was seen as sympathetic to the French; and Karl Heiges, the chief of the Bahnschutz, because he supposedly leaned toward the SPD. They also called for the dismissal of Marcell Holzer, the head of Schenker, because he was a Jew.[17] The Reich government took no action itself.[18] Instead, the matter was handled internally by the Reichsbahn in coordination with the party.

The Hitler government created a legal basis for the exclusion of officials from employment in its bureaucracy and the Reichsbahn with the promulgation of the Law for the Reconstruction of the Professional Civil Service on 7 April 1933.[19] Soon after, the DRG ordered the divisions to suspend all contracts with Jewish firms and to avoid doing business with them in the future, and issued a preliminary order to remove Jewish and leftist officials from its ranks.[20] It issued a definitive order for the implementation of the expulsions on 14 June 1933. All Communists would be removed immediately. All Jews would be retired with the exception of those who had entered the civil service before 1 August 1914 or who had served at the front during World War I. Non-Aryans were defined as those with at least one non-Aryan parent, especially Jews. All officials who had been hired after 1 August 1914 were required to prove their Aryan descent by completing a questionnaire and submitting supporting documents. The actual dismissals would be conducted by Nazi representatives, who would be placed throughout the Reichsbahn.[21] The application of this directive was discussed by the new personnel committee that was attached to the board of directors in July. It accepted the provisions of the directive and added to them that the Jews who were retained due to their early entry into the civil service or the military would be transferred from positions in which they would come in contact with the public or handle personnel, financial, or military matters. The personnel officers of the divisions would be checked to determine their racial and political backgrounds, their popularity with the employees, and their ages. If they were found wanting in any of these categories, they would be replaced by Nazis.[22] The full board approved these guidelines on 13 July 1933.[23]

On 15 May 1933 Rudolf Hess, Hitler's personal secretary and head of the Nazi Party Chancellery, created the Führerstab Reichsbahn as a subsection of the Liaison Staff (Verbindungsstab) of the party. It was charged with investigating the criticisms that had been made of the Reichsbahn's leadership. Named to chair it was Wilhelm Kleinmann. Born in Barmen on 29 May 1876, Kleinmann had served with the German field railways on the eastern front during World War I. After the war, he had been assigned to Eisenbahndirektion (EBD) Kattowitz in Upper Silesia and had participated in the struggle against the Polish acquisition of that territory. He then became the chief of Obl West in Essen. On 1 June 1933 he was named president of RBD Essen. Kleinmann had been mentioned by the Fachschaft on 6 April as one of the Reichsbahn officials whom it trusted. He began his association with the Nazi Party during the mid-1920s when he became transportation adviser to its regional organization in Essen. He joined the party on 1 October 1931, after it had won its first major electoral success, but before its control of the government was assured. He was not an old fighter, but his nationalist credentials were solid and he had joined the Nazis while it was still risky to do so, particularly in light of the Reichsbahn's explicit policies condemning political agitation.[24] On 25 June 1933 Kleinmann replaced Wilhelm Weirauch as vice general director of the DRG and assumed control of its personnel section.[25] Kleinmann was extremely energetic and ambitious. He was completely devoted to the railway and hoped to restore it to what he considered its proper position in German society, and return Germany to its former position among nations through the National Socialist revolution.[26]

Kleinmann very quickly assembled the Führerstab so that it could begin the business of cleansing the Reichsbahn of undesirable elements. He named as his secretary Gerhard Sommer, the personal assistant and friend of Dorpmüller, who had joined the party on 1 May 1933. Among the other members was Alfred Prang of the Finance Section.[27] The staff named representatives at each divisional headquarters who were relieved of their normal administrative duties so that they could devote their undivided efforts to rooting enemies of the regime out of the DRG.

The coordination of the board began on 3 May when Carl Friedrich von Siemens, its chairman, was forced to announce that Herrmann would not attend that day's board meeting because he had been arrested. He also stated that two other members, Honold, who had represented Baden, and Johannes Welker, who had represented inland waterway interests, had resigned.[28] At the end of the month, Franz Willuhn of the Reich Chancellery consulted the state secretary in the RVM, Gustav Koenigs, concerning what should be done about Siemens. Koenigs recommended leaving him as chairman of the board for the present. He praised Siemens for having kept the Reichsbahn's debt low and indicated that he could be replaced more conveniently from a political standpoint in the course of the usual rotation of board members at the end of 1933. Moreover, his continued presence would lend stability to the Reichsbahn and thereby make it easier to bring Nazis into its organization. Koenigs did agree that some members of the board should be replaced, though he did not think that they could simply be dismissed.[29]

While these preparations were under way, the street agitation directed particularly against Siemens, Dorpmüller, and Homberger continued. The Liaison Staff of the Nazi Party finally intervened to stop it. It informed the Fachschaft that Hitler had personally forbidden any further attacks on Dorpmüller. While on a train trip, Hitler had been informed that a massive demonstration was taking place outside the Main Administration in Voß Street. He stopped his train and telephoned the leaders of the rally to express his confidence in Dorpmüller and told them to call off the affair.[30] Siemens became concerned that the continued attacks, despite Hitler's expression of support, would destroy the authority of the Reichsbahn's leadership. He suggested that some old party members be taken on the board to calm the employees. He also thought that he should be replaced as chairman by a party member.[31] On 28 June Hitler discussed the matter of the Reichsbahn board with Reich transportation minister Peter Paul Freiherr von Eltz-Rübenach and Lammers, and decided that a complete reformation of the board at that moment was not possible. Instead, it would be transformed gradually over the next few months.[32]

The coordination of the board continued at its meeting on 4 July 1933. The three members who had either resigned or been removed for political reasons in May were replaced by Albert Pietzsch, a businessman from Bavaria; Kurt Freiherr von Schröder, a banker from Cologne who had helped Hitler become chancellor; and Karl Renninger, the mayor of Mannheim—all Nazis.[33] The transformation then proceeded behind the scenes over the next few months.

Coordination

One of the first targets was Vitus von Hertel, the representative of Bavaria, who was considered too old and a particularist by the youth-oriented, centralizing Nazis. The Führerstab Reichsbahn applied pressure on the Bavarian government to convince Hertel to relinquish his seat voluntarily.[34] The regime in Munich readily complied. Hertel submitted his resignation on 6 July after returning from the board meeting that had just ended in Berlin.[35] The Reich government allowed the Bavarian government a free hand in choosing whom it wished to replace von Hertel, though it asked that he be a Nazi businessman.[36]

Soon after the July board meeting, Kleinmann moved to exclude Silverberg. Immediately after the gathering, Silverberg had asked the RVM if he should leave the board. Eltz replied that he saw no need for him to do so. Then, on 10 July, Kleinmann wrote Eltz, asking that Silverberg be requested to resign so that a Nazi labor representative could be named in his place. On 28 July Eltz informed Silverberg that it was time for him to vacate his seat. Eltz apparently still doubted whether Silverberg should resign and inquired at the Reich Chancellery about Hitler's views on the matter. Hitler said that he took no interest in the Silverberg case. Against this background of moral indecisiveness, Silverberg relinquished his post on 2 August 1933.[37] Siemens wrote him on the following day to express his sympathy, telling Silverberg that he did not approve of what was taking place on the board and that he hoped to leave it as soon as possible. He predicted that a "debacle" would happen soon.[38] Despite his feelings, Siemens chaired a special meeting of the board on 10 August during which he announced the departures of Kaiser, von Hertel, and Silverberg and their replacement by three more Nazis. Georg Körner was the chief of the German Workers Association for Public Enterprises and the education officer of the County Factory Cell Organization in the NSDAP; Rolf Reiner was a Bavarian official and an officer in the Liaison Staff of the Nazi Party; and Erich Köhler was a factory owner and retired army captain.[39] Two additional changes came at the regular rotation of board members in December 1933. The Ruhr industrialist Peter Klöckner resigned, being replaced by Gustav Krupp von Bohlen and Halbach, chairman of the supervisory board of the Krupp steel firm; and Hermann Schmitz of IG Farben was replaced by Fritz Todt, the chief of the Nazi Party's office for technology and Hitler's plenipotentiary for roads.[40] Since May 1933, eight members of the board had been replaced by men who were either members of the Nazi Party or who sympathized with it.

Surprisingly, at least from his standpoint, Siemens was renominated by the government as a member of the board and, in January 1934, was reelected as chair.[41] Yet the need to maintain appearances, primarily to support Schacht's international financial maneuvers, diminished by the end of 1934. Seven members of the board were due to be replaced. The government decided that Siemens would be supplanted by the state secretary of the RVM, Gustav Koenigs. Siemens had disapproved of the racist steps taken by the Nazi regime, particularly with the Reichsbahn. But he, like so many other bourgeois Germans, had been unable to bring himself to take a clear moral stand against them. In May 1933 he had participated in a private discussion at the home of the Jewish banking family Mendelsohn concerning the anti-Semitic policies of the Hitler government. Siemens doubted that much could be done because of the wide popularity enjoyed by the Nazis. All that he could do was recommend drafting a memorandum that would demonstrate that the Jews had helped rather than harmed Germany, in the hope that this rational approach would convince the German public.[42] When it became clear to him that he would finally relinquish the post that he had tried to leave in 1930, he told Krupp that by leaving the board, he was rendering the Reichsbahn the best service that he was still capable of giving. He made no mention of the exclusion of the members of the board or DRG employees because of their race.[43] Siemens also turned to his old friend Paul Silverberg at this moment. He wrote Silverberg that his time had run out and that he was glad to be leaving, mentioning only that he had been unhappy because he had been forced to tolerate management mistakes.[44] Clearly, Siemens had developed an emotional attachment to the Reichsbahn. This, along with his views as a businessman and his patriotism, prevented him from acting against, and possibly even seeing the full implications of, the injustices that the Nazis had inflicted on Silverberg and other members of the Reichsbahn.

With Siemens's departure, seven new members of the board were named. Koenigs assumed the chair. He was not a member of the Nazi Party but was quite prepared to lead the Reichsbahn in conformance with its desires. He was technically competent but lacked the moral authority necessary to counter the use of the railway by the regime for its purposes.[45] The last of the original board members to leave was Carl Bergmann. He died in September 1935 and was replaced by the leader of the Nazi Party's office for tourism and travel, Hermann Esser.[46] Only Hermann Münchmeyer and Tilo von Wilmowsky remained from the Weimar era. Both accommodated themselves to the new circumstances until 1942.

The transformation of the board facilitated the coordination of the Reichsbahn's tenured officials. This took three forms: the exclusion of politically and racially undesirable individuals, the preferred hiring and promotion of Nazis, and the absorption of the officials' unions into the NSDAP's organizations. The process of replacing the unions with nazified bodies began immediately after Hitler came to power. The Fachschaft quickly emerged as the Nazi organization that claimed to speak for the officials. In April, Gottfried Feder, head of the Subcommission for Business, Technology, and Job Creation at the NSDAP headquarters in Munich, convinced the powerful Union of German Locomotive Engineers to join the Nazi Reich Association of German Technology.[47] At the end of June, the works councils of the officials were abolished.[48] Yet even these steps were insufficient for Kleinmann and the Nazi enthusiasts in the Reichsbahn. On 3 July 1933 Kleinmann sent a letter to Siemens demanding that the board take decisive steps to nazify the railway's work force at its meeting the next day. In particular, he told Siemens that pay would have to be raised for officials and workers alike, SA and SS members would have to be given jobs, and the board would have to be restructured and the Main Administration aryanized. Finally, Nazis would have to take control of the personnel offices of the divisions.[49] As we have seen, Siemens was not disposed to stand in Kleinmann's way. The board decided to form a special personnel committee composed of its new Nazi members Pietzsch, Schröder, Renninger, and Stieler.[50] Kleinmann, in his capacity as assistant general director, de facto chief of the Personnel Section of the Main Administration, and head of the Führerstab Reichsbahn, was named the committee's chairman. Dorpmüller attended the panel's meetings and played a prominent role in its discussions.

In October many older members of the Main Administration and the division managements were retired. Ernst Spiro, chief of the Reichsbahn Central Office for Purchasing, who was Jewish, was excluded as part of this action.[51] By the board's meeting at the end of November 1933, Kleinmann could report that of the upper officials 21 were retired due to age and 102 were transferred to new jobs. Among the middle and lower officials, 182 men were either transferred or retired. A further 280 cases were still under investigation. Among the officials transferred, 25 were divisional personnel officers who lost their positions to Nazis. In light of the agitation and excitement provoked by the Fachschaft, one is impressed by the small number of officials who were actually affected by the nazification effort, only 0.07 percent of all officials and 4 percent of the upper officials, according to Kleinmann's calculations.[52] Most of the remaining cases were resolved by September 1934. Of the 60 personnel officers at divisional and other headquarters, 46 were changed. More than a third of the people assigned to the Reichsbahn's personnel offices, chiefs and subordinates, were now Nazis.[53]

The small number of officials who lost their jobs gives no indication of the pain inflicted on those who were affected or of the extreme discomfort of those whose futures were not decided in 1933. Probably the most prominent of the individual cases was Ludwig Homberger, the chief of the Finance Section in the DRG Main Administration, who had been born into a Jewish family. He had married a German woman and become a Lutheran to please her. He had served the Royal Bavarian Railway and then the Reichsbahn loyally and with exceptional competence. He had proved his patriotism by serving as an adviser to German delegations to reparations talks, helping them lower and ultimately cancel the DRG's annuities. Because of his competence, because he was well liked, and because from the Nazi racist perspective he remained a Jew, even though he had changed his religion, Homberger immediately became an issue to be handled by the board's special personnel committee. It discussed his future at its meetings of 17 July and 9 August 1933. Stieler attended both meetings and Siemens the latter. The committee decided to retain Homberger because of his exceptional expertise and the Reichsbahn's difficult financial situation.[54] Homberger remained in his post as head of the Finance Section and continued to brief the board. However, he no longer appeared in public representing the Reichsbahn. Although no announcement was made, Alfred Prang replaced Homberger in the public's eye.

Homberger kept his job for the time being, though under degrading circumstances. Others left immediately. Wilhelm Weirauch, who was perceived by the workers as their enemy due to his role in the labor contract negotiations of the 1920s, was accused by the Fachschaft of being sympathetic to the SPD and anti-Nazi. Siemens was able to move Weirauch out of the way by appointing him head of the Reichsbahn's Main Auditing Office when Kleinmann replaced him as vice general director.[55] Dorpmüller's chief of publicity, Hans Baumann, was also moved out of the Main Administration. Because Baumann had fought at the front during World War I, he could not be dismissed, even though the Nazis considered him a racial Jew. Consequently, he was provided a job in the Reich Office for German Travel with the approval of Goebbels.[56]

The Reichsbahn's subsidiaries were also nazified and aryanized. Jews were removed from the leadership of the DVKB in May and June 1933.[57] At Schenker, an initial wave of dismissals occurred in June 1933 during which the firm's director, Marcell Holzer, was discharged. In November 1933 the Reichswehr complained that there were still too many Jews in the company's management for it to be trusted with foreign business. Dorpmüller responded that removing the remaining Jews from Schenker would cause business difficulties in eastern and southeastern Europe. He promised to make changes in the forwarder's management when the relationship between the Reichsbahn and trucks was resolved. Hitler's economic adviser, Wilhelm Keppler, raised the matter again in March 1934. Once again, Dorpmüller was able to put off any changes. Ultimately, these employees had to go as well. Incredibly, Holzer fought for his due. He brought suit against the DRG for damages in a court in New York State, which found in his favor. To avoid adverse publicity, Dorpmüller chose to settle on Holzer's terms.[58]

The third way in which the Personnel Committee's action affected the Reichsbahn's officials was preferred hiring. In August 1933 the Main Administration announced a policy of hiring members of the SA, SS, and Stahlhelm before other applicants for positions as both officials and workers. The Reichsbahn expanded these preferences in January 1934, when it announced that it would promote officials faster if they had been members of the Nazi Party prior to 30 January 1933. In March 1934, "old fighters," party members who had membership numbers below 100,000, were granted additional advantages in promotions. By March 1935 the preferences given to the Nazis were extended to men who had fought at the front during World War I. Although the Reichsbahn was attempting to reduce its work force at the time, it created jobs to fulfill these goals at an estimated cost of 900,000 RM annually. Until mid-1936, the sole reason for the increase in the number of officials with the Reichsbahn was the desire to employ and promote Nazis. Only afterward did an increase in traffic necessitate additional appointments.[59] Later, the change in the relationship of the Reichsbahn to the Reich government increased the preferences given to Nazi officials. Dorpmüller issued a directive in April 1937 providing that "proven early fighters for the national awakening" be given preference for promotions in the divisions if they possessed technical qualifications comparable with their competitors. To ensure that this directive was carried out, at least one Nazi was assigned to all promotion examination panels.[60]

By late 1937 the Reichsbahn was encountering difficulty hiring qualified officials, particularly with technical backgrounds. The regime's rearmament program had increased industrial activity, leading to wage competition for trained engineers. In the board meeting of 6 October 1937, representatives of the Personnel Section argued that the effort to hire Nazis and front veterans placed the Reichsbahn at a disadvantage in this competition. Kleinmann reassured them, saying that test scores were frequently no guide to the competence of an individual. Of equal or greater importance was the applicant's character.[61] Finally, in January 1938 the Reichsbahn further lowered the bar to entry and gave Nazis an additional advantage. Now, all members of the party who had not been members before 31 March 1936 because they had not had the opportunity to join or because they were employed in Reich, state, or local government institutions were given preference when applying for positions as officials.[62]

Despite the Reichsbahn's efforts to conform to the situation created by the Hitler government, some members of the party and especially the Fachschaft remained dissatisfied. In the summer of 1933, the Fachschaft continued to lead demonstrations in Voß Street.[63] For Dorpmüller, these antics combined with the continued political agitation directed against him and the Reichsbahn leadership in general had become intolerable. As early as May 1933, he had pleaded with the new regime to allow the Reichsbahn the freedom to manage its internal affairs itself. He called upon the Hitler government to allow the railway the "self-administration" that was traditional practice in Prussian and German administrative affairs. In return, the Reichsbahn would place itself unreservedly in the service of the government's policies.[64] At the end of June 1933, Dorpmüller complained about the chaos that was being spread into the railway by the political agitation of the Nazis. In a memorandum sent to the Reich Chancellery, Dorpmüller demanded a halt to demonstrations and politically motivated interventions in the Reichsbahn's internal administrative functions for the sake of operational safety. He insisted that discipline be restored and demanded authority to use all of his powers as general director, even against the Nazi Fachschaft and NSBO.⁶⁵ However, the coordination had still not gone far enough for Dorpmüller to be able to reassert his authority. Finally, in September 1934, he achieved the compromise that he was seeking. In the meeting of the Personnel Committee on 20 September 1934, Dorpmüller said: "The Führerstab is really a foreign body. Initially, it was necessary. But today everyone knows how they are supposed to behave. The shop stewards out in the workplaces should remain, but be named by the president of the division in consultation with the Gauleiter." Schröder then leaped to Dorpmüller's assistance and stated bluntly that the Führerstab had to be dissolved or Hess would gain excessive influence over the Reichsbahn.⁶⁶ The committee merely agreed to change the composition of the Führerstab. For Dorpmüller, this was inadequate. He wrote a letter to Eltz that day complaining of the indiscipline being caused in the Reichsbahn by Nazi agitation. Eltz brought the matter before Hess and Martin Bormann. Hess agreed to dissolve the Führerstab.⁶⁷ The compromise with the Nazi Party that Dorpmüller had proposed in May 1933 was finally concluded in September 1934. The Reichsbahn would manage its own internal affairs. In return, it would implement the party's ideological dictates and conform to the government's economic and military policies. This compromise would be observed by both sides until the collapse of the Third Reich.

The September 1934 compromise highlights the role of Dorpmüller. The general director had again survived a major shift in power in the national government. Dorpmüller's primary concern was operations. He had demonstrated before 1933 that his understanding of financial matters was limited. However, his desire to remain head of the railway was unlimited. During 1930 and 1931, Dorpmüller had attempted to build a friendly relationship with Heinrich Brüning, leading the chancellor to believe that Dorpmüller supported his policies. Yet Dorpmüller's actions in board meetings and his directives make clear that, although he detested reparations as a German nationalist, he was not prepared to bankrupt the DRG in order to eliminate them. When Brüning offered to name him Reich transportation minister in 1931, he refused, most likely because he understood that he really had very little in common with Brüning and the other members of the cabinet. The rise of the Nazis and their attacks on his beloved railway and him personally did not lessen Dorpmüller's preference for strong central authority, either in the government or in the Reichsbahn. When Hitler gained power, Dorpmüller saw an opportunity to strengthen management authority and weaken organized labor. It is unlikely that he anticipated the attacks that the Fachschaft launched against him and the DRG, let alone their ferocity. But Dorpmüller used his position to convince Hitler of his competence, winning important support in his struggle to retain his dominance over the Reichsbahn.

Dorpmüller saw the DRG as an operating agency, as an organization that ran trains to serve German society, whatever that society wanted. To serve society's needs, he thought that the experts had to be left alone to manage the complex technical apparatus necessary to move trains safely and efficiently. This narrow vision of the Reichsbahn's role in German society was the basis for the compromise with the Nazi regime. It put the Reichsbahn at the disposal of the Hitler government. So long as it was allowed to maintain its internal autonomy, the Reichsbahn would serve the regime's ends, however monstrous. Indeed, there is no record of Dorpmüller ever having considered the moral implications of the transportation requirements placed upon the Reichsbahn by the Third Reich. Dorpmüller was a one-dimensional man, interested only in running trains. This is underlined by how he conducted his private life, as much as by how he shaped the public affairs of the Reichsbahn. Dorpmüller never married. His sister ran his household until he died in 1945. He took his vacations with other railroaders, usually with his assistant Gerhard Sommer as part of the group. They did not bring women along with them. When Hermann Göring accompanied Dorpmüller on a vacation to Greece during 1934 and brought his fiancée, Dorpmüller and the other Reichsbahner were taken aback. Dorpmüller arranged for his sister to accompany him and Sommer brought his wife. Dorpmüller lived in a world filled with locomotives, trains, and tracks. Everything else was extraneous. His acceptance of the view that the Reichsbahn should serve the government of the day unreservedly made the railway vulnerable to exploitation by the Nazi regime.[68]

Dorpmüller, as befit a man who saw himself as an apolitical technician, did not join the Nazi Party when it seemed advantageous to do so in 1933. As will be seen, he had ample reason to become dissatisfied with the Hitler government during the 1930s. Consequently, he joined the party only when its treasurer contacted him on 18 January 1941 and informed him that the Reich Chancellery had ordered his induction into the NSDAP. Effective 1 February 1941, Julius Dorpmüller became a member of the Nazi Party.[69]

With the compromise of September 1934, and with Dorpmüller confident of Hitler's support, the Reichsbahn followed a policy for its officials in conformity with Nazi dictates. The leadership of the Fachschaft Reichsbahn was reformed and a less confrontational leader, Friedrich Peppmüller, brought in. In May 1935 a special committee was created to advise Dorpmüller on personnel issues involving upper-level officials. The committee included a confidential representative of Hitler, Herbert Stenger. In March 1936 dismissal from the party due to objectionable political views became grounds for the loss of an official's position with the Reichsbahn. These actions ensured that the Reichsbahn would adhere to Nazi ideological policies. The Reichsbahn implemented them itself.[70]

The final major ideological change in the way that the Reichsbahn handled its officials resulted from the promulgation of the Nuremberg laws of 15 September 1935. Kleinmann, who attended the party rally at which they were announced, immediately decided to take preliminary steps to ensure that the Reichsbahn implemented the laws itself. He reported to Dorpmüller as soon as he returned to Berlin on 17 September 1935. Within a few hours they issued directives applying the law expelling all remaining Jews from the railway. A total of thirty men were affected. Twenty-eight had already been laid off. The two remaining were temporarily kept on because they were shielded by a law designed to protect minority groups in Upper Silesia. Approximately fifty additional men who were classified as part Jews, and who had been removed from sensitive posts in 1933, were also laid off.[71]

The most prominent of the "full Jews" to lose his job in September 1935 was Ludwig Homberger. Renninger raised the Homberger issue after Kleinmann reported the final removal of the Jews from the Main Administration to the Personnel Committee on 24 September 1935. Dorpmüller explained that Homberger had been put on leave until the final implementation procedures had been decided. Until then Prang would continue to act as his substitute. Renninger expressed his satisfaction that the Homberger affair had come to an end. The situation that had existed since the spring of 1933 had been, in his words, "unbearable." Dorpmüller then interjected a comment that underscored both the human tragedy that had befallen Homberger and the others who had been expelled, and the general director's ambiguous moral position. Dorpmüller said that it was better that Homberger and his fellows were gone. Keeping them on indefinitely without assurance about their future had harmed their morale. "The man will never be happy in his life again. Shoved aside, he will awake each morning with pain and not know where he is. . . . One must have seen that with Homberger, how he had earlier devoted himself to the finances, and how he had let them drift afterward, how with each energetic comment came an aside, showing that he really didn't care anymore."[72]

Whereas Dorpmüller delayed joining the Nazi Party, even as he helped it implement its racist policies, other members of the Reichsbahn leadership did not hesitate nearly as long. There is little evidence concerning why various members of the Main Administration joined when they did. Most likely, they did so to promote their professional careers at what they considered opportune moments offered by the party. In some instances, they may have considered the Nazi Party the embodiment of their nationalist sentiments. In any case, a significant number of the highest officials in the Main Administration and the divisions joined the party. The most committed were those who, like Kleinmann, joined before it came to power in 1933. One of these was Erich Goudefroy, who was the president of RBD Mainz and who received his party membership card on 1 December 1931.[73] Another was Werner Hassenpflug, who became a member of the party a month earlier than Goudefroy. He was transferred from RBD Hamburg to a post in the Personnel Section in 1939. In 1941, he was assigned to the administrative staff directly under Dorpmüller and became head of the Personnel Section in January 1942.[74] Yet another was Maximillian Lamertz, who joined the National Socialist Motorists Corps on 1 February 1930 and became a formal member of the party on 1 April 1936. Lamertz was president of RBD Erfurt in 1933 and later became president of the important division headquartered in Essen.[75]

A number of high-ranking officials joined the party effective 1 May 1933, the last opportunity to do so before the NSDAP temporarily stopped considering membership applications. Among these were Hermann Bergmann, who became the chief of the Mechanical Section in 1936; Albert Gollwitzer, who was named division president in Munich at the insistence of the Bavarian government, after having been president of the division based in Nuremberg; and Hermann Osthoff, who had been a senior official in the Personnel Section since at least 1921. Also joining on 1 May 1933 were Alfred Prang, who succeeded Homberger as the head of the Finance Section, and Adolf Sarter, who had helped negotiate the unification of Germany's railways and who at the time was the president of RBD Trier. Finally, Karl Keller, who worked on Dorpmüller's personal administrative staff, also joined the party in May 1933.[76] When the party threw open its membership rolls again in 1937, additional high-ranking Reichsbahn officials joined. Curt Emmelius, the head of the Reichsbahn Central Office (RZA) Berlin; Wilhelm Emrich, his counterpart at the RZA Munich; Max Leibbrand, who by then was chief of the Operating Section; Wilhelm Wechmann, who was responsible for electric traction; and Kurt Tecklenburg, who had reformed the DRG's cost accounting system during the 1920s, all signed up.[77]

These officials and countless others cooperated with the party in many small but significant ways. They ordered office heads to encourage their subordinates to subscribe to the party newspaper, the *Völkischer Beobachter*, and members of the party were given time off from their railway duties to perform political work with no loss of seniority. Reichsbahn employees who held Nazi Party office were not transferred without prior approval from Rudolf Hess's office, and party members could use their oath of silence to avoid testifying at Reichsbahn disciplinary hearings.[78]

The coordination of the Reichsbahn's workers took a different course from that of the nazification of the officials. Here too the party moved deliberately, the ultimate form of its relationship with the workers not emerging until 1934. In May 1933 the unions of the Reichsbahn's workers were shut down and replaced with organizations controlled by the German Labor Front. The works councils were reformed and their socialist members replaced by people who either were members of the Nazi Party or were sympathetic to it. No further organizational changes were made until March 1934, when the Law for the Ordering of Work in the National Administrations and Enterprises was promulgated by the government. The changes attendant to this regulation resulted in pay and vacation increases for the workers. Shortly afterward, on 10 April

1934, new works councils, *Vertrauensräte*, were imposed on the Reichsbahn's workers. They were intended to infuse the railway with the party's leadership principle and the feeling of unreserved loyalty that the workers were supposed to have for their employer. Finally, at the end of the month, the existing labor contract was replaced with a modified set of work rules, which also embodied the concepts of leadership and willing subordination to authority. The Labor Front struggled to retain its place as the intermediary between the Reichsbahn's workers and the Nazi government. In 1936 it succeeded in having itself inserted into the internal mechanism for resolving worker complaints against management.[79]

The Nazis imposed on the Reichsbahn a policy of preferred hiring of workers who were party members similar to that which applied to officials.[80] Just as important, while the Reichsbahn was trying to reduce the size of its work force due to the decline in traffic, Kleinmann and Körner ensured that no workers were laid off. Indeed, even Körner lobbied for pay increases.[81] Despite his pleas, the Reichsbahn's workers received only three general wage increases after 1933. The first came in connection with the revision of the work rules in May 1934. The subsidy for family members was increased slightly, and greater weight was given to seniority.[82] Another small increase was implemented in January 1937 by raising the subsidy for children in accordance with the increases that the Reich and private industry had granted. At the same time, line maintenance, bridge repair workers, and switch operators were given overtime pay increases. These two raises cost the Reichsbahn a total of only 3.9 million RM.[83] The final pay increase resulted from the application of Reich pay scales in May 1938, leading to a 5.5 percent across-the-board pay increase for the workers.[84] Taken together, these pay raises did not permit the workers to maintain their standard of living, despite the government's control of prices. The average weekly pay of a Reichsbahn worker rose by 9.5 percent, while prices rose by about 13 percent between the end of 1932 and the end of 1938.[85]

One of the key concessions made to the workers was the change in which piecework rates were determined and piecework pay calculated. Scientific management had not been accepted by the majority of the Reichsbahn's workers. The Nazi Party, unwilling to make large wage concessions, but quite prepared to rid the railway of Western capitalist management techniques, fulfilled the workers' wishes and abolished the use of Taylor's principles in the Reichsbahn.[86] In the party's view, technical qualifications were less important than subordination to the leader and conformity to Nazi behavioral norms. The head of a facility was supposed to inspire his workers to achieve high output, not provide them with lifeless monetary incentives.[87] In December 1933 the use of time and motion studies was scaled back.[88] The new nazified main works council then demanded the reform of piecework and job assignment procedures in the repair works in April 1934. Throughout the Reichsbahn, the workers especially objected to the use of the stopwatch to measure their performance.[89] In January 1935 the Reichsbahn modified the piecework incentive system to conform with the Nazi concept of cooperation based on trust and subordination in the workplace.[90] The computation of piecework pay was relaxed and the standards lowered. In March 1937 the methods for calculating piecework pay were modified again. Greater weight was attached to individual performance than under the prior system of work groups. However, the German Labor Front participated in writing the new work rules and norms. The result was an effective pay increase for those working on an incentive basis that cost the Reichsbahn 900,000 RM.[91]

The Nazi Party also devoted considerable attention to changing the training practices of the Reichsbahn. In 1933 classes for both workers and officials were altered to include more Nazi ideology and discussions of current public events from the National Socialist perspective.[92] In December 1933 the Main Administration formed a committee to propose changes to the Reichsbahn's training manuals and courses to bring them into compliance with Nazi ideology. The committee consisted of six people, five of whom were members of the Nazi Party. The Main Administration accepted its report in April 1934 and introduced political indoctrination with anti-Semitic content into all phases of Reichsbahn internal training programs.[93] Kleinmann felt that these measures did not go far enough, so he arranged to have party speakers address the employees of repair shops and created classes on the Nazi world view that would be offered in conjunction with the German Labor Front.[94] The tenor of the training received by Reichsbahn employees is made clear by remarks made by Körner and Esser in the board meeting of 1 December 1937. The nazified teachers and guest speakers emphasized the unity of body, mind, and spirit and the primacy of the party. Otherwise, training concentrated on technical subjects and political matters. Theoretical aspects of the machines or processes that the employees used were neglected. The aim was to ensure that the Reichsbahn's people had the right political views without filling their heads with superfluous information or ideas. From his position in the Personnel Section, Osthoff made clear that in the area of training, too, the Reichsbahn and the party had come to a compromise. The party handled the ideological education of the railroaders, while the Reichsbahn looked after their technical qualifications.[95]

The Nazi desire to centralize and standardize the government had its effect on the Reichsbahn as well. It facilitated the implementation of Dorpmüller's plan to dissolve divisions and put an end to the particularist privileges enjoyed by Bavaria. The assignment of Leipzig to RBD Halle (S), which had been delayed by local political opposition, was implemented on 1 October 1934.[96] RBD Oldenburg was merged into its neighbors with little difficulty on 31 December 1934.[97] Closing RBD Ludwigshafen took longer. Eltz and the minister of the interior, Wilhelm Frick, readily approved, but the Nazi leader of the Palatinate,

Gauleiter Josef Bürckel, objected. In January 1936 the parties decided to postpone the action until after the Rhineland was remilitarized so as to avoid a loss of jobs in that depressed area. In October 1936, with the remilitarization complete, and the military spending money in the region again, Kleinmann raised the issue once more. Bürckel finally agreed, and the division was dissolved on 31 March 1937.[98]

The Nazi regime moved much more quickly to eliminate that vestige of particularism, the Group Administration (Gruppenverwaltung, or GV) for Bavaria in Munich. The resignation of the head of that organization for political reasons in June 1933 opened the possibility of eliminating it entirely. The dissolution of the GV Bavaria became entangled in the party maneuvering to have Gollwitzer named its chief. Dorpmüller overcame this problem by naming Gollwitzer president of the Munich operating division instead. Theodor Kittel, a legal expert from the Administrative Section of the Main Administration, met with the Bavarian minister-president, Ludwig Siebert, to resolve the future of the group on 7 June 1933. However, Siebert refused to compromise. At the end of August 1933, a larger meeting attended by Dorpmüller, Siebert, and representatives of the Nazi Party and the Fachschaft brought an agreement. The party representatives made it clear to Siebert that Hitler opposed the continued existence of the GV Bavaria. Facing this insurmountable obstacle, Siebert agreed to allow the group to be dissolved. In its place, a Reichsbahn central office would be located in Munich. The group was then gradually dissolved, closing on 31 December 1933.[99]

The Reichsbahn Central Office Munich was the product both of the compromise with the Bavarian government and of a new investigation into the operations of the RZA in Berlin. The RZA Munich opened its doors on 1 November 1933. Its role was then changed and expanded in August 1936. A special commission of the Main Administration had been created to investigate the acquisition practices of the RZA Berlin. It found both irregularities and inefficiencies. The irregularities were handled by the courts. The inefficiencies where addressed by modifying its organization and clarifying responsibilities for purchasing throughout the Reichsbahn. The four offices in Berlin that had been created in 1930 were combined under Kurt Emmelius. The RZA Munich was also subordinated to him. The regional purchasing offices that had been formed in the 1920s out of the vestiges of the state railways were abolished. The office in Berlin was given exclusive responsibility for purchasing steam locomotives, track materials, and other designated items for the entire railway. The RZA Munich was assigned responsibility for electric traction of all kinds as well as related electrical equipment, motor trains, and bridges.[100]

Throughout the 1920s, the states had insisted on their rights under the treaty of April 1920. They had disputed the amount of compensation that they should receive after the DRG was created in 1924, and the consequences of the inflation of 1922 and 1923 became clear. The Nazi government had no intention of becoming bogged down in similar talks. On 27 February 1934, as a provision of the Law for the Simplification and Cheapening of the Administration, the state treaty of 1920 was abrogated.[101] The transportation minister now enjoyed complete freedom to dispose over the Reich's railways without reference to the states.

The Main Administration was also reorganized. On 10 August 1933 the special Administrative Section VI A was subordinated directly to the general director to tighten his control over the internal processes of the headquarters. Many of the section's personnel were members of the Nazi Party. This in fact provided Kleinmann with a staff to support him in his work to nazify the Reichsbahn.[102] Effective 1 January 1936, the Purchasing Section was merged into the Mechanical Section as part of the simplification of the Reichsbahn's acquisition organization. The Mechanical Section set locomotive policy and design requirements, while the actual purchases were carried out by the appropriate RZA.[103]

Dorpmüller attempted to change the appearance as well as the substance of the Reichsbahn to conform with the new regime. On 15 July 1933 he ordered that the Nazi swastika symbol be applied to rolling stock and that Reichsbahn employees use the German greeting, "Heil Hitler." Officials were required to salute each other even when not on duty. If they were in uniform, they were to use a military style salute. However, if they were not wearing a hat, they would use the Nazi salute with the outstretched right arm and hand. Use of the Nazi salute led to misunderstandings and endangered operations. Some officials and workers used the salute in yards, where operating personnel mistook it as a signal. Consequently, the requirement to use the Nazi salute was relaxed to apply only to areas away from trains on 17 October. Those who avoided using either the salute or the German greeting were threatened with disciplinary measures.[104]

The Nazi attempt to transform Germany into a racist people's community reinforced the popular negative attitudes toward private property and profit. The slogan "The common good before individual good" may be seen as a cynical propaganda slogan designed to convince the German population to subordinate its desires to those of Hitler. Yet it also embodied a good deal of the rejection of private gain and the suspicion of business that was an integral component of German culture. Consequently, the Hitler government changed the economic role of the Reichsbahn to conform with its *völkisch* values. In his speech at Nuremberg on the occasion of the celebration of the one hundredth anniversary of the German railways in December 1935, Hitler characterized the Reichsbahn as a socialist enterprise that existed to serve the community. It would satisfy the transportation demands of the population safely and efficiently, while earning only enough money to pay its operating expenses and maintain its capital. Its employees would not be paid on a capitalist incentive basis but according to social standards. They would be motivated by a sense of duty to the community. As Hitler put it, "This enterprise, led according to high ethical and moral standards, is simultaneously the most progressive transportation enterprise in the world."[105] These views were essentially the same as those which were held by the Reichsbahn's officials and which had brought them into conflict with the commercial values that the Allies had attempted to implant in the Reichsbahn, and in German society, during the last half of the 1920s. Consequently, changes took place after January 1933 in the Reichsbahn's financial policies that represented a return to hallowed values rather than a departure into an unfamiliar future. The Reichsbahn would support the government's policies through its tariff, purchasing, service, and employment practices. It would attempt to cover only its production costs. It would not seek to earn an operating surplus. As Dorpmüller put it in May 1933, "Two great concepts control our tariff structure. The first is that important goods for the generality cannot be carried cheaply enough. The second is that every German region must have the same low prices for freight and passengers."[106]

Fritz Busch, who led Homberger's old office for preparation of the Reichsbahn's budget, wrote that the revision of the cost accounting system during the late 1920s "came like a spring storm over the Deutsche Reichsbahn."[107] The money-oriented outlook that cost accounting represented was rejected by the Nazis. Although he later joined the party, in 1933, Kurt Tecklenburg made a last appeal to his fellow officials to adopt his way of thinking. He wrote: "In my opinion, it would be desirable to have each component be made accountable for the relationship between its costs and its output on a continuing basis. In this way, one would take a step closer to having all components think more in terms of money than they have in the past."[108] In the atmosphere created by the Nazis, Tecklenburg's wish was hopeless.

The opposing viewpoint, that the costs of individual services did not matter, that in fact they could not even be measured, had never been abandoned by large sections of the Reichsbahn's corps of officials. Their spokesman was Walter Spieß, who was responsible for setting freight tariffs in the Main Administration from 1924 to 1945. In a series of very erudite articles, Spieß articulated the commonweal view of railway tariffs. He contended that the railway was a public utility that had to operate whether it earned revenues sufficient to pay its operating costs or not. However, in order to avoid becoming a burden on society, it should set its tariffs just high enough to cover its out-of-pocket expenses and renew its physical plant and rolling stock. Allocating capital costs to cost centers was useless since capital investments were lost in a financial sense as soon as they were made. As long as the railway met its service obligations, as long as it could run trains to the satisfaction of its customers while imposing the least economic burden upon them, it had fulfilled its duty.[109] This fundamentally noneconomic reasoning was well suited to the Nazi policy of instrumentalizing components of German society to achieve its racist, expansionist goals. Where little accountability existed, where the aim was to satisfy the common good, especially when that good was defined by a criminal leadership, the room for abuse was unlimited.

Consistent with these attitudes, the operating cost allocation system so painstakingly assembled by Tecklenburg, and so detested by the officials, was dismantled soon after the Nazis came to power. In 1933 a working group was formed in the Main Administration to modify the Reichsbahn's accounting procedures in light of the changed political circumstances. At the beginning of the meeting during which it submitted its report, Busch told the group that its draft did not accurately reflect the commonweal character of the Reichsbahn: it had assigned too great importance to "purely economic" considerations. So the proposal was altered, and during the spring and summer of 1934 the Beko (Operating Cost Account) was dismantled. As Busch explained, social considerations came before profit and the allocation of costs caused unnecessary work in light of the railway's more important social responsibilities. On 1 January 1936 the officers responsible for cost accounting at the division headquarters were reassigned to other duties. The volume of cost data that was collected was greatly reduced, and the reporting of expenses in relation to the operations that generated them was ended. At the same time, the collection of general operating statistics and the use of punched cards were scaled back.[110]

The end of the Beko accompanied the cessation of the clearing of accounts among the divisions. It had also been greatly disliked, both because of the work that it caused and because it fostered internal competition. On 31 December 1935 Busch, based on guidance from Kleinmann, issued a directive ordering the suspension of the clearing of divisional accounts.[111] As he made clear, the end of the clearing of accounts was also the end of the notion that the divisions were independent business entities. Control from Berlin would now become tighter.[112]

On 23 March 1933, in a speech to the Reichstag, Hitler called for the subordination of the Reichsbahn to the government as soon as possible as a moral responsibility.[113] This did not happen. Instead, because the substance was gained through inner coordination, because of the press of other business (due to possible difficulties concerning the Reichsbahn's foreign financial obligations), and because Eltz had his own plans, the Reichsbahn was brought under the authority of the RVM only in February 1937. As an interim measure, a new set of bylaws for the enterprise was issued on 28 November 1933. In effect, the railway reverted to the status of a government-owned and -operated enterprise that was separate from the ministerial bureaucracy.[114]

In November 1935 Kleinmann proposed to Hitler bringing the Reichsbahn directly under the Reich Transportation Ministry. Hitler expressed interest in the idea and encouraged Kleinmann to pursue it.[115] The state secretary of the Reich Chancellery, Hans Lammers, asked Dorpmüller to work with the RVM to prepare a report describing how the Reichsbahn could be subordinated to the RVM.[116] Eltz immediately raised the problems caused by the Reichsbahn's formal international obligations stemming from the Reichsbahn Law of 1930, and the rights of the foreign holders of its preferred stock. He also resurrected his proposal, initially made in 1933, to combine the transportation and postal ministries.[117] Eltz's ambitious concept went too far for Hitler at that moment. Therefore, on 16 January 1936 Hitler told him to drop the matter.[118] Eltz returned to the issue in a briefing for Hitler on 27 November 1936. The transportation minister proposed keeping the Reichsbahn as a financially independent operating organization, though subordinating it to the RVM for policy purposes. A single ministry would be organized that would be responsible for railways, roads, oceangoing shipping, inland waterways, and the post office. The transportation minister would assume the powers of the Reichsbahn board of directors. If Hitler accepted this plan, he could name a new transportation minister and his assistants in the ministry and the railway.[119] Hitler did not accept Eltz's proposal, but he did announce the subordination of the Reichsbahn directly to the RVM in a Reichstag speech delivered on 30 January 1937.[120] Hurriedly, over the next few days, the various ministries reviewed the draft of a preliminary law that would transform both the Reichsbahn and the Reichsbank into Reich agencies. The High Command of the Armed Forces (OKW) raised an objection concerning the wording of the law seeking to ensure the Reichsbahn's cooperation in time of war. Kittel quickly negotiated a compromise with the chief of staff of the OKW, General Wilhelm Keitel, and the law was promulgated on 10 February 1937. The Reichsbahn was absorbed by the Reich Transportation Ministry. The sections of the Main Administration became the railway sections of the ministry, and the board of directors was transformed into an advisory board.[121] The bylaws of the railway were changed to conform to its new legal status. Of great psychological significance was the change in the railway's name. Since January 1934, the word "Gesellschaft," or company, had been used only sparingly, indeed only when necessary on legally important documents, such as the company's annual report. Otherwise, use of the word "company" was avoided in public pronouncements on the railway. Now, the offending word "Gesellschaft" was officially dropped, and the railway's abbreviated name became DRB.[122]

Negotiations concerning a definitive Reichsbahn law became bogged down in interministerial rivalries, desires for seats on the advisory board, and the matter of the personal union of the offices of transportation minister and chief of the railway. Hess in particular sought greater influence for the party over the railway's social organizations. Finally, on 7 June 1939, Hitler approved the draft law that was promulgated on 4 July 1939.[123] It had no effect on the organization or operations of the railway.

The change in the Reichsbahn's formal legal status was also the occasion for a change in the person of the transportation minister. Although Eltz had helped impose Nazi racist policies on the Reichsbahn, he had not joined the Nazi Party and became increasingly alarmed by the direction that Hitler had taken. He met privately with Hitler to express his displeasure with the recent Hitler Youth Law on 27 November 1936. Eltz considered the law anti-Christian and feared that it would ruin the Catholic youth organizations. He asked Hitler to stop the party's campaign against the church. Hitler put him off.[124] On 2 February 1937, at the close of a cabinet meeting, Hitler distributed the golden party badge to those ministers who did not already wear it. Eltz refused to accept his. Hitler could not tolerate this direct affront to his authority. Eltz immediately resigned. Kleinmann and others promoted themselves as Eltz's successor. Possibly on the advice of Göring, Hitler instead chose Dorpmüller.[125] Dorpmüller had refused Brüning's request six years earlier. Now, due to ambition and a misplaced sense of patriotism, he accepted Hitler's call.

Having become Germany's leading railroader, Dorpmüller settled into the role of minister and successor to Carl Friedrich von Siemens as chairman of the Reichsbahn board. The group that Dorpmüller presided over was very different from its predecessor. Under the new Reichsbahn Law, the Reich transportation minister chaired the railway's board. It now functioned only as an advisory panel, not as a policy-making body. Dorpmüller also abolished the board's committees because he considered their work redundant.[126] Commensurate with its diminished role, the board was reduced in size from eighteen members to fourteen.[127] Yet, to accommodate new members from Austria, the board was expanded to sixteen seats in November 1939.[128] Despite its decline in power, a seat on the Reichsbahn board still offered prestige to its occupant.

By the summer of 1939, the Reichsbahn's relationship with the Nazi regime had stabilized. The compromise of September 1934 continued to function with minor modifications. The Reichsbahn had been returned to direct state control, and the last vestiges of the despised Western commercial management system eradicated. It conformed to the Nazi ideological program, infusing racist content into its personnel and training policies, and excluding Jews and leftists from its ranks. In return, the Reichsbahn was allowed full control over its internal technical processes. To men such as Dorpmüller, who saw the railway as an apolitical, technocratic entity, such freedom was well worth the moral price that they paid to obtain it.

Chapter Two

The Reichsbahn in the Period of Rearmament, Job Creation, and Motorization, 1933–1939

A. Passenger Service: The Flying Trains

On 20 September 1934 Julius Dorpmüller told the board of directors that, with the passing of reparations, the Reichsbahn would have to place itself more completely in the service of the national interest. The old financial priorities no longer applied.[1] Dorpmüller did not understand that, with the Nazi regime defining Germany's national interest, the Reichsbahn had begun moving down a treacherous road that would lead to its virtual destruction a decade later. The Third Reich stood for the rejection of Western values, including the interrelated institutions of representative democracy and the market as means for allocating assets in German society. It attempted to replace them with racist and militarist ideas that it claimed were more in tune with the German national character. Dorpmüller, like many nationalistic, conservative Germans, including many of his officials, accepted enough of the Nazi's values and goals to subordinate the Reichsbahn to the Hitler regime's ambitious plans for military and racial domination.

The Nazi government's rearmament and job creation programs caused a massive increase in traffic between 1933 and 1939 (Table 2.1). The Reichsbahn had difficulty adapting because it was not privy to the government's long-range plans. Consequently, its key decision makers continued to think in terms of

Table 2.1. Summary of Reichsbahn Operating Account, 1933-1939 (in billion RM)

Year	Operating Income	Operating Expenditures	Net Operating Income	Operating Ratio
1927-29 [a]	5.18	4.32	0.869	83.24
1933	2.92	3.056	−0.136	100.66
1934	3.326	3.302	0.024	99.28
1935	3.586	3.434	0.152	95.75
1936	3.985	3.513	0.472	88.16
1937	4.420	4.004	0.416	90.6
1938	5.133	4.761	0.250	92.75
1939	5.813	5.345	0.468	91.96
Percentage Change 1939 vs. 1927-29	+12.22	+23.73	−46.14	+10.48

[a] Average.
Source: DRG/DRB, *Geschäftsberichte*.

peacetime traffic until the late 1930s. An examination of the Reichsbahn's passenger service illustrates this.

During the first years of the Nazi regime, the Reichsbahn engaged in a major effort to improve the quality of its passenger service. The most prominent aspect of this program was the increase in the speed of its passenger trains. The acceleration of the Reichsbahn's passenger service was the result of work that had begun during the 1920s. As part of the renewal program, sections of track had been relocated to reduce curvature, improved switches were installed to allow trains to pass through them more quickly, and superelevation was increased in curves to counteract the centrifugal force of trains passing at higher speeds. Increasing the height of the outer rail over the inner rail enhanced both safety and passenger comfort. The Reich track design, because it was more rigid and employed longer rails than its predecessors, also helped trains run faster. Finally, the scheduled track maintenance introduced by the DRG after 1924 kept this improved track structure in excellent condition.[2]

With the implementation of the summer schedule in May 1934, the Reichsbahn greatly increased the speed of its expresses and many of its other passenger trains. The maximum track speed for expresses was raised from 100 kph to 120 kph. In addition, the schedule was tightened. Stops were shortened, and buffers that had been built into earlier schedules to allow engineers to regain time lost to delays were reduced. The schedules were calculated to six-second intervals, meaning that engineers had to bring their trains over the line so as to pass scheduled way points almost to the second, rather than to the minute.[3]

The results came immediately. The average speed for all express trains running between Berlin-Lehrte and Hamburg rose 2.2 percent compared with that in 1929. In 1929 the DRG operated only 1 train with an average speed over 90 kph. In 1934 it operated 167 trains at or above 90 kph, and 15 at average speeds over 100 kph.[4] The Reichsbahn continued to increase passenger train speeds over the next four years. In 1939 it ran the 32 fastest trains in Europe.[5] Yet, by 1937, the acceleration program had encountered difficulties. Increased traffic volume, resulting in heavier trains and the addition of many extras, slowed the rise of average speeds.[6]

Even though the DRG had not reduced passenger service commensurate with the decline in traffic during the Depression, it began increasing the number of passenger trains that it offered the public immediately after the Nazi regime came to power. In 1933, it already operated more passenger trains than it had during the years 1927 to 1929. These trains were frequently smaller than their pre-Depression predecessors. This reduction was intentional since the Reichsbahn's goal was to increase frequency of service to counter automobile competition. The effort continued right up to the last peacetime schedule prepared in late 1938 and early 1939.[7] The Reichsbahn also introduced other refinements, such as its own published passenger schedule in 1933, improved connections, and new cars built using steel and offering modern interior appointments.[8]

The increased demand for passenger service was the result of the rise in economic activity caused by the Nazi rearmament program and the closely related job creation program. Government orders to industry increased immediately in 1933 and continued to grow for the remainder of the 1930s.[9] Not only did these programs expand employment, they also led to shifts in the distribution of jobs. Although both capital goods and consumer industries participated in the boom, the emphasis in the rearmament program was on the former. Moreover, the government encouraged industries to locate new facilities in central Germany. The result was a change in passenger traffic patterns as well as an increase in travel. The political activities of the Nazi Party also caused large passenger movements. Each year, the party held a mammoth gathering in Nuremberg and smaller events at other locations. The Reichsbahn was required to transport the majority of the participants to and from these extravaganzas. It accommodated as many as possible in its regular trains, sometimes adding cars to them, or running second or third sections. When necessary it ran special trains. Leibbrand reported that for the fateful September 1935 party rally in Nuremberg, the Reichsbahn spent 1 million RM of its own money to improve the station facilities serving the gathering. It ran a total of 457 special trains and seventy-five extra sections of scheduled trains for members of the Nazi Party who attended the event. These trains carried a total of 450,000 people to and from Nuremberg. An additional 350,000 people came using regularly scheduled trains. Leibbrand planned to spend an additional 20 million RM in the future to expand the rail facilities serving the event. He also considered the heavy influx of traffic good practice for military mobilization.[10]

The 1936 Olympic games were held in Germany, imposing significant traffic demands on the Reichsbahn. The winter events took place in Garmisch-Partenkirchen in the Bavarian Alps from 6 to 16 February. To handle the anticipated influx of visitors, the Reichsbahn added a second track to parts of the line connecting Garmisch with Munich and expanded the station and holding tracks at Garmisch. The railway brought 506,000 people to and from the winter games. Based on its own observations, the Reichsbahn estimated that it carried about 61 percent of the attendees to the site of the events. The remainder traveled by road. The Reichsbahn spent 6.1 million RM to improve the rail facilities that served the winter games, an amount that it did not regain from increased traffic.[11] It also spent 1.3 million RM on construction work to prepare for the summer games that were held in Berlin from 1 to 16 August 1936. Most affected by the event was the S-Bahn, the Reichsbahn's urban commuter system in the capital, for which a new station was built and improvements made to its lines. An estimated 8 million spectators used the S-Bahn during the games, over half of the system's traffic in that period. In addition, 2,241 special trains were run to bring visitors to and from Berlin. Overall, the Reichsbahn estimated that it gained 10 million RM in new revenue as a result of the summer games.[12]

The general increase in passenger traffic was substantial by any measure. Between 1933 and 1938, the volume of passenger-kilometers delivered by the Reichsbahn rose by 95.7 percent, outpacing the expansion of the economy.[13] Yet the Reichsbahn continued to lose market share to automobiles and buses. The number of passenger cars in Germany in 1938 was twice as high as in 1929. More important, the number of passenger-kilometers delivered by these automobiles almost tripled. The prospects for the future were bleak since in 1938 passenger car purchases were four and a half times higher than in 1929. In 1929 the German public allocated about 13 percent of its transportation expenditures to vehicles that it owned itself, the remainder going to public modes of transportation. In 1938 it devoted 39.3 percent of its transportation expenditures to its own motor vehicles. Over the same period, the size of the transportation market had expanded. Total spending by the public on transportation was 56.6 percent higher in 1938 than in 1929. But most of that growth had been directed toward its own, private motor vehicles. Between 1929 and 1938, consumption of public transportation in Germany rose by only 9.6 percent, while consumption of privately owned transportation jumped by 373 percent.[14]

The Reichsbahn had largely conceded the passenger transportation market to the roads because of its acceptance of its commonweal obligation to offer cheap, convenient transportation even when it lost money doing so. Nevertheless, its response to the threat posed by the automobile was hampered by its statist attitude that much road travel was socially unnecessary. Adolf Sarter expressed this mind-set in March 1932, when he acknowledged the convenience of the private passenger automobile. Yet he thought that most long-distance trips by car were unnecessary. They were a form of sport, not serious, purposeful travel.[15] As a result of this attitude, because the Hitler regime hoped to avoid price increases to prevent domestic political discontent, and because the Reichsbahn was considered a social policy tool, the railway offered more and deeper discounts to its riders during the 1930s.

In January 1934 the government and the party pressured the Reichsbahn to cut its passenger fares. The board discussed the matter at its January meeting. Dorpmüller opposed a reduction in light of the Reichsbahn's weak financial position and the fact that passenger service had been losing about 400 million RM annually. Kleinmann pointed out that the expansion of bus service and the appearance of the Volkswagen would pose major threats to the railway and suggested that the only way that the Reichsbahn could defend itself was to cut fares. The board, however, concluded that the decline in passenger revenues was due primarily to the poor economic situation and not road competition. When the economy improved, passenger revenues would recover. At the suggestion of Siemens, it decided to propose to the government tying a 168 million RM passenger fare reduction to an arrangement that would allow the railway to retain an equivalent amount from the transportation tax.[16] The Finance Ministry rejected this proposal, claiming that it could not do without the tax revenues.[17] Eltz-Rübenach opposed a cut of this magnitude, pointing to the railway's poor finances. He proposed instead a 135.9 million RM reduction.[18] At a special meeting on 20 February 1934, the board decided again to attempt to get a rebate of the transportation tax.[19] The matter was finally resolved by Hitler on 27 February. He told Eltz that general passenger fares could be reduced when traffic increased. In the interim, a few cuts directed at particular social groups such as families could be undertaken without placing an undue burden on the Reichsbahn.[20] With this decision, the possibility of a general passenger fare cut disappeared. Instead, the Reichsbahn pursued a policy of piecemeal reductions that had the net effect of greatly reducing the cost of rail travel for most Germans. For example, people who worked at home in connection with industrial production received discounts. Party members traveling in groups of up to one hundred were charged only 1.5 Reich pfennigs per kilometer. Groups over 800, which commonly traveled to the party rallies and other events, rode for only 1 pfennig per kilometer.[21] The consequence was that average revenues per passenger-kilometer fell dramatically. In the period 1927 through 1929, the DRG collected an average of 3.03 pfennigs per passenger-kilometer. In 1933 it received only 2.81. The addition of new discounts reduced this to 2.37 by 1937. At the time, Kleinmann warned the board that there was every prospect that this trend would continue.[22] In 1937, 72 percent of all of the Reichsbahn's passengers took advantage of its discount fares.[23]

While the Reichsbahn had accepted that it would cease to be the dominant mode in the realm of passenger transportation in Germany, it was far from dropping out of the market. Its common-carrier responsibilities meant that it could not simply abandon services that caused losses. Therefore, during the early 1920s it had embarked on a program to develop motor trains. Powered by internal combustion engines, these new vehicles would be much lighter and cheaper to operate than their steam-locomotive-powered predecessors. The savings that they would yield would reduce the Reichsbahn's losses from its passenger services and thereby facilitate balancing its overall operating budget. In 1936 Kleinmann asserted that the Reichsbahn was bound by a duty of honor to become the most technologically advanced railway in the world.[24] Such expressions of Nazi bombast may have appealed to the engineers in the Reichsbahn and the nationalists outside of it, who sought technological perfectionism for its own sake. Yet sober economic calculations dictated the direction that the Reichsbahn actually took.

German development of motor trains and motor cars began before World War I. The advantages of a self-propelled car compared to a train in which a separate locomotive pulled a group of cars were obvious. The overall weight of the vehicle would be lower, necessitating less horsepower. Savings were also expected due to lower personnel requirements. Motor cars were developed that were powered by small steam engines, batteries, and diesel power plants. The steam-powered cars proved unreliable and expensive because of the difficulties in building a steam engine small enough yet powerful enough to fit into a car. Battery-powered cars were reliable but suffered from limited range, acceleration, and speed due to the heavy weight of their batteries and the need to allocate space to the cells, reducing their passenger and baggage capacity. The cars that used diesel engines encountered the problems associated with this technically immature power plant and the difficulty in transmitting its power to the rail. Other internal-combustion engines encountered the same obstacles. In 1914 both the Prussian and Saxon railways purchased diesel motor cars equipped with electric transmissions.[25] However, because the electric transmission was less energy efficient than a direct drive using gears, rods, or a hydraulic device, many German engineers, including many employed by the railways, avoided it and sought a reliable, smooth-operating direct-drive transmission.

The DRG resumed this line of development. The combination of the erosion of the railway's passenger transportation monopoly, the impossibility of having operating deficits filled by public revenues, the end of the prewar situation in which it could underpay its employees, and the need to achieve an operating surplus sufficient to meet the charges on its revenues deriving from reparations and the sale of preferred stock caused the DRG to invest in the development of the motor train. Work had been done in the period 1920 to 1923, but the unstable economic circumstances of these years made progress difficult. One significant advance had been the development of a truck that housed the motor for a self-propelled car.[26] The power truck offered the advantage of reduced weight and a lower center of gravity compared to an installation in the carbody, leading to improved ride characteristics.[27]

The new power truck was displayed to the public at a transportation exhibition held at Seddin, southwest of Berlin, in late September and early October 1924.[28] The exhibition was a landmark in the evolution of German rail technology. One of the most interesting sections showed new motor cars, including the innovative Wismar-Triebwagen that had been developed by the EVA (Eisenbahn-Verkehrsmittel-AG, Railway Transportation Device Company) in cooperation with Maybach of Friedrichshafen. EVA designed the carbody while Maybach built the diesel engine. The car was fitted with a mechanical transmission and had a heavy, riveted steel body. Yet it was clearly more advanced than its predecessors and proved reliable in commuter service between the exhibition and Wannsee.[29] The DRG purchased the car and placed it in operations, where it performed satisfactorily.

The progress made in the development of internal-combustion engines and transmissions caused the DRG to shift the emphasis of its development work away from battery-powered cars to diesel and benzol cars between 1925 and 1928.[30] It purchased a variety of different designs in small numbers and subjected them to technical and operational tests to gain experience with the new technologies.[31] It also devoted considerable attention to the internal appointments of the new cars and contemplated how their successors would appear to passengers. It employed architects and industrial designers to help determine the shape and color of seats, baggage storage facilities, and doors. Thought was even given to their external appearance. Among the first motor trains influenced by these efforts were the electric multiple units built for the Berlin S-Bahn.[32] Despite the very real progress made, however, the motor car remained in its infancy. As late as 1928, the Mechanical Section considered self-propelled cars unsuitable for large-scale operations because their motors, including those built by Maybach and MAN, were still unreliable.[33] Yet their potential was clear. Richard Anger, the chief of the Mechanical Section, was very interested in perfecting the motor car. In April 1929 he described a concept under which they would be used to reduce the cost of operating lines with weak traffic and to increase train frequency on routes with higher traffic volumes.[34]

During the Depression, the DRG pressed forward with the development of motor cars. It focused on perfecting more powerful motors and lighter construction methods for the carbodies, while still experimenting with mechanical and electrical transmissions. In 1930 Maybach introduced a diesel power plant offering 410 horsepower that was installed in three motor cars intended for accelerated train (Eilzug) service.[35] In 1931 and 1932 the DRG obtained a small number of motor cars featuring semimonocoque bodies built using light steel alloy sheets that were welded in place.[36]

While the Reichsbahn was developing motor cars for regular passenger train and accelerated train service, it was pursuing a much bolder initiative intended to retain passengers who were prepared to pay for premium service. On 12 November 1930 Friedrich Fuchs of the Mechanical Section of the Main Administration sent a memorandum to the Reichsbahn Central Office in Berlin in which he described the basic configuration of a high-speed passenger motor train. It would travel at speeds of 150 kph and use two Maybach 410 horsepower diesel engines. The RZA would prepare a draft request for proposals from industry for the construction of such a train based on these general specifications.[37] The RZA formed an office to coordinate the acquisition effort headed by Max Breuer. It completed the request quickly, and on 11 December 1930 the Main Administration ordered the RZA to begin the acquisition process. At that point, the DRG conceived of a two-car, six-axle train powered by existing diesel engines. The two cars would be articulated, that is, they would be mated over a single truck to save weight and improve ride. They would be built using light steel alloys joined using new welding techniques to form a strong semimonocoque body. The trucks would incorporate new technologies to assure a smooth ride. The two power plants would be installed in the front and rear trucks and the traction motors would be located in the middle truck, yielding superior balance allowing the train to be operated forward or backward with equal facility. Between 100 and 120 passengers would be accommodated by the new train.[38] The Waggon- und Maschinenbau AG (Wumag) of Görlitz responded with a preliminary proposal on 19 December 1930.[39] Meetings between Wumag and the RZA led to a refinement of the design and a reduction of its price over the next few weeks.[40] No other manufacturer offered a proposal to build the carbody. In contrast, BBC and Siemens-Schuckert-Werke (SSW) both submitted design studies for the traction motors and generators. SSW had been working with Maybach for years. Maybach, in turn, had been supported by Anger since at least the mid-1920s.[41]

On 30 January 1931, the RZM (Reichsbahnzentralamt für Maschinenbau, or Reichsbahn Central Office for Mechanical Engineering) chose SSW as the major subcontractor for the electrical components of the train.[42] On 10 February 1931 Dorpmüller then authorized the RZM to award a contract to Wumag for production of the carbody and for systems integration at a cost of 340,000 RM. Dorpmüller based his decision on results from preliminary wind tunnel tests using models and calculations made by SSW of the transit times that the train would achieve on the route that had already been chosen for its service introduction, the heavily traveled, flat line between Berlin and Hamburg.[43] This route had been selected because it linked Germany's two largest cities. Government officials and businessmen traveled between them frequently. The DRG hoped that professionals would be willing to pay full fare and a supplement in order to make round trips between the cities in a single day with sufficient time in either to conduct business. The higher fare would be offset by the absence of lodging expenses. From the outset, the new train was considered a test vehicle that would determine both the technical feasibility and the market acceptance of premium-priced, high-speed passenger service.[44] The Reichsbahn was careful to purchase the rights to the wind tunnel test results and the technology used to build the train's semimonocoque body.[45] By January 1932 both the cars and the motors for the new train were almost complete.[46] However, problems producing the Maybach GO 5 diesel engines delayed initial road tests until September. Then the train, which had been designed for two of the 410 horsepower engines, was test run on the Friedrichshafen-Ulm line with just one power plant. Not surprisingly, its acceleration was disappointing.[47] By the end of November 1932, the second motor had been delivered and installed in the train. Initial tests proved favorable, confirming the results of the wind tunnel calculations.[48]

At the end of January 1933, the Main Administration ordered the new train, designated the SVT (Schnellverbrennungstriebwagen, or high-speed internal combustion motor car) 877 a/b, to be brought to the test station at Grunewald. It would be run on the Berlin-Hamburg line and on the mountainous Saalfeld-Bamberg line to determine its operating characteristics. Outside observers would be kept away from the tests to minimize interruptions and distractions.[49] Dorpmüller was unable to contain his curiosity about the results of the tests. On 7 April 1933 he telephoned the chief of the RZA, Kurt Emmelius, and asked him for a progress report. Emmelius related how the little train had exceeded expectations. It offered a real speed advantage even over the long-distance express trains currently being operated by the Reichsbahn.[50] With these encouraging results, Dorpmüller and the Main Administration decided to commit the SVT 877 a/b to service on the Berlin-Hamburg line. On 15 May 1933, the train, quickly dubbed by the press and the public the "Fliegender Hamburger," made its first run.[51] The train was always sold out, indicating that there was a demand for such a service, but the new technology did not function smoothly at the outset. The Maybach engines had been chosen because they were based on a proven design. However, they had not themselves been used extensively in the form in which they were employed on the Fliegender Hamburger. Therefore, they soon developed serious problems. The difficulty was traced to faulty crankshafts that had been manufactured by Krupp. Maybach had been aware of the problem since January 1932 but had chosen not to inform the Reichsbahn so as to avoid delays. To solve the difficulty, Reichsbahn officials supervised the assembly of the crankshafts at the manufacturer.[52]

The Fliegender Hamburger also encountered ride problems. During test runs, it had bounced uncomfortably. The problem was traced to the power trucks. After adjustments were made, a demonstration was conducted on the Berlin-Hamburg route on 6 June. On the way from Hamburg, near the town of Wittenberge, three cups filled almost to the brim with water were placed in various places in both cars. When the train arrived in Berlin, the crew observed with satisfaction that not a single drop had spilled.[53] Gradually, over the next few months, the reliability of the Fliegender Hamburger, and especially its Maybach diesels, improved. However, a single small train could not protect even the limited schedule with just two runs daily. Therefore, in July 1933 the Main Administration ordered the RZM to purchase four additional trains built to a similar design.[54] Changes involved primarily the interior. Leibbrand was convinced that the designers had gone too far to save weight, resulting in a lack of comfort for the passengers. He decided that the new trains would have fewer seats, wider windows, and other amenities.[55]

Precisely how the Reichsbahn would use its motor cars and the new high-speed motor trains remained open. Leibbrand was already convinced that they represented a viable means for competing against automobiles. He therefore developed a long-range plan for the acquisition and operation of motor trains by the Reichsbahn, which the board considered during an extraordinary meeting on 29 May 1934. Leibbrand explained to the board that the main goal of the motor train program was to reduce operating expenses. Secondarily, using motor trains could slow or stop the loss of passenger traffic to automobiles, and possibly even win back some traffic. This would be achieved by increasing the frequency of train service and reducing travel time by raising operating speeds. These service improvements could not be achieved by either steam trains or electric traction at an acceptable cost. The best alternative was the construction of diesel-powered motor cars and trains. Currently, Leibbrand doubted that power plant technology had been developed sufficiently to sustain such a concept. However, if the Reichsbahn supported the industry through orders, sufficient progress would be made in the foreseeable future to make a nationwide system of motor trains feasible. Leibbrand then described the system that he proposed to build over the next seventeen years. He suggested ordering four different types of motor trains for main lines to cater to different market segments. Two would be for high-speed service at 160 kph. Smaller motor cars would be obtained to deliver service on secondary lines. Overall, he would require 4,271 motor trains and motor cars, only 71 of which would be designed for high-speed service. He anticipated converting about 80 percent of the Reichsbahn's main-line passenger service to motor trains, or carrying about two-thirds of the railway's passengers with the new vehicles. He estimated that the overall program would cost 1.5 billion RM. Due to the reduced operating costs that it would yield, however, it would result in 111.8 million RM in direct savings annually, in addition to lower pension costs resulting from a reduction in operating personnel.[56] The board discussed Leibbrand's ambitious plan in detail and decided to proceed with limited orders to perfect both the technology and the operating concept. However, it remained skeptical. Siemens and Anger still preferred electric traction. Significantly, the board remained doubtful that passenger traffic could be won back from the roads.[57]

The Fliegender Hamburger encountered additional problems with its Maybach diesels during 1934, leading Siemens to exclaim in one board meeting that electrification was still the best means of motorizing rail operations. Yet the board continued to authorize the expenditure of funds for the purchase of additional diesel motor cars and trains.[58] The Reichsbahn introduced more high-speed motor train services, creating a network that linked the major population and business centers of the country by 1938. Complementing these exclusive trains, motor cars appeared in steadily increasing numbers on secondary lines and on main lines in less urgent services.

The expansion of motor train operations was accompanied by controversy. Many passengers, including some prominent ones like Hitler and Schacht, complained about the lack of comfort on the high-speed trains. Their objections were overcome in the later, larger designs.[59] More difficult were philosophical objections raised by the Mechanical Section and the demands of claimants for the resources needed to build the cars and especially their diesel engines. The Mechanical Section opposed Leibbrand's plans and cut the allocation for motor trains in the 1935 budget.[60] It doubted that a technically mature motor train existed and questioned Leibbrand's intention to shift a large proportion of the Reichsbahn's passenger service to such trains. It went so far as to allude to a "motor train mania" prevailing in Leibbrand's Operating Section.[61] The result of these controversies was that Dorpmüller attributed only secondary importance to the high-speed motor trains and preferred that motor trains be used primarily in local traffic.[62] A small but essential part of Leibbrand's system was losing favor at the highest level. More important than these internal disputes was the increased competition for resources caused by the Nazi government's rearmament program. The production capacity of the engine manufacturers was limited. Access to this potential was sought by the navy for its submarines and by the army for its tanks and other vehicles. Kleinmann expressed the government's view when he told Bergmann to consider the cessation of motor train production to free plant resources for the military in August 1936.[63] The Air Ministry asked the Reichsbahn to cancel its orders to free manpower to work on its contracts.[64] An investigation conducted by Hermann Stroebe of the Mechanical Section concluded that the diesel engine producers did have sufficient capacity to fulfill the Reichsbahn's needs. But he too recommended placing only limited orders because diesel engines for rail applications remained immature.[65]

The consequence of internal opposition, technical problems, and the competition for resources with other agencies meant that diesel motor cars and trains provided only a small proportion of the Reichsbahn's passenger service when war broke out in September 1939. As of 31 December 1939, the DRB owned 4,651 motor cars and unpowered trailers. Of these 1,510 were diesel units and trailers for Leibbrand's system. The majority were electric multiple units used on the Berlin S-Bahn.[66] The diesel motor cars delivered 7.8 percent of the passenger-kilometers and 7.2 percent of the passenger-train-kilometers provided by the DRB in 1938, their last full year of operations before the war.[67] This represented a major increase since the early 1930s but was well below what Leibbrand had hoped to achieve. The most celebrated of the motor trains, the Fliegender Hamburger, more than covered its operating expenses, but it and its high-speed stablemates delivered only a minuscule proportion of the Reichsbahn's passenger service.[68]

The development of the Reichsbahn's high-speed motor trains was accompanied by a painful controversy concerning who should receive credit for priority of their development and over the fate of alternate designs. Franz Kruckenberg, a former airship designer, founded the Transportation Technology Company (Gesellschaft für Verkehrstechnik, or GVT) in 1924 with the purpose of revolutionizing rail transportation and winning prestige for Germany. Kruckenberg initially proposed building a propeller-driven monorail vehicle that would operate at unprecedentedly high speeds. To demonstrate the feasibility of his concept to a skeptical Reichsbahn, he built a propeller-driven rail car called the Rail Zeppelin (Schienen Zeppelin).[69] In addition to its unique propulsion system, the Rail Zeppelin featured an efficient aerodynamic shape and was built using lightweight materials and advanced techniques. In a test run made on 21 June 1931, the Rail Zeppelin achieved an impressive 230 kph.[70] Both the construction of the train and its testing were supported financially by the DRG. Impressed, but still skeptical, the Reichsbahn asked Kruckenberg to convert the Rail Zeppelin to conventional wheel drive and provided him with the money to do so.[71] The DRG also advised him to form an alliance with an established car builder so that he could produce a larger, even more advanced train for operational testing.[72]

Conversion of the Rail Zeppelin was completed in November 1932.[73] Test runs were sufficiently encouraging to justify continued work on a new, three-car train. However, progress was delayed by Kruckenberg's inability to produce suitable engineering drawings, his difficult behavior, and the allocation of production capacity by the train's builder, Westwaggon, to military contracts.[74] To accelerate the construction process, Kruckenberg turned to the Nazi Party for help, discussing his plans with Hitler in September 1934.[75] He accused the Reichsbahn of stealing his concept for high-speed rail service and specific technical features of the Rail Zeppelin.[76] None of this brought the completion of his new train any closer. Finally, the train was ready for operational testing in June 1938. However, it was plagued with axle-bearing problems that delayed the beginning of the tests until June 1939. Then it achieved 215 kph during a test run

Table 2.2. Profile of Reichsbahn Passenger Traffic and Operations, 1933-1939

Year	Passengers (billions)	Passenger-Train-Kilometers (millions)	Car-Axle-Kilometers (billions)	Average Trip (kilometers)	Passenger-Kilometers (billions)	Revenues (billion RM)	Revenues per Passenger-Kilometer (pfennigs)
1927-29[a]	1.97	392.3	10.33	23.78	46.73	1.42	3.03
1933	1.24	423.2	8.7	24.28	30.1	0.85	2.81
1934	1.36	448.4	9.3	25.62	34.8	0.92	2.63
1935	1.49	486.3	9.9	26.54	39.5	0.99	2.50
1936	1.61	506.4	10.3	27.00	43.5	1.07	2.46
1937	1.81	526.5	11.1	27.71	50.1	1.19	2.37
1938	2.04	612.7	13.0	29.00	58.9	1.33	2.37
1939	2.21	568	13.1		61.9	1.69	2.73
Percentage Change							
1939 vs. 1927-29	+12.18	+44.79	+26.82	+21.49	+32.46	+19.01	−9.9

[a] Average.
Source: DRG/DRB, *Geschäftsberichte*, 1927-39.

on the Berlin-Hamburg line but was immobilized by a broken axle two days later.[77] The cause of the repeated failures was faulty assembly of the axles by Krupp.[78] At this stage, with the impending outbreak of the war, plant capacity was unavailable to produce a replacement axle, effectively ending work on the project.[79] Over a decade, the Reichsbahn had spent 1.2 million RM on Kruckenberg's various projects.[80] It received very little in return, due largely to technical misfortunes and Kruckenberg's disorganized work style. Kruckenberg's claims that the Fliegender Hamburger incorporated technology pirated from him are without foundation. The SVT 877a/b was the result of an independent line of development. Moreover, Kruckenberg was neither the first to contemplate high-speed rail operations nor the first to propose use of an airscrew to drive a rail vehicle.[81]

The passenger traffic of the Reichsbahn increased significantly during the 1930s (Table 2.2). By 1938, it had exceeded the average for the years 1927 to 1929. However, in line with its role as serving the common good and its policy of increasing train frequency to retain traffic in its competition with the roads, the number of passenger-train-kilometers that it offered, which had not been cut during the Depression, exceeded the pre-Depression average throughout the thirties and grew faster than ridership. Indeed, in 1938, the Reichsbahn delivered 57.4 percent more train-kilometers than it had before the Depression. The size of the Reichsbahn's passenger trains as indicated by the car-axle statistics did not increase commensurately. The number of passenger-kilometers that the

DRB delivered in 1939 was 32.5 percent higher than the pre-Depression average, having grown more than the total number of riders, but less than train-kilometers. This was due to the increase in the average length of a trip, caused by travel occasioned by the armaments buildup. The increase in the Reichsbahn's passenger traffic as measured in passenger-kilometers actually outpaced the growth of the German economy as a whole. While the German net national product increased by 72.6 percent between 1933 and 1938, the DRB delivered 86.4 percent more passenger-kilometers over the same period. However, the Reichsbahn's passenger revenues did not grow to the same extent, increasing just 19 percent beyond the 1927–29 average by 1939. This was due to its policy of offering extensive discounts. The effects of the discount policy are reflected in the decline in revenues per passenger-kilometer. They reached a low of 2.37 pfennigs per kilometer in 1937 and 1938, rising slightly to 2.73 pfennigs in 1939. This was still 9.9 percent lower than the pre-Depression average. The increase in 1939 was due to the cancellation of some discounts at the end of the year and the higher tariffs of the newly absorbed Austrian, Sudeten, and Czech railways. The increase in traffic lowered the operating ratio of the Reichsbahn's passenger service to 113.7 in 1938, a major improvement compared with the 132.35 of 1933, though inferior to the pre-Depression years. The reason was that revenues rose faster than operating expenses.

B. Freight Service and Modal Competition

The Reichsbahn experienced major growth in its freight traffic as a result of the Hitler regime's rearmament program. Between 1933 and 1938, the number of ton-kilometers delivered by the Reichsbahn to the German economy increased by 87.9 percent, exceeding the rate of growth of the economy as a whole. Yet the Reichsbahn perceived itself as not benefiting fully from the increase in economic activity due to tariff reductions and the loss of traffic to its modal competitors, especially trucks. Neither the Reichsbahn nor the truck operators and forwarders were satisfied with the regulation of October 1931. The forwarders especially remained violently opposed to the railway's relationship with Schenker. When Hitler came to power, the motor vehicle interests in Germany saw an opportunity to gain political support. Hitler was quite accurately perceived as an automobile enthusiast. Consequently, the bitter dispute over the relationship between road and rail continued even after the change of government.

The forwarders attempted to convince the Nazi regime to remove the subsidies granted by the Reichsbahn to drayage companies in February 1933. Representatives of the forwarders visited Lammers in the Reich Chancellery to make their case.[1] At the same time, the Reichsbahn attempted to defend itself from the price competition of the truckers in the long-distance market. It resumed granting subsidies through Schenker to companies that would assemble less-than-carload freight (LCL) into single shipments for long-distance carriage. Reich transportation minister Eltz objected to this initiative, stating that the Reichsbahn should concentrate on bulk commodity traffic and that trucks should be used to carry smaller shipments, particularly in rural areas.[2]

Dorpmüller met with Hitler to discuss the issue of modal competition on 16 March 1933. The general director argued for a national truck monopoly controlled by the Reichsbahn on behalf of the Reich government, pointing out again that the loss of high-tariff traffic would make it impossible for the railway to offer low tariffs for bulk commodities. He also asserted that unified control of truck operations would ensure that a stock of well-maintained trucks would be available in time of war. Hitler responded that he would not allow the Reichsbahn to be destroyed by road competition, but that motor vehicles and airplanes would carry an increasing volume of traffic. He feared that the Reichsbahn would not promote the development of road traffic adequately and would entrust it with a general freight monopoly only if it assured him that it would do so. He then ordered Eltz-Rübenach to prepare a law that would create a motor vehicle monopoly.[3]

Dorpmüller interpreted Hitler's comment to mean that when the Reichsbahn showed that it would develop trucks to suit the government's needs, it would be granted the land freight transport monopoly that it sought.[4] Eltz encouraged him in this view.[5] In line with this, on 24 May 1933 the Reichsbahn reached a partial compromise with the forwarders, agreeing to end its competitive practices against them. In return, drayage prices would be set both to ensure a sufficient return for the forwarders and to permit the DRG to offer competitive door-to-door tariffs.[6] In effect, the railway sought both to please Hitler and to clear away the difficulties caused by middlemen, the forwarders, so that it could come to grips with its main competitors, the long-distance truckers. Eltz then took another step to divide the market on 1 July 1933. He ordered the Reichsbahn to stop using its own trucks for pickup and delivery service and announced that subsidies to truckers and the forwarders who worked with the railway would be abolished by the end of September 1933. He assured the Reichsbahn that he wanted it to operate trucks, but that it should do so as part of a publicly organized monopoly.[7] Dorpmüller expressed his willingness to comply but stressed that the proposed monopoly should be controlled by the Reichsbahn.[8] Eltz certainly wanted to eliminate competition in the long-distance freight transport market, but he could not decide exactly what to do. By November he was contemplating having the Reichsbahn sign long-term contracts with truckers that would ensure them business while allowing the railway to allocate traffic among them. Yet he was daunted by what he considered the disorganization of the forwarders and the uncertainty within the Reich government about how to handle the Reichsbahn.[9] Clearly, Eltz was losing the initiative on the matter of the regulation of modal competition. Dorpmüller had begun to maneuver the Reichsbahn into a position to take advantage of Hitler's attempt to realize his dream for the motorization of German society. But, in so doing, he encountered new, more resourceful competitors.

Hitler's plans to build a system of highways spanning all of Germany combined with his desire for unified control over domestic freight transportation opened before Dorpmüller's eyes the tantalizing prospect of the Reichsbahn restoring its land freight monopoly. In a meeting with the leaders of the Hamburg-Frankfurt-Basel (Hafraba) company and Dorpmüller on 10 April 1933, Hitler told the general director that "the Reichsbahn must make plans like the Hafraba to build highways itself." Dorpmüller agreed and told Hitler that the Reichsbahn would begin preparations to buy motor vehicles.[10] At the Reichsbahn board's next meeting, Homberger proposed a 15 million RM program to obtain trucks to enable the DRG to enter the freight trucking business in all arenas on a major scale. Johannes Vogt, head of the Traffic Section, warned the board that if the Reichsbahn failed to act, someone else would preempt it. The board reluctantly authorized the expenditure.[11]

Dorpmüller's effort to seize control of the trucking industry seemed to take another step forward on 29 May 1933. Hitler told a group of industrialists that the Reichsbahn would be made responsible for building the Autobahnen. This would lead to a fair division of labor between road and rail and ensure that the German transportation system would be adequately prepared for war. Moreover, the Reichsbahn would own the new highways and operate trucks on them. It would own the gasoline stations that would serve the Autobahnen and therefore be able to determine the prices charged for freight transportation in the national, commonweal interest.[12] In a subsequent conversation with Hitler, Dorpmüller asked for a law to codify Hitler's plans for the Reichsbahn and the Autobahnen. He offered to spend 50 million RM of the railway's money to begin work on highways linking Munich with Salzburg and Berlin with Stettin. Hitler agreed and asked Dorpmüller to work with Eltz to prepare a draft law that the cabinet would discuss in early June. To ensure that everything was clear to all concerned, Dorpmüller then said that the law could create a company that would build the Autobahnen. That company would be a section of the Main Administration of the Reichsbahn.[13]

The cabinet meeting promised by Hitler took place on 15 June 1933. Dorpmüller was unwilling to steer the discussion in the direction of the monopoly that he sought for the Reichsbahn, and Hitler did not. Eltz spoke of having his ministry supervise all road traffic in Germany. In the absence of a decision, Hitler announced that the matter would be raised again at a subsequent cabinet meeting.[14] That meeting came on 23 June. It was a setback for Dorpmüller. The initial draft of the Autobahn law had placed complete control of the new highways in the hands of the Reichsbahn. Then, on 21 June 1933, it was altered, removing control of the placement and design of the highways from the Reichsbahn and assigning them to a general inspector for German roadways. The cabinet meeting approved this altered draft. Six days later, on 30 June, Fritz Todt was named general inspector.[15] The law made the Reichsbahn responsible for the construction and operation of the Autobahnen through a subsidiary that it would create. The new company was given exclusive rights to build and operate the new highways. It could assess user fees with the approval of the RVM. The law made the general inspector responsible only for the design and location of the roads. The justification attached to the law stated that part of its rationale was to end the competition for freight traffic in Germany by placing the control of all commercial freight carriage under the Reichsbahn. However, the insertion of Todt meant that this aim would not be achieved. Hitler had chosen to split authority over the Autobahnen between the Reichsbahn and someone he knew to be an advocate of motorization. The wording of the law did not accurately reflect Hitler's intent. Dorpmüller had been outmaneuvered. The Reichsbahn's effort to create a land freight monopoly had suffered another setback, but it had not been completely defeated. The railway was still charged with major responsibilities in relation to the Autobahnen that it could use to

Freight Service and Modal Competition

strengthen its position. Much would depend on Dorpmüller's ability to restrict Todt's authority in the future.

Dorpmüller presented a plan to the board of directors for the creation of the Reichsautobahn-Gesellschaft (RAB) on 3 July 1933. The scheme separated the budget of the RAB from that of the Reichsbahn. The railway would provide administrative and engineering support to the new company to allow it to begin work immediately. The first stretch to be built would connect Frankfurt am Main with Heidelberg and Mannheim. A construction office had already been formed by the Reichsbahn in Frankfurt am Main to manage the effort on 24 June.[16]

In late July, Todt managed to whittle away a bit more of the Reichsbahn's authority. The Autobahn law had not provided for a board of directors for the new company. Todt, however, convinced Hitler to allow him to name one. A special committee of the Reichsbahn board then met to discuss a proposed implementing law that included provision for a board as envisioned by Todt. Siemens noticed this crucial change and pointed out that the Reichsbahn should name the board because it was the sole owner of the Autobahn company. The committee agreed to a compromise under which the board should be named by the president of the board of directors of the Reichsbahn, Siemens, together with Todt.[17] Kleinmann intimated what was in store for the Reichsbahn when he reported that Hitler had told a meeting of railroaders three weeks earlier that high-quality freight would shift to the roads while bulk commodities would remain with the Reichsbahn.[18] Work began on the first section of the Autobahn in September 1933. The Reichsbahn assigned 852 officials to the project in 1934 and 1,106 in 1935.[19]

The failure to gain effective control of the Autobahnen gave the struggle over a new overland freight transport law renewed importance. Yet here, too, Dorpmüller was unable to convince Hitler to decide in favor of the Reichsbahn. Working against him were Wilhelm Keppler, Hitler's personal economic adviser, and Todt. Eltz still advocated giving the Reichsbahn a monopoly of land freight transport. But Hitler was already moving away from this solution and postponed a decision on the matter.[20] In early May 1934 Eltz submitted a draft law that would have empowered the Reichsbahn to allocate freight among truckers.[21] Yet Dorpmüller continued to lose ground. Hitler told him on 27 June 1934 that, although the Reichsbahn would remain the "backbone of transportation," he wanted both rail and road to realize their full technological potential. Consequently, he favored a draft law prepared by Keppler under which the Reichsbahn would control only freight traffic on the Autobahnen. On all other roads competition would continue, but it would be regulated so that it would be "mild." Hitler did not want to compel the remaining opponents of a monopoly to abandon their opposition. Therefore he had chosen the route of regulation once more. Eltz had not been shown the new draft yet, so a further delay would occur.[22] Eltz and Keppler then attempted to convince Hitler to accept their respective drafts, the former providing for a monopoly controlled by the Reichsbahn, the latter for regulated competition between road and rail. The debate lasted through the summer. Hess was ready to bring the matter before the cabinet in late September, but Todt convinced him to wait yet again so that he could prevent the Reichsbahn from gaining the monopoly that it sought.[23]

Hitler finally decided the issue in late 1934. On 27 November he told Dorpmüller that he was not ready to create a land freight monopoly. To prevent truckers from undercutting the Reichsbahn's tariffs, a compulsory truck cartel would be formed instead. Hitler assured Dorpmüller that if this measure did not put an end to the cut-rate pricing of the truckers, he would take sterner measures. However, before he could do that, he had to try regulated competition based on quality of service one more time. In effect, Hitler agreed with Dorpmüller that trucks should be controlled by the state, but not through the Reichsbahn. Dorpmüller interpreted this to mean that the Reichsbahn had not been doing enough to support motorization. Ernst Brandenburg of the Transportation Ministry thought that the stumbling block had been the truckers' fear of losing their livelihoods because the Reichsbahn was operating increasing numbers of trucks itself. The forwarders had objected to a railway freight monopoly because that would have cut them out of the business. Consequently, for the foreseeable future, the Reichsbahn would operate both trucks and trains, the former on the Autobahnen. Privately owned truckers and forwarders would still compete with the Reichsbahn for traffic, but based on only the quality of their service.[24] The actual regulation was debated by the government for another six months. Hitler's decision for continued regulation, while fully within the German tradition of market organization, also fit into his leadership strategy at this stage of his rule, under which he avoided confrontations with important interest groups in order to maintain domestic political stability.

The new freight truck regulation was duly accepted by the Reich cabinet on 26 June 1935. It created a Reichs-Kraftwagen-Betriebsverband (Reich Truck Operating Association, or RKB). All truck operators and forwarders were required to join. The RKB would allocate truck space and collect fees for the transport of goods. The truckers would not actually negotiate with shippers over either price or service. The RKB would establish uniform national tariffs in negotiations with the Reichsbahn. To allow time for implementing rules to be prepared, the law was scheduled to take effect on 1 April 1936. Once again, trucks operated by manufacturers (*Werkverkehr*) were not included, robbing the regulation of much of its potential impact. In its last paragraph, the regulation provided for the cancellation of the contracts that the Reichsbahn and Schenker had concluded with forwarders under the October 1931 law. The Reichsbahn remained the owner of Schenker, but the Bahnspedition had been effectively abolished. Schenker became just one among many forwarders.[25] Dorpmüller was disappointed by the new law and continued to seek a monopoly for the Reichsbahn.[26] He and his colleagues in the Main Administration doubted that the new regulation would be enforced any more effectively than its predecessor.[27]

The legal relationship between the Reichsbahn and its modal competitors did not change again until 1938. In that year, Dorpmüller, by then Reich transportation minister, allowed the truckers to compete for carload freight in the Reichsbahn's two cheapest classes, in effect opening bulk commodity transport to the roads. He also removed the legal restriction on the replacement of money-losing train operations on secondary lines with truck service. Dorpmüller thereby set the stage for the long and painful process of line abandonment that would begin in earnest only after World War II. He also eliminated all fees and taxes on drayage charges, thus reducing the effective cost of door-to-door service for the railway.[28]

In 1933 the Reichsbahn began purchasing motor vehicles in substantial numbers for the first time. Previously, it had relied on contractors to deliver pickup and delivery service and had offered very few intercity truck or bus services. With great reluctance, the Reichsbahn began to expand its passenger bus operations after 1933. This was primarily an effort to reduce operating costs when serving remote areas that could not generate sufficient traffic to support train operations and to ensure the Reichsbahn a share of passenger traffic on the Autobahnen. In May 1933 the DRG operated 149 passenger bus lines. However, they represented only a very small portion of the market. The major change came in May 1935 when the railway began offering bus connections on the new Autobahn from Frankfurt am Main to Heidelberg. In June, the Reichsbahn began operating buses on the partially completed Autobahn from Munich to Salzburg and to resort locations south of Munich. The Traffic Section of the Main Administration still opposed operating buses over long-distance routes. However, Kleinmann instructed it to ignore economic considerations and expand bus service. The Reichsbahn, he argued, would never be able to cut fares sufficiently to attract traffic back to the rails. He and Dorpmüller, based on their knowledge of what railways in other countries had done, decided to form a subsidiary to operate the Reichsbahn's buses.[29] In 1936 the Reichsbahn added new services on the Autobahnen as they were opened where it thought that it could compete effectively with other operators. The new lines linked large cities such as Hanover and Magdeburg, or Frankfurt am Main and Karlsruhe and Stuttgart. Dorpmüller's strategy was to establish the services early and, after the highway network was complete, coordinate them with the railway's trains.[30] By the end of 1938, the Reichsbahn operated 291 bus lines with 460 buses. However, it had gained less than 1 percent of the local bus market and only about 2 percent of long-distance bus traffic.[31] Overall, the Reichsbahn's bus service remained unimportant.

During the 1930s, the Reichsbahn also greatly expanded its truck opera-

Table 2.3. Trucks Owned by the Deutsche Reichsbahn, 1929–1938

Year	Trucks	Year	Trucks
1929	35	1934	1,278
1930	45	1935	2,083
1931	66	1936	2,196
1932	135	1937	2,083
1933	144	1938	2,229

Sources: 1929-31, DRG, *Die Deutsche Reichsbahn im Geschäftsjahr 1931*, 335; 1932-37, Ref 11 to Ref 10, 11 Vkk 691, Berlin, 8 December 1937, p. 1, BA R5/3128; 1938, DRB, *Statistische Angaben 1938*, 315.

tions. Initially, the Main Administration and the board were reluctant to enter the freight trucking business. They saw the Reichsbahn as a railway enterprise, not as a transportation company.[32] However, under the pressure of Hitler's demands that the Reichsbahn support motorization, and the fear that others would gain control of road freight traffic before it could, the Reichsbahn moved into trucking (Table 2.3). In 1933 it began using trucks to replace money-losing trains on secondary lines. By the end of the next year, it had 1,127 vehicles engaged in such traffic.[33] Then, in early 1934, it began using trucks to offer new LCL services. By the end of 1936, Reichsbahn trucks served about 5,000 locations that were inaccessible by rail.[34] This expansion of the scope of the Reichsbahn's truck operations was accompanied by a change in its structure. The railway began offering an increasing number of connections between major centers already served by rail. It also increased the proportion of truck service that it offered itself, rather than through contractors. The contractor services continued to grow, but from 1935, the Reichsbahn's own truck operations dominated.[35] About one-fifth of the Reichsbahn's truck operations replaced trains. The remainder competed with commercial truckers for LCL and carload traffic.[36] On the eve of the war, the Reichsbahn anticipated that commercial trucks would ultimately challenge it for about a quarter of its freight business, cutting its revenues by a third. It would attempt to defend its hold on this traffic by using trucks itself, although it still preferred government intervention to protect it from unsocial competition from motor vehicles.[37]

The growth of road freight traffic clearly implied the failure of the truck law of 1935. The Reichsbahn concluded early that the regulation was having little effect, but its pleas for protection went unheeded.[38] The RKB itself encouraged evasion of the regulation. It arranged for shippers to receive kickbacks and stood aside when its members undercut the agreed tariff.[39] The RKB also challenged the Reichsbahn's legal right to operate trucks itself under the 1935 law.[40] The factory trucks had continued to expand their traffic, and in many cases accepted freight from others. The Reichsbahn estimated in 1939 that 200,000

Table 2.4. Tonnage Carried by Reichsbahn Truck Service, 1924-1938

Year	Total	Contractors	Reichsbahn
1924	65,323		
1925	98,769		
1926	196,382		
1927	317,512		
1928	249,346		
1929	231,911		
1930	180,132		
1931	203,568		
1932	168,522		
1933	895,980		
1934	2,972,043		
1935	4,745,295	2,129,109	2,616,186
1936	4,356,172	1,518,177	2,837,995
1937	4,306,230	1,235,523	3,070,707
1938	4,557,814	1,275,355	3,282,459

Sources: 1924-29, DIHT, *Eisenbahn und Kraftwagen*, 5; 1930-32, DRG, *Statistische Angaben 1932*, 234; 1933-34, DRG, *Statistische Angaben 1934*, 268; 1935, DRG, *Statistische Angaben 1935*, 165; 1936, DRB, *Statistische Angaben 1936*, 165; 1937-38, DRB, *Statistische Angaben 1938*, 201.

trucks were being operated by manufacturers, retailers, and others to satisfy their own needs for transportation. This was more than double the number of privately owned trucks that were engaged in local and long-distance service for hire.[41] However, by the late 1930s the Nazi rearmament boom had generated enough traffic to occupy both the Reichsbahn and all of its competitors. The difficulty became finding transportation space, not finding traffic (see Tables 2.4 and 2.5).[42]

To counter its modal competitors, the Reichsbahn also improved the quality of freight train service. This primarily took the form of increasing its speed. The improved track alignments and schedule changes that permitted the increase in running speeds for passenger trains yielded similar benefits for freight trains. The Reichsbahn also eliminated many slow orders, improved its procedures for loading cars and forming trains, and installed automated protection for grade crossings and improved signals. As with the passenger trains, the major increase in freight train speed was achieved in 1934. In 1933 the normal speed for a freight train was 65 kph. In 1934 this was raised to 70 or 75 kph depending on conditions. Some express freight trains operated at speeds up to 90 kph. The result was a significant decline in transit times. For example, in 1927 a freight train took forty-three hours to complete the run from Hamburg to Stuttgart. By 1939 the duration of the trip had been reduced to twenty-eight hours. Speeds were

Table 2.5. Reichsbahn Truck Service
Net Ton-Kilometers, 1924-1938 (in millions)

Year	Total	Contractors	Reichsbahn
1924	0.30	0.30	
1925	1.17	1.17	
1926	3.11	3.11	
1927	5.46	5.46	
1928	4.78	4.66	0.12
1929	4.77	4.39	0.38
1930	4.81	3.67	1.14
1931	4.77	2.91	1.85
1932	2.59	0.32	2.27
1933	17.39	15.15	2.25
1934	60.9	39.90	21.0
1935	93.5	45.4	48.1
1936	121.9	44.9	77.1
1937	202.3	86.9	115.4
1938	299.6	153.3	146.3

Sources: 1924-30, V., "Die Entwicklung des Reichsbahnkraftwagenverkehrs," VW 25 (8 April 1931): 248; 1931-33, "Die Entwicklung des Reichsbahnkraftwagenverkehrs seit 1929," 64. VR, 27-28 November 1934, BAC 43.01/71, Bl. 107; 1934, estimate based on DRG, Statistische Angaben 1934, 268; 1935, DRG, Statistische Angaben 1935, 165, 266; 1936-38, DRB, Statistische Angaben 1938, 201, 300.

also increased on secondary lines.[43] By 1936, however, the effort had reached its limit. Most of the Reichsbahn's freight cars were equipped with two axles. It was discovered that at speeds above 65 kph, with the technologies then in use, such cars bounced excessively, risking damage to cargo and derailments. Leibbrand ordered that the freight train schedule, in contrast to the passenger schedule, not be accelerated further in May 1936. The divisions should determine which trains could operate safely at 75 kph and slow the others back to 65 kph. At the same time it was realized that the Leig (light freight) trains that had been introduced with such great hopes during the late 1920s had failed to stop the loss of LCL to the roads.[44]

Germany was slowly emerging from the Depression in 1933 when Hitler became chancellor. He immediately instituted programs to rearm the country and expanded existing employment schemes. Rail traffic grew in 1933 for the first time since 1929. In 1934 the rearmament programs began to influence the overall level of economic activity. The Reichsbahn's freight traffic expanded significantly and continued to grow until the outbreak of the war in September 1939. Through 1937, the military operations undertaken by the Nazi regime placed little strain on the Reichsbahn. However, during 1938, combined with the demand created by the armaments boom, they imposed significant operating problems on the Reichsbahn.

Hitler's territorial acquisitions had significant effects on the Reichsbahn. The first was the return of the Saar to German sovereignty in 1935. The Reichsbahn was used to transport people to the region to swell the vote in favor of reunification. It was also used to move thousands of people to the supporting rallies that were held in places in the west, such as Koblenz. The population of the Saar voted overwhelmingly in favor of the restoration of German sovereignty. For the Reichsbahn, this meant the acquisition of an important heavy industrial region and the absorption of the area's railways. The Saar Railways, which had operated the region's railroads during the period of French administration, were dissolved and RBD Trier was moved back to Saarbrücken.[45]

The remilitarization of the Rhineland, in contrast, had little effect on the Reichsbahn. The railway was informed only at the last minute that the operation would take place. However, because the number of troops involved was small, one division and parts of another, the Reichsbahn was able to handle the deployment with no difficulties.[46]

The occupation of Austria in March 1938 was not executed as smoothly. No deployment plan existed, so the entire operation was improvised, resulting in delays and congestion on the lines leading to the country and in Austria itself.[47] The process of absorbing the Austrian Federal Railways (Österreichische Bundesbahnen, or ÖBB) by the Reichsbahn began immediately. Ludwig Röbe, formerly of the Finance Section, at that time president of RBD Wuppertal, was sent to Vienna as the Reichsbahn's commissar on 18 March 1938. Kleinmann personally supervised the process leading to the amalgamation of the two railways on 19 March. Some opposition from left-wing workers erupted but was quickly put down, and Jews were immediately removed. As in Germany, the party allowed the Reichsbahn to manage the Austrian railways as it saw fit so long as it served the regime's needs. The ÖBB had been organized differently from the Reichsbahn, so over the ensuing months the Reichsbahn converted the Austrian operating organization and divisional structure to its model, eliminating one of the four existing divisions in the process. A new Construction Section was formed in Vienna to manage the expansion and improvement of the country's lines to accommodate the increased traffic that would result from the erection of new armaments plants planned by Göring.[48]

The Reichsbahn officials who inspected the ÖBB soon after it was taken over considered it worn out. Rolling stock had not been maintained, and track had been built cheaply. Its stations required modernization, and the Reichsbahn's internal telephone network had to be installed. The DRB inherited 31,000 freight cars from the ÖBB, about two-thirds of which were equipped with air brakes. Some would be modified, and others would be confined to Austria, where they would be used in station service due to their advanced age. The

Reichsbahn also received 1,865 standard-gauge steam locomotives and 235 electric engines. They too required maintenance. The DRB quickly imposed its service organization on the Austrian system and appointed German supervisors to each repair works. About 55,000 Austrian personnel were incorporated into the Reichsbahn, many of whom were transferred to positions in Germany. German officials were placed in all of the key administrative positions in the divisions and operating offices to ensure compliance with Reichsbahn procedures. The DRB also inherited the ÖBB's annual operating deficit of about 200 million RM.[49]

The absorption of the Sudetenland in October 1938 presented the DRB with much more difficulty than the previous military operations. On 22 June 1938, the High Command of the Army (Oberkommando des Heeres, or OKH) ordered the Reichsbahn to begin expanding rail facilities in Upper Silesia, Bavaria, and Austria to support an invasion of Czechoslovakia. The work was completed in September 1938. The OKH planned to camouflage the deployment as part of the regular fall maneuvers, which that year were scheduled for the Czech border region. On 16 September, the army told the Reichsbahn to place freight cars at military installations for loading. On the following day, the DRB restricted car allocations for other purposes and began to concentrate on deploying the army. The Munich Agreement changed the operation from an invasion to an occupation. Nevertheless, the movement of the army to the Sudetenland involved a major effort by the Reichsbahn. Some army units, most notably the motorized formations, deployed by road. But the DRB was still required to move thousands of troops and to bring forward supplies for all units, including those entering the country under their own power. Reichsbahn personnel took control of the Sudeten railways on the heels of the advancing troops. The actual absorption of the lines in the region took less time than the incorporation of the ÖBB, although the Czechs disabled much equipment and removed rolling stock when they evacuated the area. The Sudeten lines were assigned to the neighboring Reichsbahn divisions.[50] In March 1939 Germany occupied the rest of Czechoslovakia and reorganized it. Portions were given to Hungary and Poland, and an independent Slovak state was established. The remainder was organized as the Protectorate of Bohemia and Moravia. The Reichsbahn established liaison offices in both states to coordinate the operations of their rail systems with its own.[51]

A final military demand placed on the Reichsbahn before the outbreak of hostilities was the building of defensive fortifications along Germany's western frontier, the Westwall. Initially, the operation was poorly planned by both the Reichsbahn and the Organization Todt, which was responsible for the actual construction work. The Reichsbahn sent additional personnel and locomotives into the area and began using unit trains to move the heavy materials to the construction sites in the Eifel Mountains. The size of the staff of RBD Saarbrücken was doubled, and 490 locomotives were sent to the region from elsewhere in Germany. The greatest obstacle standing in the way of the smooth flow of men and materials was the lack of suitable unloading facilities. Initially, there were only 197, and these were not adequately equipped. The additional Reichsbahn personnel sent to the region built 149 new facilities by the fall of 1938, expanded 73 other stations, and laid fifty-two kilometers of new track. The Obl West in Essen coordinated movements among the divisions serving the area, establishing an office in Wiesbaden to oversee the effort from nearby. Before these measures were taken, the Reichsbahn was unable regularly to meet the target of placing 6,000 cars daily for the Westwall project. Even when the target was occasionally met, many cars were not unloaded promptly, causing individual cars and whole trains destined for the area to back up elsewhere in western and central Germany. The problem was never completely solved, yet by the end of the year, an average of 7,400 cars was being unloaded daily in the Westwall construction area. At the height of the construction effort, the Reichsbahn ran 180 to 200 trains per day loaded with materials to the construction sites. They consisted primarily of gondola cars diverted from coal traffic. When preparations for the attack on Czechoslovakia began, car placings for the Westwall were temporarily reduced. By the time it ended in early 1939, the Reichsbahn had transported almost 9 million tons of freight and 400,000 laborers in connection with the fortification project.[52]

Although freight traffic had increased substantially since Hitler came to power, in the summer of 1935 the Reichsbahn suffered from increasing current liquidity problems and an operating surplus that was too small to pay anticipated charges. These problems were the result of the major discounts that the Reichsbahn had enacted as part of the Brüning deflationary program, the additional cuts made at the insistence of the Hitler regime, and the debts it incurred to finance the job creation programs of both governments.[53] Consequently, Dorpmüller began seeking support within the government for a freight tariff increase. In a meeting to discuss the matter held in the RVM on 31 July 1935, only Koenigs supported the Reichsbahn. Hess and representatives of the finance, economics, food, labor, and propaganda ministries all rejected the proposal.[54] Lammers brought the matter before Hitler in early August. He too rejected a price increase, stressing that the cost of living could not be allowed to rise. Hitler suggested instead that the Reichsbahn cut operating expenses to free cash.[55] Shortly afterward, Dorpmüller ordered the Traffic Section to prepare a thorough reform of the Reichsbahn's freight price structure with the aim of integrating the many commodity rates into the regular tariff scheme.[56] This would not increase revenues, but it would at least make clear to both the public and the government how low the Reichsbahn's tariffs really were. Meanwhile, Dorpmüller and Eltz-Rübenach continued to seek support for a freight tariff increase. The finance minister, Schwerin von Krosigk, told Eltz bluntly that the Reichsbahn would have to balance its budget on its own.[57]

By late September 1935 it had become apparent to the Main Administration that it would be unable to pay its charges on income and that the lack of cash would be even more severe in 1936. So Dorpmüller asked Eltz to help the Reichsbahn by relieving it of some of its political charges, or by letting it enter the credit market so that it could reduce the amounts that it diverted from the operating account to capital projects.[58] Schacht insisted that the Reichsbahn could not be allowed to seek credit if the Reich were to fund its armaments programs. Therefore, attention returned to either raising tariffs or reducing the charges imposed on the railway. Dorpmüller finally arranged for a cabinet meeting with Hitler during which he could make his case. The meeting was initially scheduled for 15 October 1935. At the last minute it was postponed to 17 October. It was then postponed again, this time indefinitely. Dorpmüller protested to Eltz that the situation was becoming intolerable. The Reichsbahn could not complete its budget for 1936 until it knew how its finances would be handled by the government.[59] The meeting finally occurred on 26 November 1935. Hitler, Schacht, Schwerin von Krosigk, Eltz, and Koenigs discussed the Reichsbahn's financial plight with Dorpmüller and Kleinmann. Hitler decided that the Reichsbahn should be allowed to increase its revenues, but only just enough to enable it to meet its financial obligations. He also suggested that the Reichsbahn might be allowed to obtain 100 to 150 million RM on the capital market and that the railway be relieved of the necessity of paying into its accounts for the balancing reserve and the repurchase of the preferred stock. The latter action alone would free 107 million RM. The government also canceled 26.5 million RM in debts that the Reichsbahn owed it from earlier jobs programs.[60] The Reichsbahn then prepared a tariff increase in the form of a surcharge that would be applied to selected goods so as not to raise the cost of living. The increases would yield a total of 103.5 million RM. The Traffic Section proposed that Eltz announce the increases on 17 December and that they go into effect on 1 January 1936.[61] The exact application of the surcharge was decided by Hitler in a meeting held on 12 December 1935. He excepted a few additional items, mostly food, and delayed the announcement until after the holiday season. The increase was actually implemented on 20 January 1936. On 7 October 1936 the surcharge became an integral part of the Reichsbahn's freight tariff.[62]

This was the last occasion on which the Reichsbahn raised its prices before the war. Meanwhile, it continued to grant shippers substantial discounts, particularly to support the Nazi government's arms buildup. For example, during 1937 the Four Year Plan received discounts to ship the raw materials that it used, such as iron ore, slag, and other bulk commodities. It also received special rates for shipping its products, such as synthetic gasoline and diesel fuel. By the fall

Table 2.6. Profile of Reichsbahn Freight Traffic and Operations, 1933–1939

Year	Tonnage (millions)	Freight-Train-Kilometers (millions)	Car-Axle-Kilometers (billions)	Average Haul (kilometers)	Car Placings (millions)	Ton-Kilometers (millions)	Revenues (billion RM)	Revenues per Ton-Kilometer (pfennigs)
1927–29[a]	485.3	247.3	19.36	152.5	46.0	74.1	3.33	4.79
1933	308.1	194.6	13.8	158.6	31.8	47.1	1.81	4.36
1934	365.6	216.7	16.2	158.6	35.6	56.97	2.14	4.27
1935	408.0	239.8	17.8	158	37.7	63.5	2.32	4.08
1936	452.4	257.98	19.4	158	41.2	70.7	2.64	4.15
1937	499.0	286.8	21.7	160.9	44.7	79.8	2.94	4.06
1938	547.0	336.6	24.2	171.5	47.2	88.5	3.15	3.90
1939	564.0	377	28.0	200.7	46.1	(106.2)	3.77	

Percentage Change

1939 vs. 1927–29	+16.2	+52.45	+44.6	+31.6	+0.17	+19.43	+13.21	−18.6

[a] Average.
Source: DRG/DRB, *Geschäftsberichte*.

of 1937, the annual value of the tariff reductions granted to the Four Year Plan had reached about 28 million RM.[63] By 1940, the Four Year Plan benefited from sixty-three commodity tariffs for coal alone that cost the Reichsbahn 23.4 million RM annually in forgone revenues.[64] At the end of 1938, fully 72.4 percent of the Reichsbahn's freight traffic as measured in ton-kilometers, 70.6 percent by tonnage, moved at a discount, yielding a disproportionately low 50 percent of freight revenues. All coal moved at substantial discounts.[65] About 420 commodity rates were in effect in early 1939.[66]

Despite the extensive discounts that it granted, and the fact that its operating budget was still burdened with expenses that properly belonged in the capital account, the Reichsbahn was able to earn a surplus sufficient to meet its charges for the remainder of the 1930s. Beginning in late 1935, the volume of its business, especially its freight traffic, grew faster than it expected, enabling it to earn an operating surplus that was more than adequate to pay its charges[67] (Table 2.6). It even began accumulating reserves again. Yet the Reichsbahn's freight revenues did not grow at the same rate as its traffic due to the decline in its tariffs resulting from the widespread use of discounts. In 1938 the DRB's revenues per ton-kilometer were 18.6 percent lower than the average in the three years preceding the Depression. Between 1933 and 1939, the tonnage moved by the Reichsbahn grew enormously. It exceeded the 1927–29 average for the first time in 1937. The volume of freight train service as measured in train-kilometers moved ahead of the pre-Depression average a year earlier. Owing to the redistribution of industries to areas in central Germany near raw material supplies and out of areas potentially endangered by air attack, the average distance that the DRB carried freight rose substantially. Most of the increase occurred during the last two years before the outbreak of the war. By the end of 1939, average haul was 31.6 percent higher than during the late 1920s. In effect, the Reichsbahn was moving a moderately greater tonnage a much longer distance. The figures also show that the DRB's marshaling yards were approaching the limits of their capacity by the end of the 1930s and that additional traffic could be accommodated only by implementing operating management measures to improve car utilization and by adding car space and yard capacity.

As traffic increased, the Reichsbahn began using the capacity reserves that it had accumulated during the 1920s. Indications that these reserves were being exhausted began to appear in 1937 and became serious in 1938. Car turnaround time (the period between loadings) had remained steady at about three days through the late 1920s and early 1930s. During early 1937, however, it rose to over five days. Then it receded again to about four and a half days, remaining near that mark until the end of 1938.[68] Another sign that the Reichsbahn was using all of its assets was the reduction of the share of its car fleet awaiting repairs to just 2.7 percent during the autumn of 1938.[69] While the Reichsbahn was pressing into service every car that it owned, delays developed due to the inability of receivers to unload cars fast enough. Congestion also resulted from the occupation of the Sudetenland in October 1938. Consequently, for the first time since the early 1920s, the Reichsbahn began to suffer from a backlog of trains that could not be moved into and out of its marshaling yards on schedule. The problem appeared for the first time in July 1938. During the preparations for the attack on Czechoslovakia, between 100 and 200 trains backed up, some as far west as the Ruhr.[70] The backlog reached its peak when the military traffic generated by the occupation merged with the Christmas rush of travelers, workers from the Westwall returning home, and LCL and express trains. At Christmas, 600 trains were mired in the backlog.[71]

An additional sign that the Reichsbahn's ability to satisfy demand was approaching its limit was the increase in the number of freight cars that it did not place on time. A car placing was the setting out of a car at a shipper's or receiver's freight dock or a team track for loading or unloading. Car placing totals reflected the railway's delivery of service to customers and measured the health of the marshaling yards, where freight cars were sorted and freight trains were built and disassembled. The total number of cars that the Reichsbahn placed grew steadily until 1938, when it peaked at just 2.6 percent above the pre-Depression average. It then declined slightly in 1939. This was the result of traffic restrictions imposed in September 1939 due to the initiation of hostilities by Germany and the strain on the Reichsbahn's marshaling yards. Between 1924 and 1929, the share of freight cars ordered by shippers that were not placed for loading on time had fluctuated around 1 percent. In 1928 and 1929, years of peak traffic before the Depression, the percentage of cars placed late actually fell to 0.2 percent, a sign of excellent service. The late placement percentage grew past this level only in 1936 and exceeded 1 percent for the first time in 1937. It then jumped to 10.72 percent in 1938. Most seriously affected was carload traffic. In this segment 15.4 percent of cars were placed late.[72] The increase in late placings meant that the Reichsbahn was still able to satisfy the economy's and the military's demand for car space, but only with delays.

At the advisory board meeting of 6 October 1937, Dorpmüller indicated for the first time that the Reichsbahn was having difficulty satisfying demand. He attributed this to the simultaneous occurrence of military maneuvers, the harvest, and increased industrial demand. Compounding the problem was the fact that passenger traffic had also increased, raising coal consumption and demands for time on the line. Dorpmüller concluded that the Reichsbahn's reserves of passenger cars, crews, station facilities, and locomotives were exhausted and that the supply of freight cars was extremely tight. The passenger schedule would have to be relaxed and further measures taken to ensure the smooth flow of freight.[73] Johannes Schultz, head of the Main Car Office in the Reichsbahn Central Office Berlin, and responsible for allocating freight cars throughout Germany, echoed Dorpmüller's analysis in his annual report covering 1937. He admitted that the Reichsbahn could not always meet demands for freight car space and attributed this to the major increase in traffic caused by the Four Year Plan, particularly construction, armaments production, and Wehrmacht movements. He concluded, "Traffic has now reached such proportions that it is at the limit of the Reichsbahn's ability to handle it with its current fleet of cars." He anticipated a further increase in traffic and warned that the DRB would be able to master it only if it received more freight cars.[74] Paul Sommerlatte, responsible for freight car service in the Reichsbahn headquarters' Traffic Section, openly admitted in an article published in the Reichsbahn's weekly journal that the railway had not anticipated the traffic upsurge. He called upon the government to allocate more steel to the Reichsbahn so that it could obtain more freight cars.[75]

The situation became even more difficult during the summer of 1938. Hitler accelerated rearmament, and preparations for the assault on Czechoslovakia increased industrial and military demands for car space. During the autumn, the Reichsbahn was unable to satisfy the entire demand for car space by industry, resulting in coal shortages among factories and residential consumers and a drop in its own coal supplies.[76] At the 28 September meeting of the board, Leibbrand confirmed that the DRB had been having trouble meeting traffic requirements for months. He felt that the Reichsbahn had reached the limits of its capabilities. Paul Treibe, chief of the Traffic Section, thought the problems were only temporary, but Dorpmüller was convinced that they would be lasting.[77]

The difficulties reached crisis proportions on the very day that Leibbrand warned the board of the Reichsbahn's problems. On 28 September 1938 the Reichsbahn was unable to place on time almost half of the boxcars and more than half of the open cars that industry requested. The difficulty meeting demand persisted into December. The Railway Sections again attributed it to the simultaneous efforts to build the Westwall, absorb Austria, move hundreds of thousands of people to the Nuremberg party rally, the construction projects of the Four Year Plan, the harvest, and the occupation of the Sudetenland. Exacerbating all of these difficulties was the slow unloading of freight cars by receivers. The result was that factories were threatened with closing due to coal and raw materials shortages, exports were reduced, and fertilizer was not delivered to farmers. Leibbrand summarized these individual phenomena as an increase in the sheer volume of freight traffic, its shift to areas that had not previously been major railway traffic regions, and the sudden appearance of special traffics associated with military expansion. Leibbrand now forthrightly considered the Reichsbahn's problems to be of a fundamental, systemic nature, not passing difficulties caused by bad weather.[78] Schultz of the Main Car Office agreed. In his annual review, he reported that in March and October 1938, the two occasions when the Wehrmacht had conducted operations, the Reichsbahn had been unable to satisfy completely the demand for freight transportation. It had not even been able to determine the actual scale of demand. The postponement of coal shipments during the military operations of the fall, and the need to rush them once winter began, led to major operating problems as severe cold and snow struck in December 1938.[79]

The Reichsbahn did not conceal its difficulties. On 30 December 1938 Dorpmüller took the risky step of informing Hitler in writing that the DRB had reached the limit of its potential. He stated that "the irregularities and failures to provide cars of the last few months show that the rolling stock and fixed plant of the Reichsbahn are no longer adequate to meet the demands of the Wehrmacht, passenger, and freight traffic."[80] In March 1939 Leibbrand explained the Reichsbahn's precarious position in an industry publication that was freely available inside and outside of Germany. He showed that the Reichsbahn's physical plant had not been adapted to the increase in traffic caused by Germany's rearmament and expansion.[81] Another article that appeared in the publicly available journal of the Association of Central European Railway Administrations, written by an analyst outside the Reichsbahn, concluded that the DRB had reached the limit of its ability to conduct efficient operations.[82]

To address its problems, the Reichsbahn took it upon itself to ration car space. By 1938 the Third Reich had created a controlled economy in which money was no longer the only means by which resources were allocated.[83] However, because the controls imposed by the government were incomplete and inefficient, the Reichsbahn was forced to act on its own. The DRB responded to the traffic surge of September 1938 by allocating car space to the Wehrmacht and the Four Year Plan at the expense of other claimants. Assigning cars effectively proved difficult because the government provided the railway with no indication of its priorities.[84] Finally, on 18 October 1938, again acting on its own responsibility, the DRB established a detailed set of priorities for the allocation of car space to nonmilitary users. Perishable food and then sugar beets would be moved first. Next would come fuel for the Reichsbahn, public utilities, and industry. Then, after urgent exports that would earn foreign exchange and fertilizer, 3,000 cars per day were assigned to the Westwall project.[85] In January 1939, coal was given highest priority; 42,100 cars per day were allocated to hard coal movements, primarily from the Ruhr, and 23,450 cars per day were assigned to brown coal transport, mostly in central Germany.[86] In August, the priority list again featured food in first place followed by LCL and then freight for the troops deployed on Germany's western border. Coal was assigned fourth place.[87]

Kleinmann called a meeting to discuss car space allocations on 26 July 1939. His intention was to plead once again for guidance from those who were attempting to steer the German economy and to deflect responsibility from the Reichsbahn for the problems that he saw looming on the horizon. He asked for the creation of a single office that would determine what should be moved and when. The gathering decided that representatives of the transportation, economics, and food ministries, along with delegates from the Organization Todt, the Four Year Plan, the OKW, and the OKH, would meet regularly with Sommerlatte to negotiate car space priorities.[88] But this was not what Kleinmann had sought. These were subordinate officials who could not make decisions on their own. Basic policy decisions were needed at the highest level.

C. Finances, Raw Materials, and Manpower

The operating problems that afflicted the Reichsbahn beginning in 1937 can be attributed to the way that it fit into the overall structure of the Nazi economy. The Reichsbahn was not privy to the government's rearmament and strategic plans. Instead, it was forced to react to traffic demands as they arose. In government councils, the Reichsbahn was either ignored or assigned low priority when plans were formulated. Consequently, when the Reichsbahn asked for additional resources to meet increased demand, it was denied access to them. Placing the DRB at a further disadvantage was Dorpmüller's inability to compete effectively with young energetic, ambitious, ideologically committed men such as Todt, or Paul Pleiger of the Four Year Plan Office. Nor could he follow the intrigues of Göring, Hitler, and Hess. The net result was that the Reichsbahn did not anticipate a war until sometime in early 1939. It continued to follow normal acquisition policies until late 1938, when it realized that the expansion of economic activity would continue. When war broke out in September 1939, the Reichsbahn was unprepared for the global conflict that ensued. It could have handled local wars of short duration if it had been integrated into the strategic planning apparatus and if it had abandoned peacetime operating procedures. However, it remained an outsider forced to react to developments well into the war.

The Reichsbahn's relationship with the military stretched back to the days when it was created in 1920. In August 1919 General Hans von Seeckt proposed that the new Reich Transportation Ministry include a section that would be responsible for military affairs. It would be manned by former military officers who would become civilian officials. In addition, officials in each operating division would be named who would establish contact with regional military authorities.[1] Johannes Bell, the transportation minister designate, expressed serious doubts about Seeckt's scheme.[2] In a meeting between the nascent RVM and the state railways on 15 September 1919, it was agreed that military officers could be taken into the divisional headquarters, but that on no account would a camouflaged general staff section for railway matters be established in the Transportation Ministry.[3] Seeckt finally dropped his demand in January 1920.[4] Instead, liaison was established between the military, reorganized as a result of the Versailles treaty's disarmament provisions, and the Reichsbahn. Otto Oppermann, who was responsible for the allocation of both freight cars and passenger cars in the Operating Section, maintained contact with the military, assisted by Friedrich Ebeling. On 15 February 1921, Wilhelm Groener, the Reich transportation minister, and Seeckt signed an agreement to create the Army Transportation Commission (Heerestransportkommission, or

HTK). The HTK would prepare plans for the use of Germany's railways in wartime and for the deployment of large bodies of troops on other occasions. The HTK would consist of Oppermann and the head of the Troop Office's transportation section, T7.[5] T7 was the successor to the Railway Section of the Great General Staff that had planned the railway aspects of the deployment conducted in August 1914.[6] After the creation of the DRG, Oppermann continued to be responsible for liaison with the Reichswehr and still represented the railway on the HTK. Ebeling remained in the RVM and looked after military matters from that vantage point. The military assigned liaison officers to each division. Their railway counterparts were the chiefs of operations, who were given the added title of railway plenipotentiaries (*Bahnbevollmächtigter*).[7]

The Reichsbahn was unwilling to spend money to improve its facilities for the sake of the army, a fact that the Reichswehr well knew.[8] In 1922, the Reichsbahn had canceled a number of construction projects west of the Rhine intended to improve its ability to bring troops to the border with France. It also removed second and third tracks from some lines and demolished loading ramps and bridges intended to facilitate the deployment of troops.[9] In 1923 meetings took place in Leipzig between Reichsbahn operating officials and army officers to prepare a schedule for the deployment of troops by rail. A preliminary version of this plan was completed by February 1924.[10] Then work on it stopped, and it was allowed to languish. The DRG was uninterested in such plans. It ceased printing the emergency schedule to move army formations in order to save money.[11] The HTK proposed that a new schedule be prepared in January 1925. The DRG cooperated and developed a scheme that identified those express and freight trains that would run under any circumstances, the remaining trains being canceled for the duration of the emergency. The slots freed would be used by troop and supply trains. It was also agreed that the DRG would maintain a supply of coal sufficient to operate its locomotives for forty days. In RBD Königsberg, separated from Germany in East Prussia by the Polish Corridor, stocks would be built up to 100 days.[12] In March 1925 the army officers responsible for the various deployment routes conducted an exercise to determine the ability of the railway to meet the military's needs. They uncovered no great problems but did recommend a number of improvements.[13] The Reichswehr asked the DRG to take steps to implement them. The DRG refused. When the military turned to the Reich government, it was informed that neither the finance, the transportation, nor the economics ministries could compel the DRG to expend funds against its wishes. The Finance Ministry then agreed to make the necessary moneys available and to transmit them to the DRG in a discreet manner.[14]

The DRG continued to resist military demands for assistance. In April 1928 Oppermann informed his military counterpart on the HTK that the Reichsbahn no longer maintained a comprehensive deployment schedule.[15] The military could do nothing but acknowledge this setback. Shortly afterward, the transportation officers of the army's field divisions submitted a list of construction projects that they considered necessary to enable them to use the railway effectively for deployment. The total cost was 240.4 million RM.[16] This amount was later increased to 800 million RM. The request died a silent death due to lack of funding. As one transport officer put it, "It is certain that the Reichsbahn will not do anything for us voluntarily without money." He also admitted, "We have received little support from the Reich transportation minister."[17] The most that the Reichswehr could achieve before 1930 was an agreement with the DRG to share the costs of demolition facilities installed in railway bridges. The military consented to pay for the construction of the chambers and the explosives themselves. The DRG would bear the costs of maintaining the chambers as part of its regular bridge maintenance budget.[18]

The atmosphere changed somewhat after the implementation of the Young Plan in 1930. Allied supervision of the DRG ended, giving the Reich government greater influence over its policies. This permitted closer cooperation with the Reichswehr, especially when substantial sums of money were not involved. In 1931 the Reichsbahn prepared plans for air raid protection of its facilities in cooperation with the military.[19] It also resumed preparing railway mobilization plans. By July 1932 a detailed high-performance mobilization schedule was ready for use.[20]

With the assumption of power by the Nazis, the Reichsbahn was gradually brought into a closer relationship with the armed forces, especially the army. In November 1933 a counterespionage organization was created within the Main Administration to prevent potential enemy powers from gaining access to strategically important railway information.[21] The office in the Reichsbahn responsible for liaison with the military had been vacant since 1932 when Oppermann retired. In 1933 Ebeling was brought over from the RVM to fill the post. In 1935, consonant with Hitler's proclamation of the restoration of Germany's full military sovereignty, Ebeling organized Group L (Landesverteidigung, or National Defense) in the Main Administration.[22] On 12 October 1937 Colonel Rudolf Gercke was named head of Section 5, the successor to T7. He would occupy this post until the end of the war and would decisively shape the relationship between the armed forces and the Reichsbahn. At the end of August 1939, his office was renamed, and he assumed the title of chief of military transportation (Chef des Transportwesens, or Transchef).[23] Germany was divided into transportation regions covering one or more RBD. An officer was assigned to each region, where he maintained ties between the local defense region (*Wehrkreis*) and the relevant divisions.[24] Five working groups were formed in Berlin to address the various questions that arose concerning the railway's potential role in military operations.[25] All military requests for information, resources, or policy decisions were routed through Ebeling's Group L.[26]

In April 1933 the Reichsbahn began preparation of detailed deployment plans including the allocation of schedule slots, rolling stock, and air raid protection measures.[27] An exercise was conducted to determine how both the army and the Reichsbahn would react to the loss of the Ruhr and Upper Silesia. In connection with this, the Reichsbahn conducted tests to determine the utility of using brown coal obtained from central Germany, away from Germany's borders, rather than hard coal as a locomotive fuel.[28] On 9 May 1934 military representatives discussed their requirements with Leibbrand. They expressed concern about the electrification of lines because they thought that it made them more vulnerable to air attack. They also provided details of the number of steam locomotives, freight cars, and passenger cars that they would need in the event of a mobilization. They asked Leibbrand to ensure that the railway maintained a sufficient number of steam locomotive engineers despite its increased use of diesel and electric vehicles, and asked him to obtain equipment that would enable them to use boxcars to transport men and horses.[29] The military representatives were pleased with the general ability of the Reichsbahn to move traffic. The recent efforts to increase speeds and the efficiency of stations and rolling stock indicated to them that, at that point, the Reichsbahn would have no difficulty meeting their needs.[30] The Reichsbahn also began forming units of railway personnel that would accompany the military on campaign to operate field railways and restore service on the lines in the areas captured from an enemy. These men were inducted into the military and known as "Graue Eisenbahner" (Gray Railroaders).[31]

The military identified construction projects necessary to increase the railway's ability to deploy troops away from the main lines that had been improved for commercial reasons. On 23 June 1933, a special cache, the Dorpmüller Fund, was created using money diverted from the proceeds of the transportation tax. From 1933 through 1935, 11 million RM were expended through this conduit to improve lines in Pomerania and the Rhineland.[32] In addition, the HTK allocated 3 million RM of its money for construction activities.[33] Finally, during the winter of 1933-34, the Winterbau construction program was supported with 13.5 million RM as part of the government's job creation program. It was channeled to the military through the German Company for Public Works (Deutsche Gesellschaft für öffentliche Arbeiten, or Öffa).[34] The money was used to improve rail facilities at military bases, build a bypass line in Stettin, and obtain a few cars fitted with antiaircraft guns.[35] During the following year, the Finance Ministry, the army, and the Reichsbahn together allocated a total of 27.8 million RM to the construction of military railway facilities. Of this amount, the Reichsbahn contributed only 2.29 million.[36] Hitler's announcement of the Four Year Plan and his appointment of Göring as its head with a mandate vastly to increase armaments output, and the military's knowledge of Hitler's desire to expand the size of the German field army, led the military to begin negotiations with the Reichsbahn to prepare a long-range plan to add to the railway's facilities. They mapped out a scheme that would take ten years to complete and involve the expenditure of 500 to 600 million RM.[37] That plan was never implemented because neither the Wehrmacht nor the Reichsbahn could obtain the necessary raw materials, as will be demonstrated shortly. Moreover, the duration of the plan did not correspond to Hitler's much shorter timetable.[38]

In June 1938 an emergency construction program was launched to improve railway facilities in the deployment area near the Czech border and in the Rhineland.[39] The latter was intended to facilitate the defense of the area if the Allies intervened militarily to aid Czechoslovakia. A smaller expansion plan, incorporating portions of the ten-year facility program, was already under way but had not focused on the areas where operations were imminent. The ten-year program was completely abandoned after the acquisitions of Austria and the Sudetenland rendered its strategic premises obsolete. A new railway expansion program was then laid down by the army calling for the creation of nine deployment routes leading toward Germany's eastern borders. Overall, 84.5 million RM worth of military-related railway construction was completed in 1938. For 1939, the Transchef requested an additional 81 million RM and 145,000 tons of steel.[40] Gercke's plan was immediately cut to 44 million RM by other Reich agencies. He then asked the Reichsbahn to assume the burden of funding the remainder.[41] The creation of the satellite state of the Protectorate of Bohemia and Moravia in March 1939 rendered this plan obsolete as well. Consequently, an emergency program was developed by the army to improve rail facilities in Germany's eastern provinces, Pomerania, and Upper Silesia, and in the Protectorate and Slovakia in preparation for the invasion of Poland that was then being planned. The work would involve only projects of limited scope to strengthen or expand loading platforms and sidings and to widen access roads to stations.[42]

Overall the construction and deployment planning for military purposes engaged in by the Reichsbahn prior to the outbreak of the war was limited in scope and lacked urgency. Deployment plans focused on scenarios imagined by the army, not by Hitler, leading to last-minute improvisations. The construction projects were either small or not intended to be completed during the time frame within which Hitler was operating. In short, until March 1939, they indicate that the Reichsbahn was not aware that a war was imminent. The history of the Reichsbahn's own capital programs confirms this impression.

The imposition of government controls, incomplete as they were, steadily reduced the importance of money as a means of allocating resources in the German economy. Yet, because the Reichsbahn was not privy to the Reich's war plans, it continued to shape its capital strategy in terms of monetary values until it became apparent in 1936 that the key indices had become raw materials, especially steel.

In 1933 it was not clear to the Reichsbahn's leadership that Hitler was steering Germany toward war. The railway's capital requirements seemed to be determined by the prevailing low level of traffic and the prospect that the railway would continue to lose market share to motor vehicles. Consequently, the leadership established comparatively modest goals for obtaining external capital. The primary source of debt was the government's job creation program. This source of capital was troublesome to the Reichsbahn since it could not allocate the money as it saw fit and since it consisted of short-term obligations.

The DRG's initial request for 150 million RM in credits under the regime's job creation program for 1933 was denied by the cabinet on 9 February 1933. Schwerin von Krosigk said that the Reichsbahn did not have the least claim on the government's credit resources. It would contribute to the Reich's job creation program using its own funds, particularly its own credit.[43] Through the spring of 1933, the Reich continued to refuse to support the Reichsbahn with credit while simultaneously insisting that the DRG participate in its jobs program. The DRG did not take part in the Gerecke Program that was funded with government credits. Bowing to government pressure, the Reichsbahn submitted a plan to create jobs in maintenance-of-way projects and a few new construction programs in June 1933. It would spend 250 million RM in 1933 and 310 million RM in 1934. The cabinet accepted this plan and allowed the Reichsbahn to issue bills of exchange backed by the Reichsbank to fund it. However, the cabinet made it clear that it expected the Reichsbahn to retire the debt itself.[44] The railway allocated 155 million to track renewal, 55 million toward maintenance of rolling stock, 70 million to the repair and renewal of fixed plant such as buildings and bridges, 78 million for the purchase of new locomotives and cars, 15 million for the acquisition of motor vehicles, 126 million for expansion of the Berlin S-Bahn by building a north-south tunnel under the heart of the city, and 50 million to begin work on the Autobahnen. Dorpmüller was dissatisfied with this program because the Reichsbahn was committing its own credit to projects he considered mostly unnecessary. As he told the board during its meeting on 3 July, "All of the facilities of the Reichsbahn including vehicles are in the best condition and are not being fully utilized."[45] The job creation program was continued up to the winter of 1934–35, when the Reichsbahn again used its own credit to keep workers employed through the cold months. On 14 December 1934 the RZR (Reichsbahn-Zentralamt für Rechnungswesen, Reich Central Office for Accounting) stopped issuing bills of exchange to pay for job creation, after having distributed such instruments with a total face value of 860 million RM.[46] The Reichsbahn spent a total of 1.067 billion RM on job creation projects from 1932 to early 1935, all backed by its own credit.[47]

With the end of job creation spending, the Reichsbahn resumed the search for credit to support its own capital expansion plans. In late 1934 it defined a need for 150 million RM in external credit for 1935. However, the Reichsbank informed it that the Reich government would monopolize the capital market for its own purposes. The bank recommended that the Reichsbahn turn to its employees' savings banks and insurance funds. Through a series of small transactions, the Reichsbahn had arranged for only about 80 million RM in credit.[48]

Dorpmüller persistently pursued credit for the railway during early 1935. Eltz, however, told him in March that the Reichsbahn would have to fund its capital projects through savings in the operating account.[49] Schacht also continued to bar the railway from the capital market.[50] The Reichsbahn's financial situation became increasingly serious during the spring and summer. Its revenues had not grown rapidly enough to cover its rising operating expenditures, and its short-term debts were beginning to come due. The 150 million RM bond issue from 1930 was scheduled to be repaid on 1 September, and the Finance Section lacked the cash to meet that obligation. The solution to this liquidity problem comprised two parts: the limited tariff increase, discussed earlier; and the conversion of the 6 percent bonds from 1930 into 4.5 percent bonds of the same nominal value with the redemption date pushed back to 1 September 1941.[51] These actions, along with the government's permission to forgo allocating funds to legally required reserves, effectively prevented the Reichsbahn from defaulting on its obligations and enabled it to balance its operating budget until revenues increased sufficiently to end its money worries in 1936.

Before it became clear to the Finance Section that the crisis had passed, it and Dorpmüller continued to worry about funding the Reichsbahn's limited capital plans for 1936. In August 1935 Dorpmüller asked Schacht for permission to obtain 187 million RM in external credit.[52] Again, he received only a sharply worded refusal.[53] Dorpmüller then asked Schacht to make good on his assurances given in 1933 to discount the Reichsbahn's job creation bills. Schacht denied ever having made such a commitment. He told the Reichsbahn that it would simply have to pay for its capital projects from its operating revenues and that, if it became more efficient, it would have no trouble doing so.[54]

One of the reasons Schacht refused to open the credit market to the Reichsbahn was that Hitler had given priority in access to available investment funds to the new Reichsautobahn Company. Hitler informed Dorpmüller on 18 September 1933 that he wanted a total of 6,500 kilometers of highways built at the rate of 1,000 kilometers annually. He estimated that this would cost 500 million RM each year and promised that the Reichsbank would arrange for credit to fund the project.[55] Soon afterward, Schacht informed Dorpmüller that this credit requirement would be satisfied before the Reichsbahn's needs could be considered.[56] The Reich Finance Ministry floated ideas for various financing operations during 1933 and 1934. In the meantime, the Reichsbahn spent its own money on the highway project. In March 1934 it estimated that it had already invested 200 million RM in the Autobahnen and anticipated that its stake would ultimately reach 500 million. Dorpmüller had been assured that the Reichsbank would assume this burden at some time in the future.[57] Disputes over responsibility for road transport and other financial matters stemming from the rearmament drive delayed resolution of the matter until late 1935. Then, the Reichsbahn's dire credit requirements and the effective assignment of responsibility for control of the development of the Autobahnen to Todt cleared the way for a solution. The Reichsbank arranged for a 500 million RM public loan nominally for the Reichsbahn. However, 400 million RM was actually assigned to the Reichsautobahnen. The Reichsbahn would use its reputation to attract investors to the offering. The highway administration would repay its portion of the loan. The result was that the Reichsbahn received an infusion of only 100 million RM at 4.5 percent interest, repayable in eight years.[58] This was the Reichsbahn's last large credit operation before World War II began.[59] It continued to subsidize the Autobahn project with money and by seconding skilled engineers and officials to it until the RAB was separated from the Reichsbahn on 1 June 1938. Then, most of the Reichsbahn personnel were withdrawn. However, the railway continued to pay the Autobahn company a 50 million RM subsidy annually.[60] Overall, the Reichsbahn spent at least 600 million RM of its own money on the construction of Germany's highway system between 1933 and the outbreak of the war in 1939.[61]

Between 1933 and 1936, the Reichsbahn also received a number of small credits, most of which were designed to support specific capital projects. In March 1933 the Öffa loaned the Reichsbahn 4.5 million RM, supplemented by half a million RM directly from the Reich, for the electrification of the Halle (S)-Köthen-Magdeburg line in central Germany. The Reichsbahn assumed the remaining 3 million RM in expenses necessary to complete the project.[62] In September 1933 the Reichsbahn accepted another credit from the Öffa, this time for 3 million RM to electrify the line from Augsburg to Nuremberg in Bavaria and the line from Plochingen to Tübingen in Württemberg.[63] In March 1935 the Reichsbahn accepted a loan arranged by the Merck, Finck bank of Munich for 14.5 million RM to expand its facilities serving the site of the annual Nazi Party rallies in Nuremberg.[64] Finally, in 1935, the Reichsbahn obtained a loan of 28.5 million RM from a consortium of electrical equipment companies and a loan of 12.5 million from the Reich unemployment office to electrify the line from Halle (S) to Nuremberg.[65] Cobbling together small credits in this way enabled the Reichsbahn to make substantial progress in its effort to electrify a through route from Berlin to Munich. The impressive aspect of this effort is how little money was involved and how little assistance the Reichsbahn received from the government. Overall, the Reichsbahn contracted little debt to expand its fixed plant or its collection of rolling stock. The government's bar was the major reason for this. In 1936 the Reichsbahn attempted to put the best face on its plight by informing the public that its assets were in such excellent condition, and Germany's railway network was so extensive, that no additional investments were necessary.[66] The only other major addition to the Reichsbahn's debt came not as the result of a credit operation, but due to its assumption of the Austrian railway debt of 360.5 million RM in March 1938.[67] At the end of 1938, the Reichsbahn had a total debt of 2.79 billion RM, or about 871 million RM more than at the end of 1932.[68] Considering the scale of the armaments buildup conducted by the Nazi regime and the overall capital value of the Reichsbahn, this debt increase was modest. Clearly, the Reichsbahn had not been informed of Hitler's aggressive plans and had not been assigned a high priority in preparing for their execution.

Not only did the Reich government not help the Reichsbahn financially, it drew money from the railway's operating account for its own purposes. This took the form of the Reichsbahn's paying for government-mandated capital projects such as rail facilities at military bases, the Autobahnen, and the reshaping of cities selected by Hitler with its own funds. The Brüning government had instituted the contribution to the Reich in 1931. Under this procedure, the Reichsbahn paid 70 million RM to the Reich annually. In 1934 Dorpmüller proposed a modification of this payment. He called for the cancellation of all of the Reichsbahn's political charges and their replacement by an annual lump-sum payment equivalent to 4 percent of its operating revenues. He estimated that this would save the Reichsbahn 100 million RM annually.[69] Eltz supported this proposal, but the reluctance of the other ministries to forgo income prevented it from being acted upon until late 1936. Then, effective 1 January 1937, in conjunction with the Reichsbahn being brought directly under government authority, and with its revenues growing rapidly, the contribution to the Reich was rescheduled to become 3 percent of the Reichsbahn's operating receipts up to 4 billion RM, and 9 percent of its revenues above that amount.[70]

The Reichsbahn was also required to pay the outstanding debt from the nationalization of the state railways in 1920. Under the terms of the Dawes Plan, the DRG was not responsible for this debt. Therefore, the Reich had serviced the debt itself.[71] This changed after the Reichsbahn was returned to the direct jurisdiction of the Transportation Ministry. In June 1937 Dorpmüller agreed with Schwerin von Krosigk that the Reichsbahn would assume responsibility for the debt stemming from the state treaty. The DRB then paid 94.8 million RM to the Reich annually to retire a total obligation that was valued at 2.1 billion RM at the end of 1939.[72]

The creation of mechanisms by the Hitler government to steer the German economy toward its rearmament goals had initially focused on the direction of credit to selected industries and consumers. From 1936, as rearmament accelerated, money ceased to be the primary means for allocating economic resources in Germany. Instead, state authorities, most notably the Four Year Plan Office headed by Göring, began allocating resources with the aim of achieving the ambitious expansion of the German armed forces demanded by Hitler. The shift away from the use of money as an allocating tool did not affect the position of the Reichsbahn. It continued to be assigned a low priority.

Until 1937, one of the major reasons the Reichsbahn did not receive more resources was because it did not ask for them. This can be illustrated by examining its policies concerning the purchase of rolling stock. On 1 November 1935 the Reichsbahn still had 1,280 locomotives that it did not need. It also had about 36,000 freight cars sitting idly on storage tracks. When the inefficient use of other freight cars was taken into account, the Reichsbahn estimated that it had 80,000 excess freight cars at the end of 1935.[73] The Reichsbahn's annual vehicle procurement programs were formulated accordingly. In January 1934 the Main Administration completed a supplementary plan to spend 56.7 million RM on rolling stock above the 91.1 million that it had initially intended for that year. The plan included only 52 steam locomotives and just 560 freight cars. Its emphasis was on vehicles with clearly peacetime uses such as passenger cars and diesel motor cars.[74] This plan was scaled back to 30 million RM in March and approved by the board.[75]

As traffic increased in 1935, the vehicle acquisition program was modified, but its scale was not changed. Leibbrand identified the lack of passenger cars as the most pressing need facing him. To solve the problem, the Reichsbahn stopped retiring passenger cars in March 1935. Indeed, the supply of passenger cars was so tight that the Reichsbahn had difficulty providing sufficient cars to handle the traffic caused by the Nazi Party's events.[76] Leibbrand then prepared a revised request for rolling-stock purchases for 1936. He proposed spending a total of 287.1 million RM, of which the largest amount would be devoted to acquiring passenger cars.[77] Due to the lack of credit, this program was reduced in late June 1935. A new plan to procure rolling stock was prepared, covering just the first half of 1936; the proposal was for less than half of what had been proposed in the preceding program for the entire year. The largest portion of the money sought under the plan was again assigned to the acquisition of passenger cars.[78] This program was then cut in August 1935. The plan that had been intended to cover just the first half of 1936 would now have to suffice for the entire year.[79] When Dorpmüller pleaded with Hitler for a tariff increase and access to the capital market in November 1935, he presented a plan for rolling-stock purchases based on the assumption that there would be no traffic increase. Again, the largest single component of the plan was the acquisition of passenger cars, followed by a substantial allocation for motor cars and trains.[80] The granting of a tariff increase allowed the Reichsbahn to spend 30 million RM more than it had thought possible during the depths of the summer of 1935. However, although it was becoming clear that the supply of freight cars, especially flat cars, was growing short, a large proportion of the additional money was spent on motor trains intended to test various new technologies.[81]

The dispute within the Main Administration concerning how many and what types of vehicles should be ordered erupted anew when consideration of the 1937 budget began during the spring of 1936. Bergmann, the chief of the Mechanical Section, argued that the Reichsbahn had to adapt its spending to its income, particularly because it could not predict how its revenues would develop over the long term.[82] Due to this uncertainty, he proposed a vehicle acquisition plan covering only the first half of 1937. The single largest allocation was for the purchase of passenger cars.[83] On 2 October 1936 the plan was changed to reflect the new situation created by the Four Year Plan. Koenigs visited Bergmann and told him that the Reichsbahn should quickly prepare a vehicle acquisition plan for the second half of 1937 because raw materials were becoming scarce. If it did not move fast, it might not be able to obtain the vehicles that it needed. Bergmann hurriedly prepared a program, but it was still shaped by peacetime priorities. The allocation for passenger cars, 32.2 million RM, was larger than the amounts assigned to steam locomotives and freight cars combined. Total expenditures on all types of vehicles would amount to less than 200 million RM.[84]

Dorpmüller became increasingly aware that the Four Year Plan would make greater demands on the Reichsbahn, which the railway would need more resources to meet. In a presentation to military officers, he argued that the Reichsbahn required additional raw materials if it were to satisfy traffic demands arising from rearmament. He proposed that the Reichsbahn be given priority for raw materials equal to that assigned to Four Year Plan and army projects.[85] This did not happen. Both the Reichsbahn and the RVM were excluded from the planning apparatus created by Göring, despite the fact that Dorpmüller had cultivated an acquaintance with him. Eltz complained to Göring that the Transportation Ministry had been left out of the ministerial planning committee of the Four Year Plan.[86]

The realization that things had changed came hard for the Main Administration. During the 25 November 1936 board meeting, Dorpmüller, Kleinmann, and Prang all said that the Reichsbahn had sufficient freight cars.[87] In a briefing paper for the board of directors completed in January 1937, the Main Administration still contended that the Reichsbahn's freight car fleet sufficed to meet current or foreseeable demands. It explained that the Reichsbahn's collection of freight cars was scaled to meet average demand. Owning enough freight cars to satisfy even episodic peak demands would place an unjustifiable burden on the Reichsbahn's balance sheet and was therefore rejected. When Bergmann indicated that the average age of the railway's freight cars was rising dangerously high, and that traffic was increasing due to the Four Year Plan, Dorpmüller told his subordinate that he was not worried.[88]

By July 1937 Dorpmüller had grasped that access to steel was essential for the Reichsbahn to fulfill transportation requirements. He warned the supervisory board that delays in the delivery of locomotives and freight cars would make it difficult for the Reichsbahn to meet the usual fall traffic surge, now greatly magnified by Four Year Plan traffic. He also indicated that these delays were caused by shortages of steel among the manufacturers. Kleinmann pointed out that Göring had been informed about the Reichsbahn's needs, but there was little hope for improvement because the railway was assigned a low priority.[89] At the end of the month, the Mechanical Section completed its plan for rolling-stock purchases in 1938. It provided for the expenditure of only 95.8 million RM due to the lack of steel. Only eighty-three locomotives would be ordered. Passenger car orders were slashed, and the acquisition of motor cars and trains halted. Steel was in such short supply that the Reichsbahn was already drawing on its 1938 steel allocation to build cars under its 1937 plan.[90] Kleinmann later reported, based on conversations with Göring, that the Reichsbahn's steel quota would not be increased for at least two years.[91]

In December 1937 the Mechanical Section prepared a four-year plan for the acquisition of rolling stock. This was its first significant attempt to prepare a long-range program in light of the accelerated arms buildup. Its overall cost was projected at 2.87 billion RM. It included 2,500 steam locomotives, 379 electric engines, and 118,087 freight cars. But it also included 11,940 passenger cars and restored the motor car program.[92] In many ways, this remained a peacetime proposal, although it was much better adapted to the circumstances as understood by the Reichsbahn. Bergmann's plan survived for only a few weeks. On 10 January it was drastically reduced due the inability of Dorpmüller and Kleinmann to obtain the necessary steel. Indicative of the cut was the reduction in the planned acquisition of steam locomotives to just 305 units.[93] Three days later, Dorpmüller directed the Mechanical Section to prepare an emergency program within two weeks.[94] Dorpmüller's charge led to a dispute among his subordinates that illustrates the challenges faced by the Reichsbahn. In two days of meetings chaired by Bergmann, an acquisition plan providing for the production of 1,082 steam locomotives and 41,009 freight cars was hammered out. Significantly, Bergmann still thought that it was most important to obtain express locomotives for passenger service. The representative of Group L called for the production of specific types of freight locomotives and cars. Bergmann and Leibbrand retorted that if the military wanted locomotives it would have to pay for them. They recommended that Group L think more like railroaders and less like soldiers, foreshadowing the conflicts between the Reichsbahn and the military that would erupt during the war. The key task, however, was finding a solid foundation for planning. Prang, chief of the Financial Section, argued that they could not agree to a firm plan until they were assured that enough steel would be provided actually to build the vehicles. Both Leibbrand and the Group L representative mentioned that the War Ministry had promised to give part of its steel allocation to the Reichsbahn. With this in mind, it was agreed to document a need for 2.2 million tons of steel and ask that the War Ministry increase the Reichsbahn's allocation by 900,000 tons per year. At that time, the Reichsbahn had an annual quota of 750,000 tons. It was also explicitly recognized that the Reichsbahn suffered from a shortage of locomotives and freight cars and that, if this shortage were not relieved, the DRB would not be able to handle the traffic surge that would certainly come in the autumn of 1938. The Reichsbahn simply had to have more steel. From this point onward, the Reichsbahn's capital planning was based explicitly on the availability of raw materials rather than money.[95]

The Reichsbahn was unsuccessful in its effort to obtain more steel. Dorpmüller complained that decisions concerning rearmament were being taken without consulting him. Ministries and party organizations were both bypassing the Reichsbahn.[96] Consequently, in April 1938 the Reichsbahn cut its vehicle acquisition program to 400,998 tons, or 462.6 million RM. At least Bergmann now understood that heavy freight locomotives deserved highest priority.[97]

In July 1938 Kleinmann tried to impose order on the Reichsbahn's vehicle program. He led the preparation of another long-range vehicle acquisition plan covering the years 1939 to 1943. He stated, however, that the main objective of the plan was to provide the builders with steady employment.[98] Group L, dissatisfied with the initial draft because it did not provide for the production of enough freight locomotives, proposed that the number be increased substantially to satisfy the needs of both Germany and the newly acquired regions in Austria. It also suggested that the number of flat cars and gondola cars be increased. The Mechanical Section modified its plan accordingly. To free resources, it reduced the number of express locomotives and regular passenger locomotives that would be obtained.[99] Then the Wehrmacht finally stepped in to assist the Reichsbahn. In late September, it assigned part of its steel allocation to the railway to enable it to produce the locomotives and freight cars that it so sorely needed.[100] However, Dorpmüller was still left out of the inner circles of the regime's planning. The national defense law of September 1938 was passed without his knowledge, and he was compelled to sign it against his will after the fact.[101]

The railway transportation crisis of fall and winter 1938 stimulated the government to action. In a meeting on 14 October, Göring ordered a major increase in the volume of resources allocated to the Reichsbahn.[102] The OKW requested 130,000 tons per quarter for the Reichsbahn in a meeting with Göring on 25 October 1938.[103] On 18 November 1938 Gercke and Dorpmüller proposed an even larger increase in the Reichsbahn's steel allocation to the Reich Defense Council chaired by Göring. Gercke stressed that in its current state, the DRB was not prepared for war and that the vehicle procurement plans that it had prepared in 1938 were inadequate. Göring agreed and designated the Reichsbahn's rolling-stock program as vital to the interests of the state.[104] To exploit this opportunity, the Reichsbahn prepared a massive four-year rolling-stock acquisition program, calling for the consumption of 3.2 million tons of steel and the expenditure of 3.47 billion RM. It provided for the production of 5,520 steam locomotives, 108,980 freight cars, 10,230 passenger cars and thousands of motor cars, and 30 high-speed motor trains.[105] Clearly, Leibbrand and Bergmann had realized that the scale of their acquisitions should be vastly increased and that freight traffic would continue to grow. But as the inclusion of large numbers of motor trains illustrated, they still were not aware that Hitler was leading Germany toward war in the near term. Diesel motor trains would be put out of service as soon as hostilities began owing to the military's priority in receiving scarce supplies of diesel fuel.

The Reichsbahn's ambitious rolling-stock program was cut in late December 1938, not because elements of the program were unrealistic, but because the DRB lacked bureaucratic clout. The long-term program that had just been completed was scrapped and a new plan halving annual steel consumption was prepared to replace it.[106] Then, at the end of February 1939, the Reichsbahn's allocation was suddenly increased. Hurriedly, Bergmann and his staff prepared a new acquisition plan to prevent the opportunity from being lost. For a few weeks it seemed as if most of the four-year production plan would be accomplished.[107] Then, in June, the DRB's steel supplies for the last quarter of 1939 were cut by 25 percent. In July, Bergmann was forced to stretch the program over six instead of the originally envisaged four years.[108] In the event, in 1939 the Reichsbahn received 1.59 million tons of steel for all purposes, including vehicle acquisition, building construction, and track renewal. This was 46 percent less than it had requested and 20.6 percent less than it had been allocated.[109]

The net result of the lack of guidance from the Reich government about what its planning priorities should be, its own slowness to adapt, and its lack of bureaucratic political power was that the Reichsbahn did not have enough vehicles to satisfy the demands placed upon it. As already shown, traffic demand began to exceed the Reichsbahn's capabilities in 1937 and clearly surpassed them during the last quarter of 1938. How the confused policies and lack of coordination among the leadership of both the government and the Reichsbahn affected the railway can be seen by looking at the growth of the DRB's assets from 1933 to 1939. The number of locomotives owned by the DRB in 1939, excluding the engines acquired with the Austrian railways, was only 9.57 percent greater than the number on its roster in 1933. This was about two-thirds of the increase in traffic over the same period. Considering that the Reichsbahn had a surplus of locomotives in 1933, it is reasonable to conclude that it had sufficient locomotives in 1939 to handle the traffic demands made upon it at that time. The problems that it encountered moving passengers in 1935 were due to the fact that the overall capacity of its passenger cars, 2.9 million people, was a fifth lower than it had been in 1929, 3.7 million.[110] The volume of traffic in 1935 had recovered sufficiently to overwhelm this smaller fleet of cars. The most serious difficulties

Table 2.7. Reichsbahn Rolling-Stock Acquisition Expenditures, 1933-1939 (in million RM)

Year	Steam Locomotives	Passenger Cars	Freight Cars	Total
1927-29 [a]	20.8	71.8	59.4	206
1933	23.9	9.2	12.2	88.5
1934	22.6	21.3	14.9	126.5
1935	25.8	16.5	21.0	130.3
1936	27.6	42.2	8.2	125.2
1937	28.2	51.2	14.8	138.1
1938	45.5	33.8	40.9	213.5
1939	135.0	51.7	98.3	383.3
Total	308.6	225.9	210.3	1,205.4
Percentage Change				
1939 vs. 1927-29	+1,383.6	+214.6	+254.0	+485.1

[a] Average.
Source: DRB, "Statistische Tabellen über Bestand, Ausmusterung, Beschaffung und Verkauf von Fahrzeugen der Deutschen Reichsbahn seit dem Jahre 1910," 30.73a 300. Füs 63, BA R005/12563.

arose with freight cars. Tonnage carried and ton-kilometers generated both exceeded pre-Depression levels in 1937 and continued to grow afterward. Schultz of the Main Car Office, Leibbrand of the Operating Section, and Bergmann of the Mechanical Section had all realized by mid-1938 that the Reichsbahn was having difficulty satisfying demand for freight car space: they had fewer cars while traffic had increased. In 1938 the load capacity of the Reichsbahn's freight cars was 9.49 percent lower than it had been in 1929 and 9.38 percent lower than at the end of 1932.[111] This was the result of the lack of coordination between the Reich and the Reichsbahn as reflected in the Reichsbahn's vehicle acquisition expenditures. The Reichsbahn's spending on steam locomotives exceeded the pre-Depression average from the outset of the Nazi period due to its desire to maintain a viable locomotive industry. However, because it perceived itself as having enough freight cars, its spending on them exceeded the 1927-29 average only in 1939, immediately before the outbreak of war. Despite the problems encountered in 1935, spending for new passenger cars never attained the level of the pre-Depression years. Overall, spending on vehicle acquisitions surpassed the average of the prosperous late 1920s only in 1938 (see Table 2.7).

A pattern similar to the spending on rolling stock is discernible in the Reichsbahn's expenditures on physical plant during the 1930s. Until 1938, when projects on Germany's borders preparatory to the attack on Czechoslovakia were initiated, the Reichsbahn's overall spending for expansion remained below the

Table 2.8. Capital Budget of the Deutsche Reichsbahn, 1933–1939 (in million RM)

Year	Real Expansion	New Construction	Operations Development	Reported in Balance
1927–29[a]	343.5	229.3	114.3	273.5
1933	165.1	95.8	69.3	149.9
1934	252.9	185.5	67.4	235.6
1935	182.4	181.0[b]	1.4	163.3
1936	173.1	161.3	11.8	139.7
1937	260.1	203.6	56.5	255.3
1938	437.8	368.8	69.0	409.6
1939	677.9	598.4[b]	79.5	—
Percentage Change				
1939 vs. 1927–29	+97.3	+160.9	−30.4	

[a] Average.
[b] Calculated.
Sources: DRG, *Statistische Angaben 1934*, 87; DRB, *Statistische Angaben 1938*, 122; DRG, *Voranschlag 1937*, pp. 28–29, BA RD98/14; DRB, *Wirtschaftsplan 1941*, pp. 29–30, BA RD98/14.

pre-Depression average. The distribution of the money spent shifted significantly toward new construction and away from operations development. This reflected the increase in the building of new lines and the addition of new tracks to existing lines. Here, spending exceeded the pre-Depression average in 1934. Much of this was devoted to building connectors to military installations. But the preponderance was allocated to building lines to the many new factories that were put up in previously unindustrialized localities in central Germany. Foremost among these were the many facilities of the gigantic Reichswerke Hermann Göring. New connecting tracks were built, existing stations were expanded, a new marshaling yard and two new stations were constructed, and the capacity of the lines leading to its main facility at Salzgitter was increased.[112] Despite the priority of these projects, the Reichsbahn encountered problems obtaining the materials necessary to complete them. Other armaments programs competed for steel and cement, and the government was unable to enforce its priorities. Paradoxically, the Reichsbahn was put in only fifth place on the priority list for construction materials[113] (see Tables 2.8, 2.9, and 2.10).

The Reichsbahn's low priority for raw materials also affected its track renewal program. Here, the picture is complicated by the fact that Dorpmüller and other Reichsbahn officials had consistently painted a deceptively negative picture to deceive the Allies during the 1920s. The DRG's track had never been as bad as Dorpmüller had contended, as his statements after March 1930 dem-

Table 2.9. Reichsbahn Spending for Expansion of Capital Assets, 1933–1939 (in million RM)

Year	New Line and Track	Stations	Electrification	Servicing Facilities	Small Projects	Total
1927–29 [a]	45.9	84.3	41.6	5.9	34.5	212.2
1933	26.3	32.8	19.6	0.4	9.2	88.3
1934	61.0	58.2	26.0	1.9	29.2	176.3
1935	82.5	38.6	11.1	3.4	25.9	161.5
1936	78.6	43.6	12.2	2.2	23.8	160.4
1937	80.7	57.2	14.3	4.0	34.0	190.2
1938	106.3	155.4	20.8	9.7	47.5	339.7
1939	114.8	314.8	30.7	15.4	52.3	528.0
Percentage Change						
1939 vs. 1927–29	+150.1	+273.4	−26.2	+161.0	+51.6	+148.8

[a] Average.

Sources: DRG, *Statistische Angaben 1934*, 86; DRB, *Statistische Angaben 1938*, 122; DRG, *Voranschlag 1937*, p. 29, BA RD98/14; DRB, *Wirtschaftsplan 1941*, p. 29, BA RD98/14.

onstrate. He continued to proclaim that the Reichsbahn's track was in excellent condition after the Hitler government initiated its rearmament program and caused raw materials to be kept from the railway. In May 1933 he told the board of directors that the Reichsbahn's track was in "outstanding" condition. He recounted how he had just completed an inspection trip covering all of Germany and "was astonished by its good condition."[114] In an article published in July 1933, he gave the lie to the statements that he and others had made during the 1920s when he wrote: "The condition of the track has been constantly improved through high expenditures and better maintenance methods. . . . The earlier fears that track was inferior compared to the prewar standard were cleared away by the planned work of the track specialists."[115] As late as October 1935, in the notes prepared for his meeting with Hitler to request a tariff increase, Dorpmüller was advised by these track experts: "The condition of the track can be considered at this time as completely satisfactory. This is the result of the generous renewal undertaken in the years 1926 to 1930, so during the past ten years, the renewal requirement has been completely met."[116] Not surprisingly in light of these views, the Reichsbahn never renewed as much track on an annual basis during the 1930s as it did during the years 1927 to 1929. In 1933 it began a program of partial renewal of track that it recalculated as an equivalent of complete renewal. This however was less valuable than full renewal in operating terms and can be considered a form of self-deception. The Reichsbahn renewed less track than before the Depression because it no longer had the need to create hidden reserves once the Allies were gone. Only in 1937 did lack of steel compel

Table 2.10. Reichsbahn Rolling-Stock Acquisitions, 1930–1939

Year	Steam Locomotives	Passenger Cars	Freight Cars
1927–29 [a]	193	1,554.7	9,550.3
1930	54	2,860	461
1931	88	1,303	53
1932	150	114	1,103
1933	142	101	1,517
1934	185	436	2,002
1935	135	123	3,455
1936	185	546	1,252
1937	158	836	1,615
1938	125	503	4,202
1939	660	544	13,087
Percentage Change			
1939 vs. 1927–29	+242	−65	+37

[a] Average.
Source: DRG, HV, "Statistische Tabellen über Bestand, Ausmusterung, Beschaffung und Verkauf von Fahrzeugen der Deutschen Reichsbahn seit dem Jahre 1910," 30.732.300. Füs 63, BAC R005/12563, f. 27.

the Reichsbahn to reduce its track maintenance program below what it desired. In 1939 a labor shortage caused additional problems.[117] Nevertheless, in March 1939 Dorpmüller still told the board that maintenance was adequate and that the Reichsbahn's track was perfectly safe[118] (see Table 2.11).

The DRB also experienced difficulties obtaining and retaining skilled employees. As late as March 1936, Hermann Osthoff, the chief of the Personnel Section, complained that the Reichsbahn had too many people.[119] By the end of the year, however, that had changed. In May 1937 Kleinmann ordered the divisions to reactivate retirees and to call those who were on the waiting list for employment due to a shortage of employees with civil engineering skills. He also authorized them to begin hiring women.[120] In June 1937 Reichsbahn employees were allowed to remain in their posts after they passed the normal retirement age of sixty-five. Problems attracting qualified people were especially acute in central Germany because of the expansion of industry in that region.[121] In January 1938 the Reichsbahn recalled all retired officials who were qualified to fill middle-level management and administrative positions.[122] That winter, it also increased its efforts to obtain engineers from Germany's technical colleges. It sent recruiters around the schools and took prospective applicants for tours through repair works and offered financial incentives to both the young men

Table 2.11. Reichsbahn Track Renewal, 1933–1939

Year	Kilometers		Expenditures (in million RM)	
	Full	Partial	Full	Partial
1927–29 [a]	3,613	—	234.6	—
1933	2,646	739	137.4	38.4
1934	1,545	987	84.2	53.8
1935	1,336	645	72.2	34.9
1936	1,350	645	72.6	53.0
1937	1,238	1,560	71.7	89.6
1938	1,026	1,685	63.4	103.1
1939	1,497	1,200	102.2	67.5
Percentage Change				
1939 vs. 1927–29	−58.6		−56.4	

[a] Average.
Sources: DRB, *Wirtschaftsplan*, 1936, 1938, 1941, p. 22, BA RD98/14; 1939, BAC R005/12120; DRB, *Statistische Angaben 1938*, 60; Homberger, "Wirkungen des hohen Zinsniveaus," 311, table 2.

and their schools.[123] Despite these efforts, the Reichsbahn had no choice but to lower standards for hiring and promotion. Training courses were shortened and qualifying examinations were made easier.[124] Beginning in 1936, the DRB encountered difficulty retaining skilled and unskilled workers.[125] The government labor offices frequently transferred men from locomotive sheds or track gangs to armaments factories since they enjoyed higher priorities than the Reichsbahn. Other men, attracted by the higher wages and superior benefits offered by armaments companies, changed jobs voluntarily, although that was forbidden.[126] In July 1939 Osthoff painted a bleak picture of the Reichsbahn's personnel situation to the advisory board. Obtaining laborers was extraordinarily difficult because work on the railway was hard and the pay low. The government's pay freeze, which the DRB had observed, put the Reichsbahn at a disadvantage. By this point, the Reichsbahn had hired 20,000 women to compensate for the shortage of men.[127] Morale sank under the burden of increasing traffic and longer working hours. Many officials in the upper ranks of the service pleaded to have their transfers to locations away from their homes rescinded. Kleinmann ordered them to stop sending him appeals.[128] Significantly the absentee rate due to sickness increased for officials by about a third between 1934 and the start of the war, and among workers by about a quarter.[129]

On the eve of the invasion of Poland, the Reichsbahn faced daunting challenges for which it was not fully prepared and of which it was not fully aware. The Reichsbahn's stock of vehicles and fixed plant was probably adequate to satisfy the requirements of peacetime traffic at the scale of economic activity achieved by Germany in 1938. But it could not satisfy that demand and at the same time meet the sudden, large needs of the military, as even the comparatively small operation against the Sudetenland demonstrated in October 1938. The DRB found itself in this position because the government did not consider it to be of high importance. The Reichsbahn was not included in the Hitler regime's economic and military planning due to the confusion that gripped the regime, the attitudes of Todt and sectors of the military that regarded it as obsolete, and the easy confidence on the part of Hitler and many of those around him that because the Reichsbahn had always satisfied demand in the past, it would do so again in the future. The low priority attributed to the Reichsbahn was also the result of the inability of Dorpmüller and Kleinmann to see the needs facing them before 1937. Afterward, they simply lacked the political clout necessary to convince Göring and Hitler that their needs were serious. The result was lack of coordination at the planning level and lack of resources at the acquisition level.[130]

In July 1939, at the meeting that he chaired to set priorities for the allocation of the Reichsbahn's car space, Kleinmann sounded a warning to his listeners. He told the group that he had called them together "so that they would not be surprised when a large number of requirements were not fulfilled. . . . My purpose is to give you a warning in time." His message was clear: the approaching military operations would prevent the Reichsbahn from simultaneously satisfying civilian needs. The Reichsbahn was less able to satisfy demand than it had been at the height of the transportation crisis in late 1938.[131] Kleinmann's alarm signal brought the years of peace to a somber close for the Reichsbahn. For Kleinmann, 1933 had brought new hope that Germany and the Reichsbahn would be restored to their former greatness. Kleinmann had himself worked to realize these dreams, notably by expelling some the Reichsbahn's most qualified and dedicated people, men like Homberger, from its service. Now he was tacitly admitting that the Nazi revolution had not been good to his beloved Reichsbahn, Germany's most valuable asset. Despite the glitter of the flying trains, the Reichsbahn had been starved of resources and ignored by the very government that Kleinmann, and even Dorpmüller, thought would help it.

Chapter Three

The Reichsbahn in War and Holocaust, 1939–1945

A. The Years of Conquest, 1939–1940

The Deutsche Reichsbahn played an important role in Germany's prosecution of World War II from start to finish. It deployed the military's field units and provided them with logistical support during their campaigns. It then participated in the exploitation of occupied areas by organizing their railways to satisfy Germany's needs and provided the domestic war economy with essential transportation services. From beginning to end, the DRB played a vital role in carrying out the Third Reich's racial policies, assisting in the relocation of peoples and taking millions of Jews from all over Europe to their deaths in the East. This chapter focuses on the Reichsbahn's activities during Nazi Germany's initial assault on Europe.[1]

Military traffic increased significantly early in 1939. Between January and April, Wehrmacht movements were 35 percent higher than during the same period in 1938.[2] Not all of the increased military traffic was related to the planned assault on Poland, but from early spring, the number of trains rolling eastward increased steadily. The Reich government's and the military's frequent changes to the invasion plan and the timing of its execution made planning the necessary railway movements difficult. In May the DRB began a construction program for the improvement of lines and stations in Pomerania, Silesia, Mecklenburg, Slovakia, and the Protectorate of Bohemia and Moravia. It involved only small projects that could be finished by 15 August 1939. The hurriedly prepared scheme was completed on time.[3] The planning of the railway deployment to Poland's borders took place during a meeting between Reichsbahn and Wehrmacht representatives in Oberhof from 21 to 24 June 1939. In late August, as the date for the attack neared, the Transchef, Gercke, created an office in the Wehrmacht command staff (Wehrmachtführungsstab) to improve coordination of military rail movements. On 26 August 1939 he also named a plenipotentiary commissar for war transportation in the homeland, Colonel Hans Doerr. Group L of the RVM joined the Transchef at his headquarters.[4] These steps did not eliminate the problems of coordination between the Reichsbahn, the military, and industry. Doerr immediately came into conflict with other organizations that hoped to steer the economy. Although his relationship with the Reichsbahn was friendly, the DRB resented his invasion of what it considered to be its turf. Overall, the Reichsbahn was not fully informed of the government's intentions until it was called upon to act. Most important, it was not told that the military mobilization and the economic mobilization would begin at different times. This decision hampered rail operations because the DRB planned to reduce service to the civilian sector in order to free cars, locomotives, and track time for the military. Deploying military units without restricting civilian traffic would have enormously complicated the Reichsbahn's task.[5]

The Reichsbahn began moving combat units to Germany's eastern frontiers in mid-August. The initial operation, the A-Movement, comprised 220 trains and was completed by 23 August. Prior to this, other units had been brought to their deployment positions using the peacetime schedule. The full military mobilization plan was put into effect on the night of 25–26 August 1939. The first part of this Y-Movement involved 260 trains operating in the regular schedule. Beginning on 27 August, the second component consisting of 1,700 trains was carried out using the high-intensity schedule. The transition from the regular schedule to high-intensity operations was executed smoothly. Overall, the DRB used 171,600 freight cars and 13,800 passenger cars to bring the armed forces to their jumping-off points. To support the deployment directly, 7,110 trains were run—about 250 trains per day. An additional 7,747 trains were operated to support mobilization. Because Hitler feared a possible attack from the west to aid the Poles, 1,300 trains were used to place a covering force along Germany's western borders. The Reichsbahn also operated 114 trains to evacuate 135,000 civilians from the area.[6] Without authorization from the government, the DRB returned to its regular train schedule in mid-September because operations under the high-intensity schedule had disrupted economic activity, leading to civilian complaints about inadequate rail service.[7]

The German armed forces defeated Poland in only three weeks. The brevity of the campaign meant that the Reichsbahn had no difficulty meeting the Wehrmacht's requirements. Poland was divided between Germany and the Soviet

Union in accordance with the Hitler-Stalin Pact of August 1939. Portions of the section taken by the Germans were incorporated into the Reich. To operate the railways in these areas, new divisions were formed in Posen and Danzig and some lines in eastern Upper Silesia were absorbed by RBD Oppeln.[8] The areas not incorporated into Germany were organized as the General Government under Hans Frank. The railways of the new state were subordinated to the General Directorate of the East Railway (Generaldirektion der Ostbahn, or Gedob) in Cracow. In conversations on 3 and 4 November 1939, Kleinmann and Kittel discussed with Frank and his advisers how the railways of the General Government would be handled. It was finally agreed that the Ostbahn would be a special property of the General Government, financially separate from the Reichsbahn. However, it would use DRB operating and administrative procedures, and traffic priorities would be set in Berlin. The Ostbahn would be organized along the lines of a Reichsbahn operating division and would receive a backbone of DRB personnel on secondment. The majority of the Ostbahn's employees would be Poles, and four operating divisions would be organized. Frank promulgated an order calling the Ostbahn into existence on 9 November 1939.[9] The leader of the Ostbahn throughout its existence was Adolf Gerteis, who had earned a degree in engineering from the technical college in Hanover, served in the German field railways during World War I, and occupied a variety of construction and operating positions with the Reichsbahn during the 1920s and 1930s. In September 1939 he was sent to the General Government to lead the effort to restore rail service there. In November he was named chief of operations of the Ostbahn and was then appointed its president, replacing Emil Beck, in February 1940. He had joined the Nazi Party on 1 April 1936.[10]

The relationship between the Reichsbahn and the Ostbahn was difficult from the outset. Gerteis and especially Frank sought to preserve the independence of their organization, whereas Dorpmüller attempted to absorb it completely within the DRB. The relationship began on a positive note when the Reichsbahn loaned the Ostbahn 10 million RM in October 1939, the entire sum being repaid in December.[11] From there it deteriorated rapidly. The Ostbahn complained that German firms that were repairing its lines and stations were charging it too much and were working slowly. Prang responded that the Ostbahn was supposed to be independent and that projects could not be arranged for it from Berlin.[12]

Unclear lines of authority and personal ambitions led to a dispute concerning control of the Ostbahn. In February 1941 Dorpmüller asked Hitler to assign him direct authority over Ostbahn operations, traffic, construction, and personnel in order to improve coordination between the Ostbahn and the DRB.[13] In early March, Hitler agreed so as to facilitate the buildup for the attack on the Soviet Union scheduled for that spring. In the same action, Hitler also expanded the Reichsbahn's authority over the railways of the Protectorate of Bohemia and Moravia. However, he attached the proviso that Dorpmüller had to resolve any remaining differences of opinion with Frank and the Reich protector, Konstantin von Neurath. This led to delays and prevented Dorpmüller from winning the influence over these railways that he sought. The most important result for the Ostbahn was that it was subordinated to GBL Ost in Berlin.[14]

One of the most difficult issues that confronted the Ostbahn arose due to the racial policies of the Nazi regime. From the outset, both the Reichsbahn and Frank agreed that German personnel should be used only in supervisory and policy-making positions. The vast majority of the Ostbahn's employees, and virtually all of its operating personnel, should be locals. Hitler had identified the Poles and the millions of Jews who lived in Poland as racially inferior people. The Jews were slated for liquidation. Dealing with the Poles, on the other hand, would pose constant problems. Discrimination against them had to be reconciled with maintaining their willingness and physical ability to work. This problem was insoluble. It explains in no small measure the difficulties that the Ostbahn experienced in satisfying traffic demands.

During the autumn of 1939, about 9,000 Reichsbahn personnel were sent to the General Government to restore rail service and impose the Reichsbahn's administrative and operating procedures on the Polish railways. Osthoff decided at the outset that Poles and local people of German extraction could be employed on the former Polish railways so long as they posed no political threat.[15] Initially, the Poles were confined to performing manual labor and other tasks where they could not endanger operations. It soon became clear, however, that there were simply not enough Germans available to man all of the trains and traffic control positions. Therefore, in January 1940 the Reichsbahn allowed Poles to work once again as locomotive engineers on freight trains and on some passenger trains. Poles would also be given more responsible positions in locomotive sheds and switch towers. However, they would always be supervised by Germans, and Reichsbahn employees alone would handle cash.[16] This step did not relieve the personnel shortage suffered by the Ostbahn. The principle that a Pole could not be a superior to a German placed limitations on the number of positions that could be filled by Poles. In April 1940 the DRB decided that large facilities such as repair works would be assigned a minimum of three Germans. Less important facilities would have a minimum of two Germans, one of whom would be on duty at all times.[17] By this stage, there were 36,640 Poles employed by the Ostbahn. The ratio of Germans to Poles was 1:3.9. Gercke's desire that more Reichsbahner be assigned to the Ostbahn could not be met without endangering the DRB's ability to satisfy demand in Germany.[18] The shortage of labor suffered by the Ostbahn became so acute that in May 1940 the Transchef agreed that Poles should be allowed to serve as engineers and firemen on Wehrmacht trains. They would be required to take an oath and would be paid the same amount of money as their German counterparts.[19] By the end of 1940, about 60,000 Poles were on the rolls of the Ostbahn, compared with about 5,300 Germans. In spring 1941, in preparation for the invasion of the Soviet Union, 1,200 additional Reichsbahn people were sent to the Ostbahn to ensure that the military's transport needs were fulfilled.[20] The efficiency of the Ostbahn's personnel remained low compared with that of the Reichsbahn. There were about twenty Ostbahn employees for each kilometer of its line compared with about thirteen per kilometer in Germany.[21]

The condition of the Ostbahn's Polish employees suffered due to racial discrimination by the General Government. Food was short in the German-controlled section of Poland, and the German authorities ensured that they satisfied their own needs first. The result was that the Polish railroaders were increasingly malnourished, causing them to suffer from disease and fatigue, making it difficult for them to perform their duties adequately. Trains were shortened to reduce the burden on firemen who simply lacked the strength to feed the fireboxes of locomotives pulling heavier, standard-length trains. To alleviate the problem, Gerteis made special arrangements with the local agricultural authorities and the army to obtain food for his Polish workers.[22]

The Ostbahn also suffered from a major shortage of rolling stock and damage to its fixed plant. Air attacks by the German Luftwaffe, ground combat, and demolitions by the retreating Poles caused the destruction of numerous bridges, stations, and locomotive sheds. Reichsbahn crews and German private companies were immediately committed to restore minimum rail traffic as soon as possible. By early 1940 the emergency repair effort was superseded by the Otto Program designed to prepare the Ostbahn for its role in an attack on the USSR.

While the Ostbahn's physical plant was being restored, its rolling stock was also being repaired and expanded. In mid-October 1939 Bergmann initiated a program to repair Polish locomotives and cars in Germany and ordered that German rolling stock remain in the country until the emergency had passed.[23] When it was created in November, the Ostbahn inherited a heterogeneous mix of 1,200 locomotives of sixty-two different types built in many different countries.[24] This was 225 fewer than had operated in the area under the Poles. Despite energetic efforts, 46.8 percent of the Ostbahn's locomotives were unserviceable in February 1940. The causes were inadequate repair facilities in the General Government and severe winter weather. Moreover, most of the locomotives that had been sent to Germany to be serviced had not been returned.[25] Gerteis estimated that the Ostbahn needed 1,200 locomotives to fulfill its service requirements. But the Reichsbahn initially allocated only 990 locomotives to its eastern neighbor. Gerteis succeeded in having this raised to 1,075 in October 1940.[26] At the same time, the locomotive sheds were improved and expanded in order to reduce the Ostbahn's dependence on the Reichsbahn for servicing and to prepare for the expected traffic increases.[27]

Operations on the Ostbahn were steered from Berlin. The Main Car Office allocated cars to the region, and GBL Ost supervised train movements. An office was established at the Ostbahn headquarters in Cracow to parcel out the cars that it received from Berlin. Later, in July 1943, this function was given to the Ostbahn's operating divisions.[28] Until June 1940 the Ostbahn's operations were kept to the minimum level necessary to sustain the local population and satisfy the needs of the German occupiers. Economic activity in the area was low, generating comparatively little internal traffic. Maximum speed for trains was limited to just 70 kph. No express trains were run.[29] Traffic was dominated by the Wehrmacht. Beginning in 1941, when it became clear to Hitler that the war would not be won quickly, new armaments industries were located in the area, greatly increasing transportation demand.[30] In December 1940 the Ostbahn placed a total of only 69,400 cars and generated only 2.5 million train-kilometers.[31] In January 1941 the Ostbahn could accept only 85 trains daily from Germany instead of the 100 required. Gercke concluded that the Ostbahn lacked the ability to meet the needs of the Wehrmacht's construction program in its area. This raised serious questions about its capacity to support the impending deployment of units in connection with the planned invasion of the USSR.[32] The Transchef wanted the Ostbahn to be able to handle 480 trains per day during the deployment.[33]

The Ostbahn was assigned two functions: to deliver the products of the General Government to Germany, and to handle bridge traffic between Germany and the eastern front. In 1941, the Ostbahn shipped 140,000 tons of grain, 290,000 tons of potatoes, and 20,000 tons of meat to Germany.[34] Its ability to satisfy the military demands placed upon it will be discussed shortly. Suffice it to say at this point that the Ostbahn was a constant source of difficulties for the Reichsbahn. Delays and congestion that developed there spread westward into Germany, and it sucked locomotives and freight cars eastward out of the Reichsbahn.

The German seizure of Denmark and Norway placed little burden on the DRB. Surprisingly, the same was the case for the invasion of France and the Low Countries in May 1940. Railway operations west of the Rhine remained fairly normal during the last months of 1939 and the early months of 1940. Blackout measures imposed some restrictions on marshaling activities, which usually took place at night. But the French and the British conducted few air attacks against rail facilities and, when they did, had enormous difficulty finding their targets. Due to disputes between Hitler and his military commanders about the strategy to be followed and the timing of the attack on the west, no concentrated deployment of troops took place. Divisions were exchanged between the east and west and the interior of Germany. Gradually, 136 were gathered in the jumping-off area. During the first part of the operation beginning on 10 May 1940, most of the logistical support for the Wehrmacht was handled by road. Only in early June, while the military prepared to occupy northern

France, Belgium, and the Netherlands, and to defeat the remnant of the French army in central France, did Reichsbahn personnel with about 700 locomotives move forward into the occupied areas to reestablish rail traffic. Both the men and the locomotives returned to Germany at the end of the summer.[35] While in France, Reichsbahn personnel were considered members of the Wehrmacht. This led to difficulties since the railroaders refused to submit to military discipline, felt that they were not fed adequately by the army, and retained a pride in their organization that prevented them from feeling any sense of loyalty to the Wehrmacht.[36]

German policy was to leave the operation of the railways of the western occupied areas to the local people. The Germans would supervise their activities only to ensure that they complied with occupation policy. Consequently, on 24 May 1940, an Armed Forces Transportation Division (Wehrmachtverkehrsdirektion, or WVD) was formed in Brussels to control the Belgian National Railway (Société Nationale des Chemins de Fer Belges, or SNCB). On 15 July 1940 another WVD was established in Paris to supervise the operations of the French National Railway (Société Nationale des Chemins de Fer Français, or SNCF) in occupied France. The SNCF continued to operate the railways of unoccupied France as before.[37] On 1 August 1940 control of operations was returned to both the SNCB and the SNCF except in coastal areas. Over the next few weeks, German personnel were removed from operating positions as French and Belgian railroaders gradually returned to work. Also on 1 August, the Wehrmacht established the Railway Transport Section West (Eisenbahntransportabteilung, or ETRA) in Paris under Lieutenant General Otto Kohl to coordinate railway operations throughout the occupied western areas. The occupation authorities altered the borders of France and Belgium, leading to the transfer of some sections of the French railways to the SNCB. This created difficulties coordinating the two systems because, not surprisingly, the French refused to recognize the transfer in practice. Earlier, on 15 May, the areas of Eupen, Malmédy, and Moresnet had been absorbed by RBD Cologne. On 2 August the lines in Alsace, Lorraine, and Luxemburg were taken over by RBDs Karlsruhe and Saarbrücken.[38]

The organization of WVD Paris illustrates how the German occupation authorities attempted to achieve their goal of obtaining the needed service from the local railways with minimum effort. A main supervisory office was established in Paris, and subordinate offices were formed at the headquarters of each of the operating divisions and at each operating office, locomotive shed, and construction office. The German railway personnel assigned to these duties remained members of the DRB but were responsible to WVD Paris, a military organization headed by a Reichsbahn official, Hans Münzer. He informed his subordinates that their task was simply to observe the operations of the SNCF, not to run trains themselves. They could not issue orders to French railway personnel. If the SNCF failed to move a train that was serving German traffic needs, the observers would inform the relevant French operating official and the trainmaster, who was also supervised by a German. The Germans could issue orders to the French only when absolutely necessary and could actually take over operations only to prevent sabotage. They were also forbidden from providing information about rail operations to anyone outside of the railroad, including Wehrmacht personnel. In WVD Brussels, the supervision was generally closer than in WVD Paris.[39]

Traffic in the occupied regions of the west did not reach its prewar proportions at any time during the German occupation due to the German policy of exploiting the area without regard for its economic future.[40] The French and Belgian railways were used as reservoirs of rolling stock for the Reichsbahn. On 9 August 1940 the Transchef ordered the SNCF to "loan" 1,000 locomotives and 20,000 freight cars to the DRB, while the SNCB would "loan" it 1,000 locomotives and 15,000 freight cars. After this initial installment, the SNCF would send a further 1,000 locomotives and 65,000 freight cars to the Reich.[41] These withdrawals greatly weakened both the SNCF and the SNCB. By the end of December 1940, the SNCF had lost 213,000 of its 463,000 freight cars to the Reichsbahn and WVD Brussels. Another 60,000 were being used in France to satisfy German occupation needs.[42] In addition to raiding the railways of the occupied west for rolling stock, the Reichsbahn also ordered cars from area builders and established an office in Brussels to accept them in autumn 1940. That office dealt with over 300 companies, including 12 locomotive factories and 25 car builders.[43]

The German exploitation of the occupied areas was reflected in the traffic of the two WVDs. For example, WVD Brussels operated 2,147 trains during the last two weeks of September 1940, of which 231 carried booty to Germany. The single largest group, 925, carried coal for general economic purposes, while 251 moved coal for the SNCB itself; 443 trains carried supplies for the German armed forces stationed in the region. One month later, the total number of trains run by WVD Brussels increased to only 2,615, with coal still the dominant traffic.[44] Between July 1940 and January 1941, 20,000 tons of grain and 17,500 tons of wool were shipped to Germany from the Lille operating division alone.[45]

The military campaigns of 1939 and 1940 had little direct effect on the Reichsbahn's operations in Germany. All three were of short duration, and the two that took place in 1940 did not have a large railway component. More significant was the burden imposed on the Reichsbahn in absorbing newly acquired areas into its own network and supervising the railways of the occupied and associated lands. Of equal or greater importance was the fact that the war continued. Germany's defeat in the Battle of Britain during the summer of 1940 meant that the war in the west was far from over, while Hitler's decision in July to attack the Soviet Union led to major increases in both economic and military traffic. Less apparent, but significant in the long term, was the fact that the Reichsbahn's rolling stock, especially its freight cars, circulated over a wider geographical area, making it more difficult for the Main Car Office in Berlin to control them. New flows appeared to the industries built in Germany, to the occupied areas in the west, and to the Soviet Union, the latter a result of the Hitler-Stalin Pact. All of these factors made the Reichsbahn dependent on the cooperation of the military, shippers, and the officials of the railways with which it worked in the occupied countries and their governments. The DRB had no reserves with which to meet emergencies. Thus, when shippers did not cooperate, or bad weather struck, transportation difficulties resulted.

To meet the demands placed upon it, the Reichsbahn undertook a number of organizational changes. In September 1939 the DRB proposed creating a Reich Transportation Committee. But Colonel Doerr prevented it from being formed after intervening with the Economics Ministry and complaining that the Reichsbahn was already too bureaucratic.[46] Also in September 1939 the Reich Transportation Ministry created district transportation offices to coordinate the activities of all modes of transportation within each RBD. In February 1940 the Obls were renamed General Operating Offices (Generalbetriebsleitung, or GBL) and were granted the power to issue orders to the divisions in their areas. They would also cooperate with the regional transportation offices to coordinate the activities of all transportation modes. The GBLs West and Ost would create special coal transport committees to establish liaison with the syndicates of coal producers, each of which was assigned a Wehrmacht representative.[47] On 1 April 1940 the Main Car Office was removed from the RZA Berlin and subordinated to GBL Ost, bringing it closer to the operating level.[48] In May, the Reichsbahn also formed control offices in Vienna, Warsaw, and the occupied west to resolve differences between shippers and the Wehrmacht on the one hand and the Reichsbahn and its customers on the other.[49] The district traffic offices were abolished after only one year of existence and were replaced with new offices attached to the divisions. Similar offices were created at the level of the GBLs to coordinate all forms of transportation over wider areas. Finally, a coordinating office was formed in the RVM to harmonize all three modes—rail, water, and road—throughout the Reich.[50] Adding to the plethora of offices, all with coordinating functions, Göring named transport representatives for economic matters to each RBD, who were charged with mediating between shippers and the carriers.[51]

With the outbreak of war in September 1939, the possibility of air attack on stations and trains compelled the Reichsbahn to take defensive measures. Even before the Nazis gained control of the German government, the Reichsbahn had begun studying the problem of how to reduce its vulnerability to air attack. In 1934 the Main Administration encouraged many railroad employees to join the Reich Air Protection Association (Reichsluftschutzbund). The Reichsbahn

The Years of Conquest 85

also created its own Railway Air Protection organization consisting of air raid reporting and damage repair services. Procedures were developed to protect the public and railroad personnel from bombing and strafing. Trains would be stopped in tunnels or forested areas and the passengers and crews would disembark. No train would leave a station during an air attack. Marshaling yards would work up to the last moment before an attack actually began. Concrete shelters were erected in yards for DRB employees, and reinforced cellars and covered trenches were built near passenger stations for travelers. Later in the war, large reinforced concrete surface bunkers were built to house administrative offices. The most effective means for protecting both employees and travelers was adequate early warning. Because the Reichsbahn drew information from the extensive network of ground observers, both civilian and military, that had been established by the government, and because it obtained information from the Luftwaffe's radar early-warning system, in addition to what was broadcast to the public, few railway employees and travelers were lost to air attack during the war.[52]

To the public, the most notable measure was the blackout or darkening of passenger stations and marshaling yards, which had been brightly lit at night to permit the sorting of cars. The blackout that was begun in September 1939 was soon relaxed as it became apparent that the Allied air forces were not capable of locating their targets during darkness. Passenger stations continued to be darkened, but steps were taken to make it easier for travelers to find their way around. Pillars were painted white, hand carts were removed from gate areas as much as possible, and personnel wearing luminous hat bands were assigned to the boarding platforms to provide information.[53] To enable traffic to continue to flow in spite of damage to yards and lines, alternate routing plans and preparations to redistribute marshaling were made.[54] Procedures were developed to inform train crews about the situation ahead of them. During daylight, a yellow flag with a blue stripe was displayed to warn crews that an air raid was in progress. At night, they were shown a blinking blue light. Trains that were not moving received verbal reports from station personnel. If a train was moving through an area under attack, it slowed to 40 kph. If it were damaged, or passengers injured, it would halt. Trainmasters held trains outside of stations that were under attack. If it was suspected that a line had been bombed, the train would proceed at 10 kph under conditions of good visibility. If visibility were poor, the train would stop and crew members would walk ahead to inspect the track. Later, in 1943, when air attacks on urban areas became more intense, the Reichsbahn took additional steps, such as constructing larger and heavier bunkers, preventing its employees from being drafted into clearance and repair columns, and conducting simulations to determine the best means of routing trains around bombed areas.[55] During 1939, 1940, and 1941, air raids had little effect on operations. The darkening of marshaling yards, such as the great facility at Hamm, reduced their performance by about a fifth.[56]

The outbreak of hostilities created traffic demands that the Reichsbahn did not satisfy completely. In 1939 and early 1940, the DRB was unable to adapt to the new traffic patterns created by German expansion to the east and the deployment of large numbers of troops to the combat zones while industry operated at high intensity at the same time. Cold and snow made even normal operations difficult. To help overcome the problem and prevent its recurrence, Dorpmüller appointed Ernst Emrich, president of Obl Ost in Berlin, on 8 February 1940 to examine the operations management of Obl West, its subordinate divisions, and the divisions bordering on it. It was partially at Ernst Emrich's suggestion that the more powerful GBLs replaced the Obls.[57] Emrich concluded that the Reichsbahn's traffic control mechanism had failed. In his judgment, there was no locomotive shortage, as had been claimed by many operating officers, but a failure to use properly the engines that were available. He considered the superintendents of major stations in the west incompetent, blaming the seniority system for allowing them to remain in their posts long after they should have retired. The reward system had also been abused. Bonuses were simply given on a quota basis so that everyone would get one in due time. He also found that the train offices did not perform their functions of adjusting operations to account for changing conditions. Instead, they had deteriorated into mere places where statistics were collected. The Hamburg, Münster, and Essen divisions, which handled heavy coal and iron ore traffic between the North Sea ports and the Ruhr, did not cooperate with each other. Emrich recommended a basic change in personnel policies, including placing younger, more energetic men in the train offices. Technological improvements, by themselves, he warned, would not increase the Reichsbahn's capacity to move people and freight.[58]

The sweeping changes proposed by Emrich were not made. Instead, as already noted, the General Operating Offices were created to replace the Higher Operating Offices and given the power to issue directives. In the hands of weak men, they had little positive effect. During the spring and summer of 1940, the Reichsbahn's performance improved as the weather moderated and no major demands arose. In the fall of 1940, however, the usual problems reappeared. Once again, car space became very tight. Shortages arose, especially in the east, leading to a lack of coal among some industrial users in November. After the usual decline in demand in January, the DRB again encountered problems providing shippers with car space in February 1941. Embargoes (*Sperren*) were imposed to reduce the volume of freight that was fed into the rail system. This situation persisted until the end of May 1941, when the high-performance schedule was again implemented to move the Wehrmacht to the Soviet border.

Passenger trains were cut and car space for civilian freight traffic was rationed. The situation improved only after the invasion of the USSR got under way in late June, when the military's demand for car space declined while fine weather prevailed.[59]

In the realm of passenger traffic, in November 1939 the DRB restricted the use of trains to those who could show a need to travel.[60] In January 1940 most fare discounts were ended and the surcharges for the use of express trains were increased. Shortly afterward, the maximum speed for all types of passenger trains was cut to save coal and reduce maintenance on locomotives.[61] Yet the desire to travel on the part of the public remained strong. In addition to soldiers who were authorized to visit their families when on furlough, workers who relied on the railway to commute to their jobs, and administrators who needed to visit branch plants and attend meetings, many people continued to visit their relatives, go on outings, and take vacations. The easy victories, the few hardships compared with the situation in the last years of the First World War, and the continued hope for an early peace created an atmosphere in Germany in which many people tried to live normally and were able to do so.[62] The number of passengers carried by the Reichsbahn in 1939 fell only slightly below that carried in 1938. But it rose again to a new high in 1940 and continued to rise in 1941. The DRB reduced the number of passenger-train-kilometers that it delivered in both 1939 and 1940 compared with deliveries in 1938. Although many trains were increased in size, overcrowding became the norm. The resulting heavier trains traveled more slowly and had greater difficulty adhering to their schedules.

Although passenger traffic was important for the continued functioning of the war economy, the Reichsbahn increasingly focused on freight movements. It was here that the problems that affected all of its operations developed. In July 1939, although the DRB was placing more gondola cars than it had during the same month in 1938, it was unable to meet the demand for the transport of bulk commodities. The special measures that the Reichsbahn took during peak traffic periods, such as imposing stiffer demurrage charges on shippers who failed to return freight cars during a specified time, and more frequent service to industrial spurs, had been in effect continuously since early 1939. In July the Reichsbahn's guarantee to deliver freight within a specific period was suspended indefinitely. The cause of these problems was the war. The preparations for the attack on Poland, the economic buildup, and then heavy military traffic led to unprecedented demands for car space. Moreover, because the military confiscated most motor vehicles, the Reichsbahn now had to carry the traffic that had shifted to the roadways over the preceding two decades. Finding sufficient car space to satisfy the need to move coal and high-priority finished goods simultaneously proved difficult.[63] Rather than implement the sweeping changes proposed by Ernst Emrich, the Reichsbahn chose instead to use incremental measures, such as placing restrictions on the acceptance of LCL and carload freight. It also began monitoring the movements of unit trains carrying bulk commodities and other trains carrying high-priority manufactured goods more closely. Even so, many requests for car space were not met.[64]

The attack on the west, although it included no concerted troop deployment, did place new demands for freight cars on the DRB once the Wehrmacht began drawing supplies from Germany and booty began flowing eastward to the Reich. In June 1940 the allocation of cars was tightened once again. During the summer, the situation improved as the fighting waned and traffic patterns stabilized. At the same time, the Reichsbahn learned how to use freight embargoes more selectively. Kleinmann remained reluctant to ration freight car space for all commodities throughout the Reich. He was still motivated by the peacetime desire to serve all customers promptly. However, the demands of the war compelled the DRB to place customer service behind the need to fulfill the immediate demands of the armed forces and the industries supplying them. Timeliness was sacrificed for the sake of moving large volumes of freight.[65] Increasingly, because transportation was a scarce commodity, the Reichsbahn served as a mechanism to steer economic activity in the German economy. Through the regional transportation offices, it began a campaign to transfer freight to the inland waterways, particularly bulk commodities such as coal and ores. Adolf Sarter, president of GBL West, established contact with military and industrial shippers in western Germany and the occupied areas of western Europe to develop transportation plans that encompassed all categories and movements of freight on all transportation modes in the region.[66]

In the occupied west, the transportation networks of the newly conquered areas were well developed, providing Germany with the opportunity to use them to reinforce its own war economy. The rolling stock taken from the west was used to offset the demands of traffic arising in the east. Operating these networks proved difficult because they were not fully compatible with Reichsbahn equipment, but they did result in a net increase in the DRB's transportation potential. During 1940 most of the military traffic in the east was caused by the Otto Program. To facilitate these movements, the Reichsbahn increasingly used unit trains, which it gave high priority in the assignment of crews, locomotives, and cars.[67] The traffic with the Soviet Union necessitated the improvement of stations along the newly created border in central Poland. Because the Soviet railways used a broader gauge than the Reichsbahn, facilities were built to transfer bulk commodities such as oil and grain from Soviet cars to Reichsbahn cars and coal from DRB gondolas to Soviet cars.[68] In 1940, 1,558,000 tons of freight were received by rail from the USSR and 1,533,114 tons were shipped to it.[69]

The Reichsbahn continued to allocate freight car space with as little cooperation from the Reich economic authorities as it had before the war. The Economics Ministry and the Four Year Plan Office issued a series of priority labels for the allocation of raw materials to production programs that swelled as the war continued. The Reichsbahn attempted to employ these priorities to allocate car space, but their proliferation made that difficult. In September 1939, after the conquest of Poland, the Traffic Section placed perishable food at the top of the priority list, followed by coal and coke. By February 1940 coal had returned to its usual place at the top of the list, followed by fertilizer for the spring planting. In June military demands were given highest priority, followed by food and coal. As the assault on the USSR approached, special measures were taken to free car space and to avoid congestion on the lines leading to the deployment areas. Beginning on 10 March 1941, civilian traffic in the eastern part of Germany and on the Ostbahn was reduced by 10 percent. Three days later, the same measure was applied to central Germany. Finally, during the last few weeks before the invasion, traffic in the remainder of Germany was also reduced by a tenth. Within the national target of 123,000 freight car placings per day, each division was allocated a number of car placings that it could not exceed. The seriousness of this reduction is illustrated by the fact that during 1940 the DRB had placed an average of 152,747 freight cars per day.[70]

In addition to rationing car space, the Reichsbahn had been overloading its freight cars by one ton since March 1937. The Mechanical Section in particular objected to this practice because it increased wear and the danger of mechanical failures, such as overheated wheel bearings and broken couplers. Until December 1939 the overloading of freight cars had been restricted to traffic moving over short distances. Then it was extended to all traffic. Bergmann tried to stop overloading in November 1940, pointing out that 150,000 freight cars had been obtained from the occupied West. However, the Operating Section overruled him, arguing that reducing the load of freight cars to the normal level would increase the number of cars needed to satisfy demand and therefore heighten the burden on the marshaling yards. The increased wear to cars would simply have to be tolerated.[71]

Indications that the Reichsbahn was having difficulty handling all of the traffic that it was being given were clear. The backlog of trains that could not be moved within a specified period ranging from three to six hours after scheduled departure time rose from 94 on 1 December 1939 to 1,312 on 20 January 1940. About 60,000 cars were tied up in these trains. Limiting traffic through embargoes and energetic operating measures reduced the backlog to 473 trains by 30 January, yet the problem persisted. From December 1940 the backlog never fell below 200 trains and occasionally rose to 1,000 or 1,200.[72] The situation was not catastrophic, considering that the DRB operated 25,000 to 30,000 trains daily. The most important users, particularly the Wehrmacht, could be served, but other shippers had to contend with delays.

Car turnaround time provides another indication of the strain imposed on the DRB. At the start of the war it stood at about 3.9 days. In January 1940, because of military demand and cold weather, it rose to between 6 and 7.5 days. By October 1940, it had fallen to 4.4 days, only to rise again to around 6 days by the end of the year. Winter weather and the military buildup for the war against the USSR kept turnaround near the 6-day mark until late 1941.[73] The slower circulation of cars meant that a greater number of cars was needed to move a given volume of traffic. Slower turnaround times placed a psychological burden on Reichsbahn officials such as Treibe and Leibbrand, and on shippers and receivers who had become accustomed to the 3-day circulation of cars during the 1920s.

The transition to wartime operating attitudes was difficult for most Reichsbahn officials and happened slowly. During the meeting of operating officers that took place in Leipzig on 3 September 1940, Leibbrand found it necessary to remind them that the desire to conduct operations economically had to take a back seat to achieving the highest possible car-placing totals. The group agreed to use unit trains to relieve the marshaling yards from handling as much bulk commodity traffic as possible, enabling them to concentrate on carload and LCL business.[74] Because the Reichsbahn was allocating car space in accordance with its perception of the needs of the economy and the government's numerous priorities for assigning raw materials to various production programs, it was difficult for the DRB to determine the actual demand for freight cars. Shippers ordered more cars than they needed to ensure an adequate supply. They sought priority authorizations from the various government agencies through political avenues, playing off one agency against another. Undoubtedly, there had been a real increase in demand due to the war. Yet there can also be no doubt that requests for car space were inflated. In late 1939, in the midst of a car shortage caused by military operations and severe weather, demand hovered around 200,000 cars per day. By June 1940 it receded to 187,000 cars per day. At a meeting to discuss freight car allocations on 2 December 1940, industrial and government representatives called for a total of 220,000 cars per day.[75] The Reichsbahn could not meet these demands. Indeed, its ability to deliver car space actually declined with the start of the war. During the last four months of 1939, the DRB never placed as many cars as it had during the same months in 1937, the last year not affected by military operations. It did not even place as many cars as it had during the crisis of late 1938. The worst month was September 1939, when the Reichsbahn placed 22.13 percent fewer cars than it had in September 1937. Its performance then gradually improved so that by December it placed only 6.98 percent fewer cars than in December 1937. By the late spring of 1940 car placings finally returned to their peacetime level. During the last four months of 1940, the problems of 1938 and 1939 reappeared but in much milder form. Because no military operations were under way, and the weather was not severe, the Reichsbahn was able to exceed its September 1937 performance in September 1940 by a full 10 percent. For the remainder of 1940, it placed between 5 and 6 percent more cars than it had during the same period in 1937.⁷⁶ In 1939 the Reichsbahn moved more freight than at any time in its history up to that point. It also devoted more effort to moving freight than ever before, as indicated by the record volume of freight-train and freight-car-axle-kilometers that it generated. However, while car placings stagnated, ton-kilometers continued to rise. Performance in all of these categories, except car placings, continued to increase through 1940 and into 1941.⁷⁷ Clearly, the Reichsbahn could cope with civilian and armaments industry demand so long as no military operations were under way and bad weather did not intervene.

Coal continued to dominate the DRB's freight operations, contributing just over one-third of its total freight tonnage and occupying about 58 percent of its open freight cars. Despite the effort to transfer as much of this traffic to the inland waterways as possible, the DRB remained the primary mode of conveyance for coal in Germany until the end of the war, carrying about two-thirds of all that was shipped. In September 1939 the coal mining industry requested that 78,000 units be placed for coal loading daily. Particularly during the last four months of 1939, the Reichsbahn was unable to meet this target. The Economic Group Mining labeled the shortfall a "transportation calamity."⁷⁸ Göring complained to Kleinmann that the failure of the DRB to move sufficient coal was endangering the German war effort. The Reichsbahn responded by increasing coal car placings at the expense of construction projects and the collection of the sugar beet harvest.⁷⁹ GBL West also attempted to have the mines structure their shipments to facilitate movement by unit train. The powerful Rhenish Westfalian Coal Syndicate (RWKS) resisted. It preferred to send individual cars to particular customers loaded with coal specifically blended to suit their requirements.⁸⁰ The result was that by early March 1940 conditions in the Ruhr had become so difficult that mines were granting their workers days off to allow the railway to remove the backlog of coal that had accumulated. Some party and military organizations commandeered coal from trains waiting in yards.⁸¹ During the spring and summer of 1940, the diversion of gondola cars to the west to support the Wehrmacht prevented the Reichsbahn from meeting the coal car target.⁸² Reflecting the increasing demand for energy, the coal car target was raised to 81,000 units per day in early June. Again, the Reichsbahn turned to administrative measures to try to meet the newly increased demand. Each GBL formed a coal and ore transportation committee to make the best use of the car space that was available. Göring's Four Year Plan Office dispatched representatives to each division.⁸³ Leibbrand hoped that the return of the Polish sections of Upper Silesia would increase the overall supply of coal and reduce the burden on the Ruhr. Although coal shipments from Upper Silesia doubled during 1940, they were insufficient to offset the reduced output of the Ruhr.⁸⁴ The Reichsbahn routed traffic to northwest Germany from Upper Silesia over the Coal Magistrale, a line built by the Poles with French financial and technical support during the 1920s to connect the region with Stettin on the Baltic. The Reichsbahn also began using the route that the Prussian railways had employed before World War I from Kreuzberg through Posen to Stettin. Considerable construction work was done on both of these lines to increase their capacity.[85] Kleinmann reported to the board in May 1941 that during the preceding coal economy year, running from April to March, the Reichsbahn had failed to meet its overall target by 3.8 percent.[86] The most difficult period had been the last quarter of 1939. In the worst month, coal car placings fell 26.7 percent behind the performance of the preceding year. Significant improvement came only in January and February 1940, when the Reichsbahn exceeded its performance of the previous year and moved much of the coal that had accumulated at the mines.[87] Overall, in spite of all the difficulties, the DRB moved more coal than it ever had before. Compared with results in 1937, it placed 3.6 percent more cars for coal in 1939 and 23.8 percent more in 1940, largely due to the expansion of shipments from Upper Silesia. Coal car placings in the Ruhr declined steadily, reaching only 81 percent of their 1937 total in 1940.[88] Coal traffic typified the Reichsbahn's situation on the eve of the invasion of the Soviet Union. Using its peacetime operating methods and the physical plant at its disposal, it could not deliver sufficient service when a traffic peak coincided with bad weather or some other unexpected difficulty.

B. The Attack on the Soviet Union and the Winter Crisis, 1941-1942

The German attack on the Soviet Union opened a period in which the Reichsbahn moved people and freight on an unprecedented scale over greater distances than ever before. On a much smaller scale, the Reichsbahn simultaneously transported Jews to death camps, participating in crimes against humanity. These two traffics, warlike and racist, dominate the story of the Reichsbahn during the years 1941 to 1944.

The involvement of the Reichsbahn in the planning and preparation of Operation Barbarossa was simultaneously extensive and incomplete. Detailed plans were laid for the deployment by rail of hundreds of military units to the Soviet frontier, and extensive construction projects were undertaken to expand the capacity of the lines leading to the area. At the same time, the Reichsbahn was not included in the planning for the phase of the operation that would follow the initial breakthrough. This was the result of the optimistic view held by Hitler and the Wehrmacht leadership that the campaign would be concluded swiftly due to the racial inferiority of the Red Army. The logistical demands of the brief campaign would be met by motorized supply columns. The military planners also anticipated that the Soviets would retreat so hastily that they would be unable to remove or disable their railway equipment. Therefore, the Germans would be able to use the Soviet broad-gauge railways to satisfy their needs soon after the campaign began. Against the background of these expectations, the strategists saw no need to include the Reichsbahn in their plans for the period after the deployment.[1]

To enable the railways of RBD Danzig, Königsberg, Osten, Posen, and the Ostbahn to support the deployment of troops for Barbarossa, a major construction program code-named Otto was begun in 1940.[2] The origin of the Otto Program can be traced back to a plan accepted by the Reichsbahn and Gercke on 25 April 1940. It was intended to increase the daily capacity of five through lines from Germany to the Soviet border to forty-eight trains each by the end of the summer.[3] After Hitler's decision to seize the western portion of the USSR, Gercke's office issued an order to accelerate this program.[4] On 21 July Hitler met with Field Marshal Walther von Brauchitsch, commander of the army, to discuss the strategy to be followed in the invasion of the Soviet Union. During the meeting, Hitler decided that a much larger effort should be made to improve the railway facilities serving the deployment area. Based on this decision, on 27 July the OKW issued a directive to begin the Otto Program and assigned it high priority in the allocation of raw materials and labor. Field Marshal Wilhelm Keitel, chief of staff of the OKW, demanded that the project be completed by the end of 1940.⁵ Very soon, however, it became clear that this was not possible, so the target date was pushed back to 15 April 1941.⁶

Detailed planning for the railway component of the attack on the Soviet Union began on 31 October 1940. Reichsbahn representatives met with Wehrmacht officers and sketched out an initial plan that foresaw the running of 15,000 trains to support the deployment. In subsequent meetings, this number was raised to 17,000.⁷ The Otto Program was designed to make these movements possible. It included the construction of eighty new stations; improvements to signals and communications, among them the creation of 270 new blocks; the construction of new repair shops and locomotive sheds; and the strengthening of track and bridges. When complete, the Ostbahn's five major through lines would be able to handle a total of 480 trains per day.⁸ The program encountered problems from the beginning. Although large amounts of steel were allocated to the project, deliveries began slowly because the steel mills were already inundated with orders from other claimants. Winter weather with severe frost and heavy snow delayed work into March 1941.⁹ Gercke criticized the Reichsbahn for not pressing forward with sufficient intensity, claiming that it persisted in working to peacetime standards even while the war was on.¹⁰ Another major difficulty was obtaining sufficient labor. When the program began, the Reich Labor Ministry immediately committed all of the prisoners of war available in the area covered by the project. Yet demand exceeded supply, and the struggle for labor, including Jews who were working for RBD Oppeln, continued right up to the launching of the invasion.¹¹

On 21 January 1941 Gercke met Dorpmüller in Berlin to gain the support of Germany's senior railroader for his plans to use the Reichsbahn.¹² Their discussion laid the groundwork for more detailed planning that took place during a meeting in Cracow on 4 February 1941. Here, all of the relevant officials of the Ostbahn, the Reichsbahn, and the Wehrmacht met to discuss the Barbarossa rail plan. The primary aim was to find a way to realize the full potential of the Ostbahn. Due to its location between Germany and the central section of the eastern front, the Ostbahn would play a crucial role. Through it would move the troops and supplies of Army Group Center and Army Group South, two of the three large formations that the Wehrmacht planned to launch against the Red Army. Army Group North and the northern wing of Army Group Center would be supported by RBD Königsberg. The Hungarian railways would contribute to deploying and supporting Army Group South. The Ostbahn officials reported that theoretically they could move 180 trains daily to the front. The military requested 130 in the near term. In January 1941, however, the Ostbahn actually moved only about 80 trains per day across its western border.¹³ The Army Group B staff was so dissatisfied with its performance that it proposed merging the Ostbahn with RBD Oppeln.¹⁴ For political reasons, that was impossible. Whether it would have helped matters is questionable because relations between the Reichsbahn and the military were extremely bad.

The Wehrmacht had repeatedly attempted to subordinate Reichsbahn personnel to its authority, and the railroaders resisted fiercely. The result was that Gercke decided during the spring of 1941 to create his own units charged with returning the railways of the areas immediately behind the combat units to service as quickly as possible. Gercke formed three field railway commands consisting of Reichsbahn personnel drafted into military service commanded by a cadre of regular officers. These "gray railroaders" were neither accorded sufficient time to train completely nor fully equipped before the invasion began. One command was diverted to the attack on the Balkans in April 1941, necessitating the raising of a fourth. The creation of the field railway commands exacerbated the poor relations that already existed between the Reichsbahn and the Wehrmacht. Dorpmüller and his colleagues considered them a threat.[15] In effect, Gercke had violated the cardinal rule of dealing with the Reichsbahn: not to intervene in its internal affairs. The party had learned this lesson in 1934 and, although it was dissatisfied with it in many ways, preserved the compromise that it had worked out with Dorpmüller. Gercke proved much more stubborn. The result was a prolonged dispute that was not settled until 1942.

In late March 1941 Ebeling of the Reichsbahn's Group L reported to the Transchef that the initial phase of the Otto Program would be completed on 15 April, but only on a temporary basis, meaning that the lines and stations would be usable but would require more work to enable them to withstand the rigors of the next winter.[16] In the event, the Otto Program was brought to a preliminary conclusion on 15 June 1941, just one week before the Wehrmacht jumped off. Over 30,000 workers had been committed to the effort, many of them against their will. The total cost of the program was calculated by the office of the Transchef at 307 million RM, of which the DRB bore 40 percent. Approximately 300,000 tons of steel were consumed.[17]

Despite these hurried and incomplete preparations, the actual deployment was executed without difficulty. All told, approximately 33,000 trains were run: 11,784 were used to move combat formations, while the remainder brought forward support troops and supplies, and redisposed units in the deployment area.[18] The deployment of each infantry division required about 70 trains, while the motorized and Panzer divisions used between 90 and 100 each. As the deployment progressed, the number of trains assigned to each division was raised because additional motor vehicles had been given to the units.[19] The operation was executed over six main rail routes, three of which passed through the General Government. The first phase was completed between 25 February and 14 March 1941. It involved the exchange of divisions between the east and the west. Twelve trains were run daily. Thirteen divisions left the area and eight were brought into it. In addition, 890 supply trains, 200 trains for the Luftwaffe, 60 for engineer battalions, and 25 for line-of-supply troops were run, leading to a total of about 2,500 trains operated during phase one. The second group of units began to move on 20 March 1941. The tempo of rail movements was now increased to 18 to 24 trains per day. Vacation traffic was reduced in March and eliminated entirely on 10 April. The third group began to roll on 8 April, completing its movement on 20 May. This phase of the operation was interrupted by the diversion of some field units and one of the field railway commands to southeastern Europe for the conquest of Yugoslavia and Greece. Congestion developed in the western areas of the Ostbahn because the army refused to allow troops to disembark closer to the Soviet frontier. A total of 1,400 troop trains carrying seventeen divisions ran to the deployment area during this third phase. The first part of the fourth group of divisions began its journey on 25 May 1941. For this phase of the operation, the high-intensity schedule was put into effect in Germany to free rolling stock and track capacity for the troop trains. Nine divisions plus support units moved to the deployment area during this period. The second part of the fourth group moved between 3 and 23 June 1941. This included the actual assault units, some of which were hurriedly brought north from the Balkans. Twelve Panzer and twelve motorized divisions were carried during this phase. Finally, beginning on 21 June, the day before the actual attack, another twenty-four divisions were transported eastward to move behind the spearheads. The entire operation was executed without problems. Even the Ostbahn did not use its full through capacity. The single busiest day was 7 June, when 2,588 Wehrmacht trains were on the move toward or in the deployment area. During the latter phases of the operation, it was common for about 2,500 trains to be run daily for Wehrmacht purposes.[20]

During the early days of the invasion, large quantities of Soviet rolling stock were captured and the broad-gauge lines that were overrun were hardly damaged. This early opportunity spread optimism that the logistical side of the operation would run as smoothly as the military side, yet this was not to be the case. The field railway units were unable to take advantage of this situation because supplies had not been sorted properly for loading at the dumps immediately west of the Soviet border and congestion developed on the lines leading up to the front. Behind Army Group Center, for example, trains from the Ostbahn and Germany were backed up because arrangements to unload them immediately in the rear of the advancing combat units were inadequate and because field commanders repeatedly interfered with railway operations. Finally, by 18 July, the target of twenty-four supply trains daily desired by Army Group Center was achieved. As the army group's transportation officer noted, the secret to the increased performance was the faster unloading of trains and their quicker movement over the line. These were fundamental lessons. Faster circulation of rolling stock yielded greater performance. Yet the army would have difficulty adhering to these basic rules because many field commanders ignored them. Just as ominously, it became clear that the Soviets were now withdrawing most of their locomotives. This placed a greater burden on road transport and raised the issue of altering the gauge of Soviet track.[21]

During August the railway situation remained tense, although the Wehrmacht continued its victorious advance. Again, the army's logistical units were unable to arrange for the prompt unloading of trains forwarded to them by the Ostbahn and the Reichsbahn. The army retained control of the areas to its rear, although German civilian authorities called for the transfer of these areas to them.[22] Kleinmann asked the Reich Chancellery to include a provision in the draft administrative regulation for the east that would assign control of all railways there to the RVM.[23] On 17 July Hitler issued the anticipated order, but it did little to clarify the division of responsibilities behind the front. All of the railways in the newly conquered territories were placed under the jurisdiction of the RVM. In typical fashion, however, Hitler provided that they be operated in accordance with the orders of the OKW so long as combat continued. After the fighting ended, another regulation would be issued to shape peacetime relationships.[24] In accordance with this decision, on 6 September 1941 Gercke established the Operating Office East (Betriebsleitung Ost) in Warsaw to try to improve rail service to the front. Its chief was Joseph Müller, who had previously been responsible for operations and the freight train schedule as head of office 23 in the Operating Section of the RVM. Four Main Railway Divisions (Haupteisenbahndirektionen, or HBD) were subordinated to Operating Office East, with headquarters in Riga, Minsk, Kiev, and Poltava.[25] The DRB sent liaison officers to Warsaw and also to the headquarters of the operating divisions. Meanwhile, the Reichsbahn gradually moved its people east to man the railways under the Main Railway Divisions, which in turn assumed operational control over the lines from the field railway units. Relations between the gray-clad army railroaders and blue Reichsbahner remained poor. The transport officer of Army Group South claimed that the DRB sent unqualified, poorly motivated people in insufficient numbers.[26] The HBDs proved to be unworkable because they were neither Reichsbahn organizations nor military units. Lines of command were unclear, and policy was a matter of dispute. Making the situation more difficult was the weak telecommunications system in the area that prevented the office in Warsaw from playing its role as coordinator among the HBDs.

By early September trains loaded with booty began to arrive in Germany from the newly conquered areas. During the first two weeks of the month, Army Group South sent 601 cars containing 7,950 tons of freight, including soy beans, gasoline, pigs, and paraffin, westward. This was the beginning of what Hitler and others in his government hoped would become a flood,[27] but the deluge never occurred because of bad weather and poorly maintained track.[28]

At the beginning of November 1941, the Germans were operating a total of 6,871 kilometers of railways in the occupied Soviet Union. Over half were broad-gauge.[29] A major program was begun to convert broad-gauge lines to standard-gauge, and 15,000 kilometers had been changed by the end of December 1941.[30] During November, as the front moved further away from Germany and the weather turned colder, railway operations became more difficult. The roads in the area had already been transformed into impassable morasses, forcing the military to become increasingly dependent on the railway. Yet the rail lines behind the front and in the General Government could not move enough freight to fill the gap left by the collapse of road transport. Field Marshal von Brauchitsch sent a personal letter to Dorpmüller condemning the Reichsbahn's performance. He claimed that the locomotive unserviceability rate in the east was very high and blamed the Reichsbahn for not providing sufficient repair facilities to rectify the situation. He criticized the Ostbahn in particular for failing to move enough trains through its territory.[31]

While the Wehrmacht marched deeper into the Soviet Union, and while the eastern front became a sump that sucked Reichsbahn personnel, locomotives, and freight cars into the vast, poorly organized area behind it, traffic flowed fairly normally in Germany. In July passenger traffic was heavy due to the throngs of people who flocked to vacation resorts. Most restrictions on freight loading were removed.[32] During August, although the Reichsbahn could not satisfy the entire demand for coal, freight traffic generally improved. Passenger traffic continued to be heavy, accentuated by the movement of people fleeing air attacks arriving in RBDs Mainz and Karlsruhe. However, Kleinmann warned Göring that the Reichsbahn lacked the physical resources necessary to meet all of the burdens being placed upon it.[33] Clearly, Kleinmann feared that the combination of large-scale military operations in the east and the usual fall and winter problems that had afflicted the DRB for the past three years would lead to major traffic disruptions. Yet in September there was no hint of impending disaster in Germany. Passenger traffic continued strong and coal traffic moved satisfactorily. Only a few problems appeared finding space for carload traffic.

In contrast, the Ostbahn was having considerable difficulties keeping trains moving due to the fluctuations of flows caused by the advance of the German army.[34] Traffic flowed in Germany normally through October, but difficulties arose in November. Part of the vital sugar beet crop was lost due to the transfer of locomotives and gondola cars to the increasingly troubled Ostbahn.[35] Car placings in Germany became increasingly unstable, reflecting the greater burden placed on the marshaling yards as problems rippled westward from the front through the Ostbahn into the Reich. In November, car placings slumped to 16.4 percent below the number that had been achieved in November 1940, though slightly higher than in the difficult month of November 1939. They then recovered to just 1.79 percent lower than in the preceding year in December.

The crisis struck in full force in January 1942, when car placings fell 13.8 percent below the the figure for January 1941. In February they then fell 25.4 percent below placings for the same month in 1941 and even lower than in 1938 or 1939. Congestion and delays erupted in RBD Berlin due to the loss of rolling stock to the east, the inability to send trains eastward, and heavy snow. In the west, in RBD Cologne and Essen, traffic was snarled by heavy snow and cold that froze the inland waterways, throwing an additional burden on the Reichsbahn. In February RBD Oppeln canceled passenger services. Coal accumulated at the mines in the Ruhr, and cars were backed up in RBD Halle, the hub between the east and the west. Locomotives were in short supply throughout Germany because so many had been sent east. GBL West admitted that it could not coordinate operations among its constituent divisions. Dorpmüller issued an emergency message to the division and general operating office presidents on 2 February ordering them to reduce traffic even at the price of serious disruption to economic activity.[36]

In the east, the German army, after diverting many of its armored units to a thrust toward the Ukraine at the behest of Hitler, had launched a drive to seize Moscow in late September. After another pause to allow the rain-soaked ground to freeze, the Wehrmacht resumed its advance in November. Driving far ahead of their supply lines, greatly weakened by heavy casualties, and struggling against intense cold and heavy snows, German combat units reached the suburbs of Moscow. Then, on 6 December 1941, the Soviets launched a massive counterattack that sent the Wehrmacht reeling. The combination of retreat and severe weather led to the collapse of the lines of communication leading back to Germany. Gercke blamed the Reichsbahn. On 6 November 1941 he accused the DRB of sending too few personnel to the east and of not equipping them properly. He also contended that the Reichsbahn had simply continued to feed locomotives toward the front as they were lost or disabled and had lost count of how many it had sent.[37] Meanwhile, the units in the east had taken matters into their own hands in hopes of restoring rail service. Army Group South appointed a staff to intervene in railway operations in the HBDs serving it. The result was massive bureaucratic confusion, morale problems among Reichsbahn personnel, and operational chaos.[38]

To overcome the crisis, Dorpmüller met personally with Gercke at the latter's headquarters on 20 November 1941. The aging Reichsbahn chief agreed to send more of his people to the east. However, he refused to subordinate them to the Wehrmacht as Gercke demanded. He also consented to send an additional 1,000 locomotives to the combat zone.[39] To help matters further, Dorpmüller also dispatched a personal representative with extraordinary powers to the Wehrmacht's Operating Office in Warsaw.[40] This constructive measure failed. Gercke demanded that the representative be subordinated to him and be considered a member of the military.[41] Dorpmüller again traveled east, this time to discuss transportation matters with Hitler at the Führer's headquarters in Rastenburg. The result was a bitter argument with Gercke in front of Hitler.[42]

While Dorpmüller fought both to increase the volume of supplies that reached the combat units and to preserve the Reichsbahn's institutional autonomy, his subordinates fed trains and locomotives east. In November the number of supply trains dispatched eastward from Germany was increased from 600 to 900 per day.[43] Yet because of the chaos that reigned behind the front and in the Ostbahn, few of them reached their destinations. In January 1942 Army Group Center, which required seventy-five supply trains daily, actually received only twenty-five to forty.[44] As late as mid-March, over half of the locomotives assigned to the railways of the occupied east were unserviceable.[45] Dorpmüller, Kleinmann, and their subordinates had warned the military of the impending disaster and had tried to implement remedies. The immediate cause of their problems was the enormity of the task that had been placed before them. The area that they were to serve had expanded to vast proportions, diluting the fleet of rolling stock that they had at their disposal. The particular region that had become the immediate source of operating problems, the area behind the eastern front, was not under their control, and their relationship with the authority that did have responsibility for it, Gercke, was poor. The Red Army counterattack then spread confusion in the rear of the German army. The severe weather made the problem more serious and delayed its solution. At a deeper level, the government's failure to include the DRB in its war plans and the Reichsbahn's own problems adjusting psychologically to the new situation made it extremely difficult for it to cope with the disaster.

The solution to this complex set of problems came in part from outside the Reichsbahn and in part from within it and was implemented over the first half of 1942. On 4 January 1942 Hitler ordered that the RVM should be given greater responsibility for the railways in the occupied east. The actual execution of the order was impeded by bureaucratic infighting, as was common in the Third Reich. On 14 January 1942 the Operating Office East was subordinated to the RVM and renamed Branch Office East (Zweigstelle Osten des Reichsverkehrsministeriums). The Reichsbahn became responsible for all aspects of rail operations in the occupation zone behind the field railway commands. The Main Railway Divisions were subordinated to the DRB, though they did not become a part of it.[46] Göring attempted to intervene in the matter to restore his control over the war economy. On 19 January he proposed to Hitler that the RVM be given responsibility for operating the railways of the occupied east and west and the Bohemian railways. The OKW and the Reich protector of the Netherlands, Artur Seyss-Inquart, both objected. The military wanted to retain control of its WVDs in occupied Belgium and France, while Seyss-Inquart hoped to preserve the independence of the Netherlands National Railways (Nederlandse Spoorwegen, or NS). On 23 January 1942 Hitler issued a second order that allowed the

RVM to requisition materials, rolling stock, and personnel from the Bohemian, Dutch, French, and Belgian railways and to issue operational orders to them. However, it first had to obtain the approval of the relevant German occupation authorities. In effect, Hitler had again avoided taking a clear position.[47]

In the east, Hitler's January decisions had clarified lines of authority over the railways and increased the authority of the Reichsbahn. Kleinmann, Leibbrand, and Dorpmüller began to resolve the difficulties there by sending energetic young men and additional rolling stock and materials to the areas where congestion was the worst. But progress was slow. The Reichsbahn was still using the methods that had proved so effective in peacetime. Yet they were not enough. Dorpmüller's inability to obtain sufficient raw materials for the DRB's rolling stock and facilities construction programs hampered the Reichsbahn. Moreover, the winter crisis on the eastern front had triggered a change in the leadership of the German war economy. On 9 February 1942 Hitler appointed Albert Speer minister of armaments and munitions. Speer surrounded himself with young managers drawn from private business and centralized economic policy making in his hands while decentralizing execution. The Reichsbahn did not fit into this mold because its leadership was older and because it was not fully integrated into the command apparatus steering the German economy. Speer determined to change that. Although he addressed other problems immediately after his appointment, by early March he had become fully aware of the magnitude of the Reichsbahn's difficulties and began to take steps to overcome them.

The relationship between the Reichsbahn leadership and Hitler had deteriorated significantly since the early days of the regime. Hitler had vested responsibility for the Autobahnen in Todt because he was not sure that the conservative Dorpmüller would push the development of the automobile. However, Hitler respected the railway and its leader for their clear competence at their chosen task, running trains. Because of his age, longevity of tenure, and Hitler's desire to avoid changes in the leadership of the Third Reich that might shake public morale, Dorpmüller's position was secure. But as the Reichsbahn encountered difficulties supporting Hitler's expansionist plans, those below him, especially Kleinmann, became vulnerable.

On 17 January 1942 Kleinmann briefed Hitler on the railway situation behind the eastern front. Hitler demanded that more locomotives be sent to the east. Kleinmann responded that the DRB had already sent 4,280 engines to the area. Hitler then demanded that the locomotives be given additional protection against frost. Because the DRB locomotives had been designed with the milder German winters in mind, their water pipes, pumps, and control mechanisms were mounted on the outside of their boilers, exposing them to the extreme cold of the eastern winter. Soviet locomotives had these devices placed under the boiler jackets or at other locations where they remained warm. The Reichsbahn was aware of these problems and instituted programs to rectify them. But there were not enough heated locomotive sheds available in the east to thaw frozen engines or make the necessary modifications on them. This confronted the DRB with the difficult task of returning the damaged locomotives to Germany for repair while sending more engines to the east to replace them. The result was a net decline in the number of locomotives available in the Reich itself, causing operating problems in Germany. The immobilization of engines in the east led to the loss of freight cars as well. Kleinmann informed Hitler of the Reichsbahn's efforts to overcome these problems. Hitler was not satisfied with Kleinmann's explanation. He retorted that it did not matter if the Reichsbahn lost 500 locomotives at Smolensk. Germany's fate was at stake. Reckless measures had to be taken to supply the troops.[48] In one of his nocturnal monologues on 18 January, Hitler moaned that the problem was not the winter weather but the failure of the railway to bring weapons and reinforcements to the front. If the Reichsbahn stumbled again, he threatened, it would suffer the consequences.[49]

Kleinmann again briefed Hitler on 20 February. Since their last meeting, the railway situation had deteriorated markedly. Hitler accused the Reichsbahn of failing to manage its eastern affairs properly. He became excited and claimed that Kleinmann was unwilling or unable to confront the railway's difficulties. Hitler then said that if Kleinmann did not surmount the railway problems in the east, he would have to deal with the Gestapo.[50] Hitler had clearly lost confidence in the Reichsbahn's leadership and had sent two signals that he was prepared to support the intervention of outside agencies in the internal affairs of the railway. Action was taken at two levels. In the field, Gestapo and SS officers removed Reichsbahn operating officials from their posts and sent them to prison in Germany. At Hitler's headquarters, Speer moved to reform the leadership of the DRB and incorporate it into his system for managing the German economy.

On 5 March 1942 Speer told Hitler that a major transportation crisis gripped Germany as well as the eastern front. Hitler told him that he did not think that the situation was so serious. Dorpmüller, who was present at this meeting, said nothing.[51] On 19 March Speer proposed to Hitler that a trusted member of his personal staff be chosen to be groomed as Dorpmüller's successor. Hitler, hesitating to make a major decision as was his habit, told Speer to consult Dorpmüller. Speer did so. He suggested that Kleinmann should retire due to age, but Dorpmüller would not hear of it.[52] In his regular meeting with Speer on 4 April, Hitler exclaimed that armaments production could not be allowed to slacken due to transportation problems, but he merely ordered Speer to keep him informed on this issue.[53] On 13 May 1942 Hitler finally decided that Kleinmann would go. However, the actual dismissal was delayed until a replacement could be found.[54] A few days later, Speer located a potential successor in Albert Ganzenmüller, who had successfully improved rail service in the Poltava area behind Army Group South. On 18 May Hitler ordered Ganzenmüller brought to Berlin for an interview.[55]

Albert Ganzenmüller, state secretary in the Reich Transportation Ministry and assistant general director of the Deutsche Reichsbahn, 1942–45. Courtesy of Alfred Gottwaldt.

Speer obtained Dorpmüller's consent to the change with little effort on 21 May 1942. According to Speer, Dorpmüller said that the Reichsbahn could not satisfy even the most basic needs of the German economy. Speer interpreted this as a declaration of "bankruptcy." Later in the day, Dorpmüller requested in writing that Speer become transportation dictator.[56] Ironically, the measures that had been taken by Kleinmann, Leibbrand, and their subordinates in Germany and the east had already resolved the immediate crisis. In May 1942 car placings in Germany were only 1.4 percent lower than in 1941, and even closer to the performance of 1940. They were just 2.3 percent lower than in 1937, the last year without military operations.[57] In short, when Dorpmüller allegedly made his offer to Speer, Reichsbahn freight service in Germany was close to normal. Even in the east, with the stabilization of the front and the moderation of the weather, trains were rolling again.

On 23 May 1942 Albert Ganzenmüller appeared in Speer's office in the Pariser Platz in Berlin. He had been brought to Speer's attention by one of his subordinates, Walter Brugmann, who had been assigned to Dnjepropetrovsk to assist with construction efforts to relieve train congestion behind the front. While there, he had observed Ganzenmüller in action. During a visit by Speer, Brugmann called Ganzenmüller to the newly named minister's attention. Later, Günter Schultze-Fielitz, Speer's state secretary, reminded him of Ganzenmüller. The young railroader made a favorable impression, so Speer decided to introduce him to Hitler as planned.[58]

Speer met with Hitler at his headquarters to effect the change in the leadership of the Reichsbahn on 24 May 1942. In a preliminary session, Hitler expressed his shock at Dorpmüller's refusal to take responsibility for the crisis and for assuring an adequate supply of car space in Germany. He then reaffirmed his decision to replace Kleinmann. Late in the afternoon, Hitler met with Speer, Ganzenmüller, and Erhard Milch, state secretary in the Air Ministry, who was responsible for aircraft production. Milch had gained a reputation as a forceful manager and cooperated closely with Speer. Hitler harangued them on the importance of willpower in overcoming adversity. He contended that the claim that the Reichsbahn lacked facilities was "idiocy," although he admitted that there might be a shortage of rolling stock. He called for a reduction of turnaround time by using more prisoners of war to unload freight cars and also demanded that freight movements intended to satisfy mere market demands be eliminated. He ordered that rolling stock be stripped ruthlessly from the occupied areas to satisfy Germany's needs and called for the construction of cheap, expendable cars and locomotives and improvements to the DRB's rolling-stock repair organization. Hitler asserted that the preconditions for victory were adequate supplies of coal, iron ore, and transportation service. He assigned Speer and Milch the task of assuring that these commodities were provided to the German war economy and armed forces. He then named Ganzenmüller to succeed Kleinmann and ordered a general reduction in the age of the upper leadership of the railway. Hitler next summoned Dorpmüller and Leibbrand into the room. He repeated his harangue concerning the importance of willpower and told them that "coal, iron, and transportation must be brutally put in order." Hitler ordered Dorpmüller to help Ganzenmüller achieve these goals. As they left he issued a final ominous warning: "The war must not be lost because of the transportation problem. It must be solved."[59]

On 28 May Ganzenmüller and Dorpmüller met with Speer, Milch, and their subordinates in Speer's ministry. They agreed that the repair of locomotives would be given first priority. Labor would be taken from other industries to support this initiative. They also decided to build a simplified locomotive in large numbers. A more severe rationing of car space would be instituted to enable the DRB to focus its marshaling capacity and motive power on high-priority freight. They all agreed that a major problem was inadequate car placings due to the loss of cars to the east. Organizational flaws within the DRB made solving this problem more difficult than it otherwise might have been.[60]

Two days later, Speer, Ganzenmüller, and Speer's subordinate Willi Liebel discussed the transportation situation with Hitler again. Hitler agreed to Ganzenmüller's proposal to use Italian cars for coal shipments to that country to free cars for use in Germany. Hitler also accepted Speer's proposal that the Reichsbahn be given direct operational control of the railways in the occupied west to enable it to balance car supplies throughout the area dominated by Germany. Finally, Hitler agreed to release the Reichsbahn personnel who had been arrested and placed in concentration camps.[61] The final step in the transformation process came on 28 June 1942, when Hitler ordered the replacement of other Reichsbahn leaders whom he and Speer considered superannuated: Leibbrand, Peter Kühne, who was responsible for the Reichsbahn Repair Works in the Mechanical Section, and, ironically, the Nazi president of RBD Munich, Albert Gollwitzer.[62]

Albert Ganzenmüller superseded Dorpmüller as the dominant personality in the Reichsbahn. Not only was he younger than the transportation minister, he was exceptionally energetic. At the time, Dorpmüller was weakened by intestinal ailments that confined him to the hospital in November 1942 and again in February 1945. He recovered on the first occasion and resumed his duties. Clearly, however, his strength waned and he lacked the political support in the upper reaches of the party and the government necessary to protect the Reichsbahn's interests. Ganzenmüller respected Dorpmüller and worked well with him. Dorpmüller still influenced overall policy, but Ganzenmüller ran the railway on a day-to-day basis.[63] Who was the new leader of the Reichsbahn?

Albert Ganzenmüller was born in Passau on 25 February 1905. His parents later moved to Munich, where he grew up. He received an education in the Catholic parochial schools in the city and earned a bachelor's degree in mechanical and electrical engineering from the Technical College there. He then joined the DRG as a trainee, serving with RBD Munich. After he passed the civil engineering examination in 1931, he received a permanent appointment as a Reichsbahn official. He then served in a variety of posts in Breslau, Munich, Nuremberg, and in the Mechanical Section in Berlin, specializing in electric train operations. While in Breslau, he earned a doctorate in mechanical engineering from the local technical university. He learned how to speak English and French. In June 1940 he was assigned to the WVD Paris to restore service to the extensive electric commuter network serving the French capital. He then received other appointments in Germany and Austria managing electric construction projects. He volunteered for service in the USSR and was appointed chief of the Main Railway Division East with headquarters in Poltava on 6 October 1941. Owing to his success in combating the railway difficulties that swept over his area, he was promoted to the position of general railway commissioner for the region on 16 February 1942. It was apparently during this period that he was noticed by Brugmann. Ganzenmüller had been active in radical right-wing politics since his youth. At age seventeen, he joined the Stoßtrupp Süd of the Kampfbund Reichskriegsflagge. As a member of this organization, he participated in Hitler's Beer Hall Putsch of 9 November 1923, helping to occupy the regional army (*Wehrkreis*) headquarters in Munich. For this action, he later received the Blutorden of the Nazi Party from Hitler. Ganzenmüller actually joined the Nazi Party on 1 April 1931—that is, before the waves of membership applications that flooded party headquarters when Hitler became chancellor. He was a member of the party's office for technology and participated in its athletic events, winning prizes on two occasions. In 1933 he joined the SA, leaving it only a year later.[64] In a report written on 26 August 1940, the NSDAP office in Munich judged Ganzenmüller to be fully reliable politically—just the type of high-ranking official who should be promoted by the party.[65]

After the war, Ganzenmüller claimed that he joined the Nazi Party because he was dissatisfied with economic conditions in Germany and his own prospects.[66] Fritz Schelp, who worked with Ganzenmüller as head of the Traffic Section, did not consider him a Nazi fanatic. To Schelp, Ganzenmüller was interested primarily in the railroad. Nor did he consider Ganzenmüller an anti-Semite, and pointed to Ganzenmüller's toleration of the continued employment of Jews in the RVM, such as Baumann.[67] Ganzenmüller's wartime secretary also did not consider him a Jew-hater.[68] Ganzenmüller's wife, whom he left soon after their second child was born in 1938, considered him to be a man possessed by his work who used his Nazi Party membership to promote his career. This assertion is confirmed by the Munich party office's assessment of him and his own claim that he had been preferred for promotion due to his party membership.[69] That Ganzenmüller knew that the Reichsbahn carried large numbers of Jews to their deaths cannot be disputed, although he repeatedly denied having such knowledge after the war. Hans Frank, the chief of the General Government in which many of the killings took place, discussed the matter with him on 9 December 1942.[70] After his appointment as state secretary in the RVM, he, not Dorpmüller, handled relations with the party. He later claimed that he used these opportunities to preserve the Reichsbahn's relative autonomy. Taking all of these considerations into account, it is fair to typify Ganzenmüller as a competent technician who was obsessed by his career and work with the Reichsbahn. He was not interested in moral issues. He was patriotic and gravitated to right-wing organizations because of his love of order. As the effective head of the Reichsbahn from May 1942, he focused on broad policy issues and the operational aspects of the Reichsbahn's affairs. He simply did not care about the Jews.

During the same period in which Ganzenmüller superseded Kleinmann, other changes were made in the upper reaches of the DRB leadership. Leibbrand was replaced as chief of the Operations Section by Gustav Dilli, another man of action who, like Ganzenmüller, disdained paperwork. At the time of his appointment on 1 August 1942, Dilli was fifty-one years old. Like Ganzenmüller, he received an engineering degree from the Technical College in Munich. He joined the Reichsbahn in 1922 and became an expert on freight train operations and scheduling. After serving as the president of the railway division in Brussels and with GBL West, he was appointed chief of train operations at RBD Königsberg, immediately behind Army Group North on the eastern front. In mid-January 1942 he was sent to Minsk and then Kiev to restore railway operations. Soon after his arrival, he learned that his predecessor as head of HBD Kiev had been arrested by the SS due to his failure to maintain rail service. One of his subordinates, the officer responsible for train operations, was also arrested. Both were to be executed at Hitler's order. With this encouragement, Dilli succeeded in improving rail operations in his area, earning himself the appointment as Leibbrand's successor. He had joined the NSDAP on 1 May 1933, after a long period of membership in the conservative German National People's Party. During 1932 and 1933, incredibly considering the Nazi Party's well-known views on the subject, he was a member of a Freemason lodge.[71]

Paul Treibe was replaced as chief of the Traffic Section by the forty-four-year-old Fritz Schelp. Schelp had moved up though the ranks of RBD Altona during the 1920s and 1930s. He joined the Nazi Party effective 1 May 1937. He claimed after the war that he had been forced to do so in 1938 by the president of what by then was called RBD Hamburg. He also claimed to have joined an anti-Nazi resistance group. Why Schelp was chosen is not clear. During the war he performed competently but was overshadowed by Dilli.[72]

A large number of other high-ranking Reichsbahn officials also had to vacate their posts in favor of younger men during the summer and fall of 1942. Ten division presidents were replaced, among them Kurt Tecklenburg, who had become chief of RBD Mainz. Other officials were also moved out. Wilhelm Emrich, the president of GBL South, and Robert Paul Wagner, who was the chief of the RZA Berlin's office for locomotive design, were also forced into retirement.[73]

Surveying the changes implemented within the Reichsbahn during the spring and summer of 1942, the impressive feature is how little of the DRB's fundamental operating structure and procedures was actually altered. The measures proposed by Ganzenmüller in his conference with Hitler on 28 May were hardly extraordinary and had already been proposed by Kleinmann. Nor did Dilli institute measures that departed in any fundamental way from those followed by Leibbrand. What Ganzenmüller, Dilli, Schelp, and the new division presidents brought to their jobs was a greater sense of urgency and more energy because of their youth, fortified by the knowledge that if they failed, they would not remain in their posts for long.[74] Just as important, the framework in which they operated had changed because Speer had gained Hitler's approval to give the DRB greater access to raw materials and plant capacity and to improve the allocation of transport space.

The lack of coordination among the various claimants for transportation had been a major cause of the Reichsbahn's operating problems since 1937. The difficulty of meshing rail operations in the occupied areas, especially the east, with those in Germany had been largely overcome by their operational subordination to the Reichsbahn in January 1942. The problem of allocating car space to the various claimants in the war economy was solved by Speer. On 2 June 1942 he created the Central Transportation Directorate (Zentralverkehrsleitstelle, or ZVL). Speer conceived the ZVL as the counterpart to the Central Planning committee that he chaired. Central Planning would steer the German economy by allocating raw materials among all users, especially steel. The ZVL would allocate car space and barge capacity among all shippers. It consisted of six members representing all of the major sectors of the economy, including coal mining, armaments production, and agriculture. It was chaired by the energetic and competent Ernst Emrich, president of GBL Ost. Schultz, chief of the Main Car Office, also attended its meetings.[75] The ZVL became an effective tool for managing the German transportation sector and was one of the most important results of the winter crisis.

As ordered by Hitler, Speer also created a special office to promote the more efficient use of Germany's transportation assets. It was led by Milch, although Speer, Ganzenmüller, and prominent representatives of the coal, agricultural, and industrial administrations were also members. It possessed the power to redirect flows of goods that it considered uneconomical. It particularly targeted cross-shipments of goods and tried to reduce the distances that freight was moved. Here again, market considerations were subordinated to macroeconomic and dirigiste needs to save transportation space. Consequently, companies that had purchased components from suppliers on the other side of Germany because they offered a favorable price and were supported by a commodity tariff were now compelled to obtain these goods from a nearby supplier, even if that meant paying more.[76]

In early June the railway sections of the RVM were reorganized. The two construction sections were merged and the special administrative offices directly subordinate to Ganzenmüller were reduced in number and combined with the

Personnel Section. Earlier, in January 1942, Osthoff had retired as president of the Personnel Section, to be replaced by Werner Hassenpflug, another member of the Nazi Party.[77]

The other major change undertaken as a result of the winter crisis of 1941–42 was the transfer of responsibility for the production and acquisition of the Reichsbahn's rolling stock to Speer's ministry. As we have seen, the Reichsbahn had been unable to obtain sufficient raw materials to complete even its modest vehicle production plans. This situation continued after the beginning of the war, even though the DRB was supported by Gercke.[78] In September 1939 the Reichsbahn's rolling-stock production program was suspended in the expectation that the war would be brief.[79] After the conclusion of the Polish campaign, rolling-stock construction resumed, but again only with the objective of satisfying short-term needs. Göring informed Kleinmann on 16 February 1940 that all experimentation with new types of vehicles should stop and that existing designs should be built without regard to cost or quality of finish.[80]

The DRB continued to have difficulty gaining access to plant capacity due to competition from the Wehrmacht. For example, 40 percent of the capacity of the car builders was being used to complete military orders.[81] Overall in 1940, 17 percent of the DRB's locomotive orders and 30 percent of its freight car contracts were not completed due to lack of raw materials, labor, and plant capacity.[82] The Reichsbahn attempted to remedy this situation by placing orders for locomotives and freight cars with the industries of France and Belgium. As early as July 1940, Le Creusot entered into an arrangement with the DRB to produce the heavy Class 44 freight engine and tank cars.[83] The Reichsbahn also took over the existing orders of both the SNCF and the SNCB.[84] In March 1941, three months before the invasion of the Soviet Union, the Reichsbahn anticipated that it would need a total of 900,000 freight cars, about 120,000 more than it had at the time. It foresaw a decline in demand for freight car space from the military and armaments industries and an increase in general freight traffic.[85]

After the war with the Soviet Union began, the DRB continued to plan for the future based on the anticipated victory. As of early October 1941, the DRB had 8,227 freight cars and 345 locomotives on order in France and 7,310 freight cars and 200 locomotives on order in Belgium. In addition, it had placed orders in the west for 4,720 tank cars on behalf of the Wifo (Wirtschaftliche Forschungsgesellschaft m. b. H.), a government company associated with the Four Year Plan, to move oil products from Rumania to Germany. It also had 3,000 freight cars and 50 locomotives on order in the Netherlands and 10 locomotives and 300 freight cars on order in Denmark. In Germany, it had a total of 2,114 locomotives and 31,679 freight cars on order.[86] This program was much more realistic than its predecessors but was plagued by chronic lack of resources. Kleinmann ordered the Mechanical Section to prepare a new ten-year program that would equip the Reichsbahn to serve the empire that Hitler planned to create in

Europe. It provided for the production of 60,000 freight cars and 2,500 steam locomotives each year, a colossal undertaking by any standard.[87] Yet Kleinmann was losing the battle for resources. At the same time that the ten-year plan was completed, half of the plant capacity of the car builders was being used to fulfill Wehrmacht contracts. The lead time for the delivery of a steam locomotive had stretched to fourteen months, and eight months for a freight car.[88] This situation began to change in January 1942. The winter crisis convinced Hitler to raise the priority assigned to rolling-stock production to the highest category. Kleinmann then expanded the ten-year program to include the eastern areas that had just been subordinated to the Reichsbahn. Now it called for the production of 3,500 locomotives and 80,000 freight cars annually.[89] Hitler, however, was thinking in far vaster terms and wanted results much more quickly. Therefore, he accepted Speer's proposal to remove responsibility for rolling-stock production from the Reichsbahn.

Ironically, the Reichsbahn lost control over its vehicle program because its leaders offered it to Speer. Dorpmüller recognized that he and Kleinmann lacked the political power to achieve their rolling-stock production goals. Therefore, on 2 March 1942 he asked Speer to incorporate the rolling-stock industry in his new production organization. Speer created the Main Committee for Railway Vehicles (Hauptausschuß Schienenfahrzeuge) on 7 March 1942.[90] It is likely that Dorpmüller simply hoped that the powerful new minister would help the Reichsbahn achieve its production targets by assuring it adequate supplies of raw materials and labor. Instead, the energetic head of the new main committee, Gerhard Degenkolb, seized control of the Reichsbahn's program.

At the first meeting of its special committee on locomotives on 19 March 1942, Degenkolb announced that Hitler had established a target for the production of 7,500 steam locomotives annually. Production was centered on the Class 52, a simplified version of the Class 50 freight locomotive designed to have a low axle pressure to enable it to operate on the poorly built lines in the east. The engine was also protected against the ravages of cold more effectively than its predecessors had been. Compared with producing the Class 50, producing it required fewer parts and raw materials and less labor. Its finish was not up to the standard previously demanded by the Reichsbahn, but it was designed to be built quickly and cheaply in order to satisfy immediate needs. Altogether, approximately 6,160 were completed during the war. Partcipants in the meeting identified the parts for other engines that limited production and assigned resources to eliminate these bottlenecks and gave high priority to the production of replacement parts so that the many engines damaged during the winter could be returned to service.[91] Subsequent meetings determined how production would be raised to meet the ambitious target set by Hitler. Shortly afterward, a program to build 99,400 freight cars was accepted. The overall production program was a success. It soon became apparent that it was too large,

Table 3.1. Reichsbahn Vehicle Acquisition Expenditures, 1939–1944 (in million RM)

Year	Steam Locomotives	Passenger Cars	Freight Cars	Total
1939	135.0	51.7	98.3	383.3
1940	203.97	34.3	191.0	495.5
1941	299.1	7.2	274.3	619.3
1942	418.3	10.4	278.2	757.4
1943	687.5	23.21	294.8	1,079.5
1944[a]	473.0	47.05	297.0	900.0

[a] Preliminary figures.

Sources: DRG, HV, "Statistische Tabellen über Bestand, Ausmusterung, Beschaffung und Verkauf von Fahrzeugen der Deutschen Reichsbahn seit dem Jahre 1910," 30.732.300. Füs 63, BAC R005/12563; Pless to Göring, "Anlieferung von Fahrzeugen," 39g/F 371, Geheim, Berlin, 29 August 1944, BAC R005/177 Ha, f. 115; Kreidler, Eisenbahnen im Machtbereich, 339.

however, and the program was scaled back in March 1943. In June, Speer decided to reduce the output of new locomotives in favor of producing spare parts and transferred resources to tank production.[92] The Main Committee for Rail Vehicles was merged into a new committee for all vehicles by Speer in November 1944. By that time, the Reichsbahn had been avoiding the meetings of the rail vehicle committee for months[93] (see Tables 3.1 and 3.2).

The production program initiated by Speer and managed by Degenkolb achieved significant results in remarkably short order. Steam locomotive output almost doubled in 1942 compared to 1941 and reached a peak of 4,533 in 1943. The increase in freight car production was less marked but still significant. The key contribution of the new leadership was to bring with them Hitler's backing, ensuring that sufficient resources were allocated to the builders. Degenkolb's ruthless style also ended the bickering between the Reichsbahn and the locomotive industry about the design characteristics of particular engines. In contrast, the production program was less successful in the occupied west. It was weakened by the fact that Belgium and France continued to be used as reservoirs of labor for industries in Germany because Speer was unable to gain control of labor policy. In addition, the French and Belgian workers did not give their best effort for the hated Nazi occupiers. The result was that 9,372 gondola cars, 6,210 tank cars, and 185 locomotives were completed against DRB orders in Belgium. These totals were significantly above the objectives for freight cars set by the Reichsbahn before Degenkolb appeared, and below the target for locomotives. In France, results were also mixed. Only 2,354 gondola cars and 953 tank cars were built, far fewer than planned. But 407 locomotives

Table 3.2. Reichsbahn Rolling-Stock Acquisitions, 1939–1944

Year	Steam Locomotives	Passenger Cars	Freight Cars
1939	660	544	13,087
1940	982	713	24,544
1941	1,391	104	42,924
1942	2,127	124	43,032
1943	4,533	327	51,969
1944	3,063	256	34,725

Sources: DRG, HV, "Statistische Tabellen über Bestand, Ausmusterung, Beschaffung und Verkauf von Fahrzeugen der Deutschen Reichsbahn seit dem Jahre 1910," 30.732.300. Füs 63, BAC R005/12563; Pless to Göring, "Anlieferung von Fahrzeugen," 39g/F 371, Geheim, Berlin, 29 August 1944, BAC R005/177 Ha, f. 115; Kreidler, *Eisenbahnen im Machtbereich*, 339.

were completed before the Germans were forced to evacuate the country in August 1944, a result closer to the Reichsbahn's expectations.[94]

The winter crisis of 1941–42 had seen the Reichsbahn struggle to adapt to a situation for which it was ill prepared, especially psychologically. The emergency was overcome by the application of the DRB's proven operating techniques by more energetic, more ruthless, younger men, and by the intervention of outsiders. The operating crisis had been solved by the time that Speer and Hitler intervened, though their actions prevented its recurrence. Their intervention was particularly effective in giving the DRB the raw materials that it required to obtain more rolling stock, especially locomotives. Throughout this process, the Reichsbahn had defended its freedom to deal with its affairs itself. It lost control of its rolling-stock program. But the party was unable to gain lasting influence on its leadership. Many faces had changed, but attitudes and operating procedures remained much the same. The military actually had less influence on railway operations in the summer of 1942 than it did a year earlier. While these events were taking place, the Reichsbahn became involved in another operation that, although very small in terms of the numbers of locomotives and cars involved, was of momentous moral significance and formed the darkest chapter in its history.

C. The Nazi Racial Restructuring of Europe, 1941–1944

The Deutsche Reichsbahn was involved in the Nazi program of persecution of the Jews from beginning to end. Without the provision of transport by the Reichsbahn, the Holocaust would not have been possible. About half of the Jews who died at the hands of the Nazis were brought to their deaths by the DRB. As we have seen, the Reichsbahn cooperated fully with the Nazi regime to remove Jews from its own ranks. Prior to the outbreak of the war, it also participated in the program of intensifying discrimination against the Jews.

On 8 November 1935 the Main Administration issued a directive forbidding Reichsbahn employees from shopping in Jewish-owned stores.[1] This prohibition was sharpened to include any business contact with Jews whatsoever, and with companies whose policies were influenced by Jewish investors, on 31 August 1938.[2] In March 1939 Jews were banned from using sleeping and dining cars. To avoid possible criticism, no public announcement of the policy was made. Instead, the Jewish community was informed through the Reich Representation of the Jews in Germany.[3] With the outbreak of the war, fear of criticism from foreign countries was no longer a factor influencing Nazi racial policy. Consequently, on 18 September 1941, in consonance with the police order that they wear the Star of David, Jews were required to obtain the permission of the local police to travel outside of their places of residence by rail or other public conveyance. They were still allowed to use trains within their home cities. During peak travel periods, Jews were required to let others board trains first. They were permitted only in third-class cars and could take seats only after all of the Aryan travelers had found places.[4] On 11 April 1942 these restrictions were tightened. Now, at the insistence of the Interior Ministry, Jews were allowed to ride trains only with the prior permission of the police.[5] In June they were forbidden from using waiting rooms in stations.[6] Finally, on 20 February 1943, Jews were no longer allowed to use discount fares offered by the Reichsbahn.[7] These measures humiliated and inconvenienced Germany's Jews, but most were not physically harmed by them.

The defeat of Poland in September 1939 transformed the Jewish issue for the Nazi regime. The area that came under German control was the home of about 2 million Jews, far more than the approximately 330,892 who remained in greater Germany when the war began.[8] Immediately after combat operations ceased, the SS began the process of resettling people according to their racial status. On 21 September 1939 Reinhard Heydrich, the head of the Reich Security Main Office (Reichssicherheitshauptamt, or RSHA), was ordered by his superior, Heinrich Himmler, the chief of the SS and German police, to concentrate the Jews in ghettos in the General Government. Between October 1939 and January 1940, about eighty trains brought over 90,000 Jews and a few Poles out of the areas of Posen and the Wartheland. At the same time, Ostbahn trains moved Jews into ghettos in Warsaw, Lodz, Lublin, and elsewhere.[9] On 19 November 1939 Leibbrand ordered the passenger train officers of the eastern divisions and the operating divisions of the Ostbahn to ensure that the railway carried out its duties in the relocations of people in Poland. The deportations were arranged by local police officials with the relevant division.[10]

Heydrich thought that the movements of the Jews and Poles in the General Government had not been executed smoothly. Therefore, on 21 December 1939 he named Adolf Eichmann head of office IVB4 in the RSHA with the task of organizing the movement of people to achieve the government's racist ends. In a series of meetings that took place in early 1940, Heydrich, Eichmann, and their subordinates gradually developed the procedures that they would use to transport Jews from all over Europe to the east when the time came. For example, on 4 January 1940 they decided that the optimum size for transports would be 1,000 people. The Reichsbahn was not a part of this planning process, just as it had been excluded from strategic planning for military operations. However, Eichmann did maintain close liaison with the DRB. On 22 and 23 January 1940 he attended a schedule conference in Leipzig during which Reichsbahn officials arranged to transport Jews to Lodz.[11]

The deportations of the Jews were a component in the Nazi regime's effort to remake the racial map of Europe. Other parts of the campaign involved the forced movement of non-Jews to clear areas for German settlement or to bring ethnic Germans into the Reich. The Reichsbahn played an important role in these operations as well. In late 1939 and early 1940, it moved 267,000 ethnic Germans along with their possessions in 1,300 trains from the areas of eastern Poland and the Baltic to Germany. A further 104 trains were used to bring Polish workers to Germany, and 950 trains were used to move 800,000 Poles and Jews into the General Government.[12] The relocation of people, the first steps in a program of racist social engineering, continued into 1941. For example, from 25 January to 25 March, 48,861 ethnic Germans were brought out of Lithuania to Germany in over 200 trains.[13] These trains were scheduled, allocated rolling stock, and operated by the same Reichsbahn organizations that later managed the Jewish transports.

Operation Barbarossa was simultaneously a military assault on the Soviet state and an ideological campaign to rid Europe of Jews and Bolsheviks, whom Hitler regarded as essentially the same. Therefore, the program to annihilate the Jews accelerated once the invasion began. In June 1941 Himmler ordered the construction of a death camp at Auschwitz in Upper Silesia, near Germany's eastern border and within RBD Oppeln. Then, on 31 July 1941, at Hitler's behest, Göring ordered Heydrich to solve the Jewish problem. Heydrich and Eichmann then began to plan to move the Jews from western Europe into the ghettos in the General Government as soon as possible.[14] On 4 October Heydrich and Eichmann agreed to a deportation plan, which Eichmann proceeded to implement. On 15 October 1941 Reichsbahn trains began carrying German Jews eastward. By 4 November twenty trains carrying 19,827 Jews had arrived in Minsk, where their passengers were shot by the SS.[15] These transports to Minsk were handled carefully by the Reichsbahn and HBD Center. Supervisors were made responsible for their punctual movement. Information about the trains and their passengers was distributed only to management and key operating personnel. On single-track lines, an interval of at least fifteen minutes was allowed in passing stations between the time a train moving in the opposite direction moved through and the special train carrying Jews arrived.[16] Other trains brought German Jews to Riga and Reval, where they were taken into the forests and murdered. In the General Government, more Jews were brought to the already crowded ghetto at Lodz. The careful operational arrangements should not conceal the instability that gripped planning at the highest level. Himmler, Heydrich, and Eichmann were still not certain how they should eliminate the Jews. The trains to Minsk and Riga, for example, had initially been intended for Lodz. When the ghetto there proved too crowded, they were diverted eastward. During 1941, most of the Jews who fell victim to the SS and its helpers were shot in areas recently seized from the Soviet Union. Most had lived near where they were killed. Only a small proportion were brought by rail from the west to meet their deaths in the pine forests and sand pits near Riga and Minsk. Himmler was convinced that shooting was too slow and too difficult to accomplish the task of eliminating the Jews from Europe. Until he found an acceptable method for mass killing, the transports from outside Poland would remain comparatively small in number and their destinations would vary. The railway's role consisted primarily in moving Jews to the ghettos where they awaited their fate.

During 1941, in addition to carrying Jews to their deaths, the Reichsbahn also brought Jews and other prisoners to work in slave labor camps and factories. For example, IG Farben was building a synthetic rubber plant at Dwory, near Auschwitz. Between July and December 1941, the DRB carried 158,569 prisoners between the camp and the plant. The trains were composed of captured boxcars, each of which carried 100 prisoners.[17]

The mass extermination of Jews in death camps using industrial methods began in 1942. The SS developed a system using poison gas that enabled it to kill people en masse quickly. This triggered the movement by rail of large numbers of Jews from western Europe and the ghettos of the General Government to Auschwitz and Treblinka. Eichmann created an organization designed to funnel Jews to the death factories in Poland and Silesia. Himmler set the overall direction of the project by establishing its timing and scale and by choosing where the death camps and ghettos would be located. The ghettos were consciously established in cities where adequate rail connections were available. Auschwitz,

Belzec, Sobibor, and Treblinka were chosen as the sites of death camps because they offered access to main lines as well as seclusion.[18] Eichmann formed a web of connections with local SS, police, and military formations throughout Europe that he used to bring the victims to railway stations for loading. He and local SS officials negotiated with the governments of the occupied territories to arrange for the deportation of Jews from their areas and, in some cases, for the use of the local railways. Once a plan for deportations for a certain region had been agreed upon, Eichmann would then assign his subordinate Rolf Günther the task of arranging transportation. Günther informed his subordinate, Franz Novak, of the origin and destination of the proposed movements and the number of people who would be involved. Novak then contacted office 21 in the Reichsbahn's Traffic Section, headed by the veteran official Paul Schnell.[19] Schnell was fifty-nine years old in 1942 and had been a member of the Nazi Party since 1 May 1933.[20] He was responsible for the assignment of passenger cars. His subordinate, Otto Stange, in office 211 for special trains, actually handled the allocation of car space for the Jewish transports. Once Stange determined that cars were available, the matter was handed over to GBL Ost.[21] Here the passenger car office headed by Karl Jacobi prepared a draft operating schedule that involved the circulation of groups of cars from point of origin to destination and back. Jacobi was assisted in this effort by his subordinate, Fritz Fähnrich. The drafts that they prepared were discussed at schedule conferences held four to six times annually chaired by Bruno Klemm, also of GBL Ost. Operating officials responsible for special trains from the divisions, GBLs, and the Ostbahn attended these meetings. The result was a schedule covering a period of two to three months that designated trains to be run from the places where the SS collected Jews to the places where they would be condemned to slave labor or be killed immediately. The conferences also arranged for trains to deport other peoples and to move laborers to Germany. The trains that would carry the Jews were designated Da if they originated in Germany or occupied Europe. The trains that moved within Poland were designated Pj. The latter, because they generally did not cross divisional boundaries, were handled differently. They were scheduled by the Ostbahn in conjunction with the local SS authorities within the parameters established by the overall plan shaped by GBL Ost.[22] The divisions, in accordance with the schedule formulated by the GBL Ost conference, then assigned locomotives and cars to the trains. The groups of cars were kept together and circulated between the camps and the loading locations without being broken up. Locomotives were changed approximately every 100 kilometers. During 1941 and 1942, most of the trains that left Germany and western Europe, and many that were sent from eastern Europe, excepting Poland, were composed of twenty third-class passenger cars with a second-class car for the guards. Usually, the trains headed for destinations in the occupied Soviet Union stopped at Wolkowysk in eastern Poland, where the victims were

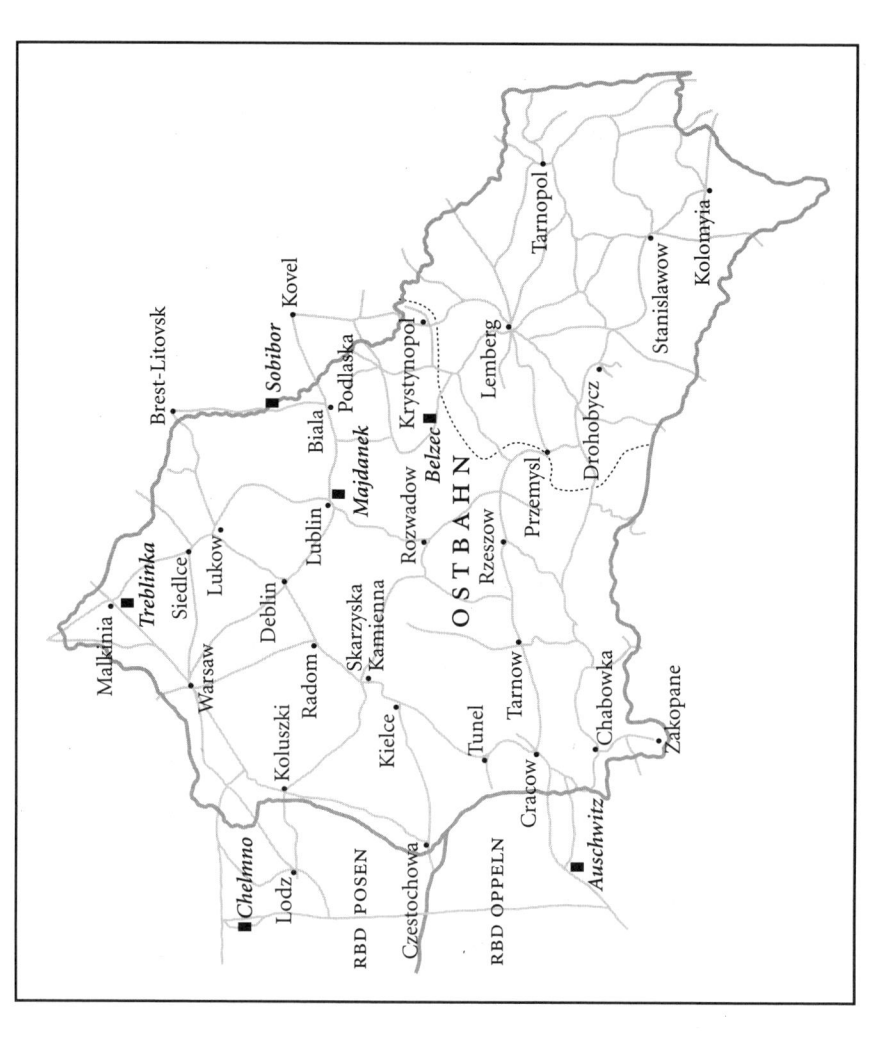

Map 3. DRB/Ostbahn Routes and Nazi Death Camps, 1942

transferred to boxcars and taken to a place such as Minsk, where they were shot. The passenger cars were cleaned and then returned empty for loading.

The Jewish transports were fitted into the Reichsbahn's operating plan as freight extras. This meant that after the regular freight trains (*Stammgüterzüge*) and the extras for priority traffics such as Wehrmacht troop movements, coal, and armaments were moved, the special trains for the extermination camps were allowed time on the through routes. The Reichsbahn insisted that the SS and its helpers have the deportees ready at the designated loading location before the scheduled time of departure. Delays frequently followed. This was the result of other, higher-priority trains being allocated slots on the main line first. Once the transports actually began their journeys, they moved slowly. Maximum speeds of just 45 kph were specified in the detailed schedules issued by the divisions. Trains composed of passenger cars moving in Germany frequently ran faster. But once they entered the Ostbahn, they slowed considerably. Initially, the trains carried 1,000 people. Later, as the SS hurried to kill as many Jews as possible before the war ended, trains carrying 2,000 or even 5,000 people became common.[23] Clearly, the planning difficulties that led to fluctuations in the flow of Jews to the work camps and extermination centers, and the decisions that determined the timing of the actions to kill Jews, took place outside of the Reichsbahn. The DRB incorporated the movement of the Jews and other people transported against their wills into its regular system for allocating car space, locomotives, and track time. The division of labor within the Reichsbahn's bureaucracy, decision by consensus at conferences, and then the execution of the overall plan in accordance with prevailing traffic conditions and maintenance plans were all standard operating procedures. The DRB, as a common carrier, made its services available to the SS as it did to any other customer.

The majority of the Jews murdered by the Nazi regime met their deaths in 1942. The heaviest movements of Jews to the death camps took place during the spring and summer. On 20 January 1942, Heydrich chaired a conference at Wannsee, a resort suburb on the west side of Berlin, to coordinate the deportation of Jews to the death camps with other Reich authorities. The Reichsbahn was not represented at this conference because there was no doubt that it would supply car space when requested to do so. The mass movement of Jews to the death camps then commenced. Trains began rolling from France in March and from Lublin in April. Later, trains brought Jews from the Netherlands, Belgium, the Warsaw Ghetto, and Croatia. The DRB encountered no significant difficulties in completing these operations, only the usual problems of temporary congestion at stations or equipment breakages. For a time, the line to Sobibor was closed for maintenance. In June, high demand by the Wehrmacht due to the offensive by Army Group South toward Kharkov led to a two-week embargo of nonessential traffic on the Ostbahn, including the special trains for Jews. But overall, from the standpoint of the Reichsbahn, the trains flowed smoothly. The plan for the period 8 August to 30 October 1942 gives an impression of how these operations were conducted. It encompassed trains for people being resettled, for harvest workers, and for Jews. The fifty trains for Jews formed the largest group. Fourteen trains departed Vienna Aspang. The next largest number left Theresienstadt, and then came Berlin with a total of eight from the Zoological Garden Station and Moabit. Four trains came from Frankfurt am Main. Two trains were scheduled to leave Darmstadt and Nuremberg. Single trains were foreseen for Karlsruhe, Cologne-Kalk, Tilsit, Breslau-East, Kassel, and Weimar. Most of the trains, twenty-six, were sent to Theresienstadt. Izbica in eastern Poland was the destination for nine, while Wolkowysk, the way-stop on the line to Minsk, was the designated end point for seven trains. Five trains traveled directly to Riga, two to Raasiku, and one to Panszew. These trains were all composed of twenty third-class passenger cars carrying fifty people each for a total of 1,000 people per train.[24]

The two most important killing centers, both in terms of the number of Jews murdered and railway operations, were Auschwitz and Treblinka. Railway-related events at the two death camps bore fundamental similarities but also had significant differences.

Auschwitz was located in the Upper Silesian industrial area in Germany. It was situated on a double-track main line that served traffic between the southwest and the north and east. From the southwest, trains came from Oderberg, an important station with lines connecting it to Vienna and other locations in southern Europe and Germany. This main line branched in two directions just north of the station in Auschwitz. One line went north to Kattowitz and the heart of the Upper Silesian heavy industrial complex. The other passed northeast to a junction with the main line from Kattowitz to Cracow. A third line connected Cracow directly with Auschwitz.[25] The death camp was located to the west of the Reichsbahn station in Auschwitz and was reached by a spur that connected with the main line to Oderberg. The transports were brought to the Auschwitz station where the road locomotive was removed. Until June 1943 the victims were unloaded in the station and then marched to the two peasant cottages that had been converted to gas chambers, where they were killed.[26] From June 1943 a Reichsbahn switching locomotive would then push the trains backward into the death camp siding. As soon as the cars were aligned along the ramp, the Reichsbahn crew departed. By April 1942 the SS borrowed a DRB switcher to serve the death camp. It had requested this engine because it did not want to give Reichsbahn personnel free access to its yard because of what was going on in the camp.[27] Many trains were backed into the camp using the road locomotive. In these cases, again, the DRB crew departed with its engine as soon as possible. Overall, operating conditions at Auschwitz did not delay the arrival of the people condemned to death. At the points of departure, occasionally delays did occur. In France in June 1942, for example, problems arose because cars and locomotives had been diverted to the military to support the offensive on the eastern front. Once this difficulty was surmounted, three trains per week departed Drancy near Paris bound for Auschwitz. Other trains came from the Netherlands and Belgium.[28] In March, April, and May, about 50,000 Jews were brought from Slovakia.[29]

Treblinka was the primary destination for Jews from the ghettos of the General Government such as Warsaw and Lublin. The operation of these trains was handled by the Ostbahn. Other trains came from Berlin, Vienna, and Prague. Treblinka was situated on a single-track secondary line. As part of the Otto Program, the capacity of this line had been expanded to twenty-four trains per day. The camp was served by the Reichsbahn station at Malkinia located on a double-track main line that ran from Warsaw to Bialystok. That line was capable of handling seventy-two trains in each direction daily. It served as a supply route for Army Group Center, carrying between thirty and forty trains per day for this purpose.[30] Trains for the death camp were brought into the yard at Malkinia. From August to early December 1942, an average of three trains arrived daily, each composed of about sixty cars. The Reichsbahn train crew handed over their work orders to the yardmaster and departed. Then, specially selected crews, most likely composed of SS personnel, broke the trains up into groups of twenty cars that were then pushed into the camp. To prevent difficulties with the public, the passenger station at Treblinka, located north of the camp, was closed to travelers on 27 August 1942. The composition of the trains differed from those destined for Auschwitz. The trains from Czestochowa, for example, were composed of two third-class passenger cars for the guards and fifty-eight boxcars for the victims. The trains, without people, weighed about 600 tons. The combined weight of thousands of people raised their burden by 200 tons. The trains were placed in a slot for through freight trains and were given seventeen hours, including a stop of two and a half hours in Warsaw, to complete the journey of about 375 kilometers. Sixty-four trains brought approximately 320,000 Jews from Radom. Upward of sixty-eight trains brought about 400,000 Jews from Warsaw and the surrounding area. Some of these trains carried as many as 7,000 people. About forty other trains brought 200,000 Jews from Galicia.[31]

Trains rolled to the other death camps in similar fashion, but in smaller numbers. For example, between June and November 1942, about twenty trains carried 100,000 people from Lublin to Sobibor and Belzec.[32] The operation to Sobibor led to an exchange between the SS and Ganzenmüller that illustrates the Reichsbahn's attitude toward the traffic in condemned Jews. The Sobibor camp was located on a comparatively little used single-track secondary line that connected Brest-Litovsk to the north with the main line between Lublin and Kowel to the south. The latter served as a main supply route for the German army fighting in the east. In July 1942 the Sobibor line was closed for maintenance. Himmler learned of this from local SS authorities and ordered the chief of his personal staff, Karl Wolff, to telephone Ganzenmüller. Ganzenmüller responded in writing on 28 July 1942. He reported that the trains scheduled for Sobibor had been redirected to Treblinka. For almost a week, one train daily had been bringing 5,000 victims from Warsaw to that alternate destination. Transports to Sobibor would resume when the track work was completed in October.[33] This exchange makes clear that Ganzenmüller was aware that the Ostbahn, which was under his supervision, was bringing Jews to their deaths. He handled the matter in a routine fashion except for his personal letter to Wolff, informing him of the steps that had been taken to address the problem. He had consulted the Reichsbahn officials on the scene through normal channels and had taken twelve days to respond. The work being done to the line leading to Sobibor was continued according the prearranged plan. The Jewish special trains were simply rerouted to another camp.

While the Reichsbahn and the Ostbahn moved hundreds of thousands of Jews to annihilation at the death camps, they also transported many more to locations behind the eastern front, where they were shot. RBD Königsberg organized the operational aspects of movements of trains to Minsk. From May to September 1942, one train was scheduled to run from Vienna weekly. Each carried 1,000 Jews in third-class passenger cars up to the Wolkowysk yard in eastern Poland. There the Jews transferred to boxcars for the remainder of the trip to Minsk. The total distance of the journey was calculated at 1,052 kilometers, for which the RBD Vienna billed the SS 20,20 RM per victim. Army Group Center stipulated that the trains come into the city after dark on weekdays, except Friday. Until they could be taken into the city, they were held on a siding outside of its suburbs. This operation was interrupted on 17 June by an embargo.[34]

While the Reichsbahn was moving hundreds of thousands of Jews eastward to their deaths, it was also moving comparable numbers of Soviet prisoners of war and civilian conscripts westward to work in Germany's factories and fields. Most of these people ultimately died as well. On 17 April 1942 Kleinmann issued an order to GBL Ost to run fifteen trains per day to bring Soviet workers to Germany. Each would carry 1,000 people. Later, the operation would be expanded to eighteen trains per day. The trains would be composed of twenty-five boxcars for the workers, two boxcars loaded with food, and one passenger car for the escort. The trains were assigned the symbol Ru.[35] No difficulty arose handling this traffic. By the end of July 1942, 1.3 million people had been brought to Germany from eastern Europe by the DRB.[36] This operation continued during 1943. During the first five months of the year, the Reichsbahn and its subordinate systems to the east brought 345,000 people to Germany from the Ukraine alone. Another 250,000 had been carried from France. Fritz Sauckel, Hitler's general plenipotentiary for labor mobilization, estimated that a total of 900,000 foreigners had been brought to Germany as part of his labor program.[37] All of them had come by rail.[38]

The flow of human beings by rail, the vast majority against their will, was interrupted by an embargo of special passenger trains lasting one month that began on 15 December 1942. The Reichsbahn took this measure to free capacity to return members of the Wehrmacht to their homes in Germany or to rest areas behind the front to celebrate the Christmas holiday. In the west, the embargo was imposed on 11 November and lasted until 9 February 1943.[39] Himmler could not tolerate this delay. On 20 January 1943, his patience at an end, he wrote a personal letter to Ganzenmüller, explaining that he wanted to remove all Jews from the area behind the German army in the USSR, Bialystok, and the General Government. He closed by writing, "Help me and get more trains for me."[40] When this elicited no response, Himmler telephoned Ganzenmüller on 3 February.[41] By then, the embargo had been lifted as planned. The winter weather in the east and the successful Soviet counterattack at Stalingrad then required the Reichsbahn to concentrate on serving the needs of the southern portion of the German front. The exigencies of the war and rail operations had brought to a close the most deadly phase of the extermination of the Jews by the Nazi regime. Yet planning for the next phase was already well under way.

In January 1943 meetings were held between the Reichsbahn and the SS to settle arrangements for the movement of Jews to the death camps during the next phase of the murder operation beginning in the first quarter of 1943.[42] For the period 20 January to 28 February, a program was prepared that included 7 Da trains and 9 Pj trains, which would carry 12,000 and over 16,000 Jews respectively. The Da trains would originate at Theresienstadt and Berlin Moabit and would travel to Auschwitz. The Pj trains began at Bialystok and Grodno and went to both Auschwitz and Treblinka.[43] The Ostbahn also sent four trains to Auschwitz from Oranczyce between 29 January and 2 February 1943. They left Brest-Litovsk at 6:55 A.M. and arrived at Czestochowa shortly after midnight. There they were handed over to RBD Oppeln for the remainder of the trip to the death camp. They were composed of twenty-five boxcars and weighed 500 tons.[44] Overall, from January to the end of March at least sixty-six trains carrying 96,450 people arrived at Auschwitz from locations in the General Government, Bialystok, Belgium, Germany, France, Theresienstadt, the Netherlands, and Greece. Among them were twenty trains with 20,000 Jews from Bulgaria. In June about 100,000 Jews were removed from the ghettos and work camps in Bialystok and brought to their deaths at Auschwitz and Majdanek near Lublin.[45] Between June and March 1943, another twenty-one trains carried 53,519 Jews to the killing center at Treblinka.[46]

By the end of 1943, most of the Jews who would lose their lives in the Holocaust had been killed by the SS and its accomplices. Only a few groups that Eichmann had not been able to reach remained. The largest of them was the Jewish community of Hungary. Eichmann and Novak along with other SS officers traveled to Budapest in March 1944 to negotiate with the Hungarian leaders for their deportation. Despite the reluctance of the Hungarian government, they carried out the operation successfully.[47] Between 15 May and 19 July, about 147 trains brought approximately 450,000 Jews to Auschwitz, where they were killed.[48] Other trains brought victims from Greece, Italy, France, and the Netherlands. In the early fall of 1944, the approach of the Red Army from the east compelled Himmler to begin shutting down and demolishing the death camps. However, he held on to the Jews under his control. Many were marched westward into Germany. Many others were taken back by rail. Seemingly irrational train movements were undertaken right up to the end of the war in an effort to keep the Jewish prisoners in German hands. Whether this was to use them as a bargaining counter or simply to find an opportune place to kill them, or because the commanders involved had not received orders to do anything else, remains unclear. Yet, even in the last desperate days of the Third Reich, the Reichsbahn helped the Nazi regime pursue its racist goals through the provision of transportation.

The geographical scope, duration, and number of trains involved in moving masses of people for racist reasons, particularly the annihilation of the Jews, raises questions about what Reichsbahn employees knew about these operations and how they reacted to them. There can be no doubt that Ganzenmüller was fully aware of the Jewish special trains and their purpose. But because of his nationalistic, technocratic attitude, and his powerful ambition, he simply did not care. Dorpmüller claimed after the war that he had heard nothing of the Jewish death trains. It is known that he visited Auschwitz in late 1944 after the Hungarian Jews had been murdered. He inspected the IG Farben plant at Dwory for a few hours and was gone by noon.[49] Certainly, while he was there, he could have seen the appalling conditions under which the slave laborers worked. Given his long railway career and the many contacts and friends he had gained over the years, it is unlikely that he had not learned of the movement of masses of Jews to their deaths.

Certainly, many operating employees of the Reichsbahn realized that the railway was transporting many thousands of people to their deaths. Oskar Diegelmann, an operations auditor based in Lublin until August 1942, admitted after the war that he had realized that nearby Belzec was a death camp when he saw piles of clothes and personal possessions that had been stored by the SS behind the locomotive shed at the station.[50] Walter Mannl was the chief of the operating office in Kattowitz, responsible for the station at Auschwitz. During a tour of Auschwitz in early 1942, he was told by the stationmaster that a large concrete building nearby was a gas chamber used to kill Jews. He did not ask for a transfer because he was having difficulties with his superiors and did not want to risk being expelled from the Reichsbahn.[51] Günther Lübbeke, who worked on construction projects in the Ostbahn, recalled after the war that he and his fellow railroaders talked about the special trains and the killings in the camps. They knew a good deal about what was happening in them, though not all of the details. Lübbeke thought that the killing of the Jews was wrong, but he did not ask for a transfer, let alone protest, because he feared the consequences.[52] Eduard Kryschak was a DRB conductor who frequently led trains to Treblinka. He stated after the war: "We knew something was wrong in Treblinka. I remember a Jewish girl who worked as a cleaning lady in Bialystok. I knew from her that she had a great fear of Treblinka. She said that one day she would not come to clean our rooms any more. That happened."[53] Hans Prause was attached to the Ostbahn divisional headquarters in Warsaw from June 1942 to June 1943. On one occasion he was in the Reichsbahn canteen at Malkinia and joined a conversation between the stationmaster and an SS officer named Michaelsen. Michaelsen told the two railroaders about the killings and invited them to visit the camp to see for themselves the humane procedures that were being used. Prause recoiled at the prospect and refused.[54] Another Reichsbahn employee was informed by the SS about the murder operation, in this case at Auschwitz. Willy Hilse was assigned to the Auschwitz station in September 1942. An SS technical sergeant told him that Jews were being brought into a room in the camp that resembled a bath and were being killed with poison gas. Afterward, their bodies were incinerated in a crematorium. Hilse quickly learned that the other Reichsbahner in Auschwitz knew that a murder operation was taking place in their immediate vicinity. Hilse also did not dare to ask for a transfer.[55] Wilhelm Fehling was the head of the operating office in Auschwitz. He had been a Nazi Party member since 1931. He speculated that he had received his job because he got along better with the SS than his predecessor. On one occasion, the SS arrested a group of Reichsbahn employees who were marshaling cars on the camp tracks. Fehling intervened with the camp commandant, Rudolf Höß, to win their release. He was certain that Jews were being murdered en masse in the camp. He stated after the war that he never considered asking for a transfer, claiming that he hoped to stay to "do some good."[56]

Very few Reichsbahner summoned the moral courage to request transfers away from the killing operation. Two examples are known. Richard Neuser, a conductor based at Bialystok, had heard from colleagues about the conditions on the Jewish transports and what happened to the Jews after they were handed over to the SS. He told the operations master that he preferred to have nothing to do with them. He was never assigned to the death trains and suffered no negative consequences.[57] Another was Alfons Glas. Glas was assigned to office 33 at the headquarters of the Ostbahn. In this position, he participated in the scheduling of trains to the death camps. He wondered what was happening to the large numbers of people who were being brought there and speculated about the health conditions that must prevail in the camps. He concluded that many of the inmates were dying and asked his superiors for a transfer. His request was granted, again without negative consequences for him.⁵⁸

As Christopher Browning has shown, it was possible for individuals to choose not to participate in the killing operation without incurring the wrath of their superiors.⁵⁹ Certainly that applied to the Reichsbahn, which had a record of protecting its own from punishment by Nazi agencies. Yet the examples discussed so far concern men at the operating level who could be easily replaced. Glas was higher in the apparatus, yet he too was able to remove himself without difficulty. What was known in Berlin, and how did the Reichsbahn officials in the headquarters building on Voß Street react? Helga Möller, who worked for Dilli as his receptionist in Kiev and Berlin, recalled that she was sure that Jews were "being systematically killed."⁶⁰ Dilli claimed after the war that he did not know for certain that masses of Jews were being murdered. Like Ganzenmüller, he probably did not care. Rolf Rückel worked in office 23, which was responsible for overall operations and for the freight train schedule. He remembered that knowledge of the killing operations was widespread in the RVM, and he knew that Schnell played a role in organizing the special trains.⁶¹ There is no record of any member of the railway sections protesting the transports, let alone asking for a transfer. Again, fear for their jobs and the safety of their families, and the simple fact that most did not care because they were not personally involved and were caught up in their duties, explains their behavior. The Reichsbahn had a corporate consciousness based on its role as a common carrier that served the public and the government whatever demands were placed on it. The psychological atmosphere, especially in the headquarters in Berlin, was bureaucratic, technocratic, and patriotic. There was pride in the Reichsbahn's accomplishments in supporting the deployment of the army and sustaining industry and the civilian population. Criticism was rejected as disloyal. Had Dorpmüller or Ganzenmüller protested, which is difficult to imagine, they would have been replaced, though neither would have suffered physical harm. Under these circumstances, it is easy to understand if not to approve of the behavior of the vast majority of DRB people in Berlin. For the men on the line, callousness and fears about job and personal security probably explain the actions of most.

The movement of the Jews to their deaths and the numerous train services that were delivered by the Reichsbahn to facilitate that process were not a financial bonanza for the DRB. The Reichsbahn billed the SS for the cost of operating the special trains. The SS directed some payments to Mitropa or, in the case of at least some trains from the occupied west, to an Account W maintained by RBD Cologne. The Reichsbahn allowed the SS to use the special tariff of one-half of the standard third-class fare reserved for groups of over 400 people.⁶² The SS calculated that the cost of moving eighteen trains from France to Auschwitz was 515,000 RM.⁶³ The nineteen trains that brought 48,533 Jews from Salonika to Auschwitz cost 1.9 million RM.⁶⁴ Given the Reichsbahn's long-standing tariff policy, it is highly unlikely that it did anything more than barely meet its operating costs from these discount fares.

The Reichsbahn not only brought Jews to the camps to be killed, it also carried away the property of the victims for use by various German organizations. Odilo Globocnik, commandant of Treblinka, reported to Himmler that 100 million RM worth of valuables were shipped to Germany in 852 freight cars during Aktion Reinhard beginning in June 1942 and lasting up to the transport embargo in December. In March 1943 Globocnik informed Himmler that during the preceding three months, a further 1,000 freight cars with clothing materials valued at 13.3 million RM had been sent to Germany. Another 1,000 cars were being used to store additional material.[65] Between January and June 1942, the camp at Chelmno sent 370 freight cars loaded with the clothes of the approximately 145,000 Jews to Germany.[66] In the west, 735 trains with 29,436 freight cars filled with furniture taken from the dwellings of deported Jews were run to Germany. The Reichsbahn took the contents of 1,576 of these cars for its own use.[67] Oswald Pohl, chief of the SS Economic-Administrative Main Office, sent a list to Himmler on 6 February 1943 showing that 825 freight cars with clothing, bed feathers, and rags had been sent to Germany from Auschwitz and Lublin. One car contained 3,000 kilograms of women's hair.[68]

Determining the total number of trains operated by the Reichsbahn for the Holocaust, given the incompleteness of the records, is impossible. The most thorough compilation was undertaken by Professor Wolfgang Scheffler during the 1960s and early 1970s. He obtained reliable evidence that at least 2,601,137 Jews were brought by the Reichsbahn to the death camps and the killing grounds of the east. Based on the number of Jews thought to have been killed in the camps, he estimated that about 3 million Jews were carried by the Reichsbahn to their deaths.[69] The single largest number, about 450,000, was moved in 147 trains from Hungary to Auschwitz in 1944. Approximately 138,325 were taken from Lodz in 110 trains from January 1942 to November 1944. Seventy-six trains carried 76,864 Jews from France to Auschwitz and Sobibor between March 1942 and August 1944. Eighty-seven trains took 94,678 Jews from the Netherlands over two years to Auschwitz and Sobibor. Based on Professor Scheffler's study and other published and unpublished sources, it is clear that Auschwitz was the destination for most of the Jewish special trains, receiving about 613. About 390 trains went to Treblinka. The other killing sites, such as Riga, Minsk, Majdanek, Chelmno, and Belzec, each received far fewer. Overall, specific evidence exists relating to the operation of 1,084 death transports. A crude estimate based on Professor Scheffler's figures indicates that about 2,000 trains were operated by the Reichsbahn and its subsidiaries, primarily the Ostbahn, to bring Jews to their deaths.[70] Other trains were run to carry materials necessary to build and maintain the camps. Individual cars were attached to freight and passenger trains to bring Jews to collection points, where they were put into trains that headed to the death camps. The SS also arranged for the transportation of Jews with particular skills between camps or to industries where they were put to work.[71] There is no tabulation of the total number of trains used to bring the booty taken from the Jews to Germany. Consequently, it is impossible to estimate the overall effort made by the Reichsbahn to support the racist assault on Europe's Jews. In absolute terms, there can be no doubt that it was substantial. However, compared with the tens of thousands of trains run for the Wehrmacht or to move coal, it was slight. Clearly, moving 3 million people to their deaths was well within the capabilities of the Reichsbahn even under wartime conditions. The operating problems that the DRB had to confront had other origins. Nevertheless, this relatively small traffic, insignificant from a transportation standpoint, remains as a large black mark on the history of Germany's most valuable asset.

D. The Years of Retreat, 1942–1944

The primary tasks facing the Reichsbahn during the years 1942 and 1943 were serving the needs of the German war economy and supporting the Wehrmacht on the eastern front. The Ostbahn was the most important connection between the railways in Germany and those in the occupied Soviet Union.

At the beginning of Operation Barbarossa, the Ostbahn operated 4,000 kilometers of standard-gauge routes of which 2,500 were considered main lines. Its headquarters remained in Cracow. It divided its territory into four operating divisions with headquarters in Cracow, Lublin, Radom, and Warsaw.[1] On 1 August 1941 the Ostbahn formed a new division in Lemberg to operate the railways of the newly conquered Galicia.[2] As part of Hitler's reassignment of responsibilities for transportation in the east, the Ostbahn was put on the level of an RBD in relation to the RVM effective 1 February 1942. Its operations were more closely integrated into those of the Reichsbahn, and its personnel were considered members of the DRB. Yet, to satisfy Hans Frank, the Ostbahn remained a special property of the General Government. Its finances were handled separately from those of the Reichsbahn, and its unique identity was maintained before the public.[3] This situation did not satisfy Dorpmüller and later Ganzenmüller, who both sought to erase any hint that the Ostbahn was an independent organization.

Dorpmüller began his campaign by gaining the support of Göring for the complete absorption of the Ostbahn by the DRB.[4] This helped him little, because, by this stage of the war, Göring had lost much of his influence with Hitler. Dorpmüller visited Frank in Warsaw at the end of July 1942 to learn the position of the head of the General Government. Frank contended that Dorpmüller assured him on this occasion that the arrangement of February was adequate.[5] However, Frank later heard rumors that Dorpmüller planned to dissolve the Ostbahn and wrote Lammers rejecting such a change. On 19 August Dorpmüller informed Lammers that coordination between the Ostbahn and RBD Oppeln had to be improved. The arrangement of February 1942 was no longer workable. Therefore, he proposed forming a general operating office that would oversee both the Ostbahn and RBD Oppeln, effectively ending what remained of the autonomy of Frank's railroad.[6] Hitler contemplated this proposal for six weeks and finally rejected it on 30 September. He agreed that the DRB should control the Ostbahn's operations, but he insisted that the Ostbahn retain its financial independence so as to serve as a source of revenue for the General Government.[7] On 16 October, Ganzenmüller then attempted to convince Hitler that only the complete incorporation of the Ostbahn by the DRB would eliminate the operating problems that continued to plague the railways in the east. Ganzenmüller made clear that the Reichsbahn was not interested in gaining access to the Ostbahn's operating surpluses. Rather, he wanted to ensure that Frank did not use the financial independence of the East Railway to influence its operating policy.[8] A week later, Hitler decided that although the Ostbahn would retain its financial autonomy, it should be fully integrated into the Reichsbahn's operating structure.[9]

Integration implied major changes in the internal organization of the Ostbahn. On 31 October Ganzenmüller ordered the abolition of the five Ostbahn divisions and their replacement by three Reichsbahn divisions to be located in Cracow, Lemberg, and Warsaw. He also intended to form a new general operating office that would include the new Ostbahn divisions and the four easternmost German divisions.[10] Ganzenmüller informed Frank of the proposed changes during a meeting in Cracow on 25 November 1942. The general governor vehemently opposed them, arguing that if he lost control of the Ostbahn, or if it appeared to the people under his rule that he had, his authority would crumble.[11] Frank's stubborn opposition delayed the implementation of Ganzenmüller's plan and ultimately weakened it. Dorpmüller, tired of Frank's opposition, attempted to confront him with a fait accompli in early May 1943. He ordered the creation of the three new divisions and named presidents to lead them. He then visited Frank on 4 May to inform him of what had happened. Frank offered such violent resistance that Dorpmüller was forced to compromise. Effective 3 June 1943, the three new divisions became operationally subordinate to the Reichsbahn but remained financially and administratively subject to the orders of the president of the Ostbahn, Gerteis. The idea of forming a new GBL was quietly dropped.[12] For the remainder of the war, the RVM attempted to reduce the independence of the Ostbahn through piecemeal measures. Yet, owing to Frank's unrelenting resistance, and then the loss of much of the area to the Soviets, it never succeeded in doing so.[13]

The Ostbahn's traffic continued to be dominated by the military operations that took place to its east. During 1942 the German army remained on the defensive on the northern and central sections of the front and advanced to the south. The result was heavy traffic through the southern part of the Ostbahn and an increase in economic traffic elsewhere. After the defeat at Stalingrad in February 1943, the German army prepared a major offensive on the central part of the front at Kursk. The failure of this drive, and the subsequent counterattack by the Red Army, forced the Wehrmacht to begin a retreat that did not end until it was defeated in Berlin in April and May 1945. By the early months of 1944, the Soviets had reached the western part of Russia. A massive offensive in June carried them to Warsaw.

To serve the traffic flow to and from the front, the Ostbahn operated about 2,700 locomotives, including recent Reichsbahn types such as the Class 52 and

41 freight engines.[14] Comparatively little traffic was generated within the General Government despite the Speer ministry's efforts to expand the armaments industry there. Shipments of agricultural goods to Germany peaked at 1.31 million tons of grain, potatoes, and meat in 1942. Then, the flow diminished to 860,000 tons in 1943 and 630,000 tons before the area was lost in 1944.[15] The Ostbahn's primary function remained handling bridge traffic to and from the eastern front. During the last month of 1941, 1,330 trains passed the Ostbahn's eastern borders into the occupied Soviet Union. During 1942, 38,556 trains moved eastward (3,213.4 per month). During the first five months of 1943, 17,472 trains followed (3,494.4 per month). An average of 40 to 45 trains crossed the border eastward at Malkinia, and 60 at Brest-Litovsk, daily. On 2 November 1942, for example, the Ostbahn sent 108 Wehrmacht trains, and 53 railway service trains, of which 32 carried locomotive coal, across its eastern borders.[16] Due to difficulties moving trains east, this traffic did not flow smoothly. On 21 October, to cite just one day, 84 Wehrmacht trains were stored on holding tracks and a further 145 were backed up in yards waiting for departure.[17]

The composition of the Ostbahn's personnel remained essentially unchanged until 1944. Poles provided virtually all of the workers and a few of the lower-ranking officials. Germans controlled the railway, although they were far outnumbered by the Poles. In August 1942, 8,419 Germans and about 150,000 non-Germans, predominantly Poles, were employed by the Ostbahn. The proportion of Germans began to rise as the Red Army neared in 1944, reaching a peak of 12 percent, or 20,188, in August.[18] Among the non-Germans who worked for the Ostbahn were Jewish slave laborers. In early September 1942, 8,568 were employed, primarily in locomotive servicing facilities. Many were skilled workers with long experience. An additional 15,383 Jews, not employees of the Ostbahn, were working on construction projects within the railway's area. The SS later removed them to a death camp, although Gerteis needed their labor.[19]

The Ostbahn's finances were managed using the same principles as the DRB. After achieving an operating ratio of 105.03 in 1940, indicating a loss, the Ostbahn had operating ratios of 94 in 1941 and 1942, a clear indication of how its expenses were manipulated to achieve an acceptably small surplus. From a financial standpoint, the Ostbahn did not cost the Reichsbahn a great deal, but it was not a source of profit either.[20]

The railways to the east of the Ostbahn were a constant source of difficulty for the Reichsbahn. The HBDs were situated in a region that was never fully secured by the Wehrmacht. Consequently, there was a constant threat of guerrilla attacks on trains or facilities, particularly along the many long lines through isolated areas. The exploitative occupation policies pursued by the various German authorities that were active in the area also made it difficult for the Reichsbahn to obtain sufficient labor. As the German armies began to retreat in 1943, partisan attacks increased, leading to major operating problems. Despite these obstacles, rail service to the armies was maintained until the very end. The winter crisis of 1941–42 was not repeated.

The Reichsbahn controlled all railway operations behind the field railway commands. The latter operated the railways in the immediate area behind the fighting front.[21] As in the case of the Ostbahn, Dorpmüller and Ganzenmüller attempted to expand their authority over the railways in the occupied USSR. Expecting victory by the German military, they attempted to position the RVM and the DRB for the postwar exploitation of the newly conquered areas. They also sought to extend their control to include the inland waterways and road traffic in the region so as to avoid a struggle between the three modes similar to that which had occurred in Germany between the two world wars. Unified control would also be beneficial while hostilities lasted.[22] Hitler accepted this reasoning and on 23 October 1942 issued an order that gave the RVM broad powers over all forms of transportation in the east. The Soviet railways became a special property of the Reich that would be administered by the RVM in the same fashion as the Reichsbahn. All of the personnel working for the various civilian transportation agencies in the east were subordinated to the RVM. On 1 December 1942, a General Transportation Directorate East (Generalverkehrsdirektion [GVD] Osten) was established in Warsaw, superseding the RVM Branch Office in that city. Josef Müller became the new directorate's chief. The GVD East was the functional equivalent of a GBL and was directly subordinate to the RVM. The Main Railway Divisions were simultaneously transformed into Reich Transportation Divisions (Reichsverkehrsdirektionen, or RVD). To facilitate control of operations behind the German armies advancing in the south, a fifth operating division had been created at Dnjepropetrovsk in November. GVD East also accepted the offer of the Transchef to assume control of economic traffic within the field railway commands in May 1943. To facilitate the management of the Reichsbahn's supply of cars, and to prevent excessive numbers of cars from being tied up in the east, the Main Car Office established a branch in Warsaw in January 1943.[23] In effect, the Reichsbahn had become responsible for all railway operations in the east except for military movements immediately behind the front. The concentration of authority in the hands of a single agency greatly reduced administrative friction and contributed significantly to the provision of adequate railway support to the Wehrmacht in the area. Yet relations with the army remained testy. Until the end of the war, the military criticized the Reichsbahn for being too safety conscious.[24]

The Reichsbahn made a major effort to improve the rail facilities that it took over in the east as a continuation of the Otto Program. Within the Ostbahn, it laid 1,700 kilometers of track between October 1939 and November 1941. In addition, it built new locomotive sheds and improved existing ones, laid telephone lines, and installed new switch towers and signals.[25] The conquest of additional territory and the transportation crisis of the winter of 1941–42 created the need for a new program. In March 1942 Gercke sketched out a long-term scheme that provided for fourteen major through routes from Germany to the conquered territories in the east. Each would be able to handle 72 trains per day under normal circumstances and up to 144 during major military operations. He anticipated that 5,000 kilometers of new lines would be built annually for years to come.[26] At the same time, the Reichsbahn prepared a program to build 10,000 kilometers of new line and eighty locomotive sheds in the east.[27] Both of these plans fell afoul of the general lack of steel and labor. Instead, the DRB initiated the Ostbau 1942 program, intended to make the repair works and locomotive sheds in the east secure against the rigors of the winter. Ostbau 1942 also included improvements to selected lines on the major transportation routes to the front to facilitate the flow of traffic. In particular, lines would be built to bypass major cities and some large yards to reduce congestion and speed through trains to their destinations. The program also contained a long-range component intended to facilitate the movement of economic traffic after the anticipated victory over the Soviets. It provided for the construction of new marshaling yards and the double tracking of major through routes over the next three years.[28] The Todt construction organization would build the lines with about 65,000 laborers. Twenty-four trains would be run daily, each with thirty cars, to support the effort.[29] The Ostbau 1942 program concentrated on the southern part of the front behind the German armies that took the offensive during the 1942 campaign. Due to delays in obtaining labor and materials, the target date for the completion of the first phase was pushed back six months to 1 April 1943.[30] By early November 1942 most of the initial objectives of the first phase of the program had been achieved.[31] The number of laborers committed to the project was massive: 89,151 workers, including 68,151 non-Germans in mid-December 1942.[32]

While the Ostbau 1942 program was being completed, new programs, Winter-Ostbau 1943 and Ostbau 1943, were begun. Winter-Ostbau required 40,000 laborers. Ostbau 1943 needed 76,000 and an average of 22.5 trains per day. The objectives of these programs were twofold: to prepare the rail lines behind the front for the Kursk offensive planned for July 1943, and to provide enough stalls in the locomotive sheds to house 80 percent of the engines operating in the east. This last measure alone would greatly reduce operating difficulties during the cold months.[33] The Ostbau 1942 program and the Winter-Ostbau were essentially completed by July 1943. The Ostbau 1943 program, like its predecessors, suffered from delays and shortages of raw materials, despite energetic efforts by the Reichsbahn to gain high priorities for them.[34] The number of people who worked on them peaked at 77,520 in March 1943. After that, the programs slowed due to the retreat of the German army and the shrinkage of the area to be served by the Reichsbahn and its subsidiaries. By 1 January 1944 the number of people working on them had dwindled to 21,464.[35]

The railway construction projects undertaken in the east can be considered a component of the Reichsbahn's overall construction effort. New construction in the Reich was reduced to the minimum necessary to support the war effort. Work that was done was concentrated on the lines leading to the east and in the divisions bordering on the area, such as RBD Oppeln. In that division, lines and yards were improved to increase the rate at which trains could flow through the region and to accommodate the coal mining areas that were retaken from Poland in September 1939.[36] By July 1941 Ebeling of Group L calculated that 128 million RM had been spent on military construction projects in the east since September 1940.[37] Within the Reichsbahn—that is, excluding the Ostbahn and the RVDs to the east—he estimated that 141.1 million RM had been spent by 1 January 1943.[38] In fiscal 1943 the DRB spent 225.5 million RM on military-related construction projects billed to its extraordinary budget. Of this, 45 million were spent in Germany and 180 million on the Ostbau program.[39] The Ostbahn, the Reichsbahn, and the Finance Ministry calculated that a total of 316 million RM had been spent on the Otto Program and 1.1 billion RM on the Ostbau program by September 1943. The Reich paid 65 percent of these bills, and the DRB the remaining 35 percent.[40]

Despite the RVDs vast size and the military operations taking place on their eastern extremities, rail traffic there was thin compared with that in Germany. On 1 January 1943 all of the RVDs combined operated a total of 6,242 kilometers of standard-gauge lines and 224 kilometers of broad-gauge lines. By June, all of the broad-gauge lines had been either lost or converted to standard-gauge. The standard-gauge network had shrunk to 2,679 kilometers by mid-December.[41] On 20 November, the RVDs had 4,305 steam locomotives, of which 28.3 percent were unavailable for service due to mechanical problems and damage.[42] More than 120,000 cars were circulating in the area.[43] The RVDs employed a total of 136,420 people as of 31 December 1942, of whom 15,930 were Germans. The number of Germans increased during 1943 while the number of non-Germans fell by almost half.[44] In December 1942 the divisions of the GVD Osten generated a total of 4.09 million train-kilometers; 53.6 percent consisted of Wehrmacht traffic.[45] In the same month, a total of 1,690 cars were placed, an indication of the low level of economic activity in the area and the predominance of through traffic.[46] On 1 January 1943, a regular work day, ninety-seven trains entered the GVD Osten and seventy-three left. Traffic remained at this level into the early summer, and then inbound traffic declined by about a quarter while outbound traffic increased.[47] During 1942, 1.4 million tons of nonmilitary freight were brought to the east by rail while 3.4 million tons left the area for Germany; 6.6 million tons of goods were moved within the area. These traffics peaked during 1943: 2.1 million tons of freight were sent to the area and 4.2 million tons left, and 8.8 million tons were carried to and from destinations within the GVD area. During 1944, due to the Soviet advance, traffic declined dramatically. In the first half of the year, only 574,687 tons of goods were brought out of the region to Germany, while 314,398 tons were sent in, consisting mostly of coal. Just 1.5 million tons were carried entirely within the area.[48] The modest volumes of economic traffic demonstrate that, despite Hitler's grandiose dreams, the Third Reich derived little economic benefit from the occupied east.

For the Reichsbahn, operating in the occupied east was bad business. To support the exploitative plans of the various Reich agencies working in the region, it charged deeply discounted tariffs. Schelp determined in mid-July 1942 that the tariffs imposed in the area did not cover the DRB's operating costs there.[49] The Wehrmacht did not pay for the services that it received during the first six and a half months of 1942. The Reich made good these charges through its extraordinary budget. In October the Reichsbahn agreed to bill the military for the transportation services that it received in the HBDs based on a crude estimate of the volume of axle-kilometers that the divisions provided to the military. The Wehrmacht would continue to be charged the low tariff of twenty Reich pfennigs per axle-kilometer. Not surprisingly, the HBDs lost heavily. For the period mid-January to 1 October 1942, they calculated their combined losses at 1.3 billion RM. The Reich Finance Ministry reimbursed them 1.1 billion RM, or 84.6 percent of their losses.[50]

Operations in the RVDs became increasingly difficult as the tide of war turned against Germany. The advance of the Red Army was coordinated with the activities of large numbers of well-equipped partisans operating in the rear areas of the German army. Their primary targets were the railways run by the Reichsbahn. Operation Citadel was the last major offensive operation undertaken by the Wehrmacht on the eastern front. During the spring of 1943, the Reichsbahn brought forward supplies and equipment, including the heavy Tiger and Panther tanks, to prepare for the attack. On the line from Minsk to Bryansk, sixty trains per day rolled eastward to support the buildup. On the Smolensk-Bryansk line another eighteen trains per day moved into the deployment area.[51] Soviet partisans conducted numerous attacks against rail lines and facilities in an attempt to hinder these movements. After the German offensive was thrown back, and the Red Army moved on the offensive, the attacks intensified. On the night of 2–3 August 1943 the partisans launched a concerted assault on lines in RVD Minsk in an attempt to aid the advancing Red Army. They cut rails at 8,422 places, interrupting traffic on five major lines, forcing the Reichsbahn to call in repair crews from Germany.[52] Attacks continued into the autumn. Operations became increasingly difficult because the constant fear of attacks necessitated slowing trains and providing special cars and personnel to search for explosives.[53] Evidence of the impact of the partisans can be seen in the accident records of RVD Kiev to the south. Until October 1942 the average

The Years of Retreat 135

number of accidents that occurred in the division per month was 40.6, most of which were due to operating errors. In October the average jumped to 105 and continued to rise, reaching 496 in July 1943. Fully 409 of these were due to sabotage.[54] Overall, partisan attacks damaged about 5,000 locomotives and 19,000 freight cars during 1943.[55] Yet this was only a foretaste of what was to come. On the night of 19–20 January 1944, partisans cut lines in 10,500 places, causing an almost complete stoppage of rail service for an entire day.[56] Reichsbahn people had been armed and stations and other facilities reinforced to offer some protection against attack. The arming of DRB personnel, who were civilians, raised questions concerning their treatment if they were captured. Yet the desperate nature of the situation and the German conviction that their enemies were subhumans who would stop at nothing overcame all doubts.[57]

While these attacks were occurring, the Reichsbahn was required to remove goods and people from the areas being relinquished to the advancing Soviets. In September 1943, just from the area behind the Dnjepr, 713 trains with 28,507 carloads of materials were sent back to Germany, followed by 743 more trains with 24,720 cars in October.[58]

Operating conditions in the west were far less perilous than in the east until the spring of 1944. Here, problems arose due to the unwillingness of many Belgians and French to cooperate with their occupiers and bureaucratic friction within the German control apparatus.

The SNCF was brought into the continental railway system that the DRB had established. On 15 June 1942, based on authority granted by Hitler, the Reichsbahn assumed control of the WVDs Paris and Brussels and renamed them Main Transportation Divisions (Hauptverkehrsdirektionen, or HVD). Hans Münzer was entrusted with HVD Paris and Colmar Bauer, HVD Brussels. On 2 July the Main Transportation Directorate for France and Belgium was established to work in parallel with the ZVL in Berlin.[59] Owing to the need to send Germans to the east, and the certainty that the Allies would not attack western Europe for the foreseeable future, the lines passing through the coastal areas were returned to both the SNCF and the SNCB in January 1943.[60]

As of 31 December 1942, the SNCF employed 414,216 people. They were supervised by a very small number of Germans, the equivalent of less than 1 percent of their total.[61] The DRB attempted to recruit SNCF employees to work for it in Germany. However, this proved difficult because of the attitude of the French railroaders, "les Cheminots," and because they well knew the treatment that awaited them.[62] The French railroaders resisted the Germans with small but effective measures that significantly reduced the performance of the SNCF, thereby hindering the German effort to exploit the French economy. In a meeting on 24 June 1943, HVD Paris officials complained to SNCF representatives that on the Le Mans–Rennes line, the express trains carrying French civilians ran on time while, due to the neglect by the SNCF trainmasters, freight trains carrying goods for the German occupiers were badly delayed.[63] A few days later, an HVD Paris official presented the SNCF with a plan to increase locomotive utilization. The French pronounced the plan unworkable because they lacked personnel. When the German representative pointed out that he had seen many French railroaders standing around locomotive sheds talking, the French told him that these were exceptions caused by poor supervision.[64] Dilli recognized that the French railroaders were of doubtful loyalty and considered this one of the major reasons for operating delays in France.[65] By late 1943 sabotage by partisans also became a major cause of train delays. In its situation report for the next to last week of November 1943, HVD Paris considered the attacks by the Maquis to be the single most significant cause of the poor car turnaround times then prevailing in France.[66]

In addition to contracting for the production of rolling stock in France, the DRB continued to remove locomotives and cars from the SNCF during 1942 and 1943. In a meeting in Paris on 6 June 1942, Ganzenmüller called upon Münzer to transfer an additional 37,000 freight cars to Germany. Münzer pointed out that the SNCF now had only 226,000 compared with the 463,000 that it had owned in 1938. The loss of cars had been a major cause of the one-third decline in car placings in France. Ganzenmüller was unimpressed and demanded 800 passenger cars and 1,100 locomotives. He also wanted 3,000 kilometers of track to be ripped out and taken to the east.[67] The Main Car Office then dictated an arrangement with the SNCF and SNCB providing that they would immediately send 50,000 freight cars to Germany.[68] The French transportation minister, Robert Gibrat, and the premier of the Vichy government, Pierre Laval, protested.[69] They were able to win a delay in the transfer of the freight cars because, at the moment, there was no shortage of car space in Germany. Yet by 1 August, 10,000 additional French cars had been sent to the Reichsbahn.[70] By September, 1,300 locomotives had arrived in Germany, including 200 from Belgium.[71] The transfer of the freight cars was completed in early 1943. At that point, 214,410 SNCF freight cars were circulating in the Reich, while 73,120 DRB cars were in France due to the normal flow of traffic, yielding a substantial net gain for the Reichsbahn.[72] A year later, at the end of February 1944, the SNCF had only 279,000 freight cars available to it, including DRB cars circulating in France. This was the greatest number achieved at any time during the war, but was still less than two-thirds the number of cars that the SNCF had used before the war. About 4,300 French locomotives were in Germany.[73] Because of these losses, and because of the shortsighted policies of the German occupiers and the efforts of the French resistance, freight traffic on the SNCF remained below prewar levels throughout the occupation. Upwards of two-thirds of this reduced traffic served the German occupiers.[74]

The Reichsbahn also used the SNCB as a reservoir of personnel and rolling stock. On 1 July 1942 HVD Brussels counted a total of 164,639 employees, of whom 92,741 were Belgians, 64,792 were Frenchmen, and only 7,106 were Germans.[75] Freight cars flowed steadily eastward out of HVD Brussels. On 5 January 1942, in the area of the SNCB, there were only 65,000 freight cars, compared with 106,000 before the war; 25,000 of the cars that it still owned were operating in Germany, and another 16,000 had already been formally transferred to the DRB. HVD Brussels also opposed sending additional cars into Germany in accordance with Ganzenmüller's demand.[76] Here, though, because of the importance of the coal mines in the region, the DRB agreed to limit the number of freight cars that it took to 40,000. This necessitated the return of some 15,000 cars that were then in Germany.[77] However, the pull of the east was too strong. Cars began flowing into Germany again so that by early March 1943, less than one-third of the boxcars that belonged to the HVD were actually available to it. This loss of car space prevented it from serving the Wehrmacht stationed in Belgium and the industries there working on German contracts.[78] In addition to losing cars to the Reichsbahn, SNCB shops were used to repair damaged rolling stock owned by the DRB. In 1941 alone, 486 locomotives underwent major servicing in the repair shops in Belgium.[79] The HVD Brussels delivered large quantities of coal to the heavy industries in southern Belgium and northern France. In June 1942 it moved a total of 1.4 million tons of coal, 75 percent of which remained within its area. It also transported a total of 933,014 tons of iron ore from the Briey field, 224,620 tons of which were sent to the Ruhr.[80] Overall, traffic to Germany reached considerable proportions. In January 1943, for example, 38,443 cars carrying 882,033 tons of freight were sent to the Reich from industries in HVD Brussels.[81] Clearly, Belgium, like France, was viewed by the Nazi occupiers as an area to be milked, not as ruthlessly as the occupied east, but milked nonetheless. It seems likely that the removal of rolling stock hindered the exploitation of the industries located in these two countries, providing another case study in the inconsistencies of Nazi imperial policy.

The ultimate purpose of the exploitation of the occupied territories was the strengthening of the German Reich. The Reichsbahn conformed to this general policy objective by concentrating on maintaining a high level of service in Germany. The Central Traffic Directorate played the decisive role in adjusting the operations of the DRB to the traffic demands made by the civilian economy and the fighting fronts. Therefore, viewing the evolution of the Reichsbahn's operations in Germany can be done best from its vantage point.

Using standard operating procedures applied by new, younger leaders, the DRB overcame the winter crisis during the course of the spring of 1942. As noted, car placings had returned to normal by April. By July the freight that had been backed up as a result of the crisis had been completely moved to its destinations.[82] Moving freight became more difficult again only during December 1942, due to the drain of rolling stock eastward to supply and reinforce the beleaguered Sixth Army at Stalingrad. Otherwise, the freight traffic situation in

Germany was generally satisfactory. There was no hint of the disaster that had struck the year before.[83] By March 1943, with the situation on the eastern front having stabilized and the weather beginning to moderate, the chairman of the ZVL, Emrich, was able to characterize the situation as good, even in the Ostbahn.[84] The situation became so satisfactory that the ZVL saw no need to meet in June 1943.[85] Problems arose again only in August, caused by the retreat after the defeat at Kursk in the east, the invasion of Italy and that country's defection from the Axis to the south, and the serious fire bombings of Hamburg in the west. These events caused congestion in marshaling yards, drew freight cars east and south, and necessitated running many trains to evacuate civilians from the regions affected by air attacks.[86] There was no change in this situation through the autumn.[87] Yet traffic levels remained high. Indeed, the Reichsbahn moved more freight in 1943 than at any other time in its history. The ZVL and the Traffic and Operating Sections of the Reichsbahn adjusted to these challenges and satisfied most demands. Then, during the spring of 1944, the operating situation began to change dramatically. The front in the east drew closer to Germany, reducing the area to be served by the DRB and its subsidiaries and the distances over which shipments traveled. The west, however, now emerged as a source of difficulty. Allied air attacks in preparation for the invasion of France disrupted rail operations, causing the HVDs Brussels and Paris to draw locomotives and freight cars out of Germany to compensate for the decline in marshaling capacity that they suffered.[88] On 1 June 1944, on the eve of the invasion, Emrich considered the operating situation satisfactory everywhere except in the areas of the west that were directly affected by air attacks.[89] The ZVL and the Reichsbahn had mastered the transportation situation in the two years between the winter crisis of 1941-42 and the Allied invasion of Normandy in June 1944.

The ZVL succeeded by adjusting the standard operating procedures that had served the DRB so well for so long. No single measure was decisive, and, at different times, different steps were more effective than others. One of the most important responsibilities of the ZVL was to set car priorities. The DRB had previously done this on its own, but without the necessary coordination with shippers. Speer's reforms enabled the Reichsbahn to adjust its service to the real needs of the centrally steered economy by bringing representatives of the shippers into constant contact with the railway. The breakdown of the price mechanism during the 1930s had been recognized by the Reichsbahn. But the various claimants for transportation space had not adjusted as quickly. The ZVL, dominated by the president of the Reichsbahn's GBL Ost, Ernst Emrich, overcame this problem.

In April 1942, before the ZVL was formed, the freight priority list was still being set by Paul Treibe, chief of the Traffic Section. Military traffic was at the top, with a large number of subcategories. Movement of oil products occupied second position. Then came car space for the railway construction programs in the east and the repair of DRB rolling stock.[90] In June the ZVL assumed responsibility for this program and adjusted it in accordance with the changing war situation. In general, Wehrmacht movements received highest priority. They were arranged between the Transchef and his subordinates behind the fighting fronts and Group L and its liaison staff at his headquarters. The ZVL had nothing to do with these movements. Among the economic traffics for which it was responsible, it allocated blocks of cars to the various coal-producing areas, the armaments industry, agriculture, and other shippers as circumstances dictated. For example, on 17 December 1943 the ZVL assigned coal first priority, allocating 70,000 coal cars per day to the mines. Next, shippers in possession of armaments program code-word authorizations from the Speer ministry would have all of their demands met. Then, the sugar beet and potato farmers would have their requirements met to the extent possible. In fourth place, farmers and millers shipping grain for bread and meal would receive 3,000 cars per day. Finally, fertilizer received 2,400 cars per day. The remaining car space was then made available for other carload freight and LCL.[91] The graduated tariff system that had been created during the early 1920s, and which encouraged long-distance shipments, was abolished in June 1942.[92] When necessary due to increased traffic or congestion, marshaling yards operated on Sunday; otherwise, the work schedule of 1938 was retained.[93] The freight train schedule that had been shaped by Leibbrand during the 1920s and 1930s also remained essentially unchanged until the summer of 1944. Regularly scheduled freight trains continued to run even if they could not be filled to capacity. Additional freight was carried by extras. Due to the disruption in the flow of traffic, marshaling activities, and the availability of locomotives, this practice was ended only on 3 July 1944.[94]

A number of problems remained constant throughout the period spring 1942 to summer 1944, although their sources changed as the war situation developed. One was the tendency for cars to be drawn out of Germany. Until the spring of 1944, cars were sucked eastward because of the vast territories to be served there and the unstable operating circumstances, and because the Wehrmacht used boxcars as storage sheds. An indication of the magnitude of the problem can be gained by considering the distribution of the Reichsbahn's freight car fleet. During the first week of August 1943, the DRB owned 808,900 serviceable freight cars. It was also using 253,251 foreign cars, either in Germany or elsewhere. Of the total, 321,846 DRB freight cars were outside of Germany, most of them in the east; 40,758 Reichsbahn cars were undergoing repairs.[95] In the spring of 1944 the geographical focus reversed as cars were drawn into France and Belgium due to the confusion caused by Allied bombing.[96]

Within Germany, the dispersal of factories to locations deemed safe from air attack caused the usage of freight cars to increase. On 14 July 1943 Hitler ordered the scattering of armaments plants to numerous smaller localities. Neither in his order nor in Speer's implementing directive was transportation mentioned. The result was that the Reichsbahn was forced to serve many more locations, placing an increased burden on the marshaling yards. Some plants were set up on secondary lines not intended to carry heavy traffic. A second wave of dispersal began in February 1944 when U.S. air attacks on plants producing fighter planes caused Speer to order their dispersal. Twenty-seven main assembly plants were scattered over about 300 locations. Schelp estimated that dispersal created a demand for an additional 2,000 car placings daily.[97] The net result of this expansion of the market through territorial conquest and dispersal was a major increase in the length of the average trip taken by a freight shipment. Between 1924 and 1929, freight traveled about 150 kilometers to its destination. During the period 1933 to 1937, this rose gradually to about 170 kilometers. With the start of the war, average haul jumped to over 200 kilometers. By the end of August 1943, it stood at 356 kilometers. During the first seven months of 1944 it declined, owing to the contraction of the front in the east, but still remained at 238.8 kilometers.[98] The increase in average haul reduced the effective number of cars available to the Reichsbahn. The freight car production program described earlier and the withdrawal of cars from the SNCF and SNCB were intended to counteract this development. Complementing new production was an extensive repair program. During June 1942, as an aftereffect of the winter crisis, the number of freight cars damaged and out of service stood at 65,000. The Reichsbahn's own repair works were already overburdened with locomotives in need of repair. Therefore, for the first time since the early 1920s the DRB contracted out the repair of freight cars to private companies.[99]

Another constant problem was the slow unloading of cars by receivers. Both industry and the Wehrmacht were guilty of tardy unloading of freight cars placed on their sidings. Four measures were undertaken to overcome this problem. More labor was assigned to the team tracks and unloading docks, including prisoners and unskilled German workers. The Reichsbahn also offered ten-mark premiums for every day early that a car was returned to circulation. If a shipper exceeded the unloading time limit, increased demurrage charges were imposed. In addition, unloading was conducted on Sunday during periods when cars were in particularly short supply. This proved to be a difficult measure to implement due to the extreme reluctance of German laborers to work on Sunday. Finally, the Reichsbahn convinced many industries to increase their storage capacity so that freight, particularly coal, could be stockpiled during the low traffic period of the summer, freeing cars for the autumn peak period.[100]

The difficulties in unloading were reflected in car turnaround time. Schultz, the head of the Main Car Office, illustrated the importance of this measurement when he pointed out that the improvement of turnaround by just one-tenth of a day effectively gained 20,000 cars for the DRB in a week.[101] Freight car turnaround time had risen to above 5 days with the beginning of the war. It then rose during the winter crisis to over 7 days. By July 1942 it had fallen to 5.3 days, and it fluctuated around this level until November and December 1943, when it rose above 6 days and remained there into the summer of 1944.[102]

To increase the work that it derived from each car, the Reichsbahn had begun overloading its freight cars in short-distance services by one ton in March 1937. The Mechanical Section opposed this measure due to the increased wear that it caused, leading to a rise in accidents. The ZVL ordered that freight cars be overloaded by two tons each during its meeting on 22 July 1942. Ore cars were to be overloaded by one ton. This measure was relaxed during early 1943 as traffic flowed more smoothly. But as the supply of freight cars tightened again later in the year, overloading was resumed. During the ZVL's meeting of 5 November 1943, Dorpmüller ordered the overloading of all freight cars except those in ore service to begin immediately and to be continued indefinitely.[103]

The expanded locomotive production program and the higher priority accorded to the Reichsbahn Repair Works in terms of raw materials and labor solved the DRB's motive power problems. Using the expanded fleet of locomotives, however, required abandoning peacetime practices. Engineers and firemen preferred to use the same locomotive all of the time, taking the engine out from their home station, remaining overnight at the destination, and returning with it coupled to another train during their next shift. This procedure, while it encouraged the careful maintenance of the engines, led to their inadequate utilization. Consequently, in September 1942 the Reichsbahn separated locomotives from crews and even specific traffics so that crews and engines could be used freely whenever power was needed.[104] This measure, which met with considerable resistance from the crews, was specifically intended to reduce the backlog of trains not moved on time. The causes of the backlog were numerous. Lack of available power and congestion in marshaling yards were the two most important factors. The failure of the locomotive shed to send an engine to a waiting train could cause delays that rippled through the system due to the Reichsbahn's practice of preparing detailed plans for the employment of engines and crews. Delays in marshaling cars—breaking up arriving trains and building new ones for departure—also caused congestion. In January 1942 the backlog reached 1,000 trains due to the winter crisis. Then it declined, falling to just 78 trains at the end of April 1942. It increased again during the fall of 1942, fluctuating around 200 to 300 trains per day. It remained around this figure through 1943, climbing briefly to 600 trains in December. During 1944 the number of trains stuck in the backlog declined until it settled to around 300 per day in May. Then it rose to over 400 in late May and early June due to the bombing and invasion in the west.[105]

Coal traffic received the special attention of the ZVL throughout the period June 1942 to June 1944. During the winter crisis, the daily coal car placing target had been set by the Traffic Section at 81,000 per day. However, the Reichsbahn was able to place only 75,000.[106] To overcome this problem, the DRB resorted to expedients such as attaching coal cars to passenger trains and using some passenger trains to return empty gondolas to the marshaling yards.[107] Complicating the DRB's coal traffic was the need to send thirty-five trains carrying 1 million tons of coal to Italy each month. Two-thirds came from the Ruhr and the Saar, the other third from Upper Silesia. This represented an outward flow away from Germany's major economic centers for which there was no reverse flow as a counterbalance, resulting in large inefficient movements of empty cars from Italy northward. Operating conditions in the Alps necessitated other awkward operating measures. The trains weighed 1,200 tons when they left the coal areas. Upon reaching the Alpine passes, they were split into two 600-ton sections. Once on the opposite side of the mountains, they were reassembled. Hours were lost in these difficult operations. The impending capitulation of Italy compelled the Wehrmacht to take over the Italian State Railways in September 1943. Although this measure reduced customs formalities at the Italian border, the rolling stock sent into the country was frequently lost to Allied air attacks.[108]

To address these problems, the ZVL adjusted the daily coal car placing target frequently. The overall number of cars devoted to coal movement was changed and the proportions allocated to the Ruhr and the Saar in the west and Upper Silesia in the east were manipulated to suit the prevailing situation. Car placings for brown coal were handled in the same fashion. In May 1942 the total number of cars to be placed for coal each day stood at 76,700. The target was raised to 83,200 on 28 May. The DRB could not meet this goal, so it was reduced to 74,220. During 1943 and 1944 the target fluctuated between 77,000 and 79,000. In May 1944 it was then raised to 84,700 per day. Until the fall of 1944, the DRB generally met the coal needs of the German economy. It did not move as much coal as the Reich Coal Association wished, but it moved enough to enable the German war economy to function without undue difficulty. In the coal economy year of 1943–44, the DRB carried 95.8 percent, 263 million tons, of the coal requested by the coal association. Using the calendar year, in 1943 the Reichsbahn moved 292.2 million tons of coal.[109]

Viewed in perspective, the Reichsbahn's freight service had recovered well after the winter crisis of 1941–42. In 1943 the DRB moved more freight than at any time in its history, 675 million tons. It did this by running more freight trains and cars than ever before. Ton-kilometers also reached the impressive peak of 178.6 billion. The Reichsbahn's traffic increased for two reasons: the tonnage to be moved rose, and the distances required to move it increased. How the DRB met these demands is instructive. The high tonnage total was achieved by increasing the number of cars running in the system and overloading them. The greater volume of train-kilometers was made possible by the increase in the size of the locomotive fleet. Trains also became larger, as indicated by the disproportionate rise in car-axle-kilometers compared with the rise in train-kilometers.

Table 3.3. Profile of Reichsbahn Freight Traffic and Operations, 1939-1944

Year	Tonnage (millions)	Freight-Train-Kilometers (millions)	Car-Axle-Kilometers (billions)	Average Haul (kilometers)	Car Placings (millions)	Operating Ton-Kilometers (billions)	Revenues (billion RM)	Revenues per Ton-Kilometer[a] (pfennigs)
1939	564	377	28.0	5.2	46.1	113.9	3.771	3.50
1940	619	448	34.4	5.35	47.1	146.9	4.720	2.99
1941	656	499	38.2	7.79	47.2	159.8	5.287	3.55
1942	644	489	35.8	9.18	45.3	164.1	5.186	3.16
1943	675	520.4	40.1	9.63	48.6	178.6	5.663	3.41
1944	625	470	35.6	11.36	43.3			

[a] Estimate calculated by determining tariff ton-kilometers as a proportion of operating ton-kilometers based on historical average of 0.93 and dividing this by revenues. Figures given are probably low.

Source: DRB, *Geschäftsberichte*.

The car placing results confirm this. In 1943 they were only 5.4 percent higher than in 1939 and just 2.97 percent higher than in 1937, the peak peacetime year. The marshaling yards had reached the limits of their potential. Service had been expanded by increasing the size of the fleet of locomotives and freight cars and running more and bigger trains over longer distances[110] (see Tables 3.3 and 3.4).

On first glance, it may seem that passenger traffic was of subordinate importance during the war. This was only partially the case. Certainly, pleasure travel was inappropriate, but the Hitler government did not attempt to eliminate it entirely for fear of harming popular morale. Moreover, passenger service was necessary to move the many millions of workers to their jobs and back to their homes daily. Passenger trains also moved people from areas threatened by air attack and carried relatives of wounded soldiers to visit them in hospitals where they were recovering. Consequently, passenger service could not be drastically cut. Instead, it too was adjusted to suit wartime circumstances.

The Reichsbahn gradually reduced the quality of its passenger service by slowing trains, allowing overcrowding, and restricting access to premium trains. It reduced the number of passenger trains that it operated and increased the size of those trains that did run. On 11 September 1941 the DRB announced that it would no longer be able to run special trains for travel groups, or even to add cars for such groups to regularly scheduled trains.[111] To conserve coal and make it easier for trainmasters to mesh the movements of passenger and freight trains, on 16 March 1942 all long-distance passenger trains were slowed by 5 percent. In addition, the duration of stops was increased and greater time was allowed for acceleration to track speed.[112] During the first two years of the war, the DRB had continued the practice of adding extra passenger trains around holidays. Due to the winter crisis, that was not possible at Easter 1942.[113] However, it was resumed for subsequent major holidays. The Reichsbahn also limited ac-

Table 3.4. Reichsbahn Freight Car Placings, 1937–1944

Year	Daily Freight Car Placings	Daily Coal Car Placings (10 ton units)
1937	146,720	62,378
1938	154,448	61,876
1939	151,868	64,619
1940	152,747	77,253
1941	153,679	73,440
1942	147,731	77,012
1943	158,352	78,801
1944	141,501	70,055

Source: Kreidler, *Eisenbahnen im Machtbereich*, 338.

cess to certain premium trains. Use of specified express trains required proof from the traveler's employer of the necessity of the trip and the purchase of a special ticket at a separate window. Access to first- and second-class sleepers was restricted using similar procedures. Some people abused these measures by obtaining letters of justification from their employers, purchasing reservations for berths, and then selling them to others at a profit.[114] The reduction in the number of trains and the increase in travel resulted in inconveniences to the public. For example, on 22 December 1943, during the Christmas rush when masses of soldiers on leave and civilians converged on the stations, some trains were jammed with twice the number of people they were intended to accommodate. In stations such as Halle (S) and Leipzig, thousands of people were left on the platforms as trains departed, bulging with passengers. Similar problems occurred during the Easter holiday in 1944.[115]

Beginning in August 1943, as a result of the fire raids on Hamburg, the Reichsbahn initiated special measures to assist the victims of urban area bombing. Trains were prepared in advance and kept in readiness loaded with medication and food at five separate locations in western Germany. They were sent automatically to a city immediately after it was bombed, thus relieving the division in which the target city was located of the worry of ordering assistance while trying to assess the situation and repair damage.[116] The DRB also provided trains of empty passenger cars to cities immediately after they were attacked to help refugees move to safe areas.

Passenger traffic rose steadily, reaching a peak of 3.7 billion people in 1944. The Reichsbahn's effort to move passengers reached its high point in 1943, when both passenger-train-kilometers and passenger-car-axle-kilometers reached their respective highs. Overall, the DRB's performance serving passenger traffic during the war, considering the simultaneous increase in freight traffic and the difficulties caused by developments on the fronts and air attacks, is remarkable (see Table 3.5).

Table 3.5. Profile of Reichsbahn Passenger Traffic and Operations, 1939-1944

Year	Passengers (billions)	Passenger-Train-Kilometers (millions)	Car-Axle-Kilometers (billions)	Average Trip (kilometers)	Passenger-Kilometers (billions)	Revenues (billion RM)	Revenues per Passenger-Kilometer[a] (pfennigs)
1939	2.21	568	13.1	23.78	61.9	1.69	2.73
1940	2.253	474	12.6		55.4	2.43	4.34
1941	2.655	520	13.7		69.4	3.25	4.68
1942	3.094	486	12.4		85.9	4.03	4.69
1943	3.539	513.7	15.1		107.3	5.262	4.90
1944	3.706	491	14.4				

[a] Estimate based on division of revenues by passenger-kilometers. Figures may be high.
Source: DRB, *Geschäftsberichte*.

The war compelled the Reichsbahn to alter its policies in two other areas besides operations: personnel and finances. The vast increase in the area served, the loss of many of its experienced employees to the armed forces or to the railways of the occupied areas, and the increased intensity of operations led to a massive increase in the number of people employed by the Reichsbahn (see Table 3.6). Many of the people who replaced those lost to the war effort were not as capable as their predecessors, either because they were physically weaker or because they worked for the Reichsbahn unwillingly. Therefore, the increase in the Reichsbahn's work force was proportionally higher than warranted by the rise in traffic.

Even before the war began, the Reichsbahn had begun recalling retirees. Then, on 1 September 1939, the day of the outbreak of the war, the DRB suspended the mandatory retirement age of sixty-five for the duration and allowed retired officials up to age seventy to return to service. However, this measure, while it gained experienced people for the railway, did not yield many additional employees. Of the 240,000 officials in retirement in 1939, only 21,000 were considered suitable for reemployment. By December 1941 only 12,000 had actually returned to railway service.[117]

Another method of gaining labor was to increase the length of the workday. On 1 June 1942 the RVM set the standard minimum workweek at sixty hours. On every second Sunday, Reichsbahn employees were required to work ten hours.[118] In addition, from January 1940 taking vacation became virtually impossible. The Reichsbahn tried to compensate by providing its people with work clothes and additional food. But these measures could not prevent labor shortages, both in skilled occupations in the Reichsbahn Repair Works and in mundane jobs unloading cars and performing track maintenance.

Throughout the war, the Reichsbahn struggled to free its employees from

Table 3.6. DRB Personnel Strength, 1937–1944

Year	Employees	Year	Employees
1937	703,546	1941	1,253,100
1938	778,374	1942	1,386,000
1939	958,000	1943	1,529,000
1940	1,145,600	1944	1,581,000

Source: DRB, *Geschäftsberichte*.

party obligations and to protect them from both the military and labor drafts. By the end of 1940, it had succeeded in shielding only 443,000 of its employees from conscription. It then won a series of increases until, in August 1944, 1,052,000 railroaders were exempt.[119] However, the Reichsbahn was still required to provide people to restore service on the railways of the countries overrun by the Wehrmacht. They too had to be replaced. In June 1940 the DRB sent 28,500 men to Belgium and France.[120] As we have seen, operations were turned over to the local railroaders as soon as possible, bringing the number of Reichsbahn personnel in the west down to 4,000 by the spring of 1941.[121] This number increased again only during the spring of 1944 as the Allied invasion approached. Then, to ensure logistical support for the military, the number of Reichsbahner assigned to the west was brought up to 33,018.[122]

The major drain on Reichsbahn manpower was the east. In September 1939 the DRB sent 50,000 of its employees to the conquered areas of Poland to restore rail service and organize the Ostbahn.[123] Although the Reichsbahn's aim here also was to use Germans only in supervisory positions, Nazi racial and occupation policies dictated that railroad people be sent to the area to Germanize it.[124] The attack on the USSR necessitated sending thousands of additional Reichsbahn employees into the east. They followed immediately behind the field railway units and operated the railways as the military moved forward. The status of these blue railroaders was a matter of rancorous dispute between the Reichsbahn and the Wehrmacht. The military considered the railroaders subject to its discipline. The Reichsbahner resisted this. Making matters worse was the fact that the Reichsbahn sent its people east without adequate preparation, forcing them to rely on the army for food, housing, and other necessities. Many soldiers considered the railroaders slovenly and undisciplined. Most of these ill feelings were the product of the clash between two groups of people with strong corporate identities and intense pride. Yet they made cooperation very difficult at times. The DRB later improved the support that it provided to its members when serving outside Germany, thereby reducing the sources of friction. The transfer of authority over virtually all railway operations in the occupied areas to the Reichsbahn also reduced tension. But the military's desire to control all elements affecting its operations, and its disdain for the Reichsbahn's deliberate methods, which seemed out of place during the wartime emergency, ensured that relations between these two important organizations remained strained.[125]

On 2 December 1941, 70,000 Reichsbahn personnel were working on the railways in the conquered east. An additional 36,000 were employed by the Ostbahn or in eastern regions incorporated into the Reich in 1939, and a further 15,789 were in the occupied west. Finally, 43,789 were serving in the armed forces. By the end of 1942, the number of men serving in uniform reached 82,329; it almost doubled to 152,217 by the end of 1943 and peaked at 201,000 in late 1944. Taking the end of 1943 as an example, an additional 73,568 were employed in the HVDs in the east and 12,053 in the west, while 9,605 were employed by the Ostbahn. Overall, including some others who were also assigned to tasks outside of Germany, the Reichsbahn had lost 249,478 employees to the war effort.[126]

Not surprisingly, these large losses caused a labor shortage within the Reichsbahn. In July 1941 the Mechanical Section calculated that it lacked 10,000 engineers, firemen, and locomotive servicing personnel. This led to delays in providing power for trains and in repairing engines.[127] At the beginning of 1942, Osthoff, the head of the Personnel Section, reported that the DRB was short a total of 120,000 employees, or about one-third of its skilled personnel.[128] The winter crisis led to a temporary change in this situation. On 20 May 1942 Sauckel, Hitler's general plenipotentiary for labor mobilization, decided to protect the DRB from further drafts and prohibited Reichsbahn employees from changing jobs merely to seek higher pay.[129] Yet the struggle for labor continued unabated. As memories of the winter crisis faded, preference in labor allocations was again accorded to other sectors. Sauckel did not fulfill his promises to provide labor to the railway, and DRB people continued to be drafted into the armed forces. When Ganzenmüller asked Lammers for an appointment with Hitler to discuss the Reichsbahn's labor problems in May 1944, Lammers told him that Hitler did not have time.[130] As the Allied armies closed in on Nazi Germany, the number of railroaders who enjoyed deferments was cut by almost 100,000 to 955,000.[131]

In addition to gaining deferments for its employees, the DRB took other steps to obtain and retain an adequate labor force. In October 1940 the Personnel Section decreed that Reichsbahner over twenty-three years of age would no longer be allowed to join the SS. This would prevent them from being distracted by political activities and ultimately drafted to serve in SS military formations.[132] The Reichsbahn also continued to reduce qualifications for hiring and promotion. For example, on 1 November 1939 it shortened the training period for switchmen. At the start of the war, the minimum age for service on a locomotive was lowered from twenty-one to eighteen years. In July 1943 the training period for engineers was reduced. Finally, in October 1944, office workers were trained to operate locomotives on Sundays or during emergencies.[133]

The Reichsbahn tapped two reservoirs of labor to compensate for its loss of German males: foreigners and German women. The employment of foreigners began slowly in 1939 because many RBDs were reluctant to take them. In a circular issued on 30 May 1940, Osthoff encouraged the divisions to use foreigners as much as possible and not just in line maintenance.[134] Initially, the foreign workers were volunteers, mostly French and Belgians who were recruited for specified periods. They received treatment similar to foreign workers employed by industry. Osthoff instructed the divisions to provide them with adequate housing and regular supplies of warm food.[135] Yet the increase in traffic and the approach of Operation Barbarossa quickly changed this situation. In February 1941 RBD Berlin was hiring prisoners from the Luftwaffe and the army.[136] The capture of hundreds of thousands of Red Army soldiers during the great battles of encirclement opened another source of cheap labor. Many of these prisoners died of exposure due to the neglect of the German military. But soon others were flowing back to Germany, frequently in open gondola cars. In October 1941 the Reich Labor Ministry gave the Reichsbahn first priority to receive these men.[137] They were used for heavy work in line maintenance and unloading freight cars.[138]

The experiences of the foreign workers varied according to their nationality owing to the racist policies of the Nazi regime. Initially, Poles were allowed to be hired only for work in the area seized by Germany in 1939. This brought many of them into the Ostbahn.[139] They were discriminated against throughout their service. On 13 January 1942, for example, they were required to wear an emblem indicating that they were Poles and to remove the buttons from their railway coats that were adorned with the Reich eagle.[140] Reichsbahner were cautioned to keep their distance from them. They should deal with the inferior people only to the extent necessary to conduct business, and under no circumstances should they be friendly toward them.[141] Despite this, circumstances dictated that the Germans and the Poles worked together. The many Reichsbahn workers who had been members of left-leaning labor unions before 1933 dealt with the Poles humanely, sharing food and clothing with them. Others treated them brutally. Whatever the case, the DRB depended on its Polish employees. RBD Posen, which had been formed in an area that had been Polish territory before the war, determined that 70 percent of its personnel, including 43 percent of its officials, were Poles in July 1942.[142]

Westerners received better treatment because they were considered more racially valuable. Yet most worked in Germany unwillingly, and therefore poorly. The Dutch workers who were assigned to the Reichsbahn in Munich rarely appeared for work, behaved badly when they did, and repeatedly reported sick.[143] In March 1941, 18,700 Italians agreed to work under contract for the Reichsbahn in Germany. They were allowed to bring their own cooks with them. They did not perform to the DRB's expectations. Yet the Reichsbahn received 15,000 Italian prisoners in September 1943.[144] The French and Belgians had learned that contract work in Germany was often very unpleasant. Consequently, a campaign to recruit 4,500 men from the SNCB in March 1942 gained only 100 applicants.[145] Overall, people of fifteen different nationalities other than German worked for the Reichsbahn during World War II. In December 1940, 70,000 were already employed by the German railroads. This number expanded to 160,000 within Germany's prewar borders by June 1943.[146] They played an important role. In RBD Posen, 75 percent of the firemen were Poles, and in RBD Stuttgart, 57 percent. In RBD Kassel, 73 percent of the people who serviced locomotives were foreigners.[147]

The other important source of labor was German women. There was much resistance to employing women in operations. Yet wartime necessity gradually broke down this barrier. On 9 September 1939 the Personnel Section authorized the divisions to hire women to perform simple tasks under easy circumstances.[148] Confusion existed as to just what these were. During a meeting of trainmasters and yardmasters on 2 November, a debate broke out as to just where and when women should be employed. Joseph Müller, chief of the operating office in the Operations Section, opposed using women as conductors, claiming that they caused disorder. Yet RBD Münster had already begun using them in this position.[149] Osthoff sent a halfhearted memorandum to the divisions on 9 December 1939, instructing them to hire more women, but only in an emergency. He then stated that the current situation should not be considered as such.[150] That attitude changed as more Reichsbahner were drafted into the armed forces during the spring of 1940. On 26 April, Osthoff ordered the divisions to make greater use of women to free men for more important tasks. He specifically stated that women could be employed as conductors on local passenger trains, as grade-crossing guards, and in repair works and locomotive sheds doing light work.[151] RBD Berlin told its male employees to put out the word that the Reichsbahn was seeking suitable women.[152] In June 1940 women were allowed to work as conductors in express and accelerated trains and as drivers of light trucks.[153] The Operating Section opposed this widening of employment for women but was overruled by the Personnel Section.[154] In April 1941 women were allowed to serve as conductors of through freight trains and in some traffic control positions in large stations.[155] In December they were permitted to work in switch towers, to supervise passenger platforms, and to serve as watch posts for work crews on the line.[156] Through these piecemeal measures, 80,000 women found jobs with the Reichsbahn by March 1942.[157]

The expansion of female employment did not stop there. The continued losses of men to the military and the occupied areas compelled the Reichsbahn to open additional job categories to women. On 13 January 1943 Werner Hassenpflug, Osthoff's successor as head of the Personnel Section, sent the divisions a comprehensive directive describing the tasks that women could be allowed to perform. In addition to jobs in administration, more operating positions would be opened to them, for example, as turntable operators. The ordinary workweek for women in all of these jobs would comprise fifty-six hours. They were not to be overworked and would be allowed time off to handle household responsibilities. He also pointed out that these jobs were all temporary. As soon as the war ended, the women would be dismissed.[158] Despite the reluctance of management to accept women, by the end of June 1943 the Reichsbahn had 190,000 women on its rolls.[159] The employment of women by the Reichsbahn continued to expand up to the end of the war. Emrich stated in a meeting of the ZVL in March 1943 that they had performed well.[160] Yet, as the temporary nature of their employment attests, they were ultimately unwelcome in what the railroaders still considered a man's world. Nazi ideology, which assigned women to the home, was incompatible with the large role given to them by the DRB during the war. Consequently, the Reichsbahn employed them only because it had no viable alternative.

The compromise that Dorpmüller devised with the Nazi Party in 1934 remained in effect until the end of the war. Many railroaders joined the party, especially officials, but the party did not influence the Reichsbahn's personnel policies.[161] In September 1940 officials were reminded that they were supposed to behave as wholehearted Nazis both on and off duty because many were not meeting the standards set by the party.[162] Due to the specialized nature of the Reichsbahn's work, the party was forced to relinquish its claim to approve appointments and promotions of officials.[163] The party also refrained from calling on Reichsbahner to attend political functions when attendance conflicted with their work schedules.[164] Yet as the war continued and the fighting became more intense, Hitler and the party attempted to increase their influence over the Reichsbahn. In June 1943 Hitler ordered that the regional leaders of the Nazi Party, the Gauleiter, indeed be consulted concerning the appointment or promotion of officials.[165] During the summer of 1943, the president of RBD Nuremberg, Ernst Geyer, was arrested by the Gestapo for making defeatist remarks. Dorpmüller and Ganzenmüller intervened to win his release. He was then retired.[166] Again, the Reichsbahn had defended its internal autonomy. Yet it was viewed suspiciously by the party as a result. Robert Ley, the leader of the German Labor Front, remarked to Ganzenmüller at the end of 1943 that the party had the impression that the Reichsbahn was a "state within the state."[167] This did not prevent the Reichsbahn from supporting Hitler's racial policies in the east or in Germany. Nor did it prevent the DRB from sustaining the German army in its war of conquest. It simply meant that the Reichsbahn insisted on conducting its affairs itself, without outside interference.

The Reichsbahn's pay policies during the war complied with the wage controls imposed by the Nazi regime. Between 1939 and 1943, officials received a modest 8.46 percent increase in their wages. Workers employed in the repair works and locomotive sheds received a 6.65 percent increase. In contrast, line maintenance workers suffered a pay cut of about 0.5 percent. Yet even the workers who received pay increases did not benefit. Although prices were controlled and necessities were rationed, inflation affected them when they turned to the black market to supplement their diets. When one considers that they all also had to work longer hours, it is clear that many Reichsbahn employees suffered an effective pay cut.[168] Those railroaders who were conscripted into the military continued to be paid and suffered no loss of seniority.[169] The foreign employees were paid according to their racial standing in the Nazi scale of human worth. Poles who had been officials of the Polish State Railway, and who performed similar functions under the DRB, were paid according to the scale for Reichsbahn officials. They were not, however, allowed to bear the title of official.[170] Otherwise, Russians, Poles, Jews, Gypsies, and prisoners were paid half of what Germans doing the same work were given. People from the Bohemian and Moravian Railway, the Dutch Railway, the SNCF, and the SNCB were paid according to the German schedules. By 1944 all Poles were put on the German pay schedule but were otherwise treated the same as the other easterners.[171]

Morale among Reichsbahn employees remained solid until the end of the war. Sabotage in Germany was negligible. During the war, the number reporting sick increased among both workers and officials. The increase among officials was small. Among workers, absenteeism due to illness rose by 43.2 percent from 1939 to 1942. But even then, it remained at 5.4 percent, which was fully acceptable under the circumstances.[172]

World War II was not a financial bonanza for the Reichsbahn. In keeping with the policy that had governed its financial affairs since it was reincorporated in the Reich administration, it was allowed to earn only a slight operating surplus, sufficient to cover its charges with the aid of extraordinary income. As before, capital expenditures were funded from current revenues and the Reichsbahn's tariffs were used to promote government policies. The Reichsbahn's credit activities were used by the Reich to soak up cash that the public could not spend on consumer goods and redirect those funds into the government's coffers. Yet the vast increase in traffic virtually ended the railway's money worries. As Fritz Busch of the Finance Section remarked, with the start of the war and the influx of revenues, costs were simply ignored.[173]

During the war, the Reichsbahn executed only four credit operations, two of which had been contemplated before the opening of hostilities. On 20 September 1938 Kleinmann wrote to the Reich Economics Ministry that the Reichsbahn could not cover all of its anticipated capital costs from operating income. While the DRB could divert 300 to 400 million RM in 1939 from its operating account, it needed to spend 1.3 billion on expansion projects.[174] This letter began a lengthy series of negotiations with the Reichsbank and the economics and finance ministries concerning the railway's credit needs. The Finance Ministry calculated that from 1939 to 1943, the Reichsbahn would have capital requirements totaling 10 billion RM, including 3.2 billion for construction associated with Hitler's plans to transform selected German cities.[175] In February 1939 Walter Funk, the economics minister, conceded that the railway should be allowed on the capital market.[176] The task then became convincing Hjalmar Schacht, the president of the Reichsbank. During a meeting on 1 March 1939, Schacht recommended that the Reichsbahn increase its operating income by eliminating commodity rates and other discounts.[177] In the meantime traffic rose, causing the Reichsbahn to revise upward its estimate of the total cost of expanding its rolling-stock fleet, and Hitler's city projects had taken on even more grandiose proportions. Prang now estimated that the Reichsbahn required a loan of 750 million RM in 1939.[178] Funk considered this excessive and joined Schacht in counseling Prang to cut discount tariffs, especially to passengers.[179] After additional negotiations, Funk finally agreed that the Reichsbahn should be allowed to obtain 500 million RM on the capital market.[180] The Finance Ministry gave its approval on 3 July.[181] Schacht dropped his objections, and the road seemed to be clear for the Reichsbahn to obtain its first major infusion of external credit since 1933. The outbreak of war, however, delayed the operation four months.[182] On 3 November 1939 the Reichsbank sold on behalf of the DRB 500 million RM in 4.5 percent bonds repayable in groups between 1945 and 1949; 200 million RM were taken by a consortium of public banks, and the remainder was offered to the public at a price of 99 RM. The entire public tranche was subscribed on the first day. As part of the agreement allowing it on the market, and because the DRB could not spend the proceeds of the bond sale immediately, it loaned 200 million RM to the Reich until 15 April 1940.[183]

The second major credit operation was the conversion of the Reichsbahn's preferred stock into bonds. In 1938 the Hitler government proposed repurchasing all outstanding preferred stock. It feared that foreigners might use their rights to influence Reichsbahn policy, even though only nonvoting certificates had been sold to the public. The DRB's response to the proposal was that conducting such a transaction would result in the railway paying 216 million RM in bonuses.[184] This temporarily stopped discussion of the issue. Once the war began, however, the Reich finance minister, Schwerin von Krosigk, raised the matter again, this time with the goal of reducing prevailing interest rates to 4 percent. Prang and Dorpmüller made clear that, although they would not block the deal, they opposed it and that the Finance Ministry would have to bear the "odium" of an early buyback.[185] With this, it was agreed that the Finance Ministry's plan, prepared in cooperation with the Reichsbank, would be implemented. The DRB would offer to exchange its outstanding preferred stock for 4 percent debentures. The Finance Ministry and the bank calculated that, because the interest rate on the debentures was 3 percent lower than the rate on the preferred stock, the DRB would realize an annual saving of 200 million RM.[186]

Table 3.7. Capital Budget of the Deutsche Reichsbahn, 1939-1944 (in million RM)

Year	Real Expansion	New Construction	Operations Development
1939	677.9	598.4	79.5
1940	694.0	627.4	66.6
1941	1,006.4	935.0	71.4
1942	870.5	788.9	81.6
1943	659.3	688.2	71.1
1944[a]	729.0	640.0	89.0

[a] Preliminary figures.
Sources: DRB, *Wirtschaftsplan 1943*, pp. 29-30, BAC R005/12122; DRB, *Wirtschaftsplan 1945*, pp. 29-30, BA RD98/14.

The transaction was conducted by the Reichsbank on 14 September 1940. The Reichsbahn sold 1.5 billion RM in 4 percent debentures, repayable in twenty-five years. Owners of Reichsbahn preferred stock received 120 RM in debentures for every 100 RM of preferred stock in their possession, plus a 7.5 percent cash payment, as compensation for one year's dividend payments.[187] The DRB paid 212 million RM in penalty fees. Holders of certificates worth 21 million RM in preferred stock did not appear to convert their paper, most likely because they lived in Allied countries. Their certificates were summarily canceled in 1941. In March 1945, with Germany crumbling around it, the Reichsbahn actually proposed retiring the 4 percent debentures.[188]

The Reichsbahn engaged in two additional, much smaller credit operations during the war. In July 1941 it converted its 150 million RM 4.5 percent bonds from 1935 into 150 million RM 3.5 percent bonds that would be due for repayment in 1966.[189] Then, in 1943, the 500 million RM bond issue that it had undertaken in 1936 was also converted. Four hundred million RM of the proceeds of this transaction had been used by the Reichsautobahnen. Dorpmüller demanded that the Reich convert this into a debt that would appear on its books and take responsibility for repaying the portion that had been allocated to the highway project.[190] The Finance Ministry rejected this idea, contending that it would create an unfavorable impression among the public. Instead, it proposed, and Dorpmüller agreed, that the debt should be converted to 3.5 percent bonds, 1 percent lower than the original issue. The Reich would assume responsibility for the DRB's 100 million RM portion because the railway could not be allowed on to the capital market in the foreseeable future. The Reichsautobahnen would repay the remaining 400 million RM debt. However, the debt would remain on the Reichsbahn's balance sheet for appearance's sake.[191] One result of this operation was that the Reichsbahn's actual debt was 400 million RM lower than the figure shown on its balance sheet. At the end of 1943, the last year for

Table 3.8. Reichsbahn Spending for Expansion of Capital Assets, 1939–1944 (in million RM)

Year	New Line and Track	Stations	Electrification	Servicing Facilities	Small Projects[a]	Total
1939	114.8	314.8	30.7	15.4	52.3	528.0
1940	144.5	280.6	18.6	16.2	48.8	508.7
1941	222.8	409.5	17.0	16.6	116.1	782.0
1942	161.6	291.6	15.1	22.6	128.5	619.4
1943	121.7	250.2	18.8	25.5	119.5	535.7
1944[b]	104.0	216.0	18.0	22.0	110.0	470.0

[a] To 1939 projects costing up to 100,000 RM, thereafter 500,000 RM.
[b] Preliminary figures.
Sources: DRB, *Wirtschaftsplan 1943*, pp. 29–30, BAC R005/12122; DRB, *Wirtschaftsplan 1945*, pp. 29–30, BA RD98/14.

which figures are available, the Reichsbahn had a total debt of 3.25 billion RM, or 16.3 percent more than it had at the end of 1938, but still quite modest considering its overall capital value and earning power.[192]

In addition to the short-term loan that the Reichsbahn made available to the Reich from the proceeds of the conversion of its preferred stock, the DRB funneled money to the Reich in other ways. The DVKB purchased Reich obligations using the money that came into its accounts through its freight credit business and from the Reichsbahn's revenue collections. In 1941 and 1942 the DRB made a total of six short-term loans to the Reich Finance Ministry. The first was for 420 million RM at 6 percent interest and was repayable in six months. The second, which was made on 10 December 1941, was for 200 million RM and was a condition for the government's acceptance of the Reichsbahn's proposed budget for 1942. It was considered a prepayment on the DRB's contribution to the Reich treasury. The interest accrued, compounded at 2.375 percent annually, would be repaid after the war. Similar deals were made in June 1942 and November 1942 for 200 million and 180 million RM each. The first was tied to acceptance of the Reichsbahn's final account for 1942 and the second to its budget proposal for 1943.[193] The DRB then loaned the Reich an additional 250 million RM on 30 November 1943 and another 250 million RM on 15 December 1943. The debts would be repaid on 25 October 1944 and bear interest of 2.65 percent.[194] In February 1944 Funk proposed that the Reichsbahn issue 5 billion RM in bonds. It would turn over the proceeds of the entire sale to the Reich but repay the debt itself. Dorpmüller, Ganzenmüller, and Prang vehemently opposed this one-sided deal, preventing it from being carried out until June 1944, when the military situation delayed discussion indefinitely[195] (see Tables 3.7, 3.8, and 3.9).

The Reichsbahn's capital budget expanded enormously during World War II

Table 3.9. Summary of Reichsbahn Operating Account, 1939–1944 (in billion RM)

Year	Operating Income	Operating Expenditures	Net Operating Income	Operating Ratio
1939	5.813	5.345	0.348	91.96
1940	7.603	7.010	0.593	93.78
1941	9.026	8.569	0.457	94.93
1942	9.797	9.288	0.509	94.81
1943	11.838	11.184	0.654	94.47
1944[a]	11.700	11.146	0.554	95.26

[a] Preliminary figures.
Sources: DRB, *Geschäftsberichte*; DRB, *Wirtschaftsplan 1945*, p. 6, BA RD98/14.

as a result of the massive building projects that it undertook to support the expansion of industry, military operations in the east, and especially the purchase of rolling stock. Virtually all of these expenditures were funded through the operating account.

Another expenditure handled through the operating account was the renewal of track. Track renewal had been a controversial issue during the 1920s when Dorpmüller and critics of reparations in the press and Reichstag had tried to argue that this vital aspect of capital maintenance, the functional equivalent of depreciation, was being neglected. Track renewal was reduced during the 1930s after the departure of the Allies, and the money freed was used to support capital expansion projects. After World War II began, track renewal was increased, but not to the levels achieved by the DRG between 1925 and 1929. The limiting factor during the war was not lack of money but the Reichsbahn's low priority for raw materials. The Wehrmacht enjoyed preferred access to steel, both for its armaments programs and for its rail expansion plans in the east. Consequently, the DRB was unable to bring track in Austria up to German standards, necessitating a reduction in train speeds there in May 1940. Even earlier, in April 1940, the Reichsbahn had begun dismantling tracks and switches in Germany in order to use them to improve the railways in the occupied territories. This practice was expanded as a result of the invasion of the USSR. In a departure from standard procedures, materials gained through the renewal of main-line track in Germany were not used to rebuild track of the second order. Instead, beginning in 1942, they were taken to the east. This lowered the quality of second-order track in Germany, lines that soon bore an increased burden of traffic due to dispersal. Additional tracks were also dismantled for use in the east. In May 1942, for example, the DRB initiated a program to remove 600 kilometers of track from less important lines for use in RBD Königsberg, the

Table 3.10. Reichsbahn Track Renewal, 1939-1944

Year	Kilometers		Expenditures (in million RM)	
	Full	Partial	Full	Partial
1939	1,497	1,200	102.2	67.5
1940	1,381	761	106.2	58.5
1941	2,077	1,186	130.0	72.8
1942	1,771	1,295	114.2	84.1
1943	2,039	1,013[b]	107.8	62.4
1944[a]	1,700	1,154.5[b]	115.0	71.0

[a] Preliminary figures.
[b] Estimate.
Sources: DRB, *Statistische Angaben 1942*, 38; DRB, *Wirtschaftsplan 1943*, p. 22, BAC R005/12122; DRB, *Wirtschaftsplan 1945*, p. 22, BA RD98/14.

Ostbahn, and the occupied USSR. One consequence of this policy was the increase in the number of broken rails. In 1942 the DRB experienced 11,000 rail breaks compared to 1,700 in 1937[196] (see Table 3.10).

The operating account was bloated by the vast expansion of revenues caused by the increase in traffic and the proportionally greater increase in the distances over which freight was shipped. As Ganzenmüller pointed out to the divisions in December 1942, the Reichsbahn was able to meet all of its financial obligations.[197] The component of revenues attributable to military traffic was enormous. In its annual statistical summary, the DRB reported that in 1940 it collected 558.1 million RM from the Wehrmacht for transportation services. In 1941 it collected 781.1 million RM, in 1942 840.6 million RM, and in 1943 1.13 billion RM from the military.[198] But actual military revenues may have been even higher. Wilhelm Weirauch, head of the Reichsbahn Main Auditing Office, stated in his review of the DRB's accounts for 1941 that 1.85 billion RM had been derived from Wehrmacht traffic, or 21.6 percent of the Reichsbahn's total revenues by his calculation.[199] However, due to the DRB's investments in new capital assets through the operating account, and its loans to the Reich, these military revenues were fed back into the war machine.

In the two years after the winter crisis of 1941-42, the Reichsbahn had fully recovered and was able to serve the transportation demands of the Nazi war machine adequately. It was also fully solvent, acting as a funnel to divert cash into the Reich's coffers and funding its expansion from its own revenues. This situation changed dramatically during the last year of the war.

E. The End of the Third Reich, 1944–1945

The Allied air attacks on marshaling yards in France, Belgium, and western Germany created havoc on the lines of communication of the German armies operating in the west. They also caused problems for the Reichsbahn in Germany. The DRB began feeding rolling stock and manpower in to HVDs Paris and Brussels to maintain rail service as the air attacks spread operating problems and as the local railway employees increasingly stayed away from work. The bombing chiefly affected marshaling yards and locomotive servicing facilities, causing congestion and delays. The rolling stock sent by the DRB into the area became mired in the morass created by the bombers. In April, May, and June 1944, it became increasingly difficult for RBDs Saarbrücken and Karlsruhe to send trains westward. By the end of the summer, Allied fighter bombers were roaming western Germany causing disruption in the area along the Rhine, while U.S. escort fighters, their tasks protecting the bombers completed, would seek railway targets on their return flights to Britain. Grave problems due to bombing in Germany began in September 1944, when the Allied air forces began attacking marshaling yards in the western part of the country. During the autumn, the assault intensified, inflicting serious damage to the major marshaling yards serving the Ruhr industrial region and other industries in western Germany.

The ZVL attempted to counter the effects of the Allied air attacks by using the procedures that had served it so well since its inception in June 1942, and the Reichsbahn for decades before. It attempted to use Upper Silesia to replace the loss of coal shipments from the Ruhr and continued to adjust priorities to suit the changing car situation and to use the inland waterways to relieve the burden imposed in the Reichsbahn. However, with the capacity of the marshaling yards dwindling, the ability of the DRB to satisfy demand shrank, rendering modifications to the priority system useless. The inland waterways were crippled by a series of air attacks in October and November, essentially eliminating them as an alternative. The ZVL also continued to use unit trains to simplify the movement of coal and used central Germany as a reservoir for empty cars that could be rushed to the coal-producing areas as needed. Yet the confusion in marshaling and the disruption of telecommunications by air attacks made it increasingly difficult to find new expedients. So the ZVL ruthlessly cut car space allocations to traffic other than coal in hopes of maintaining essential economic activity. To restore the marshaling yards and locomotive sheds, a massive repair effort was undertaken. During the fall of 1944, Reichsbahn personnel, prisoners of war, German civilians, and even workers from idled factories were committed to the effort. By November well over 100,000 people were struggling to help the

DRB maintain rail service at a minimum level, but the Allied bombers returned repeatedly to undo their work.[1]

The disruption of rail operations in the Ruhr, and the difficulty in returning empty cars to the region for loading, led to a dramatic reduction in the coal supplies available to the German economy. Manufacturing plants and utilities gradually consumed their stocks of coal beginning in September. By the end of 1944, supplies had been exhausted and production shrank due to a lack of energy. The decline in car placings also prevented the Reichsbahn from transporting semifinished and finished goods. Products, including badly needed munitions, accumulated at factories, forcing many to suspend operations in December 1944 and in the first months of 1945. The ultimate result of the breakdown in the Reichsbahn's ability to distribute freight was a shortage of weapons and other supplies for the Wehrmacht.[2]

Adding to the Reichsbahn's problems was the loss of territory. The retreats in the east up to early 1944 had the beneficial effect, from the railway's standpoint, of reducing the area that it had to serve. The ratio of rolling stock to service area increased, but the disruption of marshaling by bombing in the fall and winter of 1944, combined with territorial losses, created a situation that would have been unimaginable a few months before, a car surplus. Subsequent retreats, especially in the east, imposed massive burdens on the Reichsbahn. The DRB prepared evacuation plans well in advance, but the German civilian authorities frequently delayed using them until the last moment for fear of spreading panic among the population. Liaison with the army was adequate, but the military could not always predict when and where Soviet breakthroughs would occur and the direction that Red Army spearheads would take during the exploitation phase. The result was that the Reichsbahn had to conduct a number of hasty withdrawals, frequently under fire, of masses of panicky civilians and large quantities of industrial and military goods. By the fall of 1944, the Allied armies had reached the German border in the west and the Soviets had reached East Prussia and Warsaw. The lines stabilized here until January 1945. Then, Hitler launched a major counterattack in the Ardennes in the west. After initial success, it was thrown back by the Allies. As part of their defense, the Allied air forces launched an overwhelming attack on rail facilities in western Germany, particularly those serving the area behind the Bulge. In the east, the Red Army launched a gigantic attack in late January 1945 that took it up to the Oder River, only about seventy-five kilometers east of Berlin. This operation forced the Reichsbahn to withdraw many of its eastern divisions, including parts of RBD Oppeln. RBD Posen evacuated 2 million Germans before it was overrun. RBD Oppeln moved 1.7 million civilians away from the onrushing Red Army. To continue operations, it transferred its headquarters to Neisse on 20 January 1945.[3] The loss of Upper Silesia removed the major alternative supply of coal to the Ruhr, dealing a final, decisive blow to industry and the DRB itself. Then, during the first week of March, the western Allies vaulted the Rhine and drove deep into Germany, overrunning the divisions situated there. RBD Cologne, for example, closed its headquarters and moved to Hanover on 4 March.[4]

The disintegration of the Reichsbahn can be traced by examining a few indices of its operational performance. During the second quarter of 1944, overall freight car placings fell by 7.75 percent compared with placings for the same period in 1943. This was due to the disruption of operations in the occupied west, the effects of which reverberated eastward to the divisions along Germany's western border. During the summer of 1944, car placings recovered somewhat but remained slightly below the performance of the preceding year. Significantly, the divisions in western Germany, which were most affected by bombing, and the divisions that served as intermediaries between the west and the east, such as Halle (S) and Berlin, suffered significant declines. RBD Oppeln, because of the westward flow ahead of the advancing Red Army, was unable to compensate for the lower performance of RBD Essen serving the Ruhr. Coal car placings suffered a disproportionate decline because of the proximity of the coal-producing areas to the fronts in both east and west. Overall, coal traffic as measured in coal car placings fell during the third quarter of 1944 by 15.7 percent compared with placings in the third quarter of 1943.[5]

The collapse of traffic and, in turn, the disintegration of the German war economy began in earnest during October 1944 and accelerated during the subsequent three months. By the end of the Ardennes offensive in January 1945, overall freight car placings were 43.2 percent lower than during the same period the year before. Coal car placings in January 1945 were 55.8 percent lower than in January 1944.[6] By March 1945, freight car placings were 89.2 percent lower than a year earlier.[7]

The disintegration of marshaling and the disruption of the flow of traffic can be seen in the staggering increase in the number of trains stuck in the backlog. The air attacks in the West caused a rise in the backlog to 1,600 trains by early May 1944. This number declined as the Wehrmacht retreated to Germany and the Reichsbahn was able to consolidate operations. However, it rose steeply when the Allies focused their air attacks on marshaling yards in the western part of the country beginning in September 1944. By mid-December, the backlog had risen to 2,000 trains, and after a brief improvement at the end of the month due to poor weather that hampered the Allied bombers, then rose to about 2,800 trains at the end of February 1945.[8]

The confusion in marshaling and the disruption of the flow of traffic also caused a serious increase in car turnaround time. At the end of December 1944, it stood at 9.6 days, compared to 7.6 a year earlier. However, as Allied air attacks intensified and their armies crossed Germany's borders, it jumped to 20 days.[9] The inability to move cars in an orderly fashion—the impossibility of conducting coordinated, scheduled operations, the hallmark of the Reichsbahn's operating procedures—rebounded on the railway itself. The Reichsbahn became increasingly unable to feed its hungry locomotives with coal. Locomotive coal stocks declined from an average of 20 days in 1943 to just 6 days in January 1945, and then dwindled to almost nothing. The situation varied among the divisions. RBD Essen, in the Ruhr coal mining area, had a meager 8-day stock in early February 1945. But outlying divisions such as Stuttgart and Munich had less than a single day's supply.[10] Train performance declined accordingly. GBL South, which had delivered about 310,000 train-kilometers per day until the air offensive began, could generate a mere 95,000 train-kilometers per day at the end of March 1945.[11]

The deterioration of rail service due to air attack triggered attempts by various powers to wrench control of railway operations away from the Reichsbahn. The ambitious Speer proposed the replacement of Ganzenmüller and possibly Dorpmüller on 8 July 1944.[12] On 27 October he suggested having himself named transportation dictator so as to prevent the DRB from falling into the clutches of the Wehrmacht as the fronts neared Germany.[13] Yet Dorpmüller and Ganzenmüller were able to maintain the institutional independence and cohesion of the Reichsbahn and its personnel until the end. On 11 November 1944 Ganzenmüller named Lamertz as plenipotentiary for transportation in the Ruhr.[14] Lamertz had little success in countering the effects of Allied bombing; however, he did serve as a useful counterweight to the plenipotentiary that Speer appointed to increase the performance of the transportation apparatus. Fritz Rudorf and his subordinates were not allowed to interfere with the functioning of the GBLs and could approach the divisions and the ZVL only as representatives of shippers.[15] Finally, on 14 February 1945, Speer convinced Hitler to name him chairman of a transportation staff that would allocate car space throughout Germany. Speer contended that his intention was to protect the Reichsbahn from being gutted by the loss of its personnel to the Volkssturm.[16] Yet there can be no doubt that he was also pursuing his ambition to become the leading actor in economic affairs in Germany, to position himself for the period after the fall of the Third Reich. The Reichsbahn successfully defended itself from his attacks.

By May 1945, when Nazi Germany surrendered, the Reichsbahn had suffered a major disaster, much more serious than the disruptions of 1919 and 1920, or 1923, or during the Depression. It had supported Hitler in the pursuit of his criminal ambitions from beginning to end. As it had since it was founded, the Reichsbahn shaped and shared Germany's fate.

Conclusions

The Deutsche Reichsbahn was not consulted when the Nazi government and the Wehrmacht formulated their plans for rearmament and aggressive war. But, because it retained its central role as the major provider of transportation services in the German economy, the Reichsbahn still played an indispensable part in preparing for and prosecuting the war and in carrying out Hitler's murderous racial dreams. Its very importance meant that when it was paralyzed by Allied air attack, it contributed directly, if unwillingly, to the collapse of the Third Reich.

The Reichsbahn was a large bureaucracy that was accustomed to following standard operating procedures. It derived its identity from its ability to deliver satisfactory transportation service on demand. In return, it claimed complete internal autonomy and kept away from major political issues that did not threaten its existence. Prior to 1933 this posture had been easily assumed, because the vast majority of Reichsbahner, including its workers, were nationalists, accustomed to submission to authority. This narrow field of view allowed the Hitler dictatorship to instrumentalize the Reichsbahn for its criminal ends. The Holocaust presented no operating challenge to the DRB because the numbers of cars and engines involved were small compared with other traffics. Consequently, Dorpmüller, Ganzenmüller, and virtually everyone else in the Reichsbahn paid little attention to it. The history of the DRB's involvement in the murder of the European Jews provides a profound reminder of the powerful consequences of indifference.

It was no coincidence that the abandonment of financial responsibility accompanied the national abdication of moral responsibility. Ultimately, Walter Spieß triumphed over Kurt Tecklenburg as the DRG's cost accounting system was gutted soon after the Nazis came to power. This was the prelude to the abuse of the Reichsbahn for warlike ends. The Reichsbahn incurred debts to help the Nazi government divert private purchasing power to military expenditures, and when its revenues exploded due to the large volume of wartime traffic, it subsidized the Reich by transferring large sums to the national treasury and by moving Wehrmacht traffic at discount prices. The conversion of the Reichsbahn's preferred stock into bonds and the dismantling of its cost and financial accounting systems indicated the flight of the Nazi authorities from accountability for what they did with the German people's largest public asset. The Reichsbahn's financial history during the Third Reich is a clear example of how finances reflect not just the health of a particular enterprise but—especially in the case of such a large company, owned and operated by the government—the constitutional and moral health of the society as a whole. Diverting funds from its stated purposes, evading public accountability, and investing in projects that could be used only to prosecute aggressive war were all clear indications of the direction that the Hitler government was taking. The Reichsbahn's financial affairs were an accurate mirror of the decline of German public morals.

The Reichsbahn made an essential contribution to fighting the war. The German economy simply could not function without extensive and efficient rail transportation. Speculation about what might have happened if the Reichsbahn had been provided with more resources before the war, if it had been fully integrated into the apparatus for planning national strategy, and if less faith had been placed in motor vehicles by the military is misguided. Changes in any or all of these areas would not have solved the basic problems confronting the DRB: Hitler's ambitions were too great, the war too big, the areas to be absorbed too vast, the Allied coalition too powerful. The only solution to these problems would have been for Germany to have abandoned its aggressive plans. So long as Hitler was in power, such a change was unimaginable. The issue, then, did not lie with the Reichsbahn but with the pinnacle of the national leadership. Under these circumstances, the Reichsbahn, unaware of the stakes and the only potential solution, tried to cope as best it could by applying its proven operating techniques. It faced a major crisis in the winter of 1941-42, which it eventually mastered using its well-tried procedures. However, the winter crisis proved to be a bureaucratic defeat as it led to the DRB losing control of its rolling-stock production program. In other respects it led to gains for the Reichsbahn, such as the expansion of its control over the railways of the conquered areas. It also brought new men into its leadership. They followed the same operating procedures as their older predecessors, but applied them more energetically, sometimes ruthlessly. A second major operating crisis resulted from the Allied bombing of marshaling yards and locomotive facilities in late 1944 and early 1945. The Reichsbahn could not solve this problem itself because the crisis had military causes too strong for the railway's own operational expedients to overcome.

The history of the DRB during the war also provides evidence of the inefficiency of German occupation policies. In the west, rolling-stock programs made surprisingly small contributions to the Reichsbahn's roster. Meanwhile, its raids on the car and locomotive fleets of the French and Belgian railways reduced their ability to serve Germany's needs and masked the Reichsbahn's inefficient use of its own vehicles. In the east, one of the striking realities underscored by this account was how little was shipped back to the Reich. The rich sources of raw materials and food that drew Hitler to the region yielded comparatively little of value to the German war effort. In the same vein, this account shows the limited utility of the Nazis' labor policies. The people who labored unwillingly for the Reichsbahn were inefficient compared with their German counterparts. The labor situation with the Ostbahn was even worse. The cause of the low output of these people was the racist treatment that they suffered at the hands of the German authorities, including the Reichsbahn. Official prejudice was only partially moderated by the behavior of the minority of the Reichsbahn's workers who were sympathetic to the plight of the non-German employees. The gradual incorporation of women into the DRB's labor force, and the opposition to it, highlights the very conservative, prejudiced view of the railway's traditional officials concerning gender issues.

The Deutsche Reichsbahn was a durable organization that struggled to adapt to the social, political, and technological changes that took place around it. Until it was overwhelmed by massive force in late 1944, it mastered every operating challenge that it faced. For most of its existence, it fulfilled its reason for being by delivering efficient, reliable transportation services. Politically, the Reichsbahn was repeatedly defeated. Its traditional organizational culture bred men, like Dorpmüller, who had narrow vision. He failed to recognize Germany's responsibilities during the 1920s, failed to gain government protection from modal competition, failed to see the Hitler regime for what it was, could not obtain the resources that the Reichsbahn wanted, let alone what it needed, and cooperated meekly in executing the Nazi government's racist and aggressive program. In a very real sense, the Deutsche Reichsbahn reflected the society that it served, obsessed with its internal processes, nationalistic, and commonweal-oriented, but ultimately, concerning overriding issues of human morality, narrow and stunted. The Reichsbahn was an operating organization that met the challenge of running trains but failed as a human institution.

Appendix

Table A.1. Basic Characteristics of the Deutsche Reichsbahn (includes narrow gauge)

Year	Length of Line	Personnel	Locomotives	Freight Cars	Passenger Cars
1925–29[a]	53,545	711,666	25,401	673,393	62,807
1933	53,816	593,433	20,669	622,408	61,328
1934	53,871	630,905	21,105	594,128	59,925
1935	54,331	656,223	21,656	596,597	60,343
1936	54,458	659,943	21,792	595,360	60,339
1937	54,522	703,546	21,838	574,996	60,629
1938	62,942	778,374	25,209	650,229	68,942
1939	72,656	958,000	25,889	660,546	68,462
1940	75,553	1,145,600	28,586	779,641	70,443
1941	78,257	1,253,100	30,011	824,185	70,257
1942	78,730	1,386,000	32,243	885,906	72,448
1943	78,879	1,529,000	36,329	973,045	71,018
1944	75,763	1,581,000	37,810	987,864	70,400

[a] Average.
Source: DRG/DRB, *Geschäftsberichte*.

Table A.2. Basic Operating Statistics of the Deutsche Reichsbahn

Year	Tonnage (millions)	Passengers (billions)	Train-Kilometers (millions)
1925-29[a]	460.64	1.96	608.2
1933	308.1	1.24	625.9
1934	365.62	1.359	673.9
1935	408.00	1.488	734.3
1936	452.43	1.611	772.6
1937	499.04	1.808	823.1
1938	547	2.042	959.7
1939	564	2.212	949.1
1940	619	2.253	922.9
1941	656	2.655	998.7
1942	644	3.094	977.3
1943	675	3.539	1,034.1
1944	625	3.706	963.1

[a] Average.
Sources: DRG/DRB, *Geschäftsberichte*; DRG, *Entwicklungszahlen aus der Deutschen Eisenbahnstatistik*, 30; DRG, *Statistische Angaben 1934*, 144; DRG, *Statistische Angaben 1938*, 178; NA RG 243 200(a)143, Sheet 1.

Table A.3. Basic Financial Information Concerning the Deutsche Reichsbahn (in billion RM)

Year	Revenues	Expenditures	Cumulative Debt
1925-29[a]	4.95	4.12	1.017
1933	2.92	3.06	2.332
1934	3.33	3.30	2.742
1935	3.59	3.43	2.771
1936	3.98	3.51	2.645
1937	4.42	4.04	2.371
1938	5.13	4.76	2.792
1939	5.81	5.34	3.489
1940	7.60	7.01	3.653
1941	9.03	8.57	3.726
1942	9.80	9.29	3.853
1943	11.84	11.18	3.248
1944[b]	11.70	11.15	—

[a] Average.
[b] Preliminary figures.
Sources: DRG/DRB, *Geschäftsberichte*; DRB, "Schuldenstand der DRB seit 1924," 31 December 1943, BA R5/2549; DRB, "Wirtschaftsplan 1945," p. 8, BA RD98/14-1945.

Table A.4. Operating Accidents of the Deutsche Reichsbahn

Year	Operating Accidents per Million Car-Axle-Kilometers	Operating Accidents per Million Train-Kilometers
1925–29[a]	0.122	5.672
1933	0.09	3.22
1934	0.09	3.40
1935	0.09	3.36
1936	0.09	3.28
1937	0.09	3.71
1938	0.10	3.93
1939	0.12	5.29
1940	0.13	6.52
1941	0.12	6.41
1942	0.14	7.43
1943	0.15	8.20

[a] Average.

Sources: DRG, *Entwicklungszahlen aus der Deutschen Eisenbahnstatistik*, 58; DRG, *Statistische Angaben 1928*, p. 213; *1931*, p. 233; *1932*, p. 141; *1934*, p. 169; DRG, *Statistische Angaben 1934*, 169 for 1932–34; DRG, *Geschäftsbericht 1936*, 58 for 1935 and 1936; DR, *Statistische Angaben 1938*, 204 for 1937 and 1938; DR, *Statistische Angaben 1943*, 70 for 1941–43.

Table A.5. Organization of the Deutsche Reichsbahn, 1 September 1937

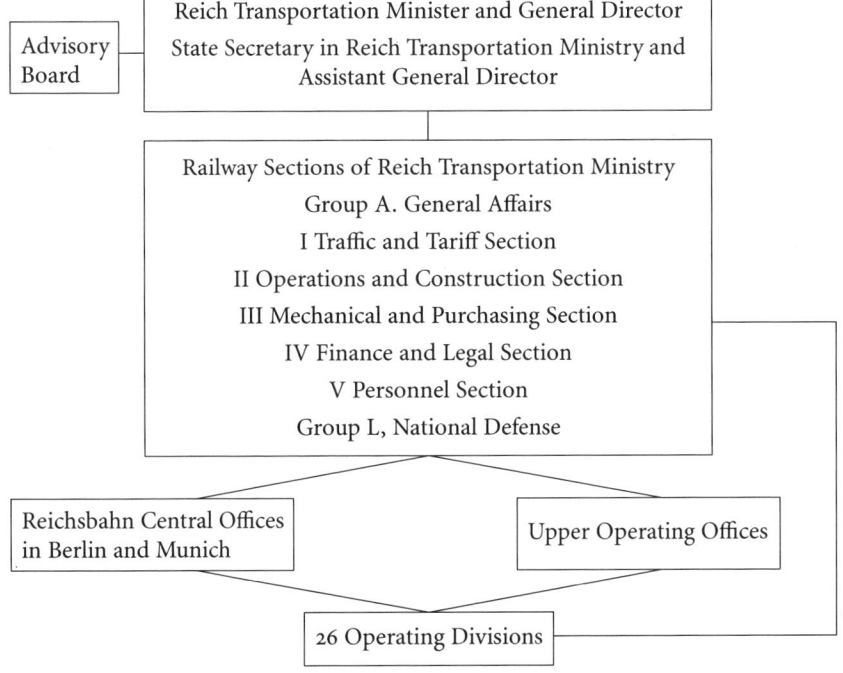

Notes

Abbreviations

In addition to the abbreviations found in the text, the following abbreviations are used in the notes.

AA	Auswärtiges Amt, Bonn
AfE	*Archiv für Eisenbahnwesen*
AR Bes.	Archiv Rankeberg, at Archivberatungsstelle Rheinland, Pulheim
Archiv Rbd Berlin	Archiv der Reichsbahndirektion Berlin (DDR)
ARK	*Akten der Reichskanzlei*, ed. Erdmann and Booms
BA	Bundesarchiv, Koblenz
BAC	Bundesarchiv, Abteilungen Potsdam, Aussenstelle Coswig (Anhalt)
BAMA	Bundesarchiv-Militärarchiv, Freiburg-im-Breisgau
BAP	Bundesarchiv, Abteilungen Potsdam
BBA	Deutsches Bergbau-Archiv (German Mining Archive), Bochum
BDC	Berlin Document Center
BHSA	Bayerisches Hauptstaatsarchiv, Munich
BR	Beirat (Advisory Council)
Doc.	Document
E-Abt.	Eisenbahnabteilungen in Reichsverkehrsministerium
ED	Eisenbahndirektion (Railway Division)
Fwi Amt	Feldwirtschaftsamt (Field Economics Office in OKW)
Gruppe L	Eisenbahnwehrmachtliche Angelegenheiten (Group for Railway-Military Affairs in RVM)
GStA	Geheimes Staatsarchiv Preussischer Kulturbesitz, Abteilung Merseburg
HV	Hauptverwaltung (Main Administration)
HWA	Hauptwagenamt (Main Car Office)
IfZ	Institut für Zeitgeschichte (Institute for Contemporary History)
IMT	International Military Tribunal
Kab	Kabinett
KL	Konzentrationslager (concentration camp)
KLK	Kriegslastenkommission (War Burdens Commission)
MA	Bayerisches Ministerium des Äussern (Foreign Ministry)

MAN	Maschinenfabrik Augsburg-Nürnberg
Mineis L	Eisenbahnwehrmachtliche Angelegenheiten (Group for Railway-Military Affairs in RVM)
MWi	Bayerisches Wirtschafts- und Verkehrsministerium (Economics and Transportation Ministry)
NA	National Archives
NL	Nachlaß (papers)
NNP	Net National Product
NSKK	Nationalsozialistisches Kraftfahrer-Korps (National Socialist Motorists Corps)
RAM	Reichsarbeitsministerium (Reich Labor Ministry)
RAW	Reichsbahn-Ausbesserungswerk (National Railway Repair Works)
Rbd	Reichsbahndirektion (National Railway Division)
RD	Reichsdrucksache
RER	Reichseisenbahnrat (Reich Railway Council)
RFM	Reichsfinanzministerium (Reich Finance Ministry)
RG	Record Group
RGBl	*Reichsgesetzblatt* (Reich Legal Gazette)
RIM	Reichsinnenministerium (Reich Ministry of the Interior)
RMfBuM	Reichsministerium für Bewaffnung und Munition (Reich Ministry for Weapons and Munitions)
RMfRuK	Reichsministerium für Rüstung und Kriegsproduktion (Reich Ministry for Armaments and War Production)
RVK	Reichsvereinigung Kohle (Reich Coal Association)
RWM	Reichswirtschaftsministerium (Reich Economics Ministry)
RZÄ	Reichsbahn-Zentralämter (Reichsbahn Central Offices)
RZE	Reichsbahn-Zentralamt für Einkauf (Reichsbahn Central Office for Purchasing)
RZM	Reichsbahn-Zentralamt für Maschinenbau (Reichsbahn Central Office for Mechanical Engineering)
SAA	Siemens-Archiv
SD	Sicherheitsdienst (of SS)
StA Dü	Staatsanwaltschaft Düsseldorf (State Prosecutor's Office, Düsseldorf)
SZD	Soviet Railways
T7	Transportation Section in Truppenamt
TMWC	*Trial of the Major War Criminals*
USHMA	United States Holocaust Museum Archives, Washington, D.C.
USSBS	United States Strategic Bombing Survey
VL	Versuchsleitung (Test Headquarters)
VR	Verwaltungsrat (Board of Directors)
VW	*Verkehrstechnische Woche* (Transportation Week)
WFSt	Wehrmacht-Führungsstab (Armed Forces Command Staff)
Wi Rü Amt	Wehrwirtschafts- und Rüstungsamt (Military Economics and Armaments Office in OKW)
WSt	Wirtschaftsstab (Economics Staff in OKW)
ZSL	Zentrale Stelle der Landesjustizverwaltungen, Ludwigsburg
ZVD	*Zeitschrift des Vereins Deutscher Eisenbahnverwaltungen* (Journal of the Association of German Railway Administrations)
ZVME	*Zeitschrift des Vereins Mitteleuropäischer Eisenbahnverwaltungen* (Journal of the Association of Central European Railway Administrations)

Preface

1. Kreidler, *Eisenbahnen im Machtbereich*; Thomas, *Wehr- und Rüstungswirtschaft*; Wehde-Textor, "Leistungen," 1-47; Schüler, *Logistik im Rußlandfeldzug*, especially chaps. 3 and 4.
2. The traditional view is presented in Teske, *Silbernen Spiegel*, 112; Stumpf, *Kleine Geschichte der deutschen Eisenbahnen*, 63-64; and Schletzbaum, *Eisenbahn*, 144.
3. Kreidler supports this thesis by omitting any mention of relations between the party and the Reichsbahn and by ignoring the Holocaust. See also Joachimsthaler, *Breitspurbahn*, 73; Bock and Garrecht, *Julius Dorpmüller — Ein Leben für die Eisenbahn*; and Gottwaldt, *Julius Dorpmüller, Die Reichsbahn und die Autobahn*, 41.
4. Goldhagen, *Hitler's Willing Executioners*; Baum, "Holocaust: Moral Indifference as the Form of Modern Evil," and *The Holocaust and the German Elite*.
5. The Bock and Garrecht book cited in note 3 is the clearest example of Dorpmüller hagiography. Interestingly, Alfred Gottwaldt, who has also published extensively on Dorpmüller and who takes a very different view from Bock and Garrecht, also subscribes to the myth of Dorpmüller as a great leader. See his *Julius Dorpmüller, Die Reichsbahn und die Autobahn*, 7; *Deutsche Reichsbahn. Kulturgeschichte und Technik*, 38; and "Fahren für Deutschlands Sieg!," 155, 158.

Chapter 1. The Coordination of the Reichsbahn, 1933-1939

1. Stieler to von Batocki, Bebenhausen, 16 August 1932, p. 3, AR Bes. E-R, 53.
2. Noakes, *The Nazi Party in Lower Saxony*, 100, 102, 104, 173-74, 178; Schönhoven, *Die deutschen Gewerkschaften*, 186; Orlow, *History of the Nazi Party, 1919-1933*, 169; Strößenreuther, *Eisenbahnen und Eisenbahner*, 2:160, quoting *Deutscher Eisenbahner*, 2 November 1930; Fischer, *Stormtroopers*, 190.
3. DRG, VR, Minutes, 22-23 September 1930, p. 2, BA R2/23090a.
4. Strößenreuther, *Eisenbahnen und Eisenbahner*, 3:18, quoting *Deutscher Eisenbahner* and *Voraus*.
5. Strößenreuther, *Eisenbahnen und Eisenbahner*, 3:20-21, citing "Beamte und NSDAP," *Der Deutsche Eisenbahn-Fahrbeamte*, 10 May 1931.
6. DRG, VR, Minutes, 24 March 1931, p. 10, BA R2/23090a.
7. DRG, VR, Minutes, 29 November 1932, p. 13, BA R2/23090b. By March 1933, the Bahnschutz had a strength of 50,000 men. Organizationally, they were subordinate to the railway police. An RVM order of 1923 had prohibited them from belonging to any union. Heiges typified the Bahnschutz as a nationalist organization. He thought that 80 percent of its members were at least sympathetic to the Nazis. DRG, Generaldirektor, "Bahnschutz," 55.568 Asc., Berlin, 18 May 1932, BA NS10/538, f. 13; "Deutscher Reichsbahnschutz," March 1933, Geheim, BA R43 I/1040, f. 193.
8. Pünder to Abegg, Rk. 5942, Berlin, 13 June 1931, BA R43 I/1052, ff. 205-6. See the similar case in Baden in Telegramm, Staatsministerium Karlsruhe to Reichskanzler, cipher, Nr. 25/1, 8 April 1932, BA R43 I/1040, f. 157; Koenigs to Pünder, "Einspruch des Badischen Innenministers gegen die Beförderung von Nationalsozialisten in Sonderzügen," E. 24. 2785, Berlin, 9 April 1932, BA R43 I/1040, ff. 159-60.
9. Günter Kausche, "Die Deutschen Eisenbahnen im zweiten Weltkrieg," p. 13, BA R5 Anh I/8.
10. Franz Bruckauf, "Die Deutsche Reichsbahn im Zweiten Weltkrieg Abschnitt Personalwesen," p. 62, BA R5 Anh I/13.
11. Joachimsthaler, *Breitspurbahn*, 73.

12. RVM, *Personalpolitik*, 4-5.
13. NSDAP, Fachschaft Reichsbahn, to RIM, Berlin, 20 March 1933, BA R43 I/1053, ff. 30-32.
14. Brademann to Lammers, 3 April 1933, BA R43 I/1053, ff. 15-21.
15. Reichskanzlei, "Vermerk, Betrifft: Reichsbahn-Gesellschaft," Rk. 3767[33], Berlin, 6 April 1933, BA R43 I/1053, f. 23; Brademann to Fabricius, Berlin, 5 April 1933, Beilage 2, pp. 2-3, BDC 3405000502, ff. 289-90; Brademann to Reichskanzlei, Rk. 3767[33], 6 April 1933, BA R43 I/1053, f. 26.
16. Fabricius to Schaub, "Aktion vom 6.4.1933 gegenüber der Hauptverwaltung der Reichsbahn," Berlin, 7 April 1933, BA R43 I/1053, ff. 24-25.
17. Ludwig, Anlage 1, BDC 3405000502, ff. 273-74.
18. RVM to Fachschaft Reichsbahn, Herrn Stubel, E. 11. 2793, Berlin, (20) April 1933, BA R43 I/1053, f. 29; Willuhn, Rk. 4234[II], Berlin, 29 April 1933, BA R43 I/1053, f. 33.
19. "Reichsgesetz zur Wiederherstellung des Berufbeamtentums. Vom 7. April 1933," *RGBl*, Teil I, Nr. 34, 1933, pp. 175-77. For the DRG's adaptation of this law, see "Wiederherstellung des Berufsbeamtentums," *Die Reichsbahn* 9 (26 April 1933): 341-43. For the questionnaire that officials had to complete, see "Wiederherstellung des Berufsbeamtentums," *Die Reichsbahn* 9 (21 June 1933): 521-30.
20. Hammer to divisions, "Vergebung von Aufträgen," 70/71 Y Rvu 247, Berlin, 24 May 1933, BAC R005/702neu.
21. Weirauch, "Wiederherstellung des Berufsbeamtentums," 52.504 Po, Berlin, 14 June 1933, BA R5/2558; Generaldirektor, "Wiederherstellung des Berufsbeamtentums," 52.504 Pada, 19 July 1933, Gruppenverwaltung Bayern, *Eisenbahn-Nachrichtenblatt*, 24 August 1933, p. 1, BA RD98/57; Generaldirektor, "Wiederherstellung des Berufsbeamtentums; hier Verbot der Zugehörigkeit zur Sozialdemokratischen und Kommunistischen Partei," 22 September 1933, Gruppenverwaltung Bayern, *Eisenbahn-Nachrichtenblatt*, 7 October 1933, BA RD98/57; RBD Berlin, "546. Wiederherstellung des Berufsbeamtentums," RBD Berlin, *Amtsblatt*, 8 August 1933, p. 271, Archiv Rbd Berlin.
22. DRG, VR, Personalausschuß, "Richtlinien für die zukünftige Personalpolitik bei der Reichsbahn," 13 July 1933, BAC R005/15033, ff. 44-46; Beyer, "Nachtrag zu den Richtlinien des Personal-Ausschusses für die zukünftige Behandlung der Personalpolitik bei der Reichsbahn," BAC R005/15028, ff. 137, 148.
23. DRG, "Richtlinien für die Handhabung der Personalpolitik bei der Reichsbahn," Drucksache Nr. 731, 10 August 1933, pp. 1-2, BAC R005/020061, ff. 27-28.
24. Kleinmann to Gaugericht der Gauleitung Groß-Berlin, Berlin, 11 June 1934, pp. 1-2, BDC 4001003460 SA-P, ff. 5-6. On Kleinmann, see Kleinmann Parteibuch, BDC; SA Parteifragebogen, October 1938, BDC; "Wechsel im Vorstand der Deutschen Reichsbahn-Gesellschaft. Reichsbahndirektionspräsident Kleinmann zum Ständigen Stellvertreter des Generaldirektors der Deutschen Reichsbahn ernannt," *Die Reichsbahn* 9 (9 August 1933): 687-88; Degener, *Degeners Wer ist's?*, 824-25; Brademann to Kleinmann, 3 April 1933, p. 7, BA R43 I/1053, f. 57; "65. Geburtstag des Staatssekretärs Kleinmann," *Die Reichsbahn* 17 (28 May-4 June 1941): 218.
25. DRG, VR, Ausserordentliche Sitzung, Minutes, 10 August 1933, p. 1, BA R2/23091; Siemens to board members, 25 July 1933, BA NL13/483, f. 235; Dorpmüller to RVM, 1 Ogvv, Berlin, 25 July 1935, AA R28725, f. 325.
26. Kleinmann, "Bericht über die . . . Arbeit . . . Beck," Berlin, 4 June 1934, p. 1, BAC R005/435neu, f. 177; Oberst i.G. Doerr, 13 June 1942, p. 3, BAMA N29/1, f. 11.
27. Weirauch, "Führerstab der NSDAP," 2 Oa 1, Berlin, 20 May 1933, BAC R005/15033, f. 23; "Bekanntgabe," *Völkische Beobachter*, 18 May 1933, BA R43 I/1053, f. 74; RBD Ber-

lin, "372. Versammlungen der Untergliederungen der NSDAP einschl. der Reichsbahnfachschaften," RBD Berlin, *Amtsblatt*, 20 May 1933, p. 183, Archiv Rbd Berlin; Reiner, Dorpmüller, Sofort, 50.506, Pwhp 415, Berlin, 17 May 1933, BAC R005/15033, f. 21; DRG, HV, "Führerstab der NSDAP," 2 Oa 1, Berlin, 28 May 1933, BAC R005/15033, f. 24; Beyer, "Beauftragte des Führerstabs bei den Reichsbahndirektionen," Sofort, 2 Oa 1, Berlin, 10 June 1933, BAC R005/15033, ff. 25–26; Gerhard Sommer, Parteibuch, BDC, RKK: 2101, Box 1077, File 13.

28. DRG, VR, Protocol, 3 May 1933, Teil 1, p. 20, BAC R005/020059, f. 336.

29. [Willuhn], "Vermerk, Deutsche Reichsbahn-Gesellschaft," Rk. 4234, Berlin, 29 May 1933, BA R43 I/1053, ff. 34–35.

30. Kleinmann to Dorpmüller, Berlin, 23 June 1933, BAC R005/15033, f. 28; *Der nationalsozialistische Eisenbahner*, Sonderausgabe, 23 June 1933, BA R43 I/1053, f. 83; Flugschrift, Fachschaft Reichsbahn, May 1933, BA R005/15033, f. 22.

31. Siemens to Batocki, 27 June 1933, SAA 4/Lf 561 (II).

32. Lammers, "Vermerk," zu Rk. 7189, Berlin, 28 June 1933, BA R43 I/1061, f. 9; "Umbildung des Verwaltungsrats der Deutschen Reichsbahn-Gesellschaft," zu Rk. 7189/33, BA R43 I/1061, f. 10.

33. Lammers, "Vermerk," Rk. 7189, Berlin, 28 June 1933, BA R43 I/1061, f. 9; "Ministerbesprechung," 30 June 1933, *ARK Kab Hitler*, vol. 1, doc. no. 175, p. 610; Eltz to Siemens, E.11. 6032, Berlin, 1 July 1933, BA R43 I/1061, f. 18; DRG, VR, Minutes, 4 July 1933, p. 1, BA R2/23091; Kleinmann, "Bericht über die . . . Arbeit . . . Beck," Berlin, 4 June 1934, p. 2, BAC R005/435neu, f. 178.

34. Kleinmann to Fischer, Berlin, 14 June 1933, BHSA, Rep. MA 106 955.

35. Siebert to von Hertel, "Verwaltungsrat der Deutschen Reichsbahn-Gesellschaft," Munich, 28 June 1933, BHSA, Rep. MA 106 955; Von Hertel to Siebert, "Verwaltungsrat der Deutschen Reichsbahn-Gesellschaft," Augsburg, 6 July 1933, BHSA, Rep. MA 106 955; Von Hertel to Eltz-Rübenach, Augsburg, 6 July 1933, BA NL13/483, f. 231.

36. "Ministerratssitzung vom 12. September 1933," BHSA, Rep. MA 106 955; Siebert to RVM, "Verwaltungsrat der Deutschen Reichsbahn-Gesellschaft," Nr. II 255 77, Munich, 14 September 1933, BHSA, Rep. MWi 8633; Eltz-Rübenach to Lammers, "Verwaltungsrat der Deutschen Reichsbahn," E 11.2822, Berlin, 23 April 1934, BA R43 I/1061, f. 72.

37. Kleinmann, "Vermerk über die Besprechung mit dem Herrn Reichsverkehrsminister am 10.7.1933," Berlin, 10 July 1933, BAC R005/15028, ff. 9–10; Kleinmann to Eltz-Rübenach, Berlin, 20 July 1933, BAC R005/15028, f. 3; Eltz-Rübenach to Silverberg, Alexisbad, 28 July 1933, SAA 4/Lf 561 (II); Lammers to Koenigs, Sts. Nr. 296/33, Ramsau b/Berchtesgaden, Persönlich, 2 August 1933, BA R43 I/1061, f. 26; Silverberg to Siemens, Cologne, 2 August 1933, SAA 4/Lf 561 (II).

38. Siemens to Silverberg, 3 August 1933, p. 1, SAA 4/Lf 561 (II), also in BA NL13/483, f. 218.

39. DRG, VR, Ausserordentliche Sitzung, Minutes, 10 August 1933, p. 1, BA R2/23091; DRG, VR, Minutes, 4 July 1933, p. 3, BA R2/23091; "Kabinettssitzung," 22 September 1933, *ARK Kab Hitler*, vol. 2, doc. no. 215, p. 825, also in BA R43 I/1061, f. 40; Eltz-Rübenach to Lammers, Berlin, 11 August 1933, pp. 2–3, BA R43 I/1061, ff. 29–30. On Körner, see Stockhorst, *Wer war was im 3. Reich*, 243; *Deutsches Führer Lexikon*, 246–47.

40. Eltz-Rübenach, "Verwaltungsrat der Deutschen Reichsbahn-Gesellschaft," E. 11. 9966, Berlin, 27 December 1933, BA R43 I/1061, ff. 44–45; DRG, VR, Minutes, 24 January 1934, pp. 1–2, BA R2/23092; "Ministerbesprechung, anschließend Kabinettssitzung," 12 January 1934, *ARK Kab Hitler*, vol. 2, doc. no. 284, and n. 17, pp. 1074–75.

41. Siemens to Hindenburg, Berlin, 24 January 1934, BA R43 I/1061, f. 70.

42. Schäffer Tagebuch, 23 May 1933, pp. 47–49, IfZ ED93, Bd. 24c, ff. 47–49.

43. Siemens to Krupp von Bohlen und Halbach, 15 December 1934, SAA 4/Lf 562.

44. Siemens to Silverberg, 21 December 1933, 21 December 1934, SAA 4/Lf 562; Siemens to Bergmann, 28 December 1934, SAA 4/Lf 560.

45. "Auszug aus der Niederschrift über die Sitzung des Reichsministeriums vom 4. Dezember 1934," Rk. 11064, p. 2, BA R43 I/1061, f. 89; DRG, VR, Minutes, 23 January 1935, pp. 2-3, BA R2/23092; Eltz-Rübenach to Koenigs, E 11. 7592, Berlin, 5 December 1934, BA R43 I/1061, f. 81; Eltz-Rübenach to Siemens, E 11. 7592, 5 December 1934, BA R43 I/1061, f. 86. On Koenigs, see Metzger, "Staatssekretär Gustav Koenigs," Abt. KSW, p 1.258/40, 20 March 1940, BA R43 II/1146b, ff. 31, 33; "Staatssekretär Gustav Koenigs," *ZVME* 75 (31 January 1935): 111.

46. On the Esser appointment, see the extensive correspondence in BA R43 II/187a and BHSA Rep. MWi 8633. On Bergmann, see DRG, VR, Minutes, 27 November 1935, p. 1, BA R2/23093.

47. Ludwig, *Technik und Ingenieure im Dritten Reich*, 111.

48. DRG, "Aufhebung der Beamtenvertretungen; Änderung der Perso und der Dienstdauervorschriften," Drucksache Nr. 755, 27-28 November 1933, BA R005/020063, ff. 131-35; "Beamtenerlaß (Aufhebung der Beamtenvertratungen)," *Die Reichsbahn* 9 (6 December 1933): 1013-14.

49. Kleinmann to Siemens, Berlin, 3 July 1933, BAC R005/15033, ff. 33-36.

50. DRG, VR, Minutes, 4 July 1933, p. 3, BA R2/23091.

51. "Personalnachrichten," *Die Reichsbahn* 9 (4 October 1933): 821-25.

52. DRG, VR, Protocol, 28 November 1933, Teil VI, p. 13, BAC R005/020063, f. 317.

53. DRG, VR, Personalausschuß, Minutes, 26 March 1934, p. 7, BA R005/435neu, f. 8; DRG, VR, Personalausschuß, Minutes, 20 September 1934, p. 5, BA R005/435neu, f. 281.

54. Stieler to Siemens, Berlin, 20 July 1933, p. 1, SAA 4/Lf 561 (III); DRG, VR, Personalausschuß, Minutes, 9 August 1933, p. 3, BAC R005/15033, f. 61.

55. E. Beck to Oberste Parteigericht der NSDAP, Berlin, 2 September 1934, p. 3, BDC 340500503, f. 342; E. Beck, "II. Fall Weirauch," Berlin, August 1934, BDC 3405000505.

56. Kleinmann to Gaugericht der Gauleitung Groß-Berlin, Berlin, 11 June 1934, pp. 8-9, BDC 4001003460, ff. 12-13.

57. DRG, VR, Protocol, 3 May 1933, Teil 1, pp. 23-24, BAC R005/020059, ff. 339-40; DVKB to Heinrich Stein, Berlin, 21 June 1933, BA R5/2557.

58. Lammers, "Vermerk," Rk. 12964, Berlin, 8 November 1933, BA R43 I/1075, ff. 141-42; Willuhn, "Vermerk," Rk. 1150, Berlin, 24 March 1934, BA R43 I/1075, f. 166; DRB to Hess, 10 Vgar (Sch H) 53, Berlin, June 1938, pp. 1-5, BAC R005/502 Ha. See also the lawyer's summary of the Holzer case in this file and Matis and Stiefel, *Das Haus Schenker*, 339-40.

59. DRG, Gruppenverwaltung Bayern, *Eisenbahn-Nachrichtenblatt*, Munich, 11 September 1933, pp. 119-21, BA RD98/57; Kleinmann to divisions, "Förderung bewährter Kämpfer für die nationale Erhebung," Sofort, 54.505 Pol/109, Berlin, 3 March 1934, BAC R005/125 Ha; DRG, VR, Personalausschuß, Minutes, 26 March 1934, p. 7, BAC R005/435neu, f. 8; DRG, VR, Arbeitsausschuß, Minutes, 27 March 1934, pp. 12-13, BA R2/23092; DRG, VR, Arbeitsausschuß, Minutes, 26 March 1935, pp. 6-10, BA R2/23092; DRB, VR, Minutes, p. 11, 25 March 1936, pp. 10-11, BA R2/23093; "Förderung bewährter Kämpfer für die nationale Erhebung," *Die Reichsbahn* 10 (24 January 1934): 81 82.

60. Otto Schumann, "Beamtenlaufbahn bei der Deutschen Reichsbahn," *Die Reichsbahn* 13 (9 June 1937): 555, 557; Dorpmüller, "Aufstiegsbeamte für Direktionsdezernate," Sofort, 1 Polü, Berlin, 14 April 1937, BAC R005/439neu.

61. DRB, BR, Minutes, 6 October 1937, pp. 6, 9, 12, BA R2/31652.

62. RBD Berlin, "50. Förderung alter Nationalsozialisten," *Amtsblatt*, 18 January 1938, p. 29, Archiv Rbd Berlin.

63. Dorpmüller, "Aktenvermerk," Berlin, 15 June 1934, BAC R005/435neu, ff. 229-30; Kleinmann to Stenger, 57.506 Pol, Berlin, 20 June 1934, BAC R005/435neu, ff. 222-23; Stenger to Kleinmann, Berlin, 23 June 1934, BAC R005/435neu, f. 224; Dorpmüller to Hess, Berlin, 8 July 1934, BAC R005/435neu, ff. 252-54.

64. Dorpmüller, "Die Reichsbahn in ihrer Verbundenheit zu Wirtschaft und Staat," *Die Reichsbahn* 9 (24 May 1933): 429.

65. Memorandum to Reichskanzlei, 29 June 1933 assigned Rk. 8253, BA R43 I/1053, f. 82.

66. DRG, VR, Personalausschuß, Minutes, 20 September 1934, BAC R005/435neu, ff. 302-3, also in BDC 340500503, ff. 358-63.

67. Eltz-Rübenach to Dorpmüller, Berlin, 26 October 1934, BAC R005/435neu, ff. 320-21; "Auflösung des Führerstabs Reichsbahn," 2 Oa 3, 2 November 1934, reprinted in *Die Reichsbahn* 10 (7 November 1934): 1122; DRG, *Hausnachrichten der Hauptverwaltung der Deutschen Reichsbahn-Gesellschaft*, 3 November 1934, p. 77, BAC R005/435neu, f. 323; DRG, VR, Personalausschuß, 27 November 1934, p. 3, BAC R005/435neu, f. 342.

68. Stieler to Siemens, Bebenhausen, 31 May 1936, SAA 4/Lf 561 (III); Notes on back of photograph of Dorpmüller and sheet with notes, BA Kl. Erw. 750; Schüler, *Logistik im Rußlandfeldzug*, 480, n. 130; Ottmann, "Ein Beitrag zur Geschichte der deutschen Eisenbahnen," 103, 106; Dorpmüller, *Rationalisierung bei der Deutschen Reichsbahn*, 6; Brüning, *Memoiren*, 427; Strößenreuther, *Eisenbahnen und Eisenbahner*, 3:48, citing *Deutscher Eisenbahner*, 25 October 1931; Schulz, *Deutschland am Vorabend der grossen Krise. Band III, Von Brüning zu Hitler*, 549-50; "Bericht bis 4. November 1931," SAA 4/Lf 561 (II).

69. [Reichsschatzmeister Schwarz] to Dorpmüller, K. Va. Schn/K., 18 January 1941, BDC 10100778700 PK; Dorpmüller's party book also in BDC 10100778700.

70. DRB, VR, Minutes, 15 May 1935, pp. 1-2, BA R2/23092; RVM, *Personalpolitik*, 4-5; RBD Berlin, "274. Austritt von Beamten aus der NSDAP," *Amtsblatt*, 17 April 1936, p. 150, Archiv Rbd Berlin. On the organization of the Fachschaft Reichsbahn, see Vogt, *Deutscher Beamten-Kalender 1936*, 253.

71. DRG, VR, Personalausschuß, Protocol, 24 September 1935, p. 14, BAC R005/435neu, ff. 430-32, 589; DRG, VR, Personalausschuß, Minutes, 26 November 1935, pp. 3-4, BAC R005/436neu, ff. 31-32; DRG, VR, Personalausschuß, Minutes, 28 January 1936, p. 5, BAC R005/436neu, f. 64; DRG, VR, Minutes, 25 September 1935, p. 23, BA R2/23092; Wilhelm Kleinmann, "Stellung und Aufgabe der Reichsbahn im nationalsozialistischen Staat," *Die Reichsbahn* 12 (18 November 1936): 1003.

72. DRG, VR, Personalausschuß, Protocol, 24 September 1935, pp. 19, 26-27, BAC R005/435neu, ff. 594, 601-2, DRG, VR, Minutes, 25 September 1935, p. 3, BA R2/23092.

73. Parteibuch Goudefroy, BDC 1030027530 PK.

74. Parteibuch Hassenpflug, BDC; RVM, "Vorschlag zur Ernennung . . . ," 1 HB 1Berlin, 5 January 1940, BA R43 II/1146b, ff. 12-15; Uchmann, Interrogation of Werner Pischel, 4 Js 564/64, Frankfurt am Main, 5 August 1966, ZSL II 206 AR-Z 15/1963, Bd. 4, f. 416.

75. Parteibuch Maximillian Lamertz, BDC.

76. Affadavit Karl Keller, 45 Js 8/62, StA Dortmund ./. Ganzenmüller, Karlsruhe, 17 February 1966, p. 1, ZSL 107(420) AR-Z 80/1962, Bd. III, f. 471; Parteibuch Hermann Bergmann, BDC; Parteibuch Hermann Osthoff, BDC; Parteibuch Alfred Prang, BDC; Parteibuch Adolf Sarter, BDC 1100031094 PK; Parteibuch Albert Gollwitzer, BDC. On Gollwitzer's appointment to RBD Munich, see the correspondence in BHSA Rep. MA 106 962.

77. Parteibuch Kurt Emmelius, Parteibuch Wilhelm Emrich, Parteibuch Max Leibbrand, Parteibuch Kurt Tecklenburg, all BDC; Parteibuch Wilhelm Wechmann, BDC RKK: 2101, Box 1348, File 20.

78. RBD Berlin, "81. Bezug der NS-Presse durch die Beamten," *Amtsblatt*, 31 January 1936,

p. 44, Archiv Rbd Berlin; Dorpmüller, "Dienstbefreiung von Beamten, Angestellten und Arbeiter für Zwecke der NSDAP, ihrer Gliederungen und angeschlossenen Verbände," 52.500 Pouo, Berlin, 25 February 1936, BAC R005/125 Ha; RBD Berlin, "957. Versetzung von Beamten, Angestellten, die Hoheitsträger der NSDAP sind," Amtsblatt, 31 December 1936, p. 526, Archiv Rbd Berlin; RBD Berlin, "186. Vernehmung von Angehörigen der NSDAP und ihrer Gliederungen," Amtsblatt, 12 March 1937, p. 83, Archiv Rbd Berlin.

79. DRG, VR, Minutes, 3 July 1933, pp. 25-26, BA R2/23092; Kleinmann, "Die neue Dienst- und Lohnordnung der Deutschen Reichsbahn," Die Reichsbahn 10 (9 May 1934): 465-66; Fromm, "Das Gesetz zur Ordnung der Arbeit in öffentlichen Verwaltungen und Betrieben," Die Reichsbahn 11 (16 January 1935): 94; Strößenreuther, Eisenbahnen und Eisenbahner, 3:135; Alexander Wulff, "Rückblick auf das Jahr 1934," ZVME 65 (3 January 1935): 3-4; Kleinmann, "Zusammenarbeit mit der Deutschen Arbeitsfront," 51.533 Plr, Berlin, 10 October 1936, Berlin, 10 October 1936, BAC R005/125 Ha.

80. RBD Berlin, "281. Dienst- und Lohnordnung für die Arbeiter der Deutschen Reichsbahn (Dilo)," Amtsblatt, 13 April 1937, p. 127, Archiv Rbd Berlin.

81. DRG, VR, Minutes, 3 May 1933, pp. 10-11, BA R2/23091; DRG, VR, Minutes, 28 November 1935, p. 12, BA R2/23091; DRG, VR, Minutes, 4 July 1934, pp. 5-6, BA R2/23092; DRG, VR, Minutes, 25 March 1936, pp. 7-9, BA R2/23093.

82. Richard Hirsch, "Die neuen Lohnbedingungen der Reichsbahnarbeiter," ZVME 74 (20 September 1934): 38.

83. DRG, VR, Minutes, 27 January 1937, pp. 12-13, BA R2/23093.

84. DRB, BR, Minutes, 4 May 1938, p. 24, BA R2/31652.

85. DRB, Geschäftsbericht 1938, 124-25; Boelcke, Die Kosten von Hitlers Krieg, 64.

86. During the mid-1920s, the Reichsbahn had adopted Frederick W. Taylor's concept of scientific management to increase labor productivity. For details, see Mierzejewski, The Most Valuable Asset of the Reich, 1:178-82.

87. Kühne, "Der Werkstättendienst der Deutschen Reichsbahn im nationalsozialistischen Staate," Die Reichsbahn 10 (10 January 1934): 54-55.

88. Anger to divisions, "Arbeitstudie," 38 Waw 77, Berlin, 31 December 1933, BAC R005/3058neu.

89. Korkamp, Hauptbetriebsrat bei der HV to DRG, HV, "Gedingeverfahren," 6843 II/Schuw, Berlin, 19 April 1934, BAC R005/3058neu.

90. RVM, Personalpolitik, 16-17.

91. DRB, BR, Minutes, 23 March 1937, pp. 10-11, BA R2/31652.

92. RIM to Obersten Reichsbehörden, DRG, Reichsbankdirektorium, "Unterrichtung der Beamten, Angestellten und Arbeiter über den Nationalsozialismus," 20 November 1933, ARK Kab Hitler, vol. 2, doc. no. 250, p. 961; Alexander Wulff, "Rückblick auf das Jahr 1933," ZVME 74 (4 January 1934): 13.

93. Robert Honold, "Das Unterrichtswesen bei der Deutschen Reichsbahn," Die Reichsbahn 10 (11 July 1934): 683; Heinrich Gland, "Die Tätigkeit der Arbeitsgemeinschaft für nationalsozialistische Schulung der Bediensteten bei der Reichsbahn," Die Reichsbahn 10 (18 July 1934): 712.

94. DRG, VR, Minutes, 21 September 1934, p. 6, BA R2/23092; DRG, VR, Minutes, 27 March 1935, p. 19, BA R2/23092.

95. DRG, VR, Minutes, 15 May 1935, pp. 1-2, BA R2/23092; DRB, BR, Minutes, 1 December 1937, pp. 16-18, BA R2/31652; DRB, BR, Minutes, 26 January 1938, p. 2, BA R2/31652.

96. DRG, VR, Arbeitsausschuß, Minutes, 20 September 1934, p. 6, BA R2/23092.

97. "Auflösung der RBD Oldenburg," Die Reichsbahn 10 (14 November 1934): 1141.

98. Lammers, "Vermerk," Rk. 10595/35, Berlin, 12 December 1935, BA R43 II/185, f. 5;

Lammers, "Vermerk über die Reichsbahndirektion Ludwigshafen," Rk. 211II/36, Berlin, 17 January 1936, BA R43 II/185, f. 6; DRG, VR, Minutes, 29 January 1936, pp. 30-33, BA R2/23093; DRG, VR, Minutes, 25 March 1936, pp. 41-42, BA R2/23093; DRG, VR, Minutes, 7 October 1936, pp. 30-31, BA R2/23093.

99. Dorpmüller to Siebert, "Reichsbahnorganisation in Bayern," 2 Ogd (Bay) 3, Berlin, 30 August 1933, pp. 1-2, BHSA Rep. MA 106 963; DRG, VR, Minutes, p. 12, BA R2/23091; DRG, Gruppenverwaltung Bayern, "Reichsbahnorganisation in Bayern," *Eisenbahn-Nachrichtenblatt*, 30 December 1933, p. 1, BA RD98/57. Eltz-Rübenach had proposed closing the GV Bayern on 8 May 1933. See Eltz-Rübenach to Lammer, "Aufhebung der bayerischen Abteilung des Reichspostministeriums und der Gruppenverwaltung Bayern der Reichsbahn in München," RVM. E. 11. Nr. 3995, Berlin, 11 May 1933, BA R43 II/1146, ff. 7-8. See the correspondence on this issue in BHSA Rep. MA 106 962.

100. DRG, Gruppenverwaltung Bayern, "Reichsbahnzentralamt München," *Eisenbahn-Nachrichtenblatt*, 3 November 1933, p. 139, BA RD98/57; Dorpmüller to divisions and RZA, "Abnahmedienst," 2 Ogb, Berlin, 13 August 1935, BA R5/2594; DRG, VR, Minutes, 25 March 1936, pp. 43-47, BA R2/23093; Kleinmann to Siebert, Berlin, 27 March 1936, BHSA Rep. MA 106 962; Siebert, "Vormerkung," Munich, 8 April 1936, BHSA Rep. MA 106 962; "Reichsbahn-Zentralämter," 2 Ogd [RZA] 12, 24 July 1936, reprinted in *Die Reichsbahn* 12 (29 July 1936): 612. See also Gottwaldt, *Geschichte der deutschen Einheitslokomotiven*, 84, 111.

101. "Rückblick auf das Jahr 1937," *ZVME* 78 (6 January 1938): 20; DRG, *Wirtschaftsführung*, 11; "Gesetz zur Vereinfachung und Verbilligung der Verwaltung. Vom 27. Februar 1934," *RGBl*, I, Nr. 22, 28 February 1934, 131.

102. DRG, "Änderung in der Gliederung der Hauptverwaltung," Drucksache Nr. 732, 10 August 1933, BAC R005/020061, ff. 33-35; "Gliederung der Hauptverwaltung der Deutschen Reichsbahn," *ZVME* 73 (21 September 1933): 790.

103. DRG, *Hausnachrichten der Hauptverwaltung der Deutschen Reichsbahn-Gesellschaft*, 30 December 1935, BAC R005/02926. See also Gottwaldt, *Geschichte der deutschen Einheitslokomotiven*, 111.

104. "Einführung des deutschen Grußes," *Die Reichsbahn* 9 (19 July 1933): 617; DRG, Gruppenverwaltung Bayern, *Eisenbahn-Nachrichtenblatt*, 18 July 1933, p. 1, BA RD98/57; DRG, Gruppenverwaltung Bayern, "Deutscher Gruß," *Eisenbahn-Nachrichtenblatt*, 25 October 1933, p. 135, BA RD98/57; Strößenreuther, *Eisenbahnen und Eisenbahner*, 3:136, citing *Reichsbahn-Beamtenzeitung*, 28 April 1934.

105. Domarus, *Hitler Reden und Proklamationen*, Bd. 1, Hlbd. 2, 559; Hitler Speech, Jahrhundertfeier, 7 December 1935, p. 1, BA R11/142, f. 203.

106. Dorpmüller, "Die Reichsbahn in ihrer Verbundenheit zu Wirtschaft und Staat," *Die Reichsbahn* 9 (24 May 1933): 428.

107. Fritz Busch, "Wandlungen im Finanzwesen der Deutschen Reichsbahn," *ZVME* 82 (1 October 1942): 512.

108. Kurt Tecklenburg, "Die Betriebskostenrechnung der Reichsbahn und ihre Auswertung für den Finanzdienst," *Die Reichsbahn* 9 (14 June 1933): 507.

109. See especially Walter Spieß, "Tariff, eine enzyklopädische Studie," *AfE* 53 (1930): 1165, 1167, 1182, 1188, 1207, 1209, 1211, 1502-3, 1512. See also his "Die subjektiven und objektiven Selbstkosten sowie die praktische Kalkulationsgrundlagen in der Reichsbahntarifpolitik," *ZVD* 63 (9 August 1923): 517-20; "Die Selbstkosten als Begriff in der Preiskalkulation (nicht als Zahlengröße)," *Die Reichsbahn* 7 (7 January 1931): 52-58; 7 (14 January 1931): 73-76; "Die Gütertarifpolitik der Reichsbahn," *ZVME* 76 (20 August 1936): 665-72; "Verkehrsleitung," *Die Reichsbahn* 14 (23 February 1938): 174-86.

110. "Niederschrift über die Besprechung der Arbeitsgemeinschaft für die Aufstellung zeit-

gemässer Vorschriften über die Wirtschaftsführung in Hannover am 1. und 2. Februar 1934," Anlage zu RBD Cologne to DRG, HV, "Arbeitsgemeinschaft für die Aufstellung zeitgemässer Vorschriften über die Wirtschaftführung," 1 F 3 Kaow, Cologne, p. 1, BA R5/2450; Fritz Busch, "Die Anforderungen des Finanzdienstes an den Dienstunterricht," *Die Reichsbahn* 10 (22 August 1934): 824; Alfred Prang, "Organisation; Finanzdienst (Abrechnung, Betriebskostenrechnung, Statistik)," 41 Ka (I) 139, Berlin, 22 January 1936, BAC R005/438neu; RBD Berlin, "112. Aenderung und Vereinfachung der Dienstvorschrift über die Fortbildung der Buchungsordnung (Fobu)," *Amtsblatt*, 8 February 1936, Archiv Rbd Berlin; DRB, "Erläuterungen zu dem Wirtschaftsplan für das Geschäftsjahr 1938," Anlage zu 41 Kmbp (1938) 2, 20 December 1937, p. 7, BAC R005/54 Ha; Kleinmann to Abteilungen II, IIA, III, IV, VII, "Ersparungsmaßnahmen auf dem Gebiete der Statistik; hier im Lochkartenverfahren," 4 Ovl, Berlin, 17 July 1935, BAC R005/020921, ff. 28-31.

111. Kleinmann, "Abrechnung unter den Reichsbahnbezirken," 41 Kb (Allg) 268, Berlin, 22 August 1935, BA R5/2457; Dorpmüller to divisions, "Aussetzung der Abrechnung unter den Reichsbahnbezirken," 41 Kb (Allg) 279, Berlin, 31 December 1935, p. 1, BA R5/2454; Kleinmann, "Zugehörigkeit der Einnahmen und Ausgaben zu den Rechnungen der Bezirke," 41 Krob 363, Berlin, 26 November 1937, p. 1, BA R005/54 Ha, also in 114 Ha and Rbd Halle (S), Reg A 1526, ff. 246-52; DRB, "Entwicklung der Bezirkl. Betriebszahlen," 41 Kb (Allg) 290, Berlin, 18 January 1938, BA R5/2458; Prang, "Buchungsvorschrift Abschnitt I; Bestimmungen über die Zugehörigkeit der Einnahmen und der Ausgaben zu den Rechnungen der Bezirke," 41 Krob 363^{II}, Berlin, 10 March 1938, Rbd Halle (S), Reg A/1526, f. 287a.

112. Fritz Busch, "Der Wirtschaftsplan der Deutschen Reichsbahn," *Die Reichsbahn* 13 (22 December 1937): 1134-35, 1141. See also Busch, "Die Vereinfachung des Finanzdienstes," *Die Reichsbahn* 12 (6 May 1936): 397-401; Busch, "Die Entwicklung der Reichsbahn-Finanzen und das Reichsbahn-Finanzwesen seit 1933," *ZVME* 77 (3 June 1937): 396; Busch, "Das formelle Finanzwesen bei der Deutschen Reichsbahn," *Die Reichsbahn* 14 (5 October 1938): 963; Busch, "Die neue Wirtschaftsvorschrift," *Die Reichsbahn* 15 (15 March 1939): 269, 271.

113. Brademann to Lammers, 3 April 1933, p. 5, BA R43 I/1053, f. 19, quoting Hitler.

114. "Geschäftsordnung der Deutschen Reichsbahn-Gesellschaft," *Die Reichsbahn* 9 (21 December 1933): 1048.

115. Willuhn, "Vermerk," Rk. 11085, Berlin, 6 December 1935, BA R43 II/185, f. 13.

116. Lammers to Dorpmüller, Rk. 11085, Berlin, 20 December 1935, BA R43 II/185, f. 14.

117. Pressestelle, RVM, "Gegenwartsaufgaben der Reichsverkehrspolitik," Berlin, 24 November 1933, pp. 12-13, AR Bes. E-R, 54; RVM to ministries, "Organisation der Reichsbahn," S.E. 11. Nr. 251, Geheim, Berlin, 31 December 1935, pp. 1-2, BA R43 II/185, ff. 16-17.

118. Lammers to Eltz-Rübenach, Rk. 46, Geheim, Berlin, 6 January 1936, BA R43 II/185, ff. 19-20; Lammers to Eltz-Rübenach, Rk. 207/36, Berlin, 15 January 1936, BA R43 II/185, f. 22.

119. Eltz-Rübenach, Berlin, 27 November 1936, AR Bes. E-R, 53.

120. Deutsches Nachrichtenbüro, "Wieder restlos unter der Hoheit des Reiches," Berlin, 12 February 1937, BA R43 II/185, f. 73.

121. "Gesetz zur Neuregelung der Verhältnisse der Reichsbank und der Deutschen Reichsbahn. Vom 10. Februar 1937," *RGBl*, Teil II, 12 February 1937, pp. 47-48. For the objection of the OKW, see the documents in BA R43 II/185, ff. 56, 59-62.

122. "Geschäftsordnung der Deutschen Reichsbahn-Gesellschaft," 2 Oavh, 15 December 1933, Gruppenverwaltung Bayern, *Eisenbahn-Nachrichtenblatt*, 29 December 1933, p. 167, BA RD98/57. See also DRG, HV, 2 Arh 17, 30 November 1935, cited in Scharf and Wenzel, *Lokomotiven für die Reichsbahn*, 1:10; Dorpmüller, "Geschäftsanweisung für die Leitung der Deutschen Reichsbahn durch die Eisenbahnabteilungen des Reichsverkehrsministeriums," Berlin, 16 February 1937, BAC R005/63/3. Note that for the first time in September 1934 and then

consistently from January 1935, the minutes of the board of directors meetings were labeled Deutsche Reichsbahn instead of Deutsche Reichsbahn-Gesellschaft. The annual report was labeled Deutsche Reichsbahn for the first time in 1935.

123. "Gesetz über die Deutsche Reichsbahn (Reichsbahngesetz), Vom 4 Juli 1939," *RGBl*, Teil I, 11 July 1939, pp. 1205-10. For the preliminary debate, see the correspondence in BA R43 II/185, ff. 111-12, 123-24, 181-92, 233.

124. [Eltz-Rübenach], memorandum, Berlin, 2 December 1936, AR Bes. E-R, 53.

125. Krauch, "Vertraulicher Informationsbericht, Zum Rücktritt des Ministers Eltz von Rübenach," Berlin, 3 February 1937, p. 2, BA ZSg. 101/30, f. 147; IMT, *Trial of the Major War Criminals*, 9:397-98; Overy, *Goering: The Iron Man*, 70.

126. Kiefer to Keitel, Berlin, 25 June 1937, BAP 21.01/B9505; DRB, BR, Minutes, 23 March 1937, p. 7, BA R2/31652.

127. "Erlaß des Führers und Reichskanzlers zur Änderung des Reichsbahngesetzes vom 7. November 1939," *RGBl*, Teil I, 14 November 1939, p. 2179; also in BA R43 II/187a, f. 61.

128. Kleinmann to Lammers, "Beirat der Deutschen Reichsbahn," 4 Ogbg, Berlin, 26 October 1939, BA R43 II/187a, ff. 55-57.

Chapter 2. The Reichsbahn in the Period of Rearmament, Job Creation, and Motorization, 1933-1939

A. Passenger Service: The Flying Trains

1. DRG, VR, Arbeitsausschuß, Minutes, 20 September 1934, p. 9, BA R2/23092.
2. Abt IIA 81 to Ref 24, Io, Berlin, February 1934, BAC R005/172.
3. Leibbrand, *Die Entwicklung des Reichsbahnbetriebes in neuer Zeit*, 28; August Urban, "Aufgaben und Ziele des Personenzugfahrplans," *ZVME* 75 (16 May 1935): 399; Alexander Wulff, "Rückblick auf das Jahr 1934," *ZVME* 65 (3 January 1935): 6.
4. "Die Geschwindigkeit der deutschen Schnellzüge," *ZVME* 65 (12 December 1935): 1058. See also Scharf and Ernst, *Vom Fernschnellzug zum Intercity*, 69.
5. Allen, *Railways of the Twentieth Century*, 98.
6. "Rückblick auf das Jahr 1937," *ZVME* 78 (6 January 1938): 8; "Rückblick auf das Jahr 1938," *ZVME* 79 (5 January 1939): 13-14.
7. Max Leibbrand, "Leistungen des Reichsbahnbetriebs," *VW* 33 (29 March 1939): 145.
8. DRG, HV, *Hundert Jahre Deutsche Eisenbahnen*, 375.
9. On Nazi rearmament, see Overy, "Hitler's War and the German Economy: A Reinterpretation," 272-91, reprinted in Overy, *War, Economy and the Third Reich*, 233-56. See also Overy, "Hitler's War Plans and the German Economy, 1933-1939," in *War, Economy and the Third Reich*, 177-204; Hans-Erich Volkmann, "Die NS-Wirtschaft in Vorbereitung des Krieges," in Deist, *Das Deutsche Reich und der Zweite Weltkrieg*, 1:177-368; Deist, *The Wehrmacht and German Rearmament*; Boelcke, *Die Deutsche Wirtschaft 1930-1938*, chaps. 1-3; Boelcke, *Die Kosten von Hitlers Krieg*, chap. 1; Bagel-Bohlan, *Hitlers industrielle Kriegsvorbereitungen, 1936-1939*; Carroll, *Design for Total War*. Less reliable are Milward, *The German Economy at War*; Kaldor, "The German War Economy"; and Klein, *Germany's Economic Preparations for War*.
10. DRG, VR, Minutes, 25 September 1935, pp. 70-71, BA R2/23092.
11. DRG, VR, Minutes, 25 March 1936, pp. 47-49, BA R2/23093.
12. DRG, VR, Minutes, 7 October 1936, pp. 27-28, BA R2/23093; Heinrich Dorpmüller, "Die Reichsbahn im Dienst der XI. Olympischen Spiele Berlin 1936," *Die Reichsbahn* 12 (9 September 1936): 737-46.
13. NNP increased in this period by 72.6 percent. Calculated from Mitchell, *European His-*

torical Statistics, 411, table J1. The percentage increase in passenger-kilometers relates only to the Altreich and the Sudetenland.

14. Based on raw data in Hoffmann, *Wachstum*, 692-95. Overy repeats an estimate that in 1935 60 percent of passenger travel took place on roads and only 32 percent on railways. See Overy, "Cars, Roads, Economic Recovery," 481.

15. Adolf Sarter, "Verkehrsfragen von wirtschaftlicher Bedeutung für die Reichsbahn," *VW* 26 (27 April 1932): 267.

16. DRG, VR, Arbeitsausschuß, Minutes, 23 January 1934, pp. 5, 7, BA R2/23092; DRG, VR, Minutes, 24 January 1934, p. 14, BA R2/23092.

17. Kleinmann, "Vermerk," 15 Tpas 61, Berlin, 16 February 1934, pp. 1, 3, BAC R005/020065, ff. 19, 21.

18. Eltz-Rübenach to Dorpmüller, E 15. 12 17, Berlin, 16 February 1934, BAC R005/020080.

19. DRG, VR, Ausserordentliche Sitzung, Minutes, 20 February 1934, pp. 2-3, 7, BAC R005/020065, ff. 4-5, 7.

20. "Vermerk über die Besprechung mit der Reichsregierung vom 28. Februar 1934," BAC R005/020066, ff. 168-71.

21. DRG, *Bestimmungen für die Beförderung der SA, SS und des NSKK auf Eisenbahnen (Besa)*, 22; DRB, BR, 23 March 1937, p. 12, BA R2/31652.

22. DRB, BR, Minutes, 6 October 1937, p. 5, BA R2/31652.

23. Busch, "Wirtschaftslage der Deutschen Reichsbahn in ihrer Entwicklung seit 1933," *VW* 32 (20 April 1938): 166.

24. Kleinmann, "Stellung und Aufgabe der Reichsbahn im nationalsozialistischen Staat," *Die Reichsbahn* 12 (18 November 1936): 1004.

25. DRG, HV, *Hundert Jahre Deutsche Eisenbahnen*, 247.

26. Friedrich Fuchs, "Der Schnelltriebwagen der Deutschen Reichsbahn-Gesellschaft," *Die Reichsbahn* 9 (4 January 1933): 7-11.

27. Kurz, *Die Triebwagen der Reichsbahn-Bauarten*, 12. Kurz's book, though it offers only a chronological description of the various cars developed, is indispensable for tracing the technological development of motor trains in Germany between the two world wars.

28. See Gottwaldt's reproduction of the exhibition catalog *Eisenbahntechnische Ausstellung Seddin 1924*.

29. Kurz, *Die Triebwagen der Reichsbahn-Bauarten*, 163-64; Gottwaldt, *Eisenbahntechnische Ausstellung Seddin 1924*.

30. DRG, HV, *Hundert Jahre Deutsche Eisenbahnen*, 250; Zschech, *Triebwagen deutscher Eisenbahnen. Band 1*, 33.

31. Przygode, "Neue Verbrennungstriebwagen," *ZVD* 66 (5 August 1926): 837.

32. RBD Berlin, Dez 25 to Dez 51, St. 25. Tm 35/462, Berlin, 23 November 1927, Archiv Rbd Berlin, Reg 2. 200, Br. 1; Zschech, *Triebwagen deutscher Eisenbahnen. Band 1*, 58.

33. DRG, HV to W. Riehm, MAN, 31 Fktv 4, Berlin, 18 February 1928, BAC R005/723/1alt, f. 159.

34. Anger to Verkehrsverband für Nordostbayern und die deutsch-böhmischen Grenzbezirke e V, "Triebwagen," 34 Bbt, Berlin, 12 April 1929, p. 1, BAC R005/723/1alt, f. 161.

35. Kurz, *Die Triebwagen der Reichsbahn-Bauarten*, 229, 231.

36. Ibid., 35, 93-94, 194.

37. DRG, HV to RZA, "Schnelltriebwagen," 31 Fktv 85, Berlin, 12 November 1930, BAC R005/022061, ff. 1-2.

38. Dorpmüller to Göring, "Dortiges Schreiben vom 16. Dezember 1940. Beschwerdeschrift der Dipl. Ing. Franz Kruckenberg," 33 Fktv 988, Berlin, 24 February 1941, p. 3, BA R5/2074,

f. 42; Gottwaldt, *Schienenzeppelin*, p. 17; Kurz, *Fliegende Züge*, 12, 14; Stroebe, "Fast Railcars of the German State Railways," 1612, 1614.

39. Wumag to DRG, RZA, "Verbrennungstriebwagen für Hauptbahnen. Schnelltriebwagen," W-Vo Kr Gesch. Nr. 1276 Proj. No. IV/1301, Görlitz, 19 December 1930, BAC R005/022061, ff. 25-37, plus the attached blueprints.

40. RZM to DRG, HV, "Schnelltriebwagen 150 km, 2 mal 400 PS," Fktves 2434, Berlin, 2 January 1931, p. 1, BAC R005/022061, f. 3.

41. Gottwaldt, *Schienenzeppelin*, 35.

42. RZM to DRG, HV, "Schnelltriebwagen für 150km Fahrgeschwindigkeit," Fktves 2434, Berlin, 30 January 1931, BAC R005/022061, f. 82.

43. DRG, HV to Mitropa, 31 Fktv 106, Berlin, 20 February 1931, BAC R005/022512, f. 64; Dorpmüller to RZM, "Schnelltriebwagen," Sofort, 31/74a Fktv 85, Berlin, 10 February 1931, BAC R005/022061, ff. 84-88; Dorpmüller to RZE, "Schnelltriebwagen," 31/74a Fktv 85, Berlin, 10 February 1931, BAC R005/022061, ff. 109-13.

44. DRG, HV to RZM and RZE, "Beschaffung eines Schnelltriebwagens," 74a/31 Fktv 85, Berlin, 2 May 1931, BAC R005/022061, f. 116.

45. RZA-M to DRG, HV, "Freigabe des für den Schnelltriebwagen angemeldeten Gebrauchsmusters No 1 150 366 Kl. 20^b," 2434 Fktves, Berlin, 23 September 1931, BAC R005/022512, f. 314; RZM to DRG, HV, "Schnelltriebwagen für 150km Fahrgeschwindigkeit," Fktves 2434, Berlin, 30 January 1931, BAC R005/022061, f. 82.

46. RZM to DRG, HV, "Dieselelektrischer Triebwagen mit 410 PS-Maybach-Motoren. Beschaffung von Ersatzstücken," 2434 Fktvel, Berlin, 29 January 1932, BAC R005/022061, ff. 132-33.

47. Helberg, VL RAW Grunberg to RZM, "Versuchsfahrten mit Schnelltriebwagen für V = 150 km/h," Fkwvt/VL Ha, Berlin-Grunewald, 21 Sept. 1932, BAC R005/022061, ff. 198-200.

48. Helberg, VL RAW Grunberg to RZM, "Versuchsfahrten mit Schnelltriebwagen," Fkwvt/VL 3, Berlin, 9 December 1932, BAC R005/022061, ff. 202-3.

49. Weirauch to GV Bayern, RBD'em Altona, Berlin, Erfurt, Halle (S), Nuremberg, RZM, "Erprobung des Schnelltriebwagen," 31 Fktv 237, Berlin, 28 January 1933, BAC R005/022061, f. 163.

50. Emmelius to (Flemming), Berlin, 8 April 1933, BAC R005/022061, f. 174; RAW Grunewald, Versuchsabteilung für Lokomotiven to RZM, "Versuche mit Schnelltriebwagen Berlin 877 a/b," Fkwvt 380/VL 3, Grunewald, 4 August 1933, BAC R005/022061, ff. 185-89.

51. Wehner, "Räder mussten rollen," 152; Immo Wendt, "Berlin-Hamburg," *ZVME* 73 (18 May 1933): 421.

52. Emmelius to DRG, HV, "Kurbenwellenbrüche an den 410 PS-Maybach-Dieselmotoren," 2434 Fktve, Berlin, 6 June 1933, p. 1, BAC R005/021843.

53. DRG, HV, "Vermerk," 31 Fklt, Berlin, 19 July 1933, p. 1, BAC R005/021843.

54. Gottwaldt, *Schienenzeppelin*, 53, 58, 88, 122; Stroebe, "Fast Railcars of the German State Railways," 1617. On the reliability issue, see Hermann Stroebe, "Neue dieselelektrische Schnelltriebwagen der Deutschen Reichsbahn," *Die Reichsbahn* 11 (15 May 1935): 572; Stroebe, "Erfahrungen mit dieselelektrischen Schnelltriebwagen in Bau und Betrieb," *VW* 30 (2 December 1936): 664.

55. Kühne, HV, "Vermerk," 31/74a Fktv 298, Berlin, 22 July 1933, pp. 1-2, BA R005/021843, also in BAC R005/022124, ff. 14-15.

56. DRG, HV, "Umstellung des Reisezugdienstes auf Triebwagen mit eigener Kraftquelle," Drucksache Nr. 795, BA R2/23092. For a more detailed discussion of this plan and the highspeed motor train system created by the Reichsbahn during the 1930s, see Mierzejewski,

"High Speed Motor Trains of the German National Railway, 1920-1945," 57-68, and "Hochgeschwindigkeitszüge in den Planungen der Reichsbahn, 1920-1945," 208-22.

57. DRG, VR, Ausserordentliche Sitzung, Minutes, 29-30 May 1934, p. 5, BA R2/23092.

58. Dorpmüller to Abt. III, Eilt, 4 Ogvsp, Berlin, 8 November 1934, BAC R005/021820, f. 347; DRG, HV, "Beschädigung der Dieselmotoren an den Triebwagenzügen der Niederlandischen Staatsbahnen," 33, Berlin, 22 November 1934, pp. 2-3, BA R005/021820, ff. 349-50; DRG, VR, Minutes, 28 November 1934, p. 3, BAC R005/020071, f. 260; Wehrmann to Bergmann, Berlin, 6 October 1934, p. 4, BAC R005/021820, f. 331. This contains a translation from the *Hag'sche Courant* from 28 August 1934 describing the problems.

59. Bergmann, "Schnelltriebwagen Bauart Hamburg. Besprechung mit Herrn Staatssekretär Kleinmann am 12. Februar 1937," Eilt, Berlin, 13 February 1937, BAC R005/022124, f. 237; (Abt. III) to Abt II, "Auf das Schreiben Bbzp 125 vom 15.2.1935," Berlin, March 1935, p. 3, BAC R005/186/2 Ha.

60. Leibbrand to Abt. II and Abt. IV, Bbzp 125, Berlin, 15 February 1935, BAC R005/186/2 Ha.

61. (Abt. III) to Abt II, "Auf das Schreiben Bbzp 125 vom 15.2.1935," Berlin, March 1935, p. 1, BAC R005/186/2 Ha.

62. Dorpmüller to ministries, "Finanzlage der Reichsbahn," 42 Kfb 419, Berlin, 17 August 1935, pp. 6-7, BA R2/23105.

63. Bergmann, "Besprechung mit dem Herrn St. GD am 24. August 1936 betreffend Rohstoff-Fragen," Eilt, Berlin, 24 August 1936, BAC R005/732/1alt, f. 4.

64. Bergmann, "Vermerk," Berlin, 25 August 1936, BAC R005/723/1alt, f. 5.

65. DRB, "Vermerk: Bedarfsplan für neue Fahrzeuge für die Jahre 1939 bis 1942 hier Triebwagen mit eigener Kraftquelle," 33 Fktv 701, Berlin, 7 January 1938, BA R5/2123.

66. RZA Munich, "Nachweisung über den Bestand an Trieb-, Steuer- und Beiwagen am 31. Dezember 1939," Munich, May 1941, p. 74, BAC R005/12884/1, f. 37.

67. "Rückblick auf das Jahr 1938," *ZVME* 79 (5 January 1939): 15.

68. Stroebe, "Fast Railcars of the German State Railways," 1618; Stroebe, "Erfahrungen mit dieselelektrischen Schnelltriebwagen in Bau und Betrieb," *VW* 30 (2 December 1936): 665.

69. Gottwaldt, *Schienenzeppelin*, 3, 6, 9, 11-12.

70. Kurz, *Fliegende Züge*, 5, 7.

71. DRG, HV, [Chronology], circa September 1934, p. 2, BAC R005/022510, f. 225.

72. DRG, HV, "Vermerk," 31/74a Fktv 298, 22 July 1933, p. 2, BAC R005/021843; DRG, HV, "Unterstützung der Arbeiten des Herrn Kruckenberg (Gesellschaft für Verkehrstechnik GVT) durch die Deutsche Reichsbahn-Gesellschaft," Berlin, November 1933, p. 2, BAC R005/022510, f. 6.

73. Kurz, *Fliegende Züge*, 7.

74. RZA Munich to DRB, "Schnelltriebwagen Bauart Kruckenberg," 2410 Fktvs (S) 1/36 Munich, p. 1, BA R5/2292.

75. Kruckenberg to Dorpmüller, Berlin, 14 September 1934, BAC R005/022510, f. 221.

76. Kruckenberg to Todt, Hanover, 6 November 1933, BAC R005/022510, ff. 5-8.

77. DRB to RZA Munich, "Schnelltriebwagen 'Bauart Kruckenberg,'" 33 Fktv 867, 30 June 1939, BA R005/022292.

78. DRB, "Wiederherstellung des Kruckenberg-Schnelltriebwagen," 33 Fktv 867, Berlin, 27 July 1939, BA R005/022292.

79. DRB, "Vermerk," 33 Fktv 867, 5 September 1939, BA R5/2292; Emrich to DRB, "Schnelltriebwagen Bauart Kruckenberg," 3515 Fktvb, Munich, 20 March 1940, BA R5/2292; DRB to RZA München, "Schnelltriebwagen Bauart Kruckenberg," 33 Fktv 988, Berlin, 30 May 1941, BA R5/2292.

80. Dorpmüller to Göring, "Dortiges Schreiben vom 16. Dezember 1940. Beschwerdeschrift des Dipl.-Ing. Franz Kruckenberg," 33 Fktv 988, p. 6, BA R005/022074, f. 42.

81. Between 1914 and 1921 the state railways had investigated streamlining trains, including conducting wind tunnel tests at the Deutsche Versuchsanstalt für Luftfahrzeuge. A propeller-driven car was tested in 1919. DRG, HV, "Die Unterstützung der Arbeiten des Herrn Kruckenbergs (Gesellschaft für Verkehrstechnik) durch die Deutsche Reichsbahn-Gesellschaft," 31 Lws 41, Berlin, 23 November 1933, p. 1, BAC R005/63 Ha. For additional information on streamlined high-speed trains, including monorails, that were proposed before Kruckenberg turned his attention to rail vehicles, see Reed, *The Streamline Era*, 21-31, and Friedrich Hasse, "Luftschraubenantrieb für Schienenfahrzeuge," *VW* 15 (14 July 1921): 227-29. For Kruckenberg's claim, see, for example, Kruckenberg to Göring, Berlin, 5 December 1940, p. 1, BA R5/2074, f. 16.

B. Freight Service and Modal Competition

1. Lammers, "Vermerk," 18 February 1933, Rk. 1369, BA R43 I/1074, f. 17.
2. Eltz-Rübenach to Lammers, "Bahnspeditionsvertrag," E. 19.1504, Berlin, 24 February 1933, pp. 4-6, BA R43 I/1074, ff. 32-33; Siemens to VR Members, "Aufzeichnung über das Verhältnis Reichsbahn/Kraftwagen betr Gewährung sogenannter fallweiser Zuschüße," Berlin, 8 March 1933, pp. 1-2, BAC R005/020058, ff. 66-67; Eltz-Rübenach to Lammers, "Bahnspeditionsvertrag. Richtlinien," E. 19.1981, Berlin, 10 March 1933, BA R43 I/1074, ff. 110-11.
3. "Vermerk des Oberregierungsrats Willuhn über einen Vortrag des Generaldirektors der Deutschen Reichsbahn-Gesellschaft zur Frage des Wettbewerbs zwischen Reichsbahn und Kraftwagen am 1. März 1933," *ARK Kab Hitler*, vol. 1, doc. no. 64, pp. 226-36, also in BA R43 I/1074, ff. 145-56.
4. DRG, VR, Protocol, 3 May 1933, Teil I, p. 12, BAC R005/020059, f. 328.
5. DRG, VR, Protocol, 3 May 1933, Teil I, pp. 21-22, BAC R005/020059, ff. 336-38.
6. Willuhn, "Vermerk, Speditionsgewerbe," Rk. 6521/6541^{II}, Berlin, 24 May 1933, BA R43 I/1074, ff. 275-76.
7. Eltz-Rübenach to DRG, HV, E 18.5718/33, Berlin, 1 July 1933, BA R43 I/1074, f. 297.
8. Dorpmüller to RVM, RWM, Lammers, "Verhandlungen mit den Spediteuren und den Vertretungen des Kraftverkehrs," 11 Vgrs 1044, Berlin, 14 July 1933, p. 3, BA R43 I/1074, f. 302.
9. Eltz-Rübenach, "Gegenwartsaufgaben der Reichsverkehrspolitik," *VW* 27 (29 November 1933): 724; Lammers, "Vermerk," Rk. 13556, Berlin, 29 November 1933, BA R43 I/1075, ff. 145-46.
10. "Besprechung des Reichskanzlers mit dem Generaldirektor der Deutschen Reichsbahngesellschaft," 10 April 1933, *ARK Kab Hitler*, vol. 1, doc. no. 95, pp. 329-32. Also in BA R43 I/1053, ff. 35-40, and R43 I/1074, ff. 188-92.
11. DRG, VR, Protocol, 3 May 1933, Teil IV, p. 14, BAC R005/020059, f. 375.
12. "Besprechung mit Industriellen über Arbeitsbeschaffung am 29. Mai 1933," BA R43 II/536, ff. 346, 351. Also in *ARK Kab Hitler*, vol. 1, doc. no. 147, pp. 511-14.
13. "Vermerk des Ministerialrats Willuhn über eine Besprechung des Reichskanzlers mit dem Generaldirektoren Dorpmüller und Hof zur Frage des Autobahnbaus am 1. Juni 1933," *ARK Kab Hitler*, vol. 1, doc. no. 153, p. 544.
14. "Chefbesprechung," 15 June 1933, *ARK Kab Hitler*, vol. 1, doc. no. 158, p. 560.
15. "Ministerbesprechung, Anschließend Kabinettssitzung," 23 June 1933, *ARK Kab Hitler*, vol. 1, doc. no. 166, pp. 584-85.
16. DRG, HV, "Reichsautobahnen," Drucksache Nr. 729, p. 3, BA NL13/535, f. 105.

17. DRG, VR, Sonderausschuß Reichsautobahnen, Minutes, 27 July 1933, pp. 2-3, BAC R005/020075, ff. 2-3.
18. DRG, VR, Sonderausschuß Reichsautobahnen, Minutes, 27 July 1933, Teil III, p. 8, BAC R005/020075, f. 37.
19. "Rückblick auf das Jahr 1935," ZVME 76 (2 January 1936): 18.
20. Lammers, "Vermerk," Rk. 13556.13562, Berlin, 29 November 1933, BA R43 I/1075, ff. 145-46.
21. DRG, VR, Arbeitsausschuß, Minutes, 8 May 1934, pp. 5-6, BA R2/23092.
22. DRG, VR, Protocol, Teil III, Heinrich II, 4 July 1934, pp. 17-19, 20, BA R005/020069, ff. 281-83, 285; DRG, VR, Minutes, 4 July 1934, pp. 11-12, BA R2/23092.
23. Lammers, "Vermerk," Rk. 6917/34, Berlin, 1 September 1934, BA R43 I/1085, f. 301; DRG, VR, Minutes, 21 September 1934, p. 7, BA R2/23092; Kopper, "Modernität oder Scheinmodernität nationalsozialistischer Herrschaft—Das Beispiel der Verkehrspolitik," 402-4.
24. DRG, VR, Minutes, 27-28 November 1934, pp. 16-17, BA R2/23092; DRG, VR, Protocol, 27-28 November 1934, Teil 6, pp. 1-6, BAC R005/020071, ff. 273-78.
25. "Gesetz über den Güterfernverkehr mit Kraftwagen. Vom 26. Juni 1935," RGBl, 1935, I, pp. 788-93; "Auszug aus der Niederschrift über die Sitzung des Reichsministeriums vom 26. Juni 1934," Rk. 5945[35], BA R43 I/1076, ff. 45-46, also in BA R43 I/1473, ff. 70-71. See also Eberhard von Beck, "Die neue Ordnung des Güterfernverkehrs mit Kraftfahrzeugen im Dritten Reich," ZVME 75 (29 August 1935): 721-32; Wilhelm Scholz, "Der Güterfernverkehr mit Kraftwagen," ZVME 76 (19 March 1936): 247-48.
26. DRG, VR, Minutes, 14 May 1935, pp. 14, 20, BA R2/23092.
27. DRG, VR, Minutes, 3 July 1935, pp. 16-17, 19, BA R2/23092.
28. DRB, BR, Minutes, 2 July 1938, pp. 17-18, 26-27, BA R2/31652; "Rückblick auf das Jahr 1938," ZVME 79 (12 January 1939): 35.
29. Memorandum circa May 1933, p. 24, BA R43 I/1074, f. 320; DRG, "Niederschrift über die Besprechung von Fragen des Kraftwagenverkehrs in der Hauptverwaltung am 2. Dezember 1935," pp. 1-3, 5, BAC R005/02438; "Die Entwicklung des Reichsbahnkraftwagenverkehrs seit 1929," BAC R005/020071, f. 108; "Rückblick auf das Jahr 1935," ZVME 76 (2 January 1936): 6.
30. DRB, BR, Minutes, 5 May 1937, p. 9, BA R2/31652.
31. A. von Neuhoff-von der Ley, "Die Entwicklung des Personen-Linienverkehrs mit Kraftfahrzeugen," AfE 62 (1939): 1416; "Rückblick auf das Jahr 1938," ZVME 79 (12 January 1939): 35.
32. DRG, VR, Protocol, 3 May 1933, p. 7, BAC R005/020059, f. 358.
33. Alexander Wulff, "Rückblick auf das Jahr 1934," ZVME 65 (3 January 1935): 6-7.
34. Wilhelm Kleinmann, "Wirtschaftliche Gegenwartsfragen der Deutschen Reichsbahn," VW 31 (17 February 1937): 76; Adalbert Baumann, "Die Eisenbahn und die neuzeitlichen Verkehrsentwicklung," VW 28 (5 December 1934): 651.
35. "Rückblick auf das Jahr 1936," ZVME 77 (14 January 1937): 23.
36. "Rückblick auf das Jahr 1938," ZVME 79 (12 January 1939): 36.
37. Kurt Trierenberg, "Organisation und Entwicklung des Kraftverkehrs der Deutschen Reichsbahn," ZVME 79 (2 March 1939): 201, 208.
38. "Rückblick auf das Jahr 1937," ZVME 78 (6 January 1938): 21; Paul Treibe, "Spediteur und Reichsbahn," ZVME 77 (2 December 1937): 863-66.
39. RBD Dresden to DRB, "Verstoß gegen das Gesetz über den Güterfernverkehr mit Kraftfahrzeugen vom 26.6.1935," 7 Vkkw, Dresden, 31 March 1937, BAC R005/020608, f. 249; Gruppe A to Abt. III, "Präsidentenkonferenz," Berlin, 8 July 1937, pp. 8-9, BAC R005/022549.
40. DRG, VR, Minutes, 7 October 1936, pp. 21-22, BA R2/23093.
41. Kleinmann, "Die Bedeutung der Verkehrsmittel im deutschen Wirtschaftsleben," VW

33 (22 March 1939): 136; Trierenberg, "Organisation und Entwicklung des Kraftverkehrs der Deutschen Reichsbahn," *ZVME* 79 (2 March 1939): 200; A. von Neuhoff-von der Ley, "Der Güterfernverkehr mit Kraftfahrzeugen im Jahre 1937," *AfE* 62 (1939): 123. In October 1936 Dorpmüller said that he was much more concerned about the Werkverkehr than line haul operators and independents. See DRG, VR, Minutes, 7 October 1936, pp. 24-25, BA R2/23093. For an informative insight into the structure of the German truck market in 1936, see "Vortrag gehalten von Dr.-Ing. W. Scholz im Reichsverkehrsministerium am 19. November 1936 über 'Aufbau des Reichs-Kraftwagen-Betriebsverbandes und die Entwicklung des Güterverkehrs mit Kraftfahrzeuge,'" BAP 46.01/584, ff. 150-203. The report notes that the Werkverkehr accounted for 77 percent of all truck traffic in November 1936. The RKB estimated that it could compete for 8.9 percent of the Reichsbahn's freight traffic as measured in tonnage, but 28.9 percent in terms of revenues.

42. Soon after the war began, on 6 December 1939, the RVM restricted long-distance truck freight traffic. Shipments over fifty kilometers, including those by trucks owned by manufacturers carrying their own freight, were subject to government approval. On 15 April 1942 the factory-owned trucks were organized by the RVM when it began allocating truck space nationwide. "Kriegseinsatz des Werkverkehrs," *Großdeutscher Verkehr* 36 (May 1942): 261.

43. Wilhelm Kleinmann, "Die Reichsbahn und die deutsche Wirtschaft," *Die Reichsbahn* 10 (21 November 1934): 1171; Julius Dorpmüller, "Schwebende Reichsbahnfragen," *Die Reichsbahn* 10 (21 November 1934): 1167; DRG, *Geschäftsbericht 1934*, 59; Wehner, "Räder mussten rollen," 156-57; Wehner, "Der Einsatz der Eisenbahnen," 36-37; Otto Ballof, "Die betrieblichen und baulichen Voraussetzungen für die Leistungssteigerungen der Reichsbahn," *Die Reichsbahn* 11 (30 October 1935): 1126-27.

44. DRG, HV, "Vermerk," 30 Fal 38, Berlin, 5 May 1936, pp. 2-3, BA R5/2179; Leibbrand, "Güterzugfahrplan," 23 Bzgg 14, Berlin, 20 May 1936, BA R5/2179; Treibe, "Allgemeine Verkehrsfragen," *Die Reichsbahn* 12 (20 May 1936): 446.

45. Hans Münzer, "Die 15 Jahre Saar-Eisenbahnen," *AfE* 58 (1935): 1462.

46. Kreidler, *Eisenbahnen im Machtbereich*, 23; Rohde, *Wehrmachttransportwesen*, 39.

47. Kreidler, *Eisenbahnen im Machtbereich*, 24; Rohde, *Wehrmachttransportwesen*, 41.

48. DRB, BR, Minutes, 4 May 1938, pp. 27-31, BA R2/31652; "Rückblick auf das Jahr 1938," *ZVME* 79 (5 January 1939): 7; Theodor Kittel, "Zum Übergang des Oesterreichischen Bundesbahnen auf das Reich," *Die Reichsbahn* 14 (23 March 1938): 273-74.

49. DRB, "Vermerk," 31 Fab 3, Berlin, 8 December 1938, BA R5/2170; Bergmann, "Werkstätten und Betrieb. Sonderarbeiten an den ehemals österreichischen Güterwagen," 30 Fkk 80, Berlin, 26 January 1939, p. 1, BAC R005/Ha 37; Prang to Referent 4, 41 Kfl 47, Berlin, 4 January 1939, Vertraulich, BA R5/2541; Philipp Wohlschläger, "Beitragsmaterial zur Ausarbeitung: die Leistungen der Eisenbahnen im 2. Weltkrieg," p. 31, Ergänzung, p. 2, BA R5 Anh II/35; Fritz, "Die Deutsche Reichsbahn im Zweiten Weltkrieg Abschnitt Werkstättenwesen," p. 26, BA R5 Anh I/12; Horn, *Reichsbahndirektion Wien*, 15.

50. DRB, BR, Minutes, 7 December 1938, pp. 31-32, BA R2/31652; Kreidler, *Eisenbahnen im Machtbereich*, 25.

51. Kausche, "Die Deutschen Eisenbahnen im zweiten Weltkrieg. (Allgemeiner und historischer Teil)," p. 15, BA R5 Anh I/18.

52. DRB, BR, Minutes, 28 September 1938, pp. 27-28, BA R2/31652; Hammersen, "Der Einsatz der Deutschen Reichsbahn beim Bau des Westwalles unter besonderer Berücksichtigung des RBD-Bezirkes Wuppertal," December 1939, pp. 1-5, BA R5 Anh I/49; "Beitrag zum Thema 'Leistungen der Deutschen Reichsbahn während des zweiten Weltkrieges,'" Cologne, 6 July 1953, pp. 1-2, BA R5 Anh I/49; "Rückblick auf das Jahr 1938," *ZVME* 79 (5 January 1939): 18; Albert Zissel, "Die Reichsbahn und die Westbefestigung," *VW* 33 (5 July 1939): 313-17.

53. "Rede des Herrn Staatssekretärs Koenigs auf dem Binnenschiffahrtstagung in Breslau am Freitag dem 28. September 1934," pp. 6–7, AR Bes. E-R 56/22/XIV; DRG, VR, Arbeitsausschuß, Minutes, 22 January 1935, pp. 6–7, BA R2/23092.

54. "Aufzeichnung über die Ressortbesprechung am 31. Juli 1935 im Reichs- und Preussischen Verkehrsministerium, betreffend die finanzielle Lage der Deutschen Reichsbahn," Anlage zu E. 12. 5423, BA R5/2540.

55. Lammers to Koenigs, Rk. 6139, Berchtesgaden, 9 August 1935, BAC R005/600alt, also in BA R5/2541.

56. Dorpmüller to RBD Berlin, "Deutscher Reichsbahn-Gütertarif," 14 Tgar 3302, Berlin, p. 1, BA R5/2594.

57. Schwerin von Krosigk to RVM, "Ausgleich der Gewinn- und Verlustrechnung der Deutschen Reichsbahn-Gesellschaft," Ve 1410/35-14Ic, Berlin, 20 September 1935, p. 1, BA R5/2541.

58. DRG, Abt. IV, "Zur Kabinettssitzung am 18. Oktober 1935," Berlin, 15 October 1935, p. 4, BA R5/2541; Dorpmüller to Eltz-Rübenach, "Finanzielle Lage der Reichsbahn," 41 Kmbp (1935) 121, Berlin, 1 October 1935, BA R5/2541.

59. Dorpmüller to Eltz-Rübenach and Lammers, 41 Kmbp (1935), Berlin, 17 October 1935, Eilt sehr!, BA R005/022541.

60. Eltz-Rübenach to Dorpmüller, Berlin, 15 October 1935, BA R5/2541; DRG, HV, "Verhandlungen mit der Reichsregierung über die finanzielle Lage der Reichsbahn im Jahre 1935," 41 Kmbp (1935) 121, Berlin, 8 January 1936, BA R5/2541; DRG, Drucksache Nr. 896, DRG, VR, Minutes, 27 November 1935, pp. 7–9, BA R2/23093; DRG, VR, Arbeitsausschuß, Minutes, 26 November 1935, pp. 5–6, BA R2/23105; Rk. 9859, Berlin, 26 November 1935, BA R43 II/187b, f. 141; DRG, VR, Minutes, 29 January 1936, p. 8, BA R2/23093; DRG, VR, Arbeitsausschuß, Minutes, 10 December 1935, p. 2, BA R2/31651; DRG, *Geschäftsbericht 1935*, 6, 21.

61. DRG, VR, Arbeitsausschuß, Minutes, 10 December 1935, p. 11, BA R2/31651.

62. DRG, VR, Minutes, 29 January 1936, p. 21, BA R2/23093; DRG, VR, Minutes, 7 October 1936, p. 7, BA R2/23093; Schnellbrief, Eltz-Rübenach to Schacht, "Reichsbahngütertarife," E 12. Nr. 8597, Berlin, 30 December 1935, BA R43 II/187b, ff. 167–68; Koenigs to Treibe, "Tariferhöhung," Berlin, 24 December 1935, BAC R005/600alt; Dorpmüller, "Tariferhöhung," Sofort, 14 Tgar 5037, Berlin, 3 January 1936, BAC R005/600alt; Pressestelle des RVM, "Reichs- und Preussischer Verkehrsminister Frhr. v. Eltz-Rübenach über 'Gütertarif der Reichsbahn' auf dem Presse-Empfang am 3. Januar 1936," BA R5/2541.

63. DRB, BR, Minutes, 6 October 1937, p. 16, BA R2/313652.

64. Leibbrand and Domsch, *Organisation und Durchführung des Betriebsdienstes und Verkehrsdienstes bei der Deutschen Reichsbahn*, 40, 43; DRG, *Wirtschaftsführung*, 54; Spiess, "Liste B (35. Fortsetzung) über die angeordnete Ausnahmetarife, die im Rahmen des Vierjahresplans in der Zeit vom 1. Oktober bis 31. Januar 1940 eingeführt worden sind," BAC R005/17 Ha, f. 80.

65. DRB, *Geschäftsbericht 1938*, p. 42.

66. "Verteilung der hauptsächlichsten Ausnahmetarifklauseln auf die einzelnen Tarife," 20 March 1939, BAC R005/17 Ha.

67. DRG, VR, Minutes, 29 January 1936, p. 4, BA R2/23093.

68. USSBS, *German Transportation*, 74–75; Otto Wehde-Textor, "Dokumentarische Darstellung der deutschen Eisenbahnen im Zweiten Weltkrieg. Teil IV. Der Verkehr," 1957, pp. 43–44, BA R5 Anh II/11.

69. DRG, *Geschäftsbericht 1938*, 152, also in "Rückblick auf das Jahr 1938," *ZVME* 79 (12 January 1939): 33. In contrast, in 1913 3.9 percent, at the end of 1921 12.8 percent, and in

1926 9.1 percent of freight cars were unserviceable in need of repairs. Von Ritter, "Rückblick auf das Jahr 1921," *ZVD* 62 (5 January 1922): 5; Dombrowski, *Wirkungen*, 110.

70. Fülling, "Leistungen der Deutschen Reichsbahn im letzten Weltkriege. Bereich Generalbetriebsleitung Süd," p. 36, BA R5 Anh I/28.

71. Kleinmann to various offices, Anlage 4 to 10 Vwb 107, Berlin, 3 August 1939, p. 2, BA R2/23108; Rohde, briefing, 26 July 1939, Anlage 4 to 10 Vwb 107, Berlin, 3 August 1939, p. 2, BA R2/23108.

72. DRG, *Geschäftsbericht 1928*, 34; DRG, *Die Deutsche Reichsbahn im Geschäftsjahr 1931*, 317; DRG, *Statistische Angaben 1934*, 261; DRG, "Übersicht über Anforderung, Stellung und nicht rechzeitige Stellung an Güterwagen im Bereich der Deutschen Reichsbahn in den Jahren 1925-1936," Tafel 6, Tafel 7, BA R005/293 Ha; DRB, *Statistische Angaben 1938*, 293.

73. DRB, BR, Minutes, 6 October 1937, pp. 17-18, 20, BA R2/23092.

74. DRB, HWA, "Jahresbericht 1937," 3353 Vwbr, Berlin, 9 June 1938, pp. 5-7, BA R005/020629.

75. Paul Sommerlatte, "Verkehrsspitzen und verkehrliche Massnahmen zu ihrer Bewältigung," *Die Reichsbahn* 13 (15 December 1937): 1107.

76. On the coal emergency, see Carroll, *Design for Total War*, 177; Boberach, *Meldungen aus dem Reich*, 2:176-77, 190-91; Gillingham, *Industry and Politics in the Third Reich*, 58-60.

77. DRB, BR, Minutes, 28 September 1938, pp. 16, 24, 26, 29, BA R2/31652.

78. DRB, "Die katastrophale Wagenlage und Ihre Gründe," 30 Fef 67, Berlin, 10 November 1938, pp. 2-5, BAC R005/021957; DRB, BR, Minutes, 8 March 1939, pp. 17-18, 20-21, BA R2/23092; Max Leibbrand, "Leistungen des Reichsbahnbetriebs," *VW* 33 (29 March 1939): 141-42. See also "Rückblick auf das Jahr 1938," *ZVME* 79 (5 January 1939): 18-19, and Wehde-Textor, "Leistungen," 5.

79. DRB, HWA, "Jahresbericht 1938," 3353 Vwbr, Berlin, 19 June 1939, pp. 5-6, BAC R005/020629.

80. Dorpmüller to Hitler, Berlin, 30 December 1938, BA R43 II/183a, f. 90.

81. Leibbrand, "Leistungen des Reichsbahnbetriebs," *VW* 33 (29 March 1939): 143.

82. Werner Kehl, "Investitionen und Finanzen," *ZVME* 79 (25 May 1939): 429. See also Hans-Erich Volkmann, "Die NS-Wirtschaft in Vorbereitung des Krieges," in Deist, *Das Deutsche Reich und der Zweite Weltkrieg*, 1:366; Kreidler, *Eisenbahnen im Machtbereich*, 31-32, 36-37; Wehde-Textor, "Leistungen," 10.

83. The Hitler government's efforts to control prices began when Carl Goerdeler was appointed price commissioner on 5 November 1934. He accomplished little due to his small staff and limited powers. His mandate expired in mid-1935. On 29 October 1938, the Reich government promulgated an ordinance creating a new office of price commissioner, placed under Josef Wagner, and imposing a price freeze, effective retroactively from 18 October 1936. Efforts to control wages began in late November 1936, culminating in an ordinance for the supervision of wages on 22 June 1938. This measure was ineffective. See Boelcke, *Deutsche Wirtschaft*, 132-33, and Deist, *Das Deutsche Reich und der Zweite Weltkrieg*, 293-98.

84. DRB, BR, Minutes, 28 September 1938, pp. 30-31, BA R2/31652. On the confusion that prevailed in Nazi economic war planning, see Herbst, *Der Totaler Krieg und die Ordnung der Wirtschaft*, 58, 92, 99; Barkai, *Das Wirtschaftssystem des Nationalsozialismus*, 15, 25; Turner, *Hitler: Memoirs of a Confidant*, 141; Deist, *Das Deutsche Reich und der Zweite Weltkrieg*, 1:185-87; Mierzejewski, "Irrationality and the Dismal Science," 36.

85. "Die katastrophale Wagenlage und ihre Gründe," 30 Fef 67, Berlin, 10 November 1938, p. 5, BAC R005/021957. See also DRB, *Geschäftsbericht 1938*, 69.

86. "Die katastrophale Wagenlage und ihre Gründe," 30 Fef 67, Berlin, 10 November 1938,

p. 2, BAC R005/021957; Funk to Dorpmüller, II Bg 20246/39 II. g, Geheim, Berlin, 31 January 1939, Anlage, p. 5, BA R41/174, f. 24.

87. Minutes of transportation discussion, Anlage 5 zu 10 Vwb 107, Berlin, 3 August 1939, p. 7, BA R2/23108.

88. Kleinmann, "Vermerk," 10 Vwb 107, and Anlage 5 zu 10 Vwb 107, Berlin, 3 August 1939, pp. 1, 5, BA R2/23108.

C. Finances, Raw Materials, and Manpower

1. Seeckt to Kriegsministerium, Reichswehrministerium, "Entmilitärisierung der Eisenbahn-Abteilung des Großen Generalstabes," Nr. 11182 E.A., Berlin, 9 August 1919, pp. 3-4, BA R43 I/973, ff. 149-49. See also Baur, "Entmilitärisierung der E.A. und Linien-Kommandanturen," Berlin, 3 September 1919, GStA, Rep. 93E/119, ff. 38-45.

2. Bell to Preussischer Minister der öffentlichen Arbeiten, "Übernahme von Offizieren in den Eisenbahndienst," Weimar, 15 August 1919, GStA, Rep. 93E/119, f. 34.

3. (RVM), "Niederschrift . . . ," zu 233/19, Berlin, 15 September 1919, GStA, Rep. 93E/119, ff. 65-67.

4. Bell to Preussischer Minister der öffentlichen Arbeiten, "Entmilitärisierung der Eisenbahnabteilungen des Grossen Generalstabs und der Linienkommandanturen," E I 3 Nr. 475, Berlin, 28 January 1920, GStA, Rep. 93E/119, f. 156.

5. Oppermann, (Halm), "Heerestransportkommission," E. IV. 42. M. 1, Berlin, 1 May 1924, BAMA II H 735.

6. Reichswehrminister to Reichsarchiv, Nr. 512, 4. 22T. 7IIa, 20 April 1922, BAMA II H 735; Groener, Seeckt, "Einrichtung einer Heerestransportkommission," Nr. E. I. 12. Nr. 337/21, p. 1, BAMA II H 731, f. 63.

7. Von Donat, "Aktenvermerk über die Besprechung der neuen Anweisung für die Grundplan vom 11.3.1931 in Braunschweig," BAMA H12/162; Kumbier, "Grundlagen für die Benutzbarkeit der Eisenbahnen," 21 G/Bm Be 1, Berlin, 26 January 1928, pp. 1, 4, BAMA H12/161.

8. T.1.IV, Berlin, 1 March 1930, BAMA II H 537, f. 368.

9. Poincaré to German Ambassador, Paris, 25 May 1922, BAMA II H 750, ff. 50-59; Hoesch to Briand, A 2538, Paris, 17 July 1929, BAMA II H 750, ff. 66-67.

10. Stieler to RBD Osten, "Abstimmung des Militärbedarfszugfahrplans," S.E. IV. 42. Nr. 23, Geheim, Berlin, 24 April 1923, BAMA H12/545; RVM, "Niederschrift über die in Braunschweig am 7. und 8. Februar 1924 abgehaltene Besprechung mit den Bahnbevollmächtigten, den technischen und militärischen Mitgliedern der Linienkommissionen über eisenbahntechnischen Angelegenheiten," E IV 42 Nr. 1312/24, Berlin, 12 March 1924, pp. 3-5, BAMA II H 537, ff. 160-61.

11. T7, Gr. II, "Tätigkeitsbericht für die Zeit vom 1.7.24-31.12.24," Nr. 274/25g, 25 May 1925, pp. 1-2, BAMA II H 735.

12. [T7], Gruppe II, "Tätigkeitsbericht für die Zeit vom 1.1.25-30.6.25," pp. 1-2, 9, BAMA II H 735.

13. Oppermann to Bahnbevollmächtigten except in demilitarized zone, 21 Nr. 2, persönlich, Berlin, 16 May 1925, p. 1, BAMA II H 550.

14. [T7], Gruppe II, "Tätigkeitsbericht, 1.7.-31.12.25," pp. 7-8, BAMA II H 735.

15. "Ergebnis der HTK-Sitzung am 3. April 1928," 17 April 1928, p. 6, BAMA II H 537, f. 322.

16. "Anmeldung der Transport-Offiziere 1.-7. Division zur Verbesserung der Leistungsfähigkeit der Eisenbahnen aus strategischen Rücksichten," [1928], BAMA II H 570/1.

17. "T.O.-Besprechung auf der Transport-Übungsreise 1932," pp. 1-2, BAMA II H 537, ff. 418-20.
18. "Vereinbarung," Se II.24 Nr. 204, Geheim, Berlin, 17 September 1929, BAMA II H 750, ff. 63-64; HTK to DRG, HV, "Kunstbauten in der Entmilitarisierten Zone," Nr. 5/27 geh, Berlin, 29 January 1927, BAMA II H 750, f. 60.
19. Dorpmüller, "Ziviler Luftschutz (Reichsluftschutz)," Vertraulich, 21 Bmvl 32, Berlin, 31 July 1931, BAC R005/020438.
20. Kumbier to RBD'en, "Planverbindungen für den Ferngüterverkehr," 21 G/Bm Bef 10, Geheim, Berlin, 29 July 1931, BAMA II H 545; Kilp to divisions, "Planverbindungen für den Ferngüterverkehr," 21 G/Bm Bef 10, Geheim, Berlin, 19 October 1931, Beilage a, BAMA II H/545; DRG, HV to divisions, "Anweisung für die Berechnung der Streckenhöchstleistungen," 21 G/Bm Bef 12, Geheim, Berlin, 18 July 1932, BA R5 Anh II/8.
21. Eltz-Rübenach to Chef Heeresorganisations-Abteilung (T 2), "Abwehr von Spionage und Verrat," W 6 geh 159/33, Geheim, Berlin, 21 November 1933, BA R5/28, f. 12; Blomberg, "Ausführungsbestimmungen für die Abwehr von Spionage und Verrat," Abw. Nr. 496/33 III L g K, Berlin, 3 November 1933, pp. 2-3, BA R5/28, ff. 9-10.
22. Wi/IF 5.335, NA T-77, R 73, FR 795031.
23. Rohde, *Wehrmachttransportwesen*, 106.
24. Blomberg, "Organisation des Transportwesens der Wehrmacht im Frieden," Nr. 2416/35g 5. Abt. Genstb. d. H. (IV), Geheim, Berlin, 11 October 1935, BAMA II H 743/1.OKW; "Organisation des Transportwesens der Wehrmacht im Frieden," Az. 43a 10. 5. Abt. (Ivf) Gen. St. d. H. Nr. 370/39g, Berlin, 31 January 1939, p. 2, BAMA H12/147.1.
25. Thomas to OKH, "Neuregelung der Zusammenarbeit mit der Reichsbahn," W.A. Nr. 937/35g J. W. Wi. (IIId), Berlin, 6 June 1935, NA T-77, R 73, FR 795013-14. Also in IfZ MA 206.
26. Dorpmüller, "Organisation der Landesverteidigung in den Eisenbahnabteilungen," 2 Ogh, Berlin, 19 May 1939, BAC R005/564alt.
27. Adam, "Arbeitsplan für das Reichsverkehrsministerium," T.A. Nr. 319/33 g. Kdos. T 2 IIIA, Berlin, 26 April 1933, NA T-77, R 73, FR 794914-23.
28. [Transchef], "Schlussbesprechung, Transport-Übungsreise 1933," Nr. 175/33 g. Kdos. T 1 IV IV, 21 April 1933, BAMA II H 595.
29. Reichsverteidigungsminister to DRG, HV, "Sicherstellung der Erfüllung der militärischen Anforderungen an die Reichsbahn im Bedarfsfalle," 1520/34 g. Kdos. T 1 IV (I), Berlin, 9 June 1934, BAMA H12/56.3.
30. Transportoffizier 3. Division to Militärisches Mitglied HTK, "Eisenbahnbauten," Nr. 31/34 geh, Berlin, 14 March 1934, BAMA H12/163.
31. Heinrich Schmeyer, Cologne, 16 September 1953, pp. 1-3, BA R5 Anh I/49.
32. "Ergebnis der Besprechung zwischen Eisenbahntechnischem Mitglied und Militärtechnischem Mitglied am 4.4.1935 in Frankfurt über weitere Verwendung des Dorpmüller-Fonds bezüglich Arbeitsgebiete von III," BAMA II H 750, f. 39; Lüttge, "Mittel für die eisenbahnmilitärische Aufgaben der Landesverteidigung," L 21 G/Bmbst 60, Geheim, Berlin, 2 October 1934, BAMA II H 750, f. 2; IIIa, "Ausbau des Eisenbahnnetzes von 1935-1939," Geheim, 4 December 1940, p. 1, BAMA H12/84.
33. Ref. O, Nr. 1185/33, geh Kdos. T1IV, 20 July 1933, BAMA II H 520/2.
34. Militärisches Mitglied HTK to Eisenbahntechnisches Mitglied HTK, "Winterbauprogramm der Deutschen Reichsbahn-Gesellschaft," Nr. 1203/33 geh. T 1 IV (III), Berlin, 8 December 1933, BAMA II H 520/2.
35. IIIa, "Ausbau des Eisenbahnnetzes von 1935-1939," Geheim, 4 December 1940, p. 2, BAMA H12/84; Kopper, "Modernität oder Scheinmodernität nationalsozialistischer Herrschaft. Das Beispiel der Verkehrspolitik," 3.

36. IIIa, "Ausbau des Eisenbahnnetzes von 1935-1939," Geheim, 4 December 1940, p. 2, BAMA H12/84; LIVb to DRG, HV, BAMA II H 750, f. 159; Ebeling to Militärisches Mitglied, Transportkommission für Eisenbahnen, "Ausbau des Eisenbahnnetzes; Mittelbereitstellung," L Gk/Bmkm 5, Berlin, 20 May 1936, BAMA II H 750, ff. 160-61.

37. Militärisches Mitglied, TK E, "Ausbau des Eisenbahnnetzes," Az. 43s 12 Gen St d H 5 Abt. (IIIa) 1892/36 g. Kdos., Berlin, 29 August 1936, BAMA H12/186; Schüler, *Logistik im Rußlandfeldzug*, 67.

38. Overy's contention that Hitler planned to launch a major war of conquest between 1943 and 1944 is based on an incorrect reading of the documents, especially the Hoßbach Memorandum. For a discussion of this issue, see Weinberg, *A World at Arms*, 29, and Mierzejewski, "Irrationality and the Dismal Science," 35-48.

39. IIIa, "Ausbau des Eisenbahnnetzes von 1935-1939," Geheim, 4 December 1940, pp. 4-5, BAMA H12/84; "Sofortprogramm zur Vorbereitung kriegsmässiger Manöver," 1938, BAMA H12/186.

40. OKH, 5. Abt., "Ausbau-Osten," Nr. 4058/38, geh. Kdos, 7 October 1938, BAMA H12/186.

41. OKH to OKW/W Stb, "Regelung der Bauwirtschaft," Az. 100 10. 5. Abt. (Ivf) Gen. St. d. H. Nr. 478.39, Berlin, 9 February 1939, BAMA H12/114.6, ff. 30-33.

42. "Ausbau-Ostgrenze," Nr. 2392/39 g Kdos., 30 March 1939, BAMA H12/186; "Beschleunigte Ausbau der Ostgrenze," Nr. 2620/39, g. Kdos., 4 May 1939, BAMA H12/186.

43. "Niederschrift über eine Sitzung des Ausschusses der Reichsregierung für Arbeitsbeschaffung," 9 February 1933, pp. 2, 12, BA R43 II/536, ff. 21, 31. Also in *ARK Kab Hitler*, vol. 1, doc. no. 19, pp. 59-60. See also Dorpmüller to Reichskommissar für Arbeitsbeschaffung, "40 Kfb. 331," Berlin, 10 March 1933, p. 1, BA R43 II/536, f. 54.

44. Dorpmüller to Eltz-Rübenach, "Zusätzliches Arbeitsbeschaffungsprogramm der Reichsbahn," 42 Kfb X 45, 14 June 1933, Anlage, pp. 6-7, BA R43 II/536, ff. 270-71; "Vermerk," Rk. 8016, Berlin, 27 June 1933, IfZ, Fa 199/12, f. 154, also in BA R43 II/536; Eltz-Rübenach to Lammers, "Zusätzliches Arbeitsbeschaffungsprogramm der Deutschen Reichsbahn-Gesellschaft," E. 13. Nr. 5715, Berlin, 23 June 1933, BA R43 II/536, ff. 283-84, also in BA R5/2511 and AA R28725, ff. 326-28; RVM to DRG, HV, RFM, RWM, RAM, Lammers, Reichsbank, "Zusätzliches Arbeitsbeschaffungsprogramm der Reichsbahn," E. 13. Nr. 5747, Berlin, 24 June 1933, BA R5/2511; Eltz-Rübenach to DRG, HV, E. 13. 5749, Berlin, 29 June 1933, p. 1, BA R43 II/536, f. 296, also in BA R5/2511.

45. DRG, VR, Minutes, 4 July 1933, pp. 9-10, Anlage 2, p. 1; BA R2/23091; DRG, VR, Arbeitsausschuß, Minutes, 3 July 1934, pp. 4-5, BA R2/23092; DRG, VR, Minutes, 9 May 1934, p. 5, BA R2/23092; Dorpmüller to RAM, "Arbeitsvorrat aus dem Arbeitbeschaffungsprogramm," 42 Kfb X 54, Berlin, 1 December 1933, BA R5/2511; Abt. IV to Abt. A (Ref 6), "Arbeitsbeschaffungsmassnahmen der Reichsbahn," Berlin, 21 November 1933, p. 2, BA R5/2511.

46. Dorpmüller to RAM, 42 Kfb X[62], Berlin, 20 September 1934, BA R2/18701; RZR to DRG, HV, "Bezahlung mit Wechseln," 0164 Kf, Berlin, 18 December 1934, BA R5/2515.

47. Dorpmüller, "Für den Vortrag beim Führer und Reichskanzler," 1 November 1935, BA R5/2541; DRG, HV, "Die wirtschaftliche Lage der Reichsbahn," Drucksache Nr. 863, 14-15 May 1935, pp. 16-17, BA R5/2540, DRG, HV to RFM, "Sonder-Arbeitsbeschaffungsprogramme der Deutschen Reichsbahn," 41 Kfb X 57, Berlin, 18 October 1934, BA R2/18701; RFM, "Die Arbeitsbeschaffungsmassnahmen der Reichsregierung 1932 bis 1935," Ar 4024 f - 5I, Berlin, 1937, pp. 54-55, BA R2/18701; Wilhelm Kleinmann, "Die Reichsbahn und die deutsche Wirtschaft," *Die Reichsbahn* 10 (21 November 1934): 1171.

48. DRG, VR, Minutes, 28 November 1934, p. 5, BA R2/23092.

49. Eltz-Rübenach to Dorpmüller, E. 13. Nr. 3492, 17 May 1935, BA R5/2540.

50. DRG, VR, Arbeitsausschuß, Minutes, 26 March 1935, pp. 3-4, BA R2/23092; DRG, VR, Minutes, 27 March 1935, pp. 2-3, 5, BA R2/23092.
51. DRG, HV, "Die wirtschaftliche Lage der Reichsbahn," Drucksache Nr. 863, 14-15 May 1935, p. 17, BA R5/2540; "Auszug aus der Aufzeichnung über die Sitzung des *Arbeitsausschusses* des Verwaltungsrats der Deutschen Reichsbahn-Gesellschaft am 2. Juli 1935," p. 2, BA R2/3879, f. 198; Dorpmüller to RWM, "Umschuldung der 6%igen Schatzanweisungen von 1930," 40 Kfb XXXI, Berlin, 19 July 1935, BA R2/3879, ff. 173-74; Reichsbank, *Verwaltungsbericht der Reichsbank für das Jahr 1935* (Berlin, 10 March 1936), 15, BA RD51/3-1935; DRG, *Geschäftsbericht 1935*, 89.
52. Dorpmüller to Reichsbank-Direktorium, "Finanzlage der Reichsbahn," 42 Kfb 419, Berlin, 17 August 1935, pp. 8-9, BA R5/2541.
53. Reichsbank-Direktorium to DRG, "Finanzlage der Reichsbahn," Nr. II 13171, Berlin, 30 August 1935, BA R2/23105.
54. RFM, "Bemerkungen zum Voranschlag der Deutschen Reichsbahn für das Geschäftsjahr 1936," no date, p. 1, BA R2/23105; [DRG], "860 Mio RBG-Wechsel," Berlin, 24 October 1935, BA R5/2541. For further evidence that Schacht was barring the DRG from the credit market, see DRG, VR, Minutes, 25 September 1935, pp. 8, 14, BA R2/23092.
55. DRG, VR, Minutes, 19 September 1933, p. 5, BA R2/23091.
56. DRG, VR, Minutes, 28 November 1933, p. 3, BA R2/23091.
57. DRG, VR, Arbeitsausschuß, Minutes, pp. 5, 7, BA R2/23092; RFM (no title, no date), BAP 21.01/B 10212, ff. 19-20.
58. DRG, VR, Arbeitsausschuß, Minutes, 10 December 1935, pp. 4-5, 9, BA R2/31651; DRG, *Geschäftsbericht 1936*, 7, 17; Prang, "Vermerk: Besprechung mit der Reichsbank wegen Aufnahme einer 500 Mio Anleihe," 40, Berlin, 16 December 1935, BA R2/3879, ff. 253-54; RFM to Reichsbank-Direktorium, Entwurf, Su 3602-50I, Berlin, 30 December 1935, BA R2/3879, f. 255; Reichsbank, *Verwaltungsbericht der Reichsbank für das Jahr 1935* (Berlin, 10 March 1936), 15, BA RD51/3-1935; Reichsbank, *Verwaltungsbericht der Reichsbank für das Jahr 1936* (Berlin, 5 March 1937), 13, BA RD51/3-1936; Volkswirtschaftliche und Statistische Abteilung der Reichsbank, "Wer hat die 4½% Schatzanweisungen der Deutschen Reichsbahn-Gesellschaft gezeichnet?," Berlin, 29 February 1936, pp. 1, 4, 9, BAP 25.01/6638, ff. 4, 7, 11.
59. The Reichsbahn arranged for small credits from foreign banks as late as June 1939. The Reich government also relieved it of responsibility of repaying the debts that it incurred to build railways in the east as part of the Osthilfe program. See the correspondence on these matters in BA R5/2502, 2529, 2580, 2581, 2806. For a list of foreign credits as of the end of 1936, see "Valutaverpflichtungen," Berlin, 4 January 1937, BA NL171/277.
60. DRB, BR, Minutes, 9 May 1939, pp. 6-7, BA R2/31652.
61. Schüler, *Logistik im Rußlandfeldzug*, 65.
62. DRG, VR, Minutes, 28 March 1933, p. 3, BA R2/23091.
63. DRG, VR, Arbeitsausschuß, Minutes, 16 September 1933, p. 3, BA R2/23091.
64. DRG, HV, 40 Kfb 383, 384, Sofort, Berlin, 23 March 1935, BA R5/2498.
65. DRB, VR, Minutes, 3 July 1935, pp. 27-28, BA R2/23092; DRG, HV to RVM, "Elektrisierung der Strecke Nürnberg-Halle-Leipzig," L 3 G/Bmeb 19, Berlin, 25 September 1935, pp. 1-2, BAMA H12/56.3.
66. Pressestelle des Reichs- und Preussischen Verkehrsministeriums, "Reichs- und Preussischer Verkehrsminister Frhr. v. Eltz-Rübenach über Gütertarif der Reichsbahn," 3 January 1936, Berlin, pp. 4-5, BA R5/2541; Fritz Busch, "Probleme der Finanzwirtschaft der Deutschen Reichsbahn," *Die Reichsbahn* 12 (23-30 December 1936): 1124-25.
67. DRB, R 40, "Schuldenstand der DRB seit 1924," BA R5/2589.
68. Ibid. See also Generalkasse der Deutschen Reichsbahn, "Geschäftsjahr 1938, Nachweis

der Bestands beim Schuldenkonto langfristig," Anlage 14 to Hauptabschluß 1938, 41 Kmüg 229, 31 December 1938, Berlin, 9 May 1939, BA R5/2581.

69. Dorpmüller, "Für den Vortrag beim Führer und Reichskanzler," 1 November 1935, p. 5, BA R5/2541; Eltz-Rübenach to Lammers, E. 13. 6628, Berlin, 4 October 1935, p. 3, AA R28725, f. 16.

70. DRB, BR, Minutes, 6 July 1937, p. 3, BA R2/31652; Alfred Prang, "Gegenwartsfragen der Finanzpolitik der Deutschen Reichsbahn," Die Reichsbahn 14 (6 April 1938): 351. See also "Rückblick auf das Jahr 1938," ZVME 79 (5 January 1939): 2; Fritz Busch, "Die Wirtschaftslage der Deutschen Reichsbahn in ihrer Entwicklung seit 1933," VW 32 (20 April 1938): 172.

71. Abt. IV, "Lasten, die das Reich für die Reichsbahn trägt," Berlin, 5 August 1935, BA R5/2541.

72. Dorpmüller to RFM, "Abrede über die Handhabung des Reichsbahngesetzes," 2 Arb 11, Berlin, 8 June 1939, p. 2, BAP 21.01/B 9505, also in BA R2/3893, ff. 6-7; Dorpmüller to Lammers, "Begründung zum Gesetz über die Deutsche Reichsbahn," 2 Arb 4, Berlin, 18 June 1937, p. 11, BA R43 II/185, f. 98; Berger to Bayrhoffer, Ve 1401-84V, Berlin, 4 December 1939, BA R2/3893; Reichsschuldenverwaltung to RFM, "Eisenbahnschulden," 6053-1, Berlin, 11 April 1940, pp. 6, 11, BA R2/3893, ff. 13, 18; RFM, Su 3656-3-Gen. B, Berlin, 20 April 1940, BA R2/3893, f. 19. The Reich's service of this debt was regulated by "Gesetz über die Ablösung öffentlicher Schulden. Vom 16. Juli 1925," RGBl, I, Nr. 32, 17 July 1925, 137-44. The debt stemming from the creation of the Reichsbahn was considered an old property-based loan (Altbesitzanleihe) because it was contracted before 1 July 1920. On 14 May 1935 the Reich ceased payment to the states on debts deriving from the Verreichlichung of 1920. However, payment to private holders of debt connected with this transaction continued, leading to the arrangement discussed in the narrative. See "Verordnung zur Abwicklung des Staatsvertrags über den Übergang der Staatseisenbahnen auf das Reich. Vom 14. Mai 1935," RGBl, II, Nr. 28, p. 437.

73. DRG, "Der Güterwagenpark der Deutschen Reichsbahn," Drucksache Nr. 963, 26-27 January 1937, p. 10, BAC R005/021755; Wilhelm Kleinmann, "Die Bedeutung der Verkehrsmittel im deutschen Wirtschaftsleben," VW 33 (22 March 1939): 132.

74. "Zusätzliches Fahrzeugprogramm 1934," Berlin, 13 January 1934, BAC R005/020064, f. 63; DRG, Voranschlag für das Geschäftsjahr 1934 (Berlin, November 1933), 24, BAC R005/020063.

75. DRG, "Zusätzliches Fahrzeugprogramm 1934," Drucksache Nr. 781, 27-28 March 1934, BAC R005/020066, f. 86; DRG, VR, Minutes, 9 May 1934, pp. 4-5, BA R2/23091.

76. DRG, HV, "Bauzüge—Einschränkungen der Verwendung von Personenwagen," 81 Io 452, Berlin, 11 June 1935, BAC R005/020923; Dorpmüller, "Ausmusterung von Personenwagen," 30 Fuv 115, Berlin, 9 March 1935, p. 1, BAC R005/88 Ha.

77. DRG, HV, "Vorläufiges Programm für die Beschaffung von Fahrzeugen 1936," Berlin, 2 June 1935, BAC R005/022549. See also DRG, "Untersuchung der Abteilung II über das Fahrzeugbeschaffungsprogramm 1936," 21 Bbzp 125, Berlin, April 1935, pp. 2, 8-9, BA R5/2541.

78. DRG, HV, "Fahrzeugprogramm 1936 für die Bestellung von neuen Fahrzeugen für das 1. Halbjahr 1936," Berlin, 28 June 1935, p. 2, BAC R005/022549; DRG, HV, "Fahrzeugbeschaffungsprogramm 1936," Drucksache Nr. 876, 2 3 July 1935, BAC R005/022549.

79. DRG, HV, "Ergebnis der Besprechung über Einschränkungsmassnahmen in der Fahrzeugbeschaffung am 16.8.1935," 41 Kmbp (1935), Berlin, 16 August 1935, BA R5/2594; Dorpmüller, "Fahrzeugbestellung," 73a Fewav 211, Berlin, 27 August 1935, BAC R005/184 Ha.

80. Abt. III and VII to Dorpmüller, "Material für die am 18. Oktober 1935 stattfindende Kabinettssitzung," Berlin, 16 October 1935, p. 1 and Anlage 3, BAC R005/022549. In the board meeting of 25 September 1935, Dorpmüller said that the Reichsbahn had sufficient freight cars.

He pointed out that 30,000 to 40,000 idle cars only increased maintenance costs. DRG, VR, 25 September 1935, p. 12, BA R2/23092.

81. DRG, HV, "Niederschrift über eine gemeinsame Besprechung der Abteilungen III und VI der HV über ein zusätzliches Fahrzeugprogramm 1936 am 5. Dezember 1935," 30.73a, Fef 45, pp. 2-3, BAC, R005/022549; Leibbrand to Abt. III, 21 Bbzp 162, Berlin, 2 January 1936, p. 1, BAC R005/022549; Abt. III, "Ergebnis der Besprechung der Abteilung III mit den Abteilungen I, II und IV am 7. Januar 1936 über die Beschaffung von Fahrzeugen aus dem Zusatzprogramm 1936 vom 30 Mill RM," pp. 1-2, BAC R005/022549; DRG, HV, "Vermerk, Beschaffung von Wagen aller Art zu Lasten des Fahrzeugbeschaffungsprogramms 1936 (Zusatzprogramm)," 30 Fewav 231, Berlin, 1 February 1936, pp. 1-2, BAC R005/022549; "Anlage zur Anmeldung der für 1936 zu beschaffenden Güterwagen," 30.73e Füv 100, 2 November 1935, pp. 1-2, BA R5/2541.

82. Abt. II to A 6, Berlin, 29 June 1936, p. 1, BAC R005/022549.

83. Bergmann to RZE, RZM, RZA Munich, "Beschaffung von Wagen aller Art zu Lasten des Fahrzeugprogrammes 1937 (1. Hälfte)," 30 Fewav 241, Berlin, 2 July 1936, pp. 3-5, BAC 43.04/334; DRB, "Fahrzeugprogramm 1. Hälfte 1937," 30 June 1936, Drucksache Nr. 932, BAC R005/022549.

84. Dorpmüller, "Vermerk. Fahrzeugbeschaffung zu Lasten des Fahrzeugprogramms 1937 (II)," 30 Fef 52, Berlin, 13 October 1936, BAC R005/022549.

85. Dorpmüller, "Stellung und Bedeutung der Deutschen Reichsbahn im Deutschen Reiche, insbesondere ihre Beteiligung an der Durchführung des Vierjahresplans und der Wehrhaftmachung Deutschlands," p. 4, BAC R005/10 Ha, f. 36.

86. Eltz-Rübenach to Göring, S 1 gen 3286, Berlin, 20 November 1936, BA R2/22980.

87. DRG, VR, Minutes, 25 November 1936, pp. 6, 10, BA R2/23093.

88. DRG, HV, "Der Güterwagenpark der Deutschen Reichsbahn," 27 January 1937, pp. 8, 10, 27-29, BAC R005/186 Ha; DRG, VR, Minutes, 27 January 1937, pp. 15-17, BA R2/23093.

89. DRB, VR, Minutes, 6 July 1937, pp. 5-7, BA R2/31652.

90. Dorpmüller, "Fahrzeugbeschaffungsprogramm 1938," 30 Fef 56, Berlin, 27 July 1937, pp. 1, 3, BAC R005/022549.

91. DRB, BR, Minutes, 6 October 1937, pp. 13, 15, BA R2/31652.

92. Bergmann to Abt. II, "Fahrzeugprogramm für mehrere Jahre," 30 Fef 58, Berlin, 1 December 1937, BA R5/2090; Bergmann to Abt. I, II, IV, Gruppe L, "Übersicht II, Bedarfsprogramm für neue Fahrzeuge für die 4 Jahre 1939 bis 1942, getrennt nach Fahrzeuggruppen, Stückzahlen und Gesamtkosten, Fall A," 30 Fef 58, Berlin, 4 January 1938, BA R5/2123.

93. Bergmann, "Anmeldung zur Beschaffung neuer Fahrzeuge für das Jahr 1939," 30 Feh 98, Berlin, 10 January 1938, p. 1, BAC R005/021920, also in BAC R005/181 Ha and BA R5/2123.

94. Kühne, to Abt II, "Sofortprogramm 1939," 30 Fef 60, Berlin, 19 January 1938, BA R5/2090.

95. Bergmann, "Sofortprogramm für Fahrzeuge," 30 Fef 62, Berlin, 24 February 1938, p. 1, BAC R005/181 Ha, also in BA R5/3158; Bergmann, "Sofortprogramm für Fahrzeuge," 30 Fef 60, Berlin, 25 February 1938, pp. 2-3, BAC R005/181 Ha; "Übersicht über das Sofortprogramm 1939 für neue Fahrzeuge," 30 Fef 60, Berlin, 31 January 1938, BA R5/2123, Minutes of Meeting, Berlin, 1 February 1938, pp. 1, 3-4, 9, BAC R005/252 Ha.

96. Dorpmüller to Ministers, "Vorträge beim Führer über Bauprojekte," 2 Arbr, Berlin, 31 January 1938, BA R43 II/1146, f. 28.

97. Bergmann, "Fahrzeugprogramm 1939," 30 Fef 63, Berlin, 20 April 1938, BAC R005/181 Ha; Bergmann, "Fahrzeugprogramm 1939," 30 Fef 65, Berlin, 11 May 1938, BAC R005/022203, also in BAC R005/181 Ha.

98. Bergmann, "Beschaffungsplan für mehrere Jahre," Berlin, 16 July 1938, BAC R005/

021957; Bergmann, "Beschaffungsplan für mehrere Jahre," 30 Fef 66, Berlin, 29 July 1938, BA R5/2090.

99. Ebeling to Abt. E III, "Fahrzeugbeschaffungsplan für mehrere Jahre," L 3g/Bmfa 4 (O), Berlin, 19 August 1938, BAC R005/021957; DRB, Ref 34, 31 to Ref 30, "Beschaffungsprogramm für mehrere Jahre," 31 Felz 85, Berlin, 2 September 1938, BAC R005/021957; Treibe to Abt. III, "Fahrzeugbeschaffungsplan für mehrere Jahre," 10 Vwah 34, Berlin, 8 September 1938, BAC R005/021957.

100. DRB, BR, Minutes, 28 September 1938, p. 32, BA R2/31652.

101. Kausche, "Die Deutschen Eisenbahnen im zweiten Weltkrieg," p. 19, BA R5 Anh I/8.

102. "Conference at the General Field Marshall Goering's at 1000, 14 October 1938," Top Secret, United States, *Nazi Conspiracy and Aggression*, 3:901, 1301-PS; Schüler, *Logistik im Rußlandfeldzug*, 72.

103. "Material for the Conference with Göring on 25 November 1938 (General Keitel, Brig. Gen. Thomas)," 27 October 1938, WiWi Id, United States, *Nazi Conspiracy and Aggression*, 3:904-6.

104. Gercke, "Sitzung des Reichsverteidigungsrats vom 18.11.38," p. 1, BA R5 Anh I/129; "Address by Göring at a meeting of the Reich Defense Council, 18 November 1938 . . . ," IMT, *TMWC*, vol. 32, pp. 414-15, 3575-PS.

105. DRB, BR, Minutes, 7 December 1938, pp. 10, 12, BA R2/31652; DRB, "Vermerk," 31 Fab 4, Berlin, 8 December 1938, p. 1, BA R5/2170; Ref 23, Baüg 42, "Übersicht I. Bedarfsprogramm für neue Fahrzeuge für die 4 Jahre 1940 bis 1943 getrennt nach Fahrzeuggattungen und Stückzahlen," BA R5/2090; "Übersicht über die für die Jahre 1940-1943 zur Beschaffung vorgesehenen Fahrzeuge aller Art (Vierjahresprogramm) . . . ," Anlage zu 30 Fef 70, Berlin, 27 December 1938, BAC R005/021957.

106. Bergmann, "Stahlkontingent und Vierjahresbeschaffungsplan Besprechung bei Herrn Staatssekretär am 22.12.1938," Berlin, 22 December 1938, BAC R005/021957; Lindermayer to Ref 30, 31, 32, 33, "Stahlkontingent," 37 Y Stwe, Berlin, 23 December 1938, BAC R005/021957; Bergmann, "Vermerk," 30 Fef 70, Berlin, 10 January 1939, BAC R005/021957; Bergmann, "Anmeldung zur Beschaffung neuer Fahrzeuge für das Jahr 1940," 30 Feh 100, Berlin, 17 January 1939, BAC R005/181 Ha, also in BA R5/2123; Bergmann to Abt. I, II, IIA, III, L, "Vierjahresplan 1940-1943," 30 Fef 71, Berlin, 25 January 1939, BA R5/2123, also in BAC R005/021957; "Übersicht I Fahrzeugprogramm für das Jahr 1940 unter Zugrundelegung einer Stahlmenge von 445,200 t," Anlage zu 30 Fef 71, Berlin, January 1939, BA R5/2123; Bergmann, "Auszug aus der Direktorenbesprechung am 2. Februar 1939," Berlin, 2 February 1939, BAC R005/021957.

107. DRB, BR, Minutes, 8 March 1939, p. 10, BA R2/31652; DRB, 30 Fef 76, Eilt sehr, Berlin, 20 February 1939, BAC R005/021957; Bergmann, "Beschaffung von Fahrzeugen nach dem Vierjahresplan 1940-1943," 30 Fef 72, Berlin, 21 February 1939, p. 1, BAC R005/021957; Bergmann to RZA, "Beschaffung von Dampflokomotiven zu Lasten der Fahrzeugprogramme 1940-1943," 31 Felz 100, Berlin, 22 February 1939, BAC R005/022402; Kleinmann, "Überbrückungsaufträge zu Lasten des Fahrzeugprogramms 1939," 30 Fef 73, Berlin, 7 March 1939, p. 1, BAC R005/021957.

108. Bergmann to Generalbevollmächtigter für die Deutsche Kriegswirtschaft, "Stahlkontingent 4. Vierteljahr 1939," 37 Y Stwe, Berlin, 21 June 1939, BAC R005/103 Ha; Bergmann, "Vermerk," 37 Y Stwe 143, Berlin, 31 August 1939, BAC R005/022166; Ackermann, "Übersicht," 30 Fewst 35, Berlin, 23 December 1939, BAC R005/186/2 Ha; DRB, BR, Minutes, 3 July 1939, p. 16, BA R2/31652.

109. DRB, Ref 37, "Stahlkontingent (Monatliche Entwicklung seit 1937)," BAC 43.04/42, f. 11.

110. DRG, HV, "Überblick über Bestand, Achsenzahlen, Eigengewicht, Ladegewichte und

Sitzplätze der vollspürigen Personen- und Gepäckwagen," Anlage 1 zu 30 Füs 34, 23 October 1929, BAC R005/652alt, ff. 90–92; DRG, "Umstellung des Reisezugdienstes auf Triebwagen," Drucksache Nr. 795, 29 May 1934, pp. 25–26, BA R2/23092; DRG, HV, *Hundert Jahre Deutsche Eisenbahnen*, 368.

111. DRG, HV, "Übersicht über Bestand, Achsenzahlen, Eigengewichte, Ladegewichte der vollspürigen Güter- und Bahndienstwagen," Anlage 2 zu 30 Füs 34, 23 October 1929, BAC R005/682alt, ff. 94–96; DRG, HV, "Ersparungsmaßnahmen bei der Reichsbahn," RER, 1 May 1939, Anlage 4, p. 46, BA RD97/5; DRG, HV, "Der Güterwagenpark der Deutschen Reichsbahn," 27 January 1937, Tafel 2, 3, BAC R005/186/2 Ha; DRB, *Statistische Angaben 1938*, 315; DRB, HV, "Vermerk," 39 Fef 132, Sofort, Berlin, 2 November 1942, Anlage 2, BAC R005/022469.

112. Schwerin von Krosigk, "Vierjahresplan: Bau einer Eisenbahn von Minden zum Wiehengebirge zur Beförderung von Eisenerzen," F 6906^k-6V, Berlin, 28 July 1937, BA R2/22990; DRB, "Bahnbau Salzgitter-Gebhardshagen," 85 I Hannover 54, Berlin, 23 December 1937, BAC R005 020723; RBD Hanover to DRB, "Neubaustrecke (Hannover)-Langenhagen-Celle," 47 Obktr 2 Io 207, Hanover, 19 February 1938, BAC R005/020935, f. 231; RBD Hanover to DRB, "Erweiterung des Bahnhofs Salzgitter," 53 Tnb 30 Nbe/(Salzgitter), Hanover, 6 April 1938, BAC R005/020723; Lamp, "Aktenvermerk über eine Besprechung am 17. August 1939 in Breitenbachsaal," 85 I Hannover (Br), Berlin, 18 August 1938, BAC R005/020723; Lamp to Leibbrand, "Bahnbau Salzgitter-Calbecht," 854 I Hannover (Br) 35, Berlin, 1 November 1938, BAC R005/020723; Wehner, *Deutsche Eisenbahnen*, 151; Werner Fischer, "Bauwesen," Minden, March 1957, p. 5, BA R5 Anh II/46.

113. Ernst Schröder, "Die zentralen Beschaffungen und Konstruktionen im 2. Weltkriege," p. 3, BA R5 Anh I/14; Werner Fischer, "Bauwesen," Minden, March 1957, p. 13, BA R5 Anh II/46.

114. DRG, VR, Protocol, Teil IV, 3 May 1933, p. 3, BAC R005/020059, f. 387.

115. Ludwig Röbe, "Das Arbeitbeschaffungsprogramm der Reichsbahn," *Die Reichsbahn* 9 (12 July 1933): 607.

116. Background paper for Dorpmüller's November 1935 briefing of Hitler, BA R5/2541. This file also appears as Abt. IIA, 16 October 1935, in BAC R005/020927, ff. 281, 283; IIA 81 to Dorpmüller, 81 Io, Berlin, 21 October 1935, BAC R005/020927, f. 281.

117. DRB, BR, Minutes, 6 July 1937, pp. 3–4, BA R2/31652; DRB, BR, Minutes, 6 October 1937, p. 2, BA R2/331652; DRB, BR, Minutes, 1 December 1937, pp. 4, 8, BA R2/23092; Kiefer, "Voranschlag der Deutschen Reichsbahn für das Geschäftsjahr 1938," Ve 1410^{37}-15V, Berlin, 2 December 1937, p. 7, BA R2/23107; DRB to RBD'en, RZÄ, "Unterhaltung und Erneuerung des Oberbaues im Geschäftsjahr 1939," 81 Iop 1650, Berlin, 15 January 1939, pp. 2, 10–11, BAC R005/152; "Rückblick auf das Jahr 1939," *ZVME* 78 (6 January 1938): 17; "Rückblick auf das Jahr 1938," *ZVME* 79 (5 January 1939): 27; Wehner, *Deutsche Eisenbahnen*, 152.

118. DRB, BR, Minutes, 8 March 1939, p. 16, BA R2/31652.

119. DRG, VR, Minutes, 25 March 1936, pp. 7–9, BA R2/23093.

120. Kleinmann to RBD'en, RZÄ, "Personalbedarf im Technischen Dienst," 50.506 Pwhp 736, Berlin, 20 May 1937, BA R43 II/187, ff. 21–23.

121. DRG to RBD'en, "Personalbedarf im technischen Dienst," 55.501, Pol 12a/717, Eilt, Berlin, 1 June 1937, BA R43 II/187, f. 20; "Rückblick auf das Jahr 1937," *ZVME* 78 (6 January 1938): 4.

122. Kleinmann, "Beschäftigung von Beamten . . . ," Streng vertraulich, 52.501 Prval, Berlin, 25 January 1938, BAC R005/125 Ha.

123. Leibbrand to RBD'en, "Verstärkte Erfassung des Nachwuchses für den technischen Dienst," 55.506 Pol 12 a/847, Berlin, 10 March 1938, BAC R005/125 Ha.

124. RBD Berlin, "421. Heranbildung jungeren Beamtennachwuchses," *Amtsblatt*, 13 May 1938, p. 198, Archiv Rbd Berlin; "Rückblick auf das Jahr 1938," *ZVME* 79 (5 January 1939): 7.
125. "Rückblick auf das Jahr 1936," *ZVME* 77 (7 January 1937): 4, 16.
126. Kleinmann, "Entziehung von Arbeitskräften...," Sofort, 50.523 Plt, 9 July 1938, p. 1, BAC R005/148 Ha; Rief, "Die Deutsche Reichsbahn im Zweiten Weltkrieg Abschnitt Personalwesen," p. 26, BA R5 Anh I/13.
127. DRB, BR, Minutes, 3 July 1939, pp. 10-13, BA R2/31652.
128. Kleinmann, "Persönliche Vorstellung von Beamten des oberen Dienstes im Reichsverkehrsministeriums," 1P, Berlin, 30 January 1939, BAC R005/564alt.
129. Kirste, "Der Krankenstand bei des Deutschen Reichsbahn," Nur für den Dienstgebrauch, Vertraulich, 1943, p. 4, BAC R005/52 Ha.
130. For other similar assessments, see Fischer, "Bauwesen," [March 1957], p. 3, BA R5 Anh II/46; Thomas, *Wehr- und Rüstungswirtschaft*; Kausche, "Die Deutschen Eisenbahnen im zweiten Weltkrieg," p. 18, BA R5 Anh I/8; Schüler, *Logistik im Rußlandfeldzug*, 66, 638.
131. Kleinmann, to various offices, "Vermerk," Sofort, 10 Vwb 107, Berlin, 3 August 1939, and Anlage 2 zu 10 Vwb 107, Berlin, 3 August 1939, pp. 1-3, BA R2/23108.

Chapter 3. The Reichsbahn in War and Holocaust, 1939-1945

A. The Years of Conquest, 1939-1940

1. Those seeking more detailed information on the Reichsbahn's involvement with German military operations should consult Kreidler, *Eisenbahnen im Machtbereich*; Pottgiesser, *Die Deutsche Reichsbahn im Ostfeldzug: 1939-1944*; Rohde, *Wehrmachttransportwesen*; Schüler, *Logistik im Rußlandfeldzug*; and Teske, *Silbernen Spiegel*.
2. Rohde, Anlage 4 zu 10 Vwb 107, 3 August 1939, p. 4, BA R2/23108.
3. "Beschleunigter Ausbau an der Ostgrenze," BAMA H12/186; Ebeling to Mineis L beim Transchef, "Aufmarschvorbereitungen," L2 g/Bamü 57, Berlin, 10 December 1940, BAMA H12/84; Scharf, *Eisenbahnen zwischen Oder und Weichsel*, 222.
4. Doerr, 13 June 1942, p. 1, BAMA N29/1, f. 9; Rohde, *Wehrmachttransportwesen*, 95-96.
5. Kausche, "Die Deutsche Eisenbahnen im zweiten Weltkrieg (Allgemeiner und historischer Teil)," pp. 17-18, 35, BA R5 Anh I/8.
6. Ebeling to Mineis L beim Transportchef, "Aufmarschvorbereitungen," L2 g/Bamü 57, Berlin, 10 December 1940, pp. 1-3, BAMA H12/84; Philipp Wohlschläger, "Beitragsmaterial zur Ausarbeitung: die Leistungen der Eisenbahnen im 2. Weltkrieg," p. 19, BA R5 Anh II/35.
7. Fritz Fülling, "Leistungen der Deutschen Reichsbahn im letzten Weltkriege, Bereich der Generalbetriebsleitung Süd," p. 40, BA R5 Anh I/28; Rohde, *Wehrmachttransportwesen*, 77-91; Teske, *Silbernen Spiegel*, 105. The numbers of trains given by Teske are low.
8. DRB, *Geschäftsbericht 1939*, 11, 17.
9. Dorpmüller to Frank, "Eisenbahnen im Generalgouvernement," 2 Arl (P), Berlin, 6 November 1939, BA R2/23810; "Verordnungsblatt des Generalgouverneurs für die besetzten polnischen Gebiete," Nr. 5, pp. 1-2, BA R2/23810; RVM, "Vermerk zur Verordnung über die Verwaltung des Eisenbahnwesens im Generalgouvernement. Vom 9. November 1939," Anlage 2 zu 2 Arl (P), 20 November 1939, BA R5 Anh II/67; Reinhardt, "Vorbemerkung, Verordnung über die Verwaltung des Eisenbahnwesens im Generalgouvernement," Ve 6040 Pol - 4V, Berlin, 25 November 1939, BA R2/23810; Adolf Gerteis, "5 Jahre Ostbahn," Bielefeld, November 1949, pp. 6-8, BA R5 Anh I/120.
10. Parteibuch Adolf Gerteis, BDC; "Die neuen Präsidenten der Reichsbahndirektionen

Posen und der Generaldirektion der Ostbahn in Krakau," *Die Reichsbahn* 15 (26 June–3 July 1940): 286–87; Pischel, "Generaldirektion der Ostbahn," 8.

11. Gerteis, "5 Jahre Ostbahn," p. 62.

12. Prang to Abt. IIA, 42 Km 86, Berlin, 15 December 1939, BAC R005/148 Ha.

13. Dorpmüller to Lammers, "Protektoratsbahnen und Ostbahnen," 2 Arl (B), Berlin, 14 February 1941, BA R43 I/637a, ff. 3–5.

14. See the correspondence in BA R43 II/637a, ff. 3–5, 7–8, 20, 22–27, 30–31, 33–34, and Dorpmüller, "Einheitlichkeit im Verkehrswesen. Ausbau des Eisenbahnnetzes," A Arl (B), Berlin, 19 March 1941, BAC R005/148 Ha; Dorpmüller to Emrich, 2 Arl (B), Berlin, 7 August 1941, BAMA H12/101.1, f. 53; Anklageschrift Ganzenmüller, 8Js 430/67, pp. 98–99, ZSL VI (420) 107 AR-Z 80/61; Gerteis, "5 Jahre Ostbahn," p. 9.

15. Telegrammbrief, Osthoff to divisions, "Personalverhältnisse im besetzten Gebiet," Pwhp, Berlin, 8 September 1939, BA R2/23810.

16. Ebeling to Transchef, "Besetzung der Dienstposten bei der Ostbahn," L2 Bmo 42, Berlin, 5 January 1940, BAMA H12/101.2, ff. 92–93.

17. Ebeling to Transchef, "Beschäftigung von Polen," L2 Bmpw 56, Berlin, 9 April 1940, BAMA H12/144.

18. Ebeling to Transchef, "Besetzung der Dienstposten bei der Ostbahn . . . ," L2 Bmpw 56, Berlin, 11 April 1940, pp. 1–2, BAMA H12/101.2, ff. 23–24.

19. Transchef to Ebeling, "Beschäftigung von Polen," Pl. Abt. Az 10 k 10/8 (Ivf) Nr. 2756.40, H Qu OKH, 20 May 1940, BAMA H12/144.

20. Franz Bruckauf, "Die Deutsche Reichsbahn im zweiten Weltkrieg, Abschnitt Personalwesen," p. 63, BA R5 Anh I/13; Gerteis, "5 Jahre Ostbahn," pp. 29–30.

21. Gerteis, "5 Jahre Ostbahn," pp. 64–65.

22. Gedob, "Vermerk über die augenblickliche Verpflegungslage der polnischen Bediensteten und die vorgesehenen Maßnahmen zur Umstellung der Verpflegung," 3H P15 Usv, Krakau, 7 October 1940, BAMA H12/63.2, ff. 444–46; Transchef, "Zusatzverpflegung für polnische Arbeiter-Otto-Programm," Nr. 03738.40, 11 October 1940, BAMA H12/631, f. 98.

23. Bergmann, "Inbetriebnahme der in Polen erbeuteten Fahrzeuge," 34 Fa 181, Berlin, 17 October 1939, BA R5/3662.

24. Gerteis, "5 Jahre Ostbahn," p. 24.

25. Gerteis to RVM, III 21 Bla M2, Cracow, 28 August 1940, p. 1, BA R5/3662; Gerteis to DRB, "Lokomotivebestand und -ausbesserung," (Pr) III 21 M1 Bla, Cracow, p. 1, BA R5/3662.

26. Gerteis to DRB, "Austausch von Lokomotiven—Unterhaltung und Betrieb," VI 63/21 W4 Ful, Cracow, 11 October 1940, BA R5/3662. Anlage 1 of this document indicates that the Ostbahn had 1,076 locomotives at the time of writing. The DRB Mechanical Section in Berlin, however, thought that it had more, 1,291 instead of the 1,075 that it had been allocated. See Abt. III to Abt. IVA, 34 Bla, Berlin, 29 November 1940, BA R5/3662.

27. Gerteis, "5 Jahre Ostbahn," pp. 48, 50.

28. Ibid., p. 19.

29. Gedob to DRB, "Verteilung der ehemaligen polnischen Schnellzuglok der Gattung Pt 31," Pr III 21 Bla, Cracow, 3 June 1940, BA R3662.

30. Gerteis, "5 Jahre Ostbahn," p. 17.

31. Fernschreiben, Etra Ost 231 to Transchef, 3 January 1941, BAMA H16/63,1, f. 7.

32. Leibbrand, "Niederschrift über die Besprechung unter dem Vorsits des Transchefs am 6. Januar 1941 . . . ," 21g/Baü 30, Geheim, Berlin, 11 January 1941, p. 3, BAMA H12/63,1.

33. Ebeling to Transchef, "Otto-Bauvorhaben in Generalgouvernement," L5 g Rs/Bmbst 449, Geheime Reichssache, Berlin, 9 January 1941, BAMA H12/63,1, f. 89.

34. Pischel, "Generaldirektion der Ostbahn," 22.

35. Kreidler, *Eisenbahnen im Machtbereich*, 55.

36. Hans Münzer, "Deutsche Eisenbahner im besetzten Frankreich," *ZVME* 81 (20 February 1941): 105-6.

37. Wohlschläger, "Bericht über den Einsatz der WVD Brüssel," p. 89, BA R5 Anh I/93; Rohde, *Wehrmachttransportwesen*, 240-41.

38. Eisenbahn-Betriebsdirektion Brüssel to all Maschinenämter, "Beschäftigung des deutschen Lokpersonals," 21, Brussels, 13 August 1940, BA R5 Anh I/97; WVD Brussels, "Niederschrift über die Besprechung mit den Vertretern der SNCF am 29.10.1940, 9.30 Uhr im Gebäude der WVD Brüssel," 30, Brussels, 30 October 1940, p. 1, BA R124/25; Spalding to all offices, "Rückgabe der Betriebsführung im Bereich der EBD Lille an die SNCF ausnahmlich der Küstenzone," 31 B 3, Lille, 1 November 1940, p. 1, BA R124/106; Poenicke, "Überwachung des Betriebsdienstes und Aufgaben der Überwachungsstellen," Hirson, 19 November 1940, BA R124/25; Kreidler, *Eisenbahnen im Machtbereich*, 58-60.

39. Wohlschläger, "Bericht über den Einsatz der WVD Brüssel," p. 87, BA R5 Anh I/93; Spalding, "Vorläufige Dienstanweisung für die Überwachungstätigkeit bei der Oberzugleitung und den Zugleitungen der EBD Lille," January 1941, pp. 1-2, BA R124/100; Spalding, "Vorläufige Dienstanweisung für die Überwachungsdienststellen der EBD Lille," 31 January 1941, pp. 1-2, BA R124/103; Münzer, "Vorläufige Dienstanweisung für die Überwachungszentralstellen der WVD Paris, Abt. Eisenbahnen," no date, pp. 1-2, BA R5 Anh I/113.

40. Milward, *New Order*, 199; Kehrl, *Krisenmanager*, 189-97; Kroener, Müller, and Umbreit, *Das Deutsche Reich und der Zweite Weltkrieg*, 5.1:221-26; Thomas, *Wehr- und Rüstungswirtschaft*, 213-23; Mollin, *Montankonzerne und "Drittes Reich,"* 220-75.

41. Telegramm, Bergmann to GBL West, etc., "Abgabe von belgischen und französischen Lokomotiven und Güterwagen," 31 Fkl 1010, Berlin, 9 August 1940, p. 1, BAC R005/57 Ha; Kühne to divisions, "Werkstätten. Erhaltung der Güterwagen; französische und belgische Leihgüterwagen," 38 Wbü 131, Berlin, 30 August 1940, p. 1, BAC, R005/57 Ha; Kreidler, *Eisenbahnen im Machtbereich*, 61.

42. Milward, *New Order*, 199.

43. Roth, "Abnahmedienst in den besetzten Westgebieten Belgien und Frankreich," pp. 1-2, BA R5 Anh I/100.

44. Wohlschläger, "Bericht über den Einsatz der WVD Brüssel," p. 66, BA R5 Anh I/93.

45. EBD Lille, "Erfahrungen aus dem Dezernat 7," pp. 1-2, BA R5 Anh I/100.

46. Doerr, 13 January 1942, p. 2, BAMA N29/1, f. 10.

47. Dorpmüller, "Umwandlung der Oberbetriebsleitungen in Generalbetriebsleitungen," Eilt, 2 Ogd (Obl) 2, Berlin, 24 February 1940, BAC R005/564alt; Bahndiensttelegramm, Emrich to divisions, (February 1940), BA R5 Anh II/52; Günter Kausche, "Die Deutschen Eisenbahnen im zweiten Weltkrieg (Allgemeiner und historischer Teil)," p. 29, BA R5 Anh I/8.

48. Dorpmüller to divisions, HWA, 2 Ogd (Ogl) 3, Eilt, Berlin, 29 March 1940, BA R5 Anh II/67; Kausche, "Die Deutschen Eisenbahnen im zweiten Weltkrieg," p. 27; Kreidler, *Eisenbahnen im Machtbereich*, 202-3.

49. Kausche, "Die Deutschen Eisenbahnen im zweiten Weltkrieg," pp. 27-28.

50. Dorpmüller, "Verkehrsorganisation. Einsetzung von Verkehrsleitungen," 19 Val 2, Berlin, 18 September 1940, BAC R005/564alt; Dorpmuller, "Verkehrsorganisation. Einsetzung von Verkehrsleitungen. Zweiter Durchführungserlaß," 19 Val 3, Berlin, 17 October 1940, BA R5/3649; Kausche, "Die Deutschen Eisenbahnen im zweiten Weltkrieg," p. 28; Kreidler, *Eisenbahnen im Machtbereich*, 204.

51. Göring, V.P. 12101/2/1, Berlin, 2 August 1940, BAMA H12/131.

52. Dorpmüller, "Ziviler Luftschutz (Reichsluftschutz)," Vertraulich, 21 Bmvl 32, 31 July 1931, BAC R005/020438; HV to divisions, "Reichsluftschutzbund," 52.504 Pa, Berlin, 24 Sep-

tember 1934, BA R5 Anh II/31; Hampe, *Ziviler Luftschutz*, 86-89, 314-15, 488-92; Kreidler, *Eisenbahnen im Machtbereich*, 17, 222, 251-52; USSBS, *German Transportation*, 52.

53. Leibbrand to divisions, "Ordnung auf den Bahnhöfen; hier: Nachprüfung des Beleuchtungsstandes vom Standpunkt des Betriebsdienstes," 21 Baü 71, Berlin, 5 February 1940, BA R5 Anh II/31.

54. RBD Frankfurt am Main to E-Abt., "Maßnahmen zur Bedienung des Reisezugverkehrs bei Zerstörung der Bahnanlagen durch Bombenabwurf," 31 612 Bau, Frankfurt am Main, 17 September 1941, BA R5 Anh II/31.

55. Dilli to divisions, "Betriebliche Maßnahmen bei Fliegerangriffen," 24 Bavf 400, Berlin, 14 October 1942, pp. 1-3, BA R5 Anh I/63; Ebeling to divisions, "Selbst- und Gemeinschaftshilfe bei Bombenschäden," L 4 Bmasle 401, Berlin, 15 February 1943, pp. 11-12, BA R5 Anh II/31; "Auszug aus der Niederschrift über die 29. Betriebsleiterbesprechung der Deutschen Reichsbahn am 16. und 17. März in Eisenach," BA R5/2102.

56. Dez 32, "Höchstleistungen der Ablaufberge und Bahnhöfe bei Verdunklung und ungünstige Witterung," Essen, October 1941, BA R5 Anh II/33.

57. Telegrammbrief, Emrich to divisions, Obl's, HWA, Essen, 8 February 1940, BA R5 Anh II/42.

58. Emrich, March 1940, BA R5 Anh II/42.

59. See the very informative monthly summaries of reports from the divisions for November 1940 through June 1941 in BA R2/23731 and Telegramm, RVM to Gbl's and divisions, Nr. 284, Berlin, 2 February 1942, BA R5 Anh II/44.

60. USSBS, *German Transportation*, 42; Kreidler, *Eisenbahnen im Machtbereich*, 238.

61. Telegramm, RVM to divisions, etc., "Aufhebung von Fahrpreisermäßigungen; Änderung des Schnellzugzuschlags," 15 Tpl 56, Berlin, 10 January 1940, BA R43 II/637, f. 88, also in BA R43 II/189, ff. 31-32; Fritz Busch, "Grundzüge der Finanzpolitik der Deutschen Reichsbahn," *ZVME* 80 (25 July 1940): 376, 380; "Geschäftsbericht der Deutschen Reichsbahn," *ZVME* 81 (26 June 1941): 361.

62. Boberach, *Meldungen aus dem Reich*, 3:681; Kershaw, *Popular Opinion and Political Dissent in the Third Reich*, 281, 317. Steinert, *Hitler's War and the Germans*, 93-94, claims that Germans suffered many hardships during this period, although the grumbling that she reports seems fairly innocuous. For additional information, see USSBS, *The Effects of Strategic Bombing on German Morale*; Beck, *Under the Bombs*; Janis, *The Psychological Impact of Air Attacks*; Iklé, *The Social Impact of Bomb Destruction*; Iklé, "The Effect of War Destruction upon the Ecology of Cities."

63. HWA, "Jahresbericht 1939," 3353 Vwbr, p. 1, BAC R005/020629; DRB, *Wirtschaftsplan für das Geschäftsjahr 1942* (Berlin, November 1941), p. 39, BAC R005/12121; Sommerlatte, briefing notes, 26 July 1939, Anlage zu 10 Vwb 107, Berlin, 3 August 1939, pp. 1, 4, BA R2/23108.

64. RFM, Ve 1410-39-33V, h.v. O 13563 A1-1558, Berlin, 18 January 1940, BA R2/23108; Telegrammbrief, Leibbrand to divisions, "Güterzugbetrieb," 23 Baü 83, Berlin, BA R5 Anh II/44.

65. Kleinmann to GBLs, divisions, etc., "Kontingentierung der Verkehrsmengen in schwierigen Betriebslagen," 23 Baü 128, Berlin, 7 December 1940, BA R5 Anh I/61; Richard Couvé, "Auf jeden Wagen kommt es an!," *Die Reichsbahn* 16 (21-28 August 1940): 352; Wohlschläger, "Eisenbahnen im 2. Weltkrieg," p. 22; HWA, "Jahresbericht 1940," WD 149, p. 5, BAC R005/020629.

66. Sarter to DRB, C 81 Vgbm 3964, Essen, 3 December 1940, Anlage, "Besprechung am 20. November in Metz über die Erz-, Kohlen und Koksversorgung der Saar, Lothringen, Belgien, Luxemburg und Nordfrankreich," pp. 1-4, BA R5/3638; Wehde-Textor, "Leistungen," 14; Adolf

Sarter, "Die Verkehrsleitung der Generalbetriebsleitung West und der Gebietsverkehrsleitung West," pp. 5, 7, 10, 18, BA R5 Anh I/100.

67. Bahndiensttelegramm, DRB to Gbl Ost, divisions, 26 Baüg 61, Berlin, 22 February 1941, BA R5/2090.

68. Gauge is the railway term for the distance between the heads of the two rails. The Reichsbahn used the standard gauge of 1,435 millimeters (4 feet, 8.5 inches). The SZD used a broad gauge of 1,524 millimeters (5 feet).

69. Schnellbrief, Treibe to Auswärtigesamt, etc., "Güterverkehr mit der UdSSR," 10 Vagl (UdSSR) 90, Berlin, 15 January 1941, BAC R005/2/6 Ha.

70. Sussdorf, GBW 6/6785/39, Berlin, 21 September 1939, BAMA H12/114.6, f. 7; GB Bau, "Sicherstellung des Waggonbedarfs für vordringliche Bauten," Nr. GB 191/39g, Berlin, 25 October 1939, BAMA H2/114.6, ff. 51–52; Telegrammbrief, Treibe, "Wagenstellung; Reihenfolge der Zuteilung auf die Bestellungen," 10 Vwb 219, Berlin, 13 February 1940, BAC R005/020624, also in BA R5 Anh II/44; Treibe to divisions, "Richtlinien für die Wagenverteilung," 10 Vwb 281, Berlin, 1 June 1940, BA R5/819; Telegrammbrief, Treibe to divisions, etc., 10 Vwb 544, Berlin, 3 July 1941, BA R5/2090; DRB, BR, Minutes, 25 March 1941, Geheim, p. 13, BA R2/31653; Kreidler, *Eisenbahnen im Machtbereich*, 119, 338.

71. Telegrammbrief, Bergmann, "Ausnutzung der Güterwagen," 30 Fkwg 564, Berlin, 9 March 1940, BAC R005/89 Ha, also in BA R5/2090; Treibe, "Ausnutzung der Güterwagen," 10 Vwh 22, Berlin, 11 December 1939, BA R5/2090; Bergmann, "Ausnutzung der Güterwagen," 30 Fkwg 573, Berlin, 29 November 1940, BA R5/2090; Abt. II to Abt. III, "Ausnutzung der Güterwagen," 23 Baüg 41, Berlin, 7 December 1940, BA R5/2090; USSBS, Dilli Interrogation, p. 4, NA RG 243, 200(a)127; Ernst Schröder, "Die zentralen Beschaffungen und Konstruktionen im 2. Weltkriege," p. 11, BA R5 Anh I/14; "Geschäftsbericht der Deutschen Reichsbahn über das Jahr 1940," *ZVME* 81 (26 June 1941): 362.

72. DRB, BR, Minutes, 30 January 1940, Geheim, p. 7, BA R2/31653; DRB, BR, Minutes, 25 March 1941, Geheim, p. 18, BA R2/31653.

73. DRB, BR, Minutes, 1 October 1940, Geheim, p. 9, BA R2/31653; DRB, BR, Minutes, 27 May 1941, Geheim, p. 32, BA R2/31653.

74. DRB, "Niederschrift 26. Betriebsleiterbesprechung der Deutschen Reichsbahn am 3. September 1940 in Leipzig," 23 Babh 33, Berlin, 21 September 1940, pp. 4, 9, BA R5 Anh I/61.

75. DRB, BR, Minutes, 30 January 1940, Geheim, p. 9, BA R2/31653; "Vortrag des Herrn Ministerialdirektor Treibe über die Verkehrslage," Anlage b to Minutes of 78. Präsidentenkonferenz, 4 June 1940, p. 1, BA R5 Anh I/69; DRB, 23 Baüg, Berlin, 2 December 1940, BA R5/2090; Otto Wehde-Textor, "Dokumentarische Darstellung der deutschen Eisenbahnen im Zweiten Weltkrieg. Teil IV. Der Verkehr," p. 36, BA R5 Anh II/11.

76. Calculated from raw data in DRB, *Statistische Monatsberichte*, 1937–40, BA RD98/72.

77. To save labor, the Reichsbahn stopped calculating the volume of tariff ton-kilometers delivered in 1939. It still recorded the number of operating ton-kilometers generated.

78. Wirtschaftsgruppe Bergbau to RVM, Abt. II, "Vermeidung von Förderausfälle im Steinkohlenbergbau infolge Wagenmangels," Na 31, Berlin, 7 December 1939, p. 1, BA R7/627, f. 20. Sarter, "GBL West," p. 16. Coal car placings were calculated in ten-ton units. Most coal cars could carry twenty tons.

79. Dorpmüller to Gauleiter Stürtz, "Wagenstellung für Kohlen," 10 Vwb (Kohlen), Sofort, Berlin, 28 December 1939, BAC R005/020624, also in BA R7/627, f. 16.

80. Jacobshagen, "Niederschrift über die Besprechung am 9.2.1940 . . . ," pp. 2–4, BA R5 Anh II/42.

81. Sarter, "GBL West," p. 9.

82. Telegramm, Dorpmüller to divisions, etc., Nr. 2534, Berlin, 19 February 1940, BA R5

Anh II/42; Eigen to Reichsbeauftragte für Kohle, "Wagenstellung für Kohle," II Bg 209/89[40], Berlin, 6 March 1940, BA R7/627, ff. 31-32.

83. "Zur Kohlenlage Anfang September 1940," Geheim, BA R41/174, f. 280.

84. Kleinmann, "Vermerk über das Ergebnis der Sitzung über die Einsetzung von Kohlen- und Erztransportausschüssen am 8. Juni 1940," Anlage 1 zu 10 Vgbm (Kohlen) 56, 12 June 1940, BA R5/3649; Kurt Friebe, "Verkehrsleitung," VW 34 (20-27 November 1940): 311, 313; "Vortrag des Herrn Ministerialdirektor Treibe über die Verkehrslage," Anlage b to Minutes of 78. Präsidentenkonferenz, 4 June 1940, p. 1, BA R5 Anh I/69.

85. DRB, BR, Minutes, Geheim, 26 November 1940, pp. 14-15, BA R2/31653; Dorpmüller, "Verkehrsaufbau im Osten," VW 34 (14-21 February 1940): 51; Philipp Mangold, "Beitrag zur Eisenbahngeschichte des Zweiten Weltkrigs hier: Aufgaben der Betriebsabteilung der General- betriebsleitung Ost, Berlin," p. 3, BA R5 Anh I/26.

86. DRB, BR, Minutes, Geheim, 27 May 1941, p. 35, BA R2/31653.

87. USSBS, "Carloads Coal (all types)," NA RG 243, 200(a)143.

88. Computed from raw data obtained from RVK, *Statistischer Bericht Nr. 13*, Berlin, February 1945, pp. 18-19, BBA 15/1103.

B. The Attack on the Soviet Union and the Winter Crisis, 1941-1942

1. For a detailed discussion of the involvement of the Reichsbahn in Operation Barbarossa, see Schüler, *Logistik im Rußlandfeldzug*.

2. Ebeling to Abt. I, II, IV, "Otto-Bauvorhaben," L 5g Rs/Bmbst 370 (O), Berlin, 9 December 1941, BA R5/2084.

3. Transchef to Ebeling, "Ausbau von Strecken im Generalgouvernement," Pl. Abt. Az. 43s - 30 (IIIa) Nr. 593/40g. Kdos, 25 April 1940, BAMA H12/83, f. 40.

4. Planungsabteilung, Transchef, "Aktennotiz über die Besprechung im Reichsverkehrs- ministerium am 19.7.1940," Az. 43s - 43 (IIIa) Nr. 2218/40 geh. Kdos., 25 July 1940, p. 1, BAMA H12/63.2.

5. OKW, "Ausbau des Eisenbahn- und Strassennetzes im Osten Stichwort: Otto," Az.: 43s - 30 Chef Trspw./Pl. Abt. (IIIa/S) Nr. 2220/40g Kdos, Berlin, 25 July 1940, BAMA H12/63.2, ff. 132-33; Transchef, Chefgruppe C2 to Planungsabteilung IIIA, "Otto-Programm, Führer- bauten," Az. C 2 allg. Nr. 0870/40g. Kdos., 13 September 1940, BAMA H12/63.2, f. 243; OKW to RAM, "Ausbau des Eisenbahn- und Strassennetzes im Osten (Programm Otto)," Az.: 43s - 30 Chef Trspw./Pl. Abt. (IIIa/S), Nr. 2237/40 geh. Kdos, 27 July 1940, BA R41/193, f. 1; Pischel, "Generaldirektion der Ostbahn," 25-26, 38.

6. Ebeling to Transchef, "Bauprogramm Otto," L5 g Rs/Bmbst 417, Berlin, 25 November 1940, BAMA H12/63/.2, f. 466; Elchlepp, "Bemerkungen des Herrn Transportchefs anläßlich seiner Ost-Reise," 5 October 1940, BAMA H12/63,1; "Aktennotiz über die Besichtigungsreise des Herrn Transportchefs im General-Gouvernement in der Zeit vom 28. Sept. bis 1. Okt. 40," p. 1, BAMA H12/67.2; Transchef to Thomas, "Otto-Programm und Lok- und Wagenpro- gramm," Pl. Abt. Az.: 10 o 14 e (Ivf) Nr. 5538/40 geh, 11 September (1940), BAMA H12/63.2, f. 240.

7. Kreidler, *Eisenbahnen im Machtbereich*, 117-18.

8. Frank Tagebuch, 20 September 1940, p. 3, IfZ, MA-120/2, f. 885; Haeseler to Transchef, "Bauvorhaben im Generalgouvernement," L5 g Rs/Bmbst 406, Berlin, 18 November 1940, BAMA H12/63,1; Kreidler, *Eisenbahnen im Machtbereich*, 52, 115, 118.

9. Köhle to Gruppe L, "Bauvorhaben Otto," 30 Bbv L9 g Rs/Bmbst, Krakau, 3 January 1941, p. 4, BAMA H12/63/1 (a), f. 49.

10. Glasl to Ebeling, "Erreichung von Höchstleistungen im Ottoprogramm," Az. 43s - 30 Pl. Abt. (IIIa) Nr. 7234/40 geh, (Berlin), 16 January 1941, BAMA H12/63,1a, f. 9.

11. RAM to OKW, "Einsatz von Kriegsgefangenen bei dem Bauprogramm 'Otto,' " Va 5230/4468/40 g. Rs., Berlin, 17 August 1940, BA R41/193, f. 2; Glasl to OKW, "Einsatz von Kriegsgefangenen beim Otto-Programm," Pl. Abt. Az. 43s - 30 (IIIa), Nr. 5014/40 geh, Berlin, 18 August 1940, BA R41/193, f. 7; Transchef to OKW, "Kriegsgefangene für das Otto-Programm," Pl. Abt. Az. O 14/O (IIIS)IIIa, Nr. 5298/40 geh, Berlin, 30 August 1940, BA R41/193, f. 14; Transchef to RAM, "Einsatz von Kriegsgefangenen bzw. Juden für Otto-Programm," Pl. Abt. Az. 43s - 30 (IIIa) Nr. 6812/40 geh, Berlin, 26 November 1940, BAMA H12/63,1, f. 81; RAM, "Sicherstellung des Kräftebedarf für das Programm 'Otto,' " Va 5431/7562/40g, Berlin, 11 December 1940, BA R41/193, f. 50; Letsch to Transchef, "Sicherstellung des Kräftebedarfs für 'Otto'-Programm," Va Nr. 5431/230/41g, Berlin, 21 January 1941, BAMA H12/63,1, f. 82; RAM to Taege, "Dringlichkeit des Otto-Programms," Va Nr. 5230/2455/41g, Berlin, 2 April 1941, BAMA H12/67.2, f. 69.

12. Teske, *Silbernen Spiegel*, 102.

13. Zellermann, in his memorandum of 5 February 1941, indicated that 130 trains were crossing the border of the General Government from Germany daily instead of the theoretically possible 180. See Zellermann, Etra-Ost, Gruppe I, "Akten-Notiz," 230/41 geh, Litzmannstadt, 5 February 1941, p. 1, BAMA H12/63,1. See also Ebeling to Transchef, "Otto-Bauvorhaben in Generalgouvernement," L5 g Rs/Bmbst 449, Geheime Reichssache, Berlin, 9 January 1941, BAMA H12/63,1, f. 89. See also Teske, *Silbernen Spiegel*, 102.

14. Bv.T.O. Heeresgruppenkommando B to Transchef, "Besprechung am 4.2. bei Gedob in Krakau," Tgb.-Nr. 33/41 geh, H.Qu., 5 February 1941, BAMA H12/131.

15. Schüler, *Logistik im Rußlandfeldzug*, 195, 197, 203-4.

16. Ebeling to Transchef, "Weiterführung des Bauprogramms 'Otto,' " L 5 g Rs/Bmbst 417 (g), Berlin, 28 March 1941, BAMA H12/67.2, f. 77.

17. Ebeling to Transchef, "Ostbauprogramm aus besonderem Anlaß 1940 Otto-Programm," L 5 g Rs/Bmbst 417, Berlin, 16 September 1940, BAMA H12/63.2, f. 216; [Transchef], "Übersicht zur Haushaltsmeldung 1943/44," [14 November 1942], p. 1, BAMA H12/77, f. 65; Gerteis, "5 Jahre Ostbahn," pp. 53-54, BA R5 Anh I/120.

18. Teske, *Silbernen Spiegel*, 105; Kausche, "Eisenbahnen im zweiten Weltkriege," p. 61, BA R5 Anh I/8.

19. Teske, *Silbernen Spiegel*, 102.

20. Teske, who participated in this operation as a general staff officer in the army, provides statistics and a periodization that differs substantially from that provided by Pischel. Kreidler relied on Pischel for his account. Pischel enjoyed the benefit of being able to read all of the accounts listed here and documents at the Federal Military Archive in Freiburg-im-Breisgau. He was assigned to the Ostbahn during this period and later. Pischel, "Generaldirektion der Ostbahn," 38-39; Kreidler, *Eisenbahnen im Machtbereich*, 118-19; Teske, *Silbernen Spiegel*, 103-5.

21. Bv. T.O. beim H. Gr. Mitte, "Eisenbahnlage Stand 3.7.41 abends," Geheim, H. Qu. 3 July 1941, pp. 1-2, BAMA H12/94; Bv. T.O. beim H. Gr. Mitte, "Verstopfung auf der Bahn," H. Qu., 8 July 1941, p. 1, BAMA III2/94; Bv. T.O. beim H. Gr. Mitte, "Eisenbahnlage Stand 10.7 abends," H.Qu., 10 July 1941, pp. 1-2, BAMA H12/94; Bv. T.O. beim H. Gr. Mitte, "Eisenbahnlage (Nr. 6) Stand 27.7 abends," H. Qu., 27 July 1941, p. 1, BAMA H12/94.

22. Bv.T.O. beim H. Gr. Mitte, "Eisenbahnlage (Nr. 7) Stand 1.8. abends," H. Qu., 1 August 1941, p. 1, BAMA H12/94.

23. Kleinmann to Willuhn, "Verwaltung des Verkehrswesens in den neuen Ostgebieten," 2 Arl (O), Berlin, 27 June 1941, pp. 3-4, BA R6/21, ff. 91-92.

24. "Erlaß des Führers über die Verantwortung der neu besetzten Ostgebiete. Vom 17. Juli 1941," BA R6/21, ff. 123-24.

25. The HBDs are sometimes referred to as HEDs in the surviving documents. Kleinmann to Syrup, "Organisation des Verkehrswesens in den neu besetzten Ostgebieten," Geheim, Berlin, 7 July 1941, NA T-178, R-18, FR 3674107-11; Rohde, *Wehrmachttransportwesen*, 219-20; *Eisenbahnen im Machtbereich*, 211-12; Pottgiesser, *Reichsbahn im Ostfeldzug*, 26.

26. Schmidt, "Absinken der Leistung der Eisenbahn im Bereich der Heeresgruppe Süd nach dem 1. September 1941," p. 1, BAMA H12/99; Teske, *Silbernen Spiegel*, 129-30.

27. H.Gr. Süd, Abt. Ib Wi, "Zusammengefassten Tätigkeitsbericht vom 1.-15.9.1941 der Abteilung Ib Wi," 16 September 1941, BAMA H12/99.

28. Wehrmachttransportleitung Ost, "Berichterstattung über Versorgung und Betriebslage. 1.9.41-18.9.41," O.U. 17 September 1941, BAMA H12/99.

29. Wehrmachttransportleitung Ost to Transchef, "Statistik der in Betrieb befindlichen Strecken. Stand 1.11.1941," Az. 43S-Gruppe III, O.U., 3 November 1941, BAMA H12/99.

30. "Auszüge aus den Kriegstagebüchern des Wi Stabes Ost," Rep 502FC-38 (Blatt 61-70), p. 2, BA R5 Anh I/171.

31. Von Brauchitsch to Dorpmüller, Nr. 001394.41 Chef Trspw, H. Qu. OKH, 17 November 1941, BAMA H12/101.1, f. 33.

32. DRB, "Auszug aus den Lageberichten der Reichsbahndirektionen für Juli 1941," 41, Berlin, 25 August 1941, BA R2/23731.

33. Kleinmann to Göring, "Beeinträchtigung von Betrieb und Verkehr bei der Deutschen Reichsbahn infolge der Umnagelung der Strecken in den besetzten Ostgebieten," 26g/Baü 43, Berlin, 27 August 1941, pp. 1, 4, BA R5 Anh II/44; DRB, "Auszug aus den Lageberichten der Reichsbahndirektionen für August 1941," 41, Berlin, 22 September 1941, p. 1, BA R2/23731.

34. DRB, "Auszug aus den Lageberichten der Reichsbahndirektionen für September 1941," 41, Berlin, 20 September 1941, BA R2/23731.

35. Prang, "Auszug aus den Lageberichten der Reichsbahndirektionen für November 1941," 41, Berlin, 11 January 1942, BA R2/23731.

36. Telegramm, Dorpmüller to GBL's, divisions, 26 Baü 181, Berlin, 2 February 1942, BA R5/2085; DRB, "Auszug aus den Lageberichten der Reichsbahndirektionen für Januar 1942," 41, Berlin, 28 February 1942, pp. 1, 3, 5, BA R2/23731; DRB, "Auszug aus den Lageberichten der Reichsbahndirektionen für Monat Februar 1942," 41, Berlin, 14 April 1942, pp. 1, 3-7, BA R2/23731; Sarter to RVM, "Betriebs- und Verkehrslage der Generalbetriebsleitung West," Pr Aü, Essen, 9 February 1942, pp. 1, 6, BA R5/2085.

37. Gercke to Dorpmüller, 6 November 1941, pp. 1-3, BAMA H12/101.1, ff. 34-36.

38. Klein, "Vorschlag zur Klärung und Verbesserung des Arbeitsverhältnisses mit dem Eisenbahn-Pionierbaustab," Lemberg, 15 November 1941, p. 2, BAMA H12/99.

39. Dorpmüller, Gercke, "Vermerk über die Besprechung des Herrn Reichsverkehrsministers mit dem Transport-Chef in Anna am 20.11.1941," pp. 1-2, BAMA H12/101.1, f. 31.

40. Telegramm, Dorpmüller to Transchef, "Einsetzung eines Personalreferent," 39048, 5 December 1941, BAMA H12/101.1, ff. 31-32.

41. Fernschreiben, Transchef to Dorpmüller, "Einsetzung eines Personalreferenten," 13 December 1941, BAMA H12/101.1, f. 30.

42. Halder to Haustein, Königstein/Ts, 29 September 1949, p. 11, BA R5 Anh II/65.

43. Kleinmann, "Vermerk über Abteilungsleiterbesprechung am 27. November 1941," Berlin, 27 November 1941, BA R5/2084.

44. Interrogation of Wilhelm Logemann, Essen, 11 August 1971, p. 1, ZSL II 206 AR-Z 15/963, vol. 4, f. 575.

45. Leibbrand to Ref 125, Berlin, 13 March 1942, BA R5 Anh I/129.

46. Dorpmüller to GBLs, divisions, etc., "Übernahme von Eisenbahnen im besetzten Ostraum durch den Reichsverkehrsminister," 2 Arl (O), Berlin, 13 January 1942, BA R5 Anh I/127; Prang, "Abrechnung der Leistungen für die Eisenbahnen im Bereich der HBD'en (besetztes Ostraum)," 41 Kbl 101, Berlin, 10 February 1942, p. 1, BA R005/114 Ha; RVM Zweigstelle Osten to HVDs, "Geschäftsverkehr und Besprechungen zwischen den HBDen und der Gedob," MD 1.103 Oav, Warsaw, 2 April 1942, BA R5 Anh I/127; Schüler, *Logistik im Rußlandfeldzug*, 565-66.

47. Görnert to Lammers, Berlin, 19 January 1942, BA R43 II/637a, ff. 36-39; Fernschreiben, Lammers to Göring, Führer-HQ, 22 January 1942, p. 2, BA R43 II/637a, f. 44; Lammers to Dorpmüller, Rk. 1348, Führer-HQ, 30 January 1942, BA R43 II/637a, f. 80; Lammers, Rk. 1348B, Führer-HQ, 30 January 1942, GStA, Rep. 115 I c/11166; Hitler, "Erlaß des Führers über Vereinheitlichung in der Leitung des Einsatzes der Eisenbahnen des Protektorats, der besetzten niederländischen Gebiete, Belgiens und des besetzten Frankreichs für die Kriegführung," Fü. H.Q., 23 January 1942, BA R5/2085; Kreidler, *Eisenbahnen im Machtbereich*, 356-57.

48. Kleinmann, "Vermerk über den Vortrag beim Führer am 17. Januar 1942 13^{30} Uhr im Führerhauptquartier," Berlin, 19 January 1942, pp. 1-2, BA R2/22499.

49. Picker, *Hitlers Tischgespräche*, 85.

50. Halder to Haustein, Königstein/Ts, 29 September 1949, pp. 8-9, BA R5 Anh II/65.

51. Anklageschrift Ganzenmüller, pp. 188-89, ZSL VI (420) 107 AR-Z 80/61; Gehrke to Müller, Az. II 2 14 Pl Ost (II), Nr. 0281/41g, 13 January 1942, NA T-175, R-124, FR 2699480-1; Müller, "Leistungen der Eisenbahn auf den ehemaligen russischen Bahnstrecken," Berlin, 21 February 1942, NA T-175, R 124, FR 2599473-75; Müller to Dorpmüller, "Abteilungspräsident Landenberger," Warsaw, 1 March 1943, NA T-175, R 125, FR 2599483-85; Boelcke, *Deutschlands Rüstung*, 71.

52. Speer-Chronik, 1942, 19 May 1942, p. 35, BA R3/1736, f. 41; Boelcke, *Deutschlands Rüstung*, 80.

53. Boelcke, *Deutschlands Rüstung*, 87.

54. Ibid., 118.

55. Ibid., 123.

56. Speer-Chronik, 1942, 21 May 1942, p. 37, BA R3/1736, f. 43; Speer, *Inside the Third Reich*, 222-23.

57. Raw data from DRB, *Statistische Monatsberichte*, for the relevant years.

58. Vernehmung Speer, Heidelberg, 24 October 1969, p. 3, Anklageschrift Ganzenmüller, pp. 180, 241, ZSL VI (420) 107 AR-Z 80/61; StA Dü, URI 4/67 (G), (8 Js 750/67) gegen Stange, 8 Ks 1/71, Band XIX (Ganzenmüller), f. 155, StA Dü.

59. "Besprechung im Führer-Hauptquartier am 24. Mai 1942," Streng Vertraulich, 26 May 1942, BAMA RH4/v.67, ff. 1-5; Boelcke, *Deutschlands Rüstung*, 124.

60. "Sitzung beim Reichsminister Speer am 28. Mai 1942," BA R41/257.

61. Boelcke, *Deutschlands Rüstung*, 130-32. For an account from one of the railroaders who was arrested, see Hahn, *Eisenbahner in Krieg und Frieden*, 64-86.

62. Boelcke, *Deutschlands Rüstung*, 142.

63. Prang to Saemisch, Berlin, 24 December 1942, p. 2, BA NL171/182, f. 12; Affadavit Erna Kirste, 45 Js 8/62, Frankfurt am Main, 15 February 1966, p. 3, ZSL 107 (420) AR-Z 80/1962, Band III, f. 464; Boelcke, *Deutschlands Rüstung*, 469.

64. NSDAP Reichsleitung to Hauptamt für Technik, Fi/Ha 13040, Munich, 27 March 1940, BDC 1020082950 PK; Parteibuch Ganzenmüller, BDC; Personalfragebogen Ganzenmüller, BDC; Dorpmüller to Lammers, 1 HB 1, Berlin, 27 May 1942, BA R43 II/1146b, ff. 67-70; Anklageschrift Ganzenmüller, 8 Js 430/67, pp. 48-57, ZSL VI (420) 107 AR-Z 80/61; "Dr.-Ing. Albert Ganzenmüller," *Großdeutscher Verkehr* 36 (1942): 259.

65. Klessing to Gauleitung München-Oberbayern, Munich, 26 August 1940, p. 3, BDC 10200082950 PK.
66. Anklageschrift Ganzenmüller, pp. 241-42, ZSL VI (420) 107 AR-Z 80/61.
67. Anklageschrift Ganzenmüller, pp. 187, 244-45, 247-50, ZSL VI (420) 107 AR-Z 80/61.
68. Anklageschrift Ganzenmüller, pp. 231-32, ZSL VI (420) 107 AR-Z 80/61; Ulrich Meyer, "Vernehmungsniederschrift," V 4 SK 9378, Philadelphia, 3 December 1968, p. 5, ZSL 208 AR-Z 230/59, vol. 16, f. 4426.
69. Hesse, "Verfügung," 45 Js 8/62, Dortmund, 12 August 1966, ZSL 107 (420) AR-Z 80/1962, vol. III, f. 515; "Vernehmungsniederschrift, . . . Gertrud Ganzenmüller," Munich, 11 May 1966, 45 Js 8/62, p. 2, Sta Dü, 8 Ks 1/71, vol. VII, f. 42; Interrogation of Else Fritz, 45 Js 8/62, Bonn, 1 April 1966, Sta Dü 8 Ks 1/71, vol. VII, ff. 30-32; Anklageschrift Ganzenmüller, pp. 184-85, ZSL VI (420) 107 AR-Z 80/61.
70. Anklageschrift Ganzenmüller, p. 239, ZSL VI (420) 107 AR-Z 80/61; Frank, *Das Diensttagebuch des deutschen Generalgouverneurs in Polen 1939–1945*, 588.
71. VR, "Information," *Die Bundesbahn* (December 1971): 5; Parteibuch Dilli, BDC 1010067822 PK; Schwedersky, Interrogation of Dilli, UR I 4/67 (G), Frankfurt am Main, 8 May 1969, p. 3, ZSL 208 AR-Z 230/59, vol. 17, f. 4533; Speer-Chronik, 23 May 1942, p. 38, BA R3/1736, f. 44; Dilli to Uchmann, "Bericht des Ministerialdirektors a.D. Gustav Dilli," Füssen, 29 August 1967, p. 6, ZSL II 206 AR-Z 15/1963, vol. 4, f. 587.
72. Affadavit Fritz Schelp, 4 Js 8/62, Frankfurt am Main, 16 February 1966, ZSL 107 (420) AR-Z 80/1962, vol. III, ff. 467-70. Parteibuch Schelp, BDC 1160003391 PK; Schelp to Uchmann, Frankfurt am Main, pp. 2-3, ZSL II 206 15/1963, vol. 4, ff. 532-33; Anklageschrift Ganzenmüller, p. 187, ZSL VI (420) 107 AR-Z 80/61. RBD Altona was renamed RBD Hamburg in July 1937. Wechmann, "Umbenennung der Reichsbahndirektion Altona," 30 Fen 71, Berlin, 30 July 1937, BAC R005/88 Ha.
73. Kleinmann was given the comfortable post of head of the managing board of Mitropa. Leibbrand was named head of an office that prepared plans for the broad-gauge railway that Hitler intended to build to connect the conquered areas in the east with major cities in Germany after the war. Willuhn to Lammers, "Reichsverkehrsministerium," Rk. 9900B, Berlin, 10 July 1942, p. 1, BA R43 II/637a, f. 187; "In den Ruhestand getreten," *Die Reichsbahn* 18 (7-14 October 1942): 317; Mühl, *Mitropa*, 61, 71-72.
74. Kreidler, *Eisenbahnen im Machtbereich*, 207, comes to the same conclusion.
75. Ganzenmüller, "Einstellung einer Zentralverkehrsleitstelle," 19 Val 140, Berlin, 2 June 1942, BAC R005/020627; Ganzenmüller to Emrich, "Tätigkeit der Zentralverkehrsleitstelle," 10 Vwb 902, Berlin, 8 June 1942, BAC R005/020627; J.-F. Wernich, "Persönliche Erfahrungen und Erinnerungen hinsichtlich der Behandlung wehrwirtschaftliche Transporte im 2. Weltkrieg," pp. 2-3, BA Kl. Erw. 496, ff. 14-15; "Einsetzung einer Zentralverkehrsleitstelle," *Die Reichsbahn* 18 (17-24 June 1942): 214-15; Kreidler, *Eisenbahnen im Machtbereich*, 234-35; Wehde-Textor, "Leistungen," 15.
76. Speer-Chronik, 1942, 24 June 1942, p. 44, BA R3/1736, f. 51; USSBS, Speer Interrogation, 17 May 1945, p. 12, NA RG 243 40 (c) 26; Gerhard Simon, "Verkehrsausweitung, Verkehrslenkung und Transportentflechtung," 428-33; Kreidler, *Eisenbahnen im Machtbereich*, 194-95, 206.
77. Parteibuch Hassenpflug, BDC; Dorpmüller to E-Abt, "Gliederung der Eisenbahnabteilungen," 2 Oph, Berlin, 4 June 1942, BAC R005/Ha 92/1; Dorpmüller, "Organisation," 2 Oph Berlin, 5 June 1942, BAC R005/Ha 92/1.
78. Transchef to OKW/WStb, "Stahlkontingent für die Reichsbahn im Mob. Fall," Az. 10014.12(Ivf) No. 4414/39, g. Kdos, 5 September 1939, p. 1, BAMA N12/114.6, f. 2; Bergmann, "Festlegung desjenigen Teiles der noch unerledigten Aufträge auf Wagen aller Art, aus den Be-

schaffungsprogrammen bis einschliesslich 1939. Zusatz, der zu Ende geführt werden soll," 30 Fewav 301, Berlin, 17 October 1939, p. 1, BA R5/2123, also in BAC R005/54/2 Ha; "Beschaffung von Güterwagen zu Lasten des Fahrzeugprogramms 1940 (Zusatz)," 30 Fewgv 170, Berlin, 29 November 1939, p. 1, BAC R005/45/a Ha; Solveen to Stahlwerks-Verband, Berlin, 10 January 1940, BAC R005/022329; Glasl to Wi Rü Amt, "Dringlichkeitsstufen," Pl. Abt. Az.: D(V), Nr. 5027/40 geh, 15 August 1940, BAMA H12/114.4, f. 6; Glasl to OKW/Wi Rü Amt, "Dringlichkeit der Fertigungsprogramme der Wehrmacht," Az. 10 o 14 Pl. Abt (IVf) Nr. 212/41g, 15 January 1941, p. 2, BAMA H12/114.4, f. 62. See also the important correspondence in BAC R005/022329.

79. DRB to RZA, "Einstellung des Baues von Wagen aller Art aus dem Programm 1940," 30 Fef 82, Berlin, 12 September 1939, BAC R005/103 Ha.

80. Bergmann, "Auszug aus der Abteilungsleiter-Besprechung vom 16. Februar 1940," Berlin, BAC R005/022166.

81. DRB, "Aufstellung des Fahrzeugprogramms 1940," 31 Fef 103, Berlin, 2 September 1940, BAC R005/45/2 Ha.

82. RZA, "Anlieferung von Fahrzeugen," W-SF 30, Berlin, 10 January 1941, BAC R005/15004, Anlage 3; Leibbrand, "Anlieferung von Fahrzeugen im Dezember 1940," 39 Füg 143, Berlin, 18 January 1941, BAC R005/Ha 10/2, f. 2.

83. Emmelius to DRB, "Feststellung der Liefermöglichkeiten der Firma Schneider & Co in Le Creusot und Chalons sur Saone," L-SF 31, Berlin, 19 July 1940, p. 1, BAC R005/022254, f. 66.

84. Emmelius to DRB, "Anlieferung von Fahrzeugen," W-SF 30, Berlin, 8 November 1940, p. 2, Anlage 4, BAC 43.04/42, ff. 70, 74.

85. DRB, "Unterlagen für die Aufstellung eines Wagenbauprogramms auf lange Sicht (10-Jahresplan)," 30 Fef 112, 8 March 1941, pp. 1-2, BA R5/2090.

86. Emmelius, "Fahrzeugindustrie in den besetzten Gebieten," SF 01-SF 35, Berlin, 1 October 1941, BAC R005/022254, ff. 317, 321; DRB, "Übersicht II zum Fahrzeugprogramm 1941," 30 Fef 103, Berlin, 21 October 1941, BAC R005/2303neu.

87. DRB, "Zehnjahresplan der Fahrzeugbeschaffung," 30 Fef 112, Berlin, January 1942, pp. 6-8, BAC R005/45/2 Ha; E III, "Vorschlag der Abteilung III für einen Zehnjahresplan," 30 Fef 112, Berlin, 18 November 1941, BAC R005/022203.

88. Bergmann, "Vermerk," 39 Füg 163, Berlin, 11 December 1941, BAC R005/177 Ha, f. 49; DRB, "Zehnjahresplan der Fahrzeugbeschaffung," 30 Fef 112, Berlin, January 1942, p. 5, BA R5/2173.

89. OKW, "Dringlichkeit des kriegswichtigen Programms der Reichsbahn," Nr. 105/42g, Berlin, 14 January 1942, NA T-77, R-521, FR 1749289-90; DRB, "Vermerk," 30 Fef 112, Berlin, February 1942, BAC R005/45/2 Ha.

90. Dorpmüller to Speer, "Fahrzeugbeschaffung der Reichsbahn," Persönlich, 31 Fkl 1177, Berlin, 2 March 1942, BA R5/3624; Speer to Dorpmüller, "Hauptausschuss Verkehr und Industrierat," Nr. M. 1296/42, Berlin, 23 March 1942, BA R5/3624.

91. Hauptausschuss Schienenfahrzeuge, Sonderausschuss Lokomotiven, "Niederschrift über die Sitzung des Sonderausschusses Lokomotiven am 19. März im Lokomotiv-Haus, Berlin," Anlage zu 31 Fkl 1177, Berlin, 10 May 1942, pp. 4, 7, 9, BA R5/3624; Gottwaldt, *Deutsche Kriegslokomotiven 1939-1945*, 37-42, 150; Scharf and Wenzel, *Lokomotiven für die Reichsbahn*, 1:78-91.

92. Bergmann, "Kriegsprogramm 1943 für Fahrzeugbeschaffung," 30 Fef 126, Berlin, 14 May 1942, BAC R005/45/2 Ha; Hauptausschuss Schienenfahrzeuge, "Aktenvermerk, Kurzung des Kontingents der Reichsbahn für II/43," Berlin, 8 March 1943, BAC R005/022469; Gottwaldt, *Kriegslokomotiven*, p. 89.

93. RMfRuK to Witte, Persönlich, Berlin, 10 November 1944, BA R5/2170; Arbeitsausschuß Reichsbahn to DRB, Berlin, 14 November 1944, BA R5/2170.
94. Roth, "Der Abnahmedienst in den besetzten Westgebieten Belgien und Frankreich," Siegen, 25 June 1953, pp. 4-6, BA R5 Anh I/100.

C. The Nazi Racial Restructuring of Europe, 1941–1944

1. RBD Berlin, "809. Einkauf des Bediensteten in jüdischen Geschäften," *Amtsblatt*, Nr. 104, 8 November 1935, p. 393, Archiv Rbd Berlin.
2. RBD Berlin, "741. Jüdische Gewerbebetriebe," *Amtsblatt*, Nr. 79, 9 September 1938, pp. 318-19, Archiv Rbd Berlin.
3. Dorpmüller to Stellvertreter des Führers Stab, "Verbot der Benutzung von Schlaf- und Speisewagen durch Juden," 21 Bba 10, Berlin, 25 March 1939, GStA, Rep. 115 I c/11169.
4. Kleinmann, "Benutzung der Verkehrsmittel durch Juden," 15 Vpa 21, Berlin, 18 September 1941, BA R2/23731, also in IfZ Fa 506/14, ff. 21-22, BHSA, Rep. MWi 8514.
5. Schnellbrief, Kleinmann, "Benutzung der Verkehrsmittel durch Juden," 15 Vpa 23, K 11.8914/42, Berlin, 11 April 1942, BHSA, Rep. MWi 8514.
6. Ganzenmüller, "Benutzung der Verkehrsmittel durch Juden," 15 Vpa 23 K 11 13906, Berlin, 6 June 1942, BA R2/23731.
7. Leibbrand, "Gewährung von Fahrpreisermässigungen an Juden," 15 Toe 68, Berlin, 20 February 1943, GStA, Rep. 115 I c/11168.
8. Hilberg, *Destruction of the European Jews*, 1:157.
9. Yahil, *Holocaust*, 137.
10. Anklageschrift Ganzenmüller, 8 Js 430/67, pp. 110-11, ZSL VI (420) 107 AR-Z 80/61.
11. Seidl, "Vermerk. Besprechungen zwischen SS-H' Stuf. Eichmann und SS-Hauptscharführer Seidl am 22. und 23. Januar 1940 in Berlin Kurfürstenstrasse 116," 253140, 25 January 1940, IfZ, Eichmann-Prozess, doc. 1400; Anklageschrift Ganzenmüller, 8 Js 430/67, pp. 112, 114, ZSL VI (420) 107 AR-Z 80/61.
12. Dorpmüller, "Verkehrsaufbau im Osten," *VW* 34 (14-21 February 1940): 51; Pischel, "Generaldirektion der Ostbahn," 36.
13. Friedrich Käss, "Die Deutsche Reichsbahn und die Umsiedlung der Volksdeutschen aus Litauen," *Die Reichsbahn* 17 (28 May-4 June 1941): 207-9.
14. Himmler to Greiser, Tgb. Nr. A/29/59/41, Fü.-Hq., 18 September 1941, BA NS19neu/2655, f. 3.
15. Yahil, *Holocaust*, 294, 302-3, 312.
16. Telegrammbrief, Völcker, "Fahrplananordnung No. 11," 33 Bfp/Bfsr, Minsk, 8 November 1941, USHMA, RG-53.002M, R 1, doc. 5, f. 378/117.
17. RBD Oppeln to DRB, "Beförderungen von Häftlingen des Konzentrationslagers Auschwitz," III 6 V 2 Tpe, Oppeln, 28 February 1942, BA R5/3055.
18. Hilberg, *Destruction of the European Jews*, 1:192, 3:875, 881; Yahil, *Holocaust*, 148; Raul Hilberg, "Auschwitz and the Final Solution," in Gutman and Berenbaum, *Anatomy of the Auschwitz Death Camp*, 83; Jean-Claude Pressac and Robert-Jan van Pelt, "The Machinery of Mass Murder at Auschwitz," in Gutman and Berenbaum, *Anatomy of the Auschwitz Death Camp*, 213.
19. Landesgericht für Strafsachen Wien, "Zeugvernehmung, Franz Novak," 33 a Hs 3484/61, 15 June 1961, pp. 3-8, ZSL 107 (420) AR-Z 80/1961, ff. 153-58; Anklageschrift Ganzenmüller, 8 Js 430/67, pp. 121-22, 131, ZSL VI (420) 107 AR-Z 80/61.
20. Paul Schnell, Parteibuch, BDC.

21. Anklageschrift Ganzenmüller, 8 Js 430/67, pp. 96-97, ZSL VI (420) 107 AR-Z 80/61.

22. DRB, "Geschäftsplan der Generalbetriebsleitung Ost Berlin," Ausgabe August 1940, pp. 4, 7-9, BAC R43.16/1; Der Leitende Oberstaatsanwalt bei dem Landgericht Hamburg, "Vernehmung Stier," Frankfurt am Main, 13 April 1965, StA Dü 8 Ks 1/71, vol. VI, p. 4, f. 115; Staatsanwalt Flensburg, "Niederschrift Walther Stier," 2 Js 117/63, Frankfurt am Main, 6 March 1964, pp. 3-4, StA Dü Js 430/67, vol. V, ff. 203-4; Staatsanwalt Uchmann, "Vernehmung Stier," 4 Js 564/64, Frankfurt am Main, 11 July 1967, pp. 4-6, ZSL II 206 AR-Z 15/1963, vol. 4, ff. 583-85; Anklageschrift Ganzenmüller, 8 Js 430/67, pp. 103, 120, 146, 147, 150-51, ZSL VI (420) 107 AR-Z 80/61; Hilberg, *Destruction of the European Jews*, 2:408-12; Mangold, "GBL Ost," p. 1, BA R5 Anh I/26.

23. Anklageschrift Ganzenmüller, 8 Js 430/67, pp. 125-26, 169, 197, ZSL VI (420) 107 AR-Z 80/61; Blank, "Abschlußbericht, Betr.: Walter, Heinisch, Theodor Stier," 6 AR-Z 15/63, Ludwigsburg, 24 July 1963, pp. 3-6, ZSL 107 (420) AR-Z 80/1961, ff. 399-402; Gedob, "Fahrplananordnung Nr. 567, Da-Züge; Sonderzüge mit Umsiedlern," 30 H Bfp 17 Bfsv, Nur für den Dienstgebrauch, Cracow, 26 March 1943, ZSL II 206 AR-Z 15/1963, ff. 29-30; Günther, "Richtlinien zur technischen Durchführung der Evakuierung von Juden *nach dem Osten* (KL Auschwitz)," IV B 4 a 2093/42g (391), Berlin, 20 February 1943, pp. 4-5, IfZ, Eichmann-Prozess, doc. 1282; "Richtlinien zur technischen Durchführung der Evakuierung von Juden in das Generalgouvernement (Trawniki bei Lublin)," pp. 3-4, IfZ, Eichmann-Prozess, doc. 1279; RBD Königsberg, "Fahrplananordnung Nr. 81," 33 Bfp 9 Bfsv, Nur für den Dienstgebrauch, Königsberg, 14 August 1942, BA R5/3618, f. 99.

24. Telegrammbrief, Jacobi, to RBD'en, Ostbahn HBD Mitte, HBD Nord, "Sonderzüge für Umsiedler, Erntehelfer und Juden in der Zeit vom 8. August-30. Oktober 1942," PR 112 Bfsv, Berlin, 8 August 1942, BA R5/3618.

25. "Übersichtskarte des Bezirks der Generaldirektion der Ostbahn," 8 January 1941, BA R5/3307.

26. Franciszek Piper, "Gas Chambers and Crematoria," in Gutman and Berenbaum, *Anatomy of the Auschwitz Death Camp*, 162.

27. DRB, Bahnhof Auschwitz to Kommandantur des Konzentrationslagers in Auschwitz, Auschwitz, 24 April 1942, USHMA, RG-11.001M, R 32, folder 183, f. 140; Fricke to RBD Oppeln, "Privatgleisanschluß Auschwitz," III/2/8201/Dr. Hd./Hu, 11 April 1942, USHMA, RG-11.001M, R 32, folder 183, ff. 142-43; Uchmann, Questioning of Wilhelm Fehling, 4 Ja 564/64, Recklinghausen, 8 June 1967, ZSL II 206 AR-Z 15/1963, p. 7, vol. 4, f. 454.

28. Fernschreiben, Dannecker to RSHA IVB4, "Judentransporte aus Frankreich," IV J - Sachakt SA 24 Dan/S, Geheim, Paris, 16 June 1942, IfZ, Eichmann-Prozess, doc. 52, reprinted in Hilberg, *Sonderzüge*, Anlage 19, 167-68; Telegramm, Eichmann to Knochen, "Evakuierung von Juden aus Frankreich," Nr. 14542, Berlin, 18 June 1942, IfZ, Eichmann-Prozess, doc. 57; "Evakuierung von Juden," IV J - SA 225a, Paris, 5 September 1942, IfZ, Eichmann-Prozess, 120, Anklageschrift Ganzenmüller, 8 Js 430/67, pp. 143-44, 176, ZSL VI (420) 107 AR-Z 80/61.

29. Günther to Rademacher, "Abschiebung der Juden aus der Slovakei," IVB4a 2145/42g (1090), Berlin, 15 May 1942, IfZ, Eichmann-Prozess, doc. 839.

30. EHD Mitte to Transchef, "Ausbauforderungen," 31 BBv/31 H g, Minsk, 11 September 1941, BAMA H12/96; Teske, *Silbernen Spiegel*, 104; Map, "Otto-Programm Geforderte Regelleistungen auf den Strecken der Ostbahn," BA R5 Anh II/50, reprinted in Pischel, "Generaldirektion der Ostbahn," 22; Richter, Gedob, to Stations, etc., "Fahrplananordnung Nr. 594," Nur für den Dienstgebrauch, 33 H Bfp 16 Bfsv, Cracow, 21 September 1942, BA NS4 Anh 9; Telegrammbrief, Massute, Gedob, "Zugverteiler ab 2.11. 1942," 30 Bbv B 20 g/Bmba (nfD), Cracow, 2 November 1942, BA R5 Anh II/50. According to Kurt Becker, who was an operating official with the Ostbahn from November 1939 to October 1944, forty to forty-eight trains moved east-

ward on the Warsaw-Malkinia line daily. Oberstaatsanwalt Hamburg, "Protokoll, Vernehmung Kurt Becker," Kassel, 8 April 1965, p. 4, StA Dü 8 Ks 1/71, vol. VI, f. 90. "Eisenbahnverkehr im Osten im zweiten Weltkrieg," Section B, Anlage, indicates that in 1942 an average of 18.5 trains daily crossed the border from the General Government to the occupied Soviet Union at Malkinia. This number increased to 22.6 during the first five months of 1943. BA R5 Anh II/50. Malkinia was the second busiest border crossing point toward the east on the Ostbahn.

31. Gedob to all Stations on Siedlce-Scharfenwiese line, etc., "Fahrplananordnung Nr. 243," Cracow, 27 August 1942, BA NS4 Anh/9; Abraham Goldfarb, 14 June 1960, Petach Tikwa, p. 5, ZSL 208 AR-Z 230/59, vol. 8, f. 1611, Anklageschrift Ganzenmüller, 8 Js 430/67, p. 4, ZSL VI (420) 107 AR-Z 80/61; Bruno Klemm, "Protokoll über die in Berlin am 26. und 28. September 1942 abgehaltene Konferenz, betreffend die Evakuierung der Juden des Generalgouvernements und die Verschiebung der Juden Rumäniens in das Generalgouvernement," ZSL II 206 AR-Z 15/1963, ff. 5-6, copied from United Restitution Organization, *Dokumente über Methoden der Judenverfolgung im Ausland*, 75-76; L. Lukaszkiewicz and J. Maciejewski, "Bericht über das Ergebnis der vom 24. September 1945 bis zum 22. November 1945 durchgeführten Ermittlungen betreffend das Vernichtungslager Treblinka (Lager Nr. II)," translation from the Polish, Siedlce, 22 November 1945, pp. 4, 6, ZSL 208 AR-Z 230/59, vol. 5, ff. 827, 829; Landgericht Düsseldorf, Interrogation of Richard Neuser, UR I 21/59, Siegen, 4 July 1961, p. 1, ZSL 208 AR-Z 230/59, vol. 9, f. 1834; Stanislaw Kohn, Aktz: Kps 425/45, Lodz, 7 October 1945, ZSL 208 AR-Z 230/59, vol. 8, f. 1654; Zentralarchiv der jüdischen Geschichtskommission in Polen, Translation of Statement by Oskar Strawczynski, 1066 Kps 435/45, Lodz, 7 October 1945, ZSL 208 AR-Z 230/59, vol. 4, f. 732; Jakob Wiernik, Rishon Le Zion, 28 August 1960, pp. 3-4, ZSL 208 AR-Z 230/59, vol. 8, ff. 1635-36; Schwedersky, Interrogation of Eduard Kryschak, UR I 21/59, Bremen, 12 December 1960, p. 3, ZSL 208 AR-Z 230/59, vol. 7, f. 1526; Wolfgang Scheffler, "Übersicht über Eisenbahntransporte in die Vernichtungslager vom Juli 1942 bis zum Frühjahr 1943," Berlin, May 1973, pp. 14-18, 22, StA Dü, 8 Ks 1/71, vol. XXIX, ff. 242-46, 250; Yahil, *Holocaust*, 378-80.

32. Wolfgang Scheffler, "Übersicht über Eisenbahntransporte in die Konzentrationslager vom Juli 1942 bis zum Frühjahr 1943," Berlin, May 1973, p. 24, StA Dü, 8 Ks 1/71, vol. XXIX, f. 252.

33. Anklageschrift Ganzenmüller, 8 Js 430/67, p. 209, ZSL VI (420) 107 AR-Z 80/61; Ganzenmüller to Wolff, Geheim, Berlin, 28 July 1942, BA NS19neu/2655, f. 57, also in BDC 1020082950, and reprinted in Hilberg, *Sonderzüge*, 177, Anlage 26; Hilberg, *Destruction of the European Jews*, 2:491.

34. Exner, "Fahrplananordnung Nr. 12," 33 Bfp 9 Bfsv, Nur für den Dienstgebrauch, Königsberg, 7 May 1942, USHMA RG-53.002M, 378/1/784, also in BA R5/3618, ff. 3-4; Kayser, to Stations on Wolkowysk-Baranowitsche-Minsk Gbf line, 33 Bfp 5 Bfsv, Minsk, 13 May 1942, BA R5/3618, ff. 11-12; Bahndiensttelegramm, Kayser to Stations, 22 May 1942, BA R5/3614, f. 24; Kommandeur, SS SD Weissruthenien to RBD [sic] Mitte, "Vereinbarung über Judentransporte aus dem Reich," IIB, Minsk, 23 May 1942, BA R5/3618, f. 27, also in USHMA, RG-53.002M, 378/1/784; "Fahrplan A. 46," p. 3, BA R5/3618, f. 47; Schnellbrief, Schober to Stations, etc., "Da-Züge Wien Aspangbahnhof-Minsk," 33 B Bfp 41 Bfsv, Nur für den Dienstgebrauch, Vienna, 13 May 1942, BA R5/3614, f. 25; RBD Königsberg to P, Minsk, "DA-SDZ," W (?) 593, 17 June 1942, USHMA, RG-53.002M, 378/1/784.

35. Telegrammbrief, Kleinmann, "Beförderung russischer ziviler Arbeitkräfte von den besetzten Ostgebieten nach dem Reich (Ru - Transporte)," 21 Bfsv 435, Berlin, 17 April 1942, pp. 2-5, 7, BA R5 Anh II/44; RBD Berlin, "552. Sonderzüge mit russischen Arbeitern - Ru-Züge-," *Amtsblatt*, Nr. 78, 21 July 1942, p. 280, Archiv Rbd Berlin.

36. Sauckel, "Einsatz fremdländischer Arbeitskräfte in Deutschland. Stand 27.7.1942," G.Z.

Va 5780/1644, p. 1, IfZ, Fa 511, f. 92. For additional information, see Herbert, *History of Foreign Labor in Germany*, 149–53, table 10, p. 154, and Homze, *Foreign Labor in Nazi Germany*, 81, table VII, p. 83.

37. RVD Kiew, "Vermerk," 2 P 31 Pwhk, Kiev, 11 June 1943, BAMA H12/59.

38. Reliable statistics for the total number of non-Jewish foreign civilians and prisoners who worked in Germany are not available. In August 1944, 7.6 million worked in Germany. All of them had been brought there by rail. See Herbert, *History of Foreign Labor in Germany*, table 12, 156.

39. Telegramm, Krüger to Himmler, kr/fi. 1240/42, eh., 5 December 1942, BA NS19neu/2655, f. 69; Berger (?) to AA, 3001/42g, Geheim, Brussels, 5 January 1943, IfZ, Eichmann-Prozess, GO 1, doc. 1072; Anklageschrift Ganzenmüller, 8 Js 430/67, pp. 136, 217, ZSL VI (420) 107 AR-Z 80/61; Pischel, "Generaldirektion der Ostbahn," 44.

40. Himmler to Ganzenmüller, I 195/43 A (g), 20 January 1943, BA NS19/2774, also in StA Dü, 8 Ks 1/71, vol. XIV, ff. 55–56; Anklageschrift Ganzenmüller, 8 Js 430/67, pp. 222–23, ZSL VI (420) 107 AR-Z 80/61.

41. Anklageschrift Ganzenmüller, 8 Js 430/67, pp. 223–24, ZSL VI (420) 107 AR-Z 80/61; see also Hilberg, *Destruction of the European Jews*, 2:492.

42. Telegramm, Eichmann to Knochen, "Beförderung von Juden aus Frankreich," Nr. 35391, Berlin, 19 December 1942, IfZ, Eichmann-Prozess, doc. 121.

43. Telegrammbrief, Jacobi to divisions, etc., "Sdz für Umsiedler in der Zeit vom 20.1 bis 28.2.1943," PW 113 Bfsv, Berlin, 16 January 1943, BA R5/3618, ff. 114–19.

44. Bahndiensttelegramm, Gedob to RVD Minsk, Nr. 16, 28 January 1943, USHMA, RG-53.002M, 378/1/784, doc. 2.

45. RVM to AA, "Bezahlung der Judentransporte aus Griechenland," 17 Tpe Or 29, Berlin, 24 November 1944, BA R2/23492; Alexander Belev, Theodor Dannecker, "Vereinbarung," Sofia, 22 February 1943, IfZ, Eichmann-Prozess, G 01, doc. 417; Scheffler, "Übersicht über Eisenbahntransporte in die Vernichtungslager vom Juli 1942 bis zum Frühjahr 1943," Berlin, May 1973, p. 34, StA Dü, 8 Ks 1/71, vol. XXIV, f. 262; Anklageschrift Ganzenmüller, 8 Js 430/67, p. 4, ZSL VI (420) 107 AR-Z 80/61.

46. Scheffler, "Übersicht über Eisenbahntransporte in die Vernichtungslager vom Juli 1942 bis zum Frühjahr 1943," Berlin, May 1973, p. 35, StA Dü, 8 Ks 1/71, vol. XXIV, f. 263.

47. For a detailed description of these talks, see Pätzold and Schwarz, *"Auschwitz war für mich nur ein Bahnhof,"* 44–50.

48. Damrau, Rehse, "Vernehmungsniederschrift Adolf Johann Barthelmäs," LKA Baden-Württemberg, I/7(NSG) Tgb-Nr. I.7-16-31/67, Stuttgart, 11 April 1967, p. 4, ZSL VI 107 (420) AR-Z 80/1961, vol. IV, f. 570; Anklageschrift Ganzenmüller, 8 Js 430/67, pp. 228–29, ZSL VI (420) 107 AR-Z 80/61. For additional details, see Randolph L. Braham, "Hungarian Jews," in Gutman and Berenbaum, *Anatomy of the Auschwitz Death Camp*, 463–65.

49. Damrau, Rehse, "Vernehmungsniederschrift Adolf Johann Barthelmäs," LKA Baden-Württemberg, I/7(NSG) Tgb-Nr. I.7-16-31/67, Stuttgart, 11 April 1967, p. 7, ZSL VI 107 (420) AR-Z 80/1961, vol. IV, f. 573; Amstgericht Kiel, Interrogation of Otto Pleß, Az. 12 gs 396/67 -, Kiel, 15 March 1967, p. 2, StA Dü 8 Ks 1/71, vol. XIII, f. 43; Anklageschrift Ganzenmüller, 8 Js 430/67, p. 297, ZSL VI (420) 107 AR-Z 80/61.

50. Hessisches LKA, "Vernehmung Oskar Diegelmann," Neukirchen, 12 December 1961, ZSL II 206 AR-Z 15/1963, f. 6.

51. Uchmann, Interrogation of Walter Mannl, 4 Js 564/64, Siegburg, 24 April 1967, ZSL II 206 AR-Z 15/1963, vol. 4, f. 477.

52. J. J. Blomeyer, "Vernehmungsniederschrift (Günther Lübbeke)," Washington, D.C., 5 December 1968, pp. 3–5, ZSL 208 AR-Z 230/59, vol. 16, ff. 4431–33.

53. Schwedersky, Interrogation of Eduard Kryschak, UR I 21/59, Bremen, 12 December 1960, pp. 2-3, ZSL 208 AR-Z 230/59, vol. 7, ff. 1526-27.

54. Schwedersky, Interrogation of Hans Prause, UR I 4/67 (G), Düsseldorf, 9 October 1968, pp. 1, 4, ZSL 208 AR-Z 230/59, vol. 15, ff. 4274, 4277.

55. Uchmann, Interrogation of Willy Hilse, 4 Js 564/64, Frankfurt am Main, 5 July 1967, pp. 5-6, ZSL II 206 AR-Z 15/1963, vol. 4, ff. 509-10.

56. Uchmann, Interrogation of Wilhelm Fehling, 4 Ja 564/64, Recklinghausen, 8 June 1967, pp. 4-6, ZSL II 206 AR-Z 15/1963, vol. 4, ff. 453-55.

57. Landgericht Düsseldorf, Interrogation of Richard Neuser, UR I 21/59, Siegen, 4 July 1961, p. 2, ZSL 208 AR-Z 230/59, f. 1835.

58. Schwedersky, Interrogation of Alfons Glas, UR I 21/59, Munich, 21 October 1960, p. 6, ZSL 208 AR-Z 230/59, vol. 7, f. 1397; Uchmann, Interrogation of Alfons Glas, 4 Js 564/64, Garmisch-Partenkirchen, 17 August 1967, p. 3, ZSL II 206 AR-Z 15/1963, vol. 4, f. 394.

59. Browning, "One Day in Jozefow"; Browning, *Ordinary Men: Reserve Police Battalion 101 and the Final Solution in Poland*; Browning, *The Final Solution and the Foreign Office*, 178-81.

60. Anklageschrift Ganzenmüller, 8 Js 430/67, pp. 290-91, ZSL VI (420) 107 AR-Z 80/61.

61. Anklageschrift Ganzenmüller, 8 Js 430/67, p. 291, ZSL VI (420) 107 AR-Z 80/61.

62. Siegert to DRB, "Beförderungskosten für Polentransporte," SIE/Nr. 152/41-239-, Berlin, 1 March 1941, BA R5/3055; Eichmann to DRB, "Polentransporte," IVD4 164/41, Berlin, 20 February 1941, BA R5/3055, f. 57, Anklageschrift Ganzenmüller, 8 Js 430/67, pp. 97, 105, ZSL VI (420) 107 AR-Z 80/61; Hilberg, *Destruction of the European Jews*, 2:467, 643; Hilberg, "German Railroads/Jewish Souls," 63.

63. Schnellbrief, Siegert to RFM, "Kosten bei der Evakuierung von Juden aus Frankreich," S II C 1 Nr. 869/42-238-10-, Vertraulich, Berlin, 17 August 1942, BA R2/12158, f. 74; Hilberg, *Destruction of the European Jews*, 2:644.

64. Kiefer to Breyhahn, Ve 6040 Griech-8V, Berlin, 20 October 1944, BA R2/23492; Yahil, *Holocaust*, 414.

65. Anklageschrift Ganzenmüller, 8 Js 430/67, pp. 97, 105, ZSL VI (420) 107 AR-Z 80/61; Yahil, *Holocaust*, 367.

66. Yahil, *Holocaust*, 323.

67. Hilberg, *Destruction of the European Jews*, 2:659.

68. Anklageschrift Ganzenmüller, 8 Js 430/67, pp. 89, 105, ZSL VI (420) 107 AR-Z 80/61.

69. Scheffler to Spiess, Berlin, 30 November 1969, StA Dü, Sonderband X, Teil IV; StA Dü, Anklageband, 8 Ks 1/71, vol. XXII, p. 178; Anklageschrift Ganzenmüller, 8 Js 430/67, pp. 3, 105, ZSL VI (420) 107 AR-Z 80/61.

70. The estimate of the total number of trains is based on Scheffler's estimate of 3 million people having been brought to their deaths by rail and an estimate of an average of 1,460.117 people per train. Dividing the estimated number of victims by the number of victims per train yields a total of 2,054.63 trains. It must be stressed that this number gives only a rough idea of the Reichsbahn's overall effort to carry this traffic. These estimates and the figures presented in the text are based on Anklageschrift Ganzenmüller, 8 Js 430/67, pp. 86, 105, ZSL VI (420) 107 AR-Z 80/61; "Gutachten des Sachverständigen Dr. Scheffler in der Strafsache gegen Dr. Ganzenmüller," I-32/72, p. 52, StA, Dü 8 Ks 1/71, vol. XXVIII, f. 95; Wolfgang Scheffler, "Übersicht über Eisenbahntransporte in die Vernichtungslager vom Juli 1942 bis zum Frühjahr 1943," Berlin, May 1973, p. 31, StA Dü 8 Ks 1/71, vol. XXIX, f. 32; Wolfgang Scheffler, "Vorläufige Übersicht über Eisenbahntransporte in die Vernichtungslager 1941-1944," StA Dü, 8 Js 430/67, Sonderband X, Teil IV; Anklageschrift Ganzenmüller, 8 Js 430/67, pp. 177-78, ZSL VI (420) 107 AR-Z 80/61; Yahil, *Holocaust*, 361, 391-434, 525, 537.

71. Lagerkommandant Buchenwald, "Häftlingsüberstellung," Weimar-Buchenwald, 14 Oc-

tober 1942, BA NS4 Bu/133; Waffen-SS, Kommandantur, KL Buchenwald, "Transportbefehl, Häftlingsüberstellung," Weimar-Buchenwald, 27 April 1943, BA NS4 Bu/133; RBD Hanover to DRB, "Leihweise Abgabe von Personenwagen," 33H Bfp 30 Bbg, Hanover, 13 April 1944, BA R5/2117; DRB to RBD Hanover, "Leihweise Abgabe von Personenwagen," 21 Bbz, 29 April 1944, BA R5/2117. For additional information in the movements of Jews to and from work camps and factories, see Berben, *Dachau, 1933–1945*, 96–101, 242–48, 261, 264, 266, 268.

D. The Years of Retreat, 1942–1944

1. Gerteis, "Die Ostbahn," *ZVME* 81 (3 July 1941): 374.
2. Gerteis, "5 Jahre Ostbahn," p. 10, BA R5 Anh I/120; *Verordnungsblatt für das Generalgouvernement*, Nr. 68, 1 August 1941, pp. 448–49, BA R2/23810.
3. Dorpmüller to GBL's, divisions, "Ostbahn," 2 Arl (O), Berlin, 13 May 1942, BA R2/23810; Lammers, "Ostbahn," Rk. 556 BII, Berlin, 19 January 1942, GStA, Rep. 115 Ic/11166; Kiefer, "Vermerk, Übernahme von Betrieb und Verwaltung der Ostbahn," Ve 6040 Russl - 14 V, Berlin, 28 January 1942, BA R2/23810; Gerteis, "5 Jahre Ostbahn," p. 10.
4. Lammers, "Einverleibung der Ostbahn in die Deutsche Reichsbahn," Rk. 11096B, Noch heute, Berlin, 7 August 1942, BA R43 II/184a, f. 28; Pischel, "Generaldirektion der Ostbahn," 11.
5. Fernschreiben, Frank to Lammers, Nr. 151, Cracow, 12 August 1942, p. 2, BA R43 II/184a, f. 43; Pischel, "Generaldirektion der Ostbahn," 12.
6. Dorpmüller to Lammers, "Ostbahn," 2 Ogd, Berlin, 19 August 1942, BA R43 II/184a, ff. 55–56.
7. Lammers, "Zweiter Erlaß des Führers über die Ostbahn," Rk. 11782, Berlin, 30 September 1942, BA R43 II/184a, f. 57.
8. Willuhn, "Ostbahn," Rk. 1513, Führer Hauptquartier, 18 October 1942, BA R43 II/184a, ff. 82–83.
9. Lammers to Dorpmüller, "Ostbahn," Rk. 15132B, Feldquartier, 26 October 1942, BA R2/23495, also in BA R43 II/184a, ff. 87–88.
10. Ganzenmüller to E-Abt., "Ostbahn," 2 Arl (P), Berlin, 31 October 942, BA R2/23495.
11. Frank-Tagebücher, 25 November 1942, IfZ, MA-120/4-3, FR 1263-67.
12. Frank-Tagebücher, 4 May 1943, Cracow, IfZ, MA-120/10, FR 249-61; Anklageschrift Ganzenmüller, 8Js 430/67, p. 105, ZSL VI (420) 107 AR-Z 80/61; Günther Wien to Uchmann, "Ermittlungssache gegen Dr. Geitmann," Frankfurt am Main, 28 July 1967, p. 5, ZSL II 206 AR-Z 15/1963, vol. 4, f. 552; Gerteis, "5 Jahre Ostbahn," pp. 12–13; Kiefer, "Organisation der Ostbahn im Generalgouvernement," Ve 6040 Pol-72V, Berlin, 3 June 1943, BA R2/23495.
13. Frank-Tagebücher, 9 July 1943, IfZ, MA-120/10, FR 661-63; Frank-Tagebücher, 14 July 1944, IfZ, MA-120/13, FR 246-48. On this see Pischel, "Generaldirektion der Ostbahn," 12–14.
14. Gerteis, "5 Jahre Ostbahn," pp. 46–47.
15. Pischel, "Generaldirektion der Ostbahn," 22.
16. "Eisenbahnverkehr im Osten im zweiten Weltkrieg," Anlage, BA R5 Anh I II/50; Der Leitende Oberstaatsanwalt bei dem Landgericht Hamburg, "Protokoll, Vernehmung Kurt Becker," Kassel, 8 April 1965, pp. 2, 4, StA Dü 2 Ks 1/71, vol. VI, ff. 88, 90; Telegrammbrief, Erwin Massute, "Zugverteiler ab 2.11.1942," 30 Bbv B 20 g/Bmba (nfD), Cracow, 2 November 1942, BA R5 Anh II/50.
17. Gerteis to Mineis L b, Transchef, etc., "Beseitigung der Betriebsschwierigkeiten im Gedob-Bereich hier: Durchführung des Wehrmachtnachschubs," 30/30H Baü, Cracow, 30 October 1942, p. 4, BA R5 Anh II/59.

18. DRB to Gedob, "Abrechnung der Personalleistungen für die Ostbahn im August 1942," 41 Kbl 193, Berlin, 12 October 1942, BA R5/3279; DRB to Gedob, "Abrechnung der Personalleistungen für die Ostbahn im August 1944," 41 Kbl (Ostbahn) 31, Berlin, 27 October 1944, BA R5/3279; Gerteis, "5 Jahre Ostbahn," p. 35.

19. Gerteis to RVM, "Jüdische Arbeitkräfte bei der Ostbahn," 4 P 30g/Pldav, Cracow, 16 September 1942, BAC R005/023128, f. 42; Gerteis to Höheren SS- und Polizeiführer, Krakau," 4 P30g/Pldav, Cracow, 16 September 1942, BAC R005/023128, ff. 43-44. On the conflict between economic rationality and racist policies in Nazi labor policies, see Naasner, *Neue Machtzentren in der deutschen Kriegswirtschaft*, 155-58, 380, 451.

20. Ostbahn, Jahresabschlüße 1940, 1941, 1942, BA R2/23495; Frank-Tagebücher, 9 July 1943, IfZ, MA-120/10, FR 663, 718.

21. "Organisation und Tätigkeit der Deutschen Reichsbahnverwaltung in den besetzten russischen Gebieten," 7 August 1954, p. 2, BA R5 Anh I/142.

22. Willuhn (?), "Führererlasse Bahn und Post," Rk. 12810B, Berlin, 16 September 1942, BA R43 II/184a, ff. 63-64, 71-72.

23. Schnellbrief, Schelp to Transchef, "Steuerung der Wirtschaftstransporte im Ostraum," 10 A Vgal (Ostland) 100, Berlin, 7 January 1943, p. 1, BA R5/2086; Schnellbrief, RVM Zweigstelle Osten, "Übergang der Aufgaben der Feldbetriebsleitung auf die GVD Osten," 60 Bg Rz/Ja 36 (g), Warsaw, 9 March 1943, BAMA H12/72; "Auszüge aus den Kriegstagebüchern des Wi Stabes Ost," Rep 502 FC-38 (Blatt 61-71), p. 7, BA R5 Anh I/171; Dorpmüller to divisions, etc., "Verkehrswesen in den besetzten Ostgebieten," 2 Arl (O), Berlin, 10 November 1942, BA R5 Anh II/52, also in BA R2/23499; RVM Zweigstelle Osten, "Einrichtung der Generalverkehrsdirektion Osten und der Reichsverkehrsdirektionen," MD 1. 103 Og 25, Warsaw, 30 November 1942, BA R5 Anh I/127; Wendler, "Vermerk," 10 Vw (Ostland) 15 Berlin, 18 January 1943, pp. 2-3, BA R5/2092, also in BAC R005/89 Ha; GVD Osten, "Geschäftsanweisung für die Generalverkehrsdirektion in Warschau, Vom 1. April 1943," BA R5 Anh I/127; Kreidler, *Eisenbahnen im Machtbereich*, 324.

24. Teske, *Silbernen Speigel*, 200.

25. Ebeling to Transchef, "Stand der Bauten und der Streckenleistungen des Otto-Programms," L 5 g Rs/Bmbst 429, Berlin, 23 December 1941, BAMA H12/68; Alfred Simon, "Die Entwicklung der Wirtschaft im neuen Deutschen Ostraum und ihre Auswirkung auf die Verkehrsträger," *Großdeutscher Verkehr* 36 (March 1942): 114.

26. Transchef to Ebeling, Az. 43s 30 Pl. Abt. III 1. St. Nr. 0405/42, g. Kdos., 12 March 1943, BAMA H12/110.

27. Schaefer, "Vermerke aus der Besprechung beim Vpr am 23.3.42 über den Nachschub Osten auf masch. techn. Gebiet," +SF - SF 45-, Berlin, 24 March 1942, BAC 43.04/163, f. 11.

28. Gercke, "Befehl," Az. 43s 30 Pl Abt. III 1 St, Nr. 01542 geh, [Berlin], 26 March 1942, p. 1, BA R41/208, f. 118.

29. RVM, Zweigstelle Osten, "Niederschrift der Besprechung über das Ostbauprogramm 1942 beim Chef des Transportwesens am 12. Mai 1942," MD 60 B Sa (Ostbau 42) 2, Warsaw, 15 May 1942, BAC R005/020762.

30. Gercke, "Befehl für den weiteren Ausbau der Eisenbahnen im Osten: 'Winter-Ostbau 1942/43,'" AZ. 43s 30 Pl. Abt. (III op) 1. St, Nr. 04682/42 geh, [Berlin], 6 September 1942, p. 2, BA R41/271, f. 23.

31. Massute to Gruppe L, "Fertigstellung der Bauvorhaben im 'Winter-Ostbau 1942/43,'" 30 Bbv 41 g Rs Bmbst 191 (g), 9 November 1942, BAMA H12/109.2; "Vortragsnotiz über den Stand des Ostbaues 1942," 23 September 1942, BAMA H12/109.2.

32. DRB, 70 Ia (Russland) 5, Berlin, 26 September 1942, BAC R005/020763; DRB, 70 Ia (Russland) 5, Berlin, 6 January 1943, BAC R005/020763.

33. RVM Zweigstelle Osten, "Niederschrift über die Besprechung beim Chef des Transportwesens, Planungsabteilung, am 9. und 10.11.1942 betreffend 'Winter-Ostbau 1942/43,'" MD 60 B Ja (Ostbau) 104, Warsaw, 14 November 1942, pp. 3-4, 9, BA R41/278, ff. 9-10, 13; GVD Osten to DRB, "Winterostbau 1942/43, hier: Arbeitkräfte," 5 OA 527 Pwhk 41, Warsaw, 23 December 1942, BA R41/271, ff. 28-29; GDV Osten to Transchef, "Baulich gesicherte Leistungen," 60 B g Rs/Ia 31 (g), Warsaw, 10 March 1943, pp. 1-2, BAMA H12/230; Wuthmann, to GVD Osten, "Baulich gesicherte Leistungen," 43s 30 Pl Abt (IIIop), Nr. 01722/43 geh, 19 April 1943, p. 3, BAMA H12/230; Transchef, "Niederschrift über die Besprechung beim Chef des Transportwesens, Planungsabteilung am 2. und 23 April 1943 betreffend 'Ostbau 1943,'" 14 May 1943, p. 8, BAMA H12/66; Pischel, "Generaldirektion der Ostbahn," 27; Gerteis, "5 Jahre Ostbahn," pp. 56-58, BA R5 Anh I/120.

34. Beauftragte der Organisation Todt beim Transchef, "Auszugsweise Abschrift aus dem Bericht der OT-Einsatzgruppe Russland Mitte für die Zeit vom März bis Mai 1943," Nr. 1457.43, 12 July 1943, BAMA H12/59; Lamp to Abt. II, III, Gruppe L, "Schwierigkeiten in der Durchführung der Bauvorhaben durch Verknappung der Oberbaustoffe," VI 71 Nae 1087, Berlin, 30 July 1943, BAC R005/021319; HVD Paris, "Mitteilungsblatt über die Verkehrs- und Wagenlage für die 47. Woche," E 7 H V 1 Vw, Paris, 29 November 1943, p. 4, BA R124/154; Rudolphi, "Dringlichkeitseinstufung kriegswichtiger Bauvorhaben, Rangliste 1944," 71 Nae 1944, Berlin, 29 February 1944, BAC R005/021319.

35. DRB, 70 Ia (Russland) 5, Berlin, 9 November 1943, BAC R005/020763; "Vortragsnotiz. Betr.: Kräfteeinsatz der GVD Osten im Ostbauprogramm," 8 March 1944, BAMA H12/59.

36. Göring to Dorpmüller, Berlin, 17 February 1942, BA R5/2805; Abt. VII to Abt. II, "Bauprogramm der Deutschen Reichsbahn," 70 Nae 1294, Berlin, 8 April 1942, Anlage, "Vermerk über die Besprechung am 24.3.42 über das Bauprogramm der Deutschen Reichsbahn," Berlin, 25 March 1942, BA R5/2085; Telegrammbrief, Doll, "Einschränkung der Bautätigkeit; Anmeldung der Bauten für die Zeit vom 1. April 1942 bis 31. Dezember 1942," 171 Nae 1322, Berlin, 4 April 1942, BAC R005/021319; RBD Oppeln, "Bericht über die Besprechung bei der Wirtschaftskammer Oberschlesien, Kattowitz, am 16. Juli 1942," Kattowitz, 16 July 1942, BA R5/3530.

37. Ebeling to Transchef, "Anmeldung der Bauten aus besonderem Anlaß für das 3. Kriegswirtschaftsjahr," L 5 g Rs/Bmbst 370, Berlin, 29 July 1941, BAMA H12/69.

38. Ebeling to Transchef, "Kostenzusammenstellung des Otto-Programms (ausschliesslich Generaldirektion der Ostbahn)," L 5, g Rs/Bmbst 41 (O), Berlin, 1 April 1942, BAMA H12/63/1 (a), f. 146.

39. RVM to OKW WFSt, "RV-Massnahmen: ausserordentlicher Reichshaushalt 1943," L g Rs/Bmkm 32 (g), Berlin, 1 June 1944, BAMA H12/77, f. 169.

40. Gerteis, Kiefer, Prang, "Aufzeichnung über die Verhandlung in Krakau vom 9.-12. September 1943 zur Frage der Finanzierung des Otto- und Ostbauprogramms," Cracow, 12 September 1943, Anlage zu L 5g/Bmkm 13 (O), 12 October 1943, BAMA H12/77, f. 152; Pischel, "Generaldirektion der Ostbahn," 33.

41. [GVD Osten], Betriebslängen, BA R5 Anh I/141.

42. Müller to DRB, "Betriebsmaschinendienst; hier Reisebericht Min Rat Günther," 30 L 314 Bl, Warsaw, 10 February 1943, BA R5 Anh I/129.

43. Estimate based on Teske, *Silbernen Spiegel*, 205.

44. [GVD Osten], "Personalstand," BA R5 Anh I/141.

45. GVD Osten, "Monatl. Zugkilometer in Mio," BA R5 Anh I/141.

46. [GVD Osten], "Güterwagenstellung, getr. n. Gattungen (tägl. Durchschnitt)," BA R5 Anh I/141.

47. GVD Osten, "Übernommene u. Übergebene Züge 1943," BA R5 Anh I/141.

48. Wernich, "Wirtschaftverkehr der besetzten Ostgebiete Juli 1941-Juni 1944," 1944, BA R5 Anh I/125, also in BA Kl. Erw. 496, ff. 21-22.

49. Schelp to Rosenberg, "Eisenbahn-Gütertarife in den besetzten Ostgebieten," 12 Tgal 2395, Berlin, 15 July 1942, p. 1, BA R2/23499.

50. Kiefer, "Vermerk, Abrechnung der Beförderungsleistungen der Eisenbahnen im Bereich der Haupteisenbahndirektionen. Wehrmachtverkehr im besetzten Ostraum," Ve 6040 Russl - 69V, 60, 58, 27, 53, 52, 31, 26V, Berlin, 12 September 1942, BA R2/23499; RVM, "Abschluß der Eisenbahnsondervermögen für die besetzten Ostgebiete für das Geschäftsjahr 1942," draft, [16 October 1943], p. 7, BA R2/23499.

51. Teske, *Silbernen Spiegel*, 179-81.

52. RVD Minsk to GVD Osten, "Betriebslagemeldung vom 3.8.43," 30 Ozl Bamt, Vertraulich, Minsk, 3 August 1943, p. 1, BA R5 Anh I/144; RVD Minsk to GVD Osten, "Betriebslagemeldung vom 4.8.43," 30 Ozl Bamt, Vertraulich, Minsk, 4 August 1943, p. 1, BA R5 Anh I/144; Teske, *Silbernen Spiegel*, 195.

53. RVD Minsk to GVD Osten, "Betriebslagemeldung vom 10.10.43," 30 Ozl Bamt, Vertraulich, Minsk, 10 October 1943, p. 1, USHMA, RG-53.002M, R 2, 378/1/400, doc. 38.

54. [GVD Osten], "Betriebsunfälle im Bezirk der RVD Kiev. Ursachen der Unfälle," BA R5 Anh I/141.

55. Kausche, "Eisenbahnen im zweiten Weltkriege," pp. 65-66, BA R5 Anh I/8.

56. Teske, *Silbernen Spiegel*, 218.

57. As of 3 September 1942, DRB personnel in the east had been issued 23,000 rifles and 21,000 pistols. Görnert to Bodenschatz, Br. B. Nr. 773/42o, 3 September 1942, NA T-84, R-6, IfZ MA-144/3, ff. 5392-5392A. Also see Kommandantur des Sicherungsgebietes Weißruthenian, "Anordnung zur Bandenbekämpfung," Minsk, 7 September 1942, USHMA, RG-53.002M, 378/1/789.

58. Teske, *Silbernen Spiegel*, 197, 200.

59. Telegrammbrief, Dorpmüller to WVD Paris, Brussels, "Übernahme der Eisenbahnen in den besetzten französischen Gebieten und Belgien," 2 Arl (W), Berlin, 13 June 1942, BA R5 Anh I/127; Dorpmüller, Speer, "Einrichtung der 'Haupt-Verkehrs-Leitstelle Frankreich/Belgien,'" 2 Ogv/Az 43 a/b (Westen) Gr. Verkehr Nr. 5497/42, Berlin, 2 July 1942, BAC R005/020619.

60. EBD Lille to Ständige Vertretung der SNCF, "Rückgabe der Betriebsführung im Küstengebiet," 31 B 3 Bao, Lille, 2 December 1942, BA R124/138.

61. HVD Paris, "Niederschrift über die Besprechung bei der HVD Paris am 10.3.43 über den Bericht der Kommission Dr. Bartsch," 30 TÜW 1, Paris, 11 March 1943, p. 2, BA R124/3; Münzer, "Die Französische Eisenbahnen im Jahre 1942," *ZVME* 84 (2 March 1944), BA R5 Anh I/111.

62. "Notiz betreffend die Bedungungen der Abordnung von SNCF-Bediensteten in den Dienst der Deutschen Reichsbahn," Lt/LL-, 20 April 1942, p. 1, BA R124/121; WVD Paris, "Anweisung von SNCF-Bediensteten für die Deutsche Reichsbahn," 3 A i (SNCF), Vertraulich, Paris, 14 May 1942, BA R124/121.

63. HVD Paris, "Aktenvermerk über die Besprechung am 26.6.1943 in Paris betr. Maßnahmen zur Steigerung der Dampflokleistungen im Bereich der SNCF," Paris, 12 July 1943, pp. 1-2, BA R124/142.

64. HVD Paris, "Aktenvermerk über die Besprechung am 30.6.1943 in Paris betr. Maßnahmen zur Steigerung der Dampflokleistungen im Bereich der SNCF," Paris, 17 July 1943, p. 3, BA R124/142.

65. DRB, "Niederschrift 30. Betriebsleiterbesprechung, 18.-19. August 1943," 26 Babh 37, Berlin, p. 9, BA R5 Anh I/63; also in BA R5/2782.

66. HVD Paris, "Mitteilungsblatt über die Verkehrs- und Wagenlage für das 47. Woche," E 7 HV 1 Vw, Paris, 28 November 1943, p. 2, BA R124/154. See also Durand, *La SNCF*.

67. Rohde, "Niederschrift über die Besprechung am 18 Juni 1942," Lr 31 HA 6, Paris, 18 June 1942, p. 102, BAC R005/020619; Bergmann, "Abgabe von französischen und belgischen Güterwagen," 30 Fkwg 618, Berlin, 9 June 1942, BAC R005/89 Ha, also in BAC R005/020619; Münzer, "Aktenvermerk über die Besprechung bei den Eisenbahnabteilungen des RVM in Berlin am Samstag, den 6.6.1942," Lr A6, Berlin, 6 June 1942, BAC R005/020619.

68. HWA, "Vereinbarung," WE 205 Vw, Berlin, 12 June 1942, p. 1, BAC R005/020619.

69. Fernspruch, Münzer to Mineis L, 17 June 1942, 8:30, BAC R005/020619.

70. Wendt, "Niederschrift über die 1. Sitzung . . . 31. Juli 1942," E 7 V7 Val, Paris, 6 August 1942, p. 3, BA R124/140.

71. GVL West, "Niederschrift zur Besprechung . . . am 24. September 1942," C 91 Val Westen, Essen, 1 October 1942, BAC R005/020619.

72. DRB to HWA, "Bestand deutscher Güterwagen in Frankreich," 10 Vw (Westen) 93, Berlin, 14 January 1943, BAC R005/020619.

73. HVD Paris to DRB, "Rückführung deutscher Wagen nach dem Reich," Pr(7) V6 Vw, Paris, 25 March 1944, p. 1, BAC R005/020619; Milward, *New Order*, 281.

74. Milward, *New Order*, 282, table 64; Milward, *War, Economy and Society*, 144.

75. HVD Brüssel, "Wissenswerte Angaben," p. 10, BA R5 Anh I/93.

76. Schlumprecht, "Abgabe von 12 500 Wagen aus Belgien nach dem Reich," Gr. VI/Transp. St. Hlf, 5 June 1942, BAC R005/020619.

77. Schnellbrief, Baur to DRB, "Rücklauf belgischer Güterwagen aus Deutschland," Lr 7 V8 Vw, Brüssel, 15 October 1942, BAC R005/020619.

78. Schnellbrief, Bauer to HWA, "Bestand an belgischen G-Wagen in Deutschland," Lr 7 V8 Vw, Brussels, 26 March 1943, BAC R005/020619.

79. HVD Brüssel, "Wissenswerte Angaben," p. 56, BA R5 Anh I/93.

80. HVD Brüssel, "Wissenswerte Angaben," p. 24, BA R5 Anh I/93.

81. Schnellbrief, HVD Brüssel to Wehrmachttransportleitung, "Awi-Transporte," Lr 7 V 5 Vgbm, Brussels, 13 February 1943, p. 6, BAC R005/020580.

82. DRB, "Auszug aus den Lageberichten der Reichsbahndirektionen für Monat Juli 1942," 41, Berlin, 3 September 1942, p. 1, BA R2/23731.

83. Emrich, ZVL, Minutes, 22 December 1942, Vertraulich, Berlin, 24 December 1942, pp. 2-3, BA R5 Anh II/38; DRB, "Auszug aus den Lageberichten der Reichsbahndirektionen für Monat Dezember 1942," 41, Berlin, 23 January 1943, pp. 1, 5, BA R2/23731.

84. Emrich, ZVL, Minutes, 16 March 1943, Vertraulich, Berlin, 23 March 1943, pp. 1, 3, BA R5 Anh II/38.

85. Emrich, ZVL, Minutes, 15 May 1943, Vertraulich, Berlin, 18 May 1943, pp. 6, 10, BA R5 Anh II/38.

86. Emrich, ZVL, Minutes, 13 August 1943, Vertraulich, Berlin, 16 August 1943, pp. 1-2, 4, BA R5 Anh II/38.

87. Emrich, ZVL, Minutes, 15 October 1943, Vertraulich, Berlin, 21 October 1943, p. 1, BA R5 Anh II/38.

88. Emrich, ZVL, Minutes, 9 March 1944, Vertraulich, Berlin, 15 March 1944, pp. 1, 3, BA R5 Anh II/38; Emrich, ZVL, Minutes, 28 April 1944, Vertraulich, Berlin, 3 May 1944, pp. 1, 5, BA R5 Anh II/38.

89. Emrich, ZVL, Minutes, 1 June 1944, Vertraulich, Berlin, 1 June 1944, p. 1, BA R5 Anh II/38.

90. Telegrammbrief, DRB, "Wagenstellung für die Stichwörte 'Fahrzeugprogramm,' 'Fahr-

zeugunterhaltung,' und 'Reichsbahn,'" 10 Vwb 825, Berlin, 30 April 1942, BAC 43.04/163, f. 20, also in BA R5/3624.

91. Emrich, ZVL, Minutes, 17 December 1943, Vertraulich, Berlin, 22 December 1943, p. 6, BA R5 Anh II/38.

92. Emrich, ZVL, Minutes, 11 June 1942, Vertraulich, Berlin, 12 June 1942, p. 1, BA R5 Anh II/38.

93. Telegrammbrief, Schelp to divisions, "Güterwagenstellung an den Sonntagen," 10 Vwb 1287, Berlin, 8 April 1944, BA R5/2086.

94. RBD Berlin, "305. Güterfahrplan-Stammgüterzüge," Amtsblatt, Nr. 39, 2 June 1944, p. 123, Archiv Rbd Berlin.

95. HWA, "Wochenbericht über die Wagenlage," 1-7 August 1943, BA R5 Anh II/39.

96. Emrich, ZVL, Minutes, 10 November 1942, Vertraulich, Berlin, 14 November 1942, p. 1, BA R5 Anh II/38; Emrich, ZVL, Minutes, 5 January 1943, Vertraulich, Berlin, 5 January 1943, pp. 1, 2, BA R5 Anh II/38; Emrich, ZVL, Minutes, 2 February 1943, Vertraulich, Berlin, 6 February 1943, p. 2, BA R5 Anh II/38; Emrich, ZVL, Minutes, 14 April 1943, Vertraulich, Berlin, 20 April 1943, pp. 1, 3, BA R5 Anh II/38; Emrich, ZVL, Minutes, 17 December 1943, Vertraulich, Berlin, 22 December 1943, pp. 1-2, BA R5 Anh II/38; Emrich, ZVL, Minutes, 28 April 1944, Vertraulich, Berlin, 3 May 1944, pp. 6-7, BA R5 Anh II/38.

97. Hitler, "Erlaß," Führerhauptquartier, 28 June 1943, RMfBuM, "Betriebsverlagerung und Verlegung von Lagern, Parks, Depots," Rü A Nr. 17 501/43g Rü II/4a, Berlin, 14 July 1943, BA R5/3216; Emrich, ZVL, Minutes, 17 September 1943, Vertraulich, Berlin, 23 September 1943, p. 6, BA R5 Anh II/38; Emrich, ZVL, Minutes, 26 January 1944, Vertraulich, Berlin, 31 January 1944, pp. 1-2, 8, BA R5 Anh II/38; DRB, "Niederschrift über den Rundspruch am 21. Juli und die Fernsprech-Präsidentenkonferenz am 24. Juli 1944," 2 Aasp 83, Geheim, August 1944, p. 12, BA R5 Anh I/69, f. 394; USSBS, Ganzenmüller Interrogation, 30 May 1945, p. 3, NA RG 243, 200(a)127; USSBS, *German Transportation*, 51; USSBS, *Aircraft Division Industry Report*, 24.

98. Emrich, ZVL, Minutes, 31 August 1943, Vertraulich, Berlin, 4 September 1943, p. 1, BA R5 Anh II/38; DRB, BR, Minutes, 24 March 1942, Nur für den Dienstgebrauch, p. 3, BA R2/31653; Kreidler, *Eisenbahnen im Machtbereich*, 227; Wehde-Textor, "Leistungen," 13.

99. Emrich, ZVL, Minutes, 11 June 1942, Vertraulich, Berlin, 12 June 1942, p. 1, BA R5 Anh II/38; Emrich, ZVL, Minutes, 25 June 1942, Vertraulich, Berlin, 27 June 1942, pp. 5, 6, BA R5 Anh II/38.

100. Göring, V.P. 9712/2, Berlin, 31 May 1942, BA R43 II/637a, ff. 186-87, also in GStA, Rep. 115 Ic/11169; RVM to divisions, etc., "Prämienverfahren für vorzeitige Rückgabe von Wagen," 10 Vgba 256, Berlin, 5 June 1942, BA R5 Anh II/44; Emrich, ZVL, Minutes, 25 June 1942, Vertraulich, Berlin, 27 June 1942, pp. 2-3, BA R5 Anh II/38; Emrich, ZVL, Minutes, 22 September 1942, Vertraulich, Berlin, 26 September 1942, p. 8, BA R5 Anh II/38; Emrich, ZVL, Minutes, 5 January 1943, Vertraulich, Berlin, 9 January 1943, p. 7, BA R5 Anh II/38; Emrich, ZVL, Minutes, 12 May 1943, Vertraulich, Berlin, 18 May 1943, pp. 1, 5, BA R5 Anh II/38; Sarter, "GBL West," p. 7, BA R5 Anh I/100.

101. Emrich, ZVL, Minutes, 2 February 1943, Vertraulich, Berlin, 6 February 1943, p. 1, BA R5 Anh II/38.

102. DRB, BR, Minutes, 1 December 1942, Nur für den Dienstgebrauch, p. 14, BA R2/31653; DRB, BR, Minutes, 15 February 1943, Geheim, p. 13, BA R2/31653; USSBS, Dorpmüller Interrogation, 29 May 1945, p. 3, NA RG 243, 200(a)127; DRB, "Niederschrift über die 91. Präsidentenkonferenz am 6. Dezember 1943," 2 Aasp 91, Geheim, Berlin, 5 January 1944, BA R5 Anh I/69; Wochenberichte of the Hauptwagenamt, March-June 1943, BA R5 Anh II/39; Wehde-Textor, "Dokumentarische Darstellung," pp. 43-44, BA R5 Anh II/11; Kreidler, *Eisen-*

bahnen im Machtbereich, 284, 286. The figures given in USSBS, *German Transportation*, 74-75, seem high.

103. Emrich, ZVL, Minutes, 22 July 1942, Vertraulich, Berlin, 22 July 1942, p. 3, BA R5 Anh II/38; Emrich, ZVL, Minutes, 5 November 1943, Vertraulich, Berlin, 10 November 1943, p. 3, BA R5 Anh II/38; Wehde-Textor, "Dokumentarische Darstellung," pp. 39-40.

104. Dilli to divisions, etc., "Niederschrift, 28. Betriebsleiterbesprechung," 26 Babh 35, Berlin, 16 September 1942, pp. 2, 6-7, BA R5 Anh I/62.

105. Derived from HWA, Wochenberichte, BA R5/2092, BA R5 Anh II/39. See also Kreidler, *Eisenbahnen im Machtbereich*, 275, 276, 279, 285-88.

106. Wehde-Textor, "Dokumentarische Darstellung," p. 36.

107. Leibbrand to divisions, etc., "Kohlenwagen in Personenzügen," 23 Baü 187, Berlin, 19 March 1942, BA R5/2085.

108. RBD Munich, "Kohlenverkehr Deutschland—Italien über den Brenner," B ktr, Munich, 3 April 1940, pp. 1-3, 7, BA R5 Anh II/36; GBL South, "Italiakohlenverkehr im Juni 1943," G 42/44 Bjgmk, Munich, 3 June 1943, pp. 1-2, BA R5 Anh II/36; GBL South, "Niederschrift zur Besprechung über den Wirtschaftsverkehr mit Italien am 17. März 1944 in Verona," C 73 Vgal, Nur für den Dienstgebrauch, Munich, 31 March 1944, p. 3, BA R5 Anh I/116; Michaelsen, "Die Kriegsschauplätze Balkan und Italien," pp. 27-29, BA R5 Anh I/23; Fülling, GBL Süd, pp. 18-20; Wohlschläger, "Eisenbahnen im 2. Weltkrieg," p. 11, BA R5 Anh II/35; "Tätigkeit der Betriebsüberwachung der GBL West im 2. Weltkrieg," p. 5, BA R5 Anh I/27.

109. Schultz, HWA, Wochenbericht, 15 May 1942, p. 4, BA R5/2092; Central Planning, Minutes, 28 May 1942, Geheim, Berlin, 29 May 1942, p. 2, NA T-83, R-76, FR 3447777; Schelp, 10 Vwb (Kohlen) 209, Berlin, 24 October 1942, BA R5/3630; Schultz, HWA, Wochenbericht, 9 April 1943, p. 3, BA R5 Anh II/39; Schultz, HWA, Wochenbericht, 8 January 1944, BA R5 Anh II/39; Meinberg, "Der grossdeutschen Kohlenverkehr im 1. Halbjahr des KWJ 1943-44," TB 1250/43g, Berlin, 21 October 1943, Anlage 1, Anlage 2, BA R5/57; Schultz, HWA, Wochenbericht, 13 May 1944, BA R5 Anh II/39; Telegrammbrief, DRB to divisions, etc., 10 Vwb (Kohlen) 228, Berlin, 24 May 1944, BA R5/3181; Emrich, ZVL, Minutes, 5 January 1943, Vertraulich, Berlin, 9 January 1943, Anlage 1, p. 7, BA R5 Anh II/38; Emrich, "Verteilung der Massengütttransporte auf das ganze Jahr entsprechend der Leistungsfähigkeit der Verkehrsträger," Pr (Z) 81 Val 5, Berlin, 31 May 1944, Anlage 5, p. 1, BA R5/3173, also in BA R5 Anh II/38; Wehner, "Einsatz," 113, based on DRB, *Statistische Angaben*, 1938-43.

110. The total load-bearing capacity of the DRB's freight car fleet increased from 9.71 million tons in 1939 to 12.12 million tons in 1942. Of the 952,000 freight cars used by the DRB as of January 1942, one-third were not of German origin. DRB, "Zehnjahresplan der Fahrzeugbeschaffung," 30 Fef 112, Berlin, January 1942, p. 4, BA R5/2123; DRB, "Vermerk," 39 Fef 132, Sofort, Berlin, 2 November 1942, Anlage 2, BAC R005/022469.

111. Dorpmüller, "Einschränkung des Reiseverkehrs, hier: Verbot von Veranstaltungen, Tagungen und Kongressen," 20 g Bfp 13, Geheim, Berlin, 11 September 1941, BA R2/23731.

112. Leibbrand to divisions, etc., "Vorbereitung zur Verlängerung der Fahrzeiten der Reisezüge," 20 Bfp 247, Berlin, 16 March 1942, BA R5/2085.

113. Kleinmann to ministries, etc., "Reiseverkehr zu Ostern," 20 Bfsf 184, Berlin, 20 March 1942, BA R43 II/637a, f. 114.

114. Ganzenmüller to Reich agencies, etc., "Schlafwagenbenutzung," 15 Vpsch 32, Berlin, 6 June 1942, BA R43 II/637a, ff. 129-30; Schelp to Reich agencies, etc., "Schlafwagenbenutzung," 15 Vpsch 32, Berlin, 14 August 1942, BA R43 II/637a, f. 136; Schnellbrief, Leibbrand to Reich agencies, etc., "Reisebeschränkungen," 15 Vpe 36, Berlin, 14 August 1942, p. 2, BA R43 II/637a, f. 138; Schelp to Reich agencies, etc., "Schlafwagenbenutzung," 15 Vpsch 46, Berlin, 7 October 1943, BA R43 II/637a, ff. 157-58.

115. GBL Ost, Wochenbericht, 12-24 December 1943, Vertraulich, Berlin, 25 December 1943, p. 2, BA R5 Anh II/40; GBL Ost, Wochenbericht, 8-14 April 1944, Vertraulich, Berlin, 15 April 1944, p. 2, BA R5 Anh II/41.

116. Telegrammbrief, Ganzenmüller to divisions, etc., "Soforteinsatz; hier: Verpflegungszüge," 26 Baü 231, Berlin, 21 December 1943, BA R5/3055; DRB, "Niederschrift 30. Betriebsleiterbesprechung, 18.-19. August 1943," 26 Babh 37, Berlin, 10 November 1943, p. 10, BA R5 Anh I/63, also in BA R5/2782.

117. Rödl, "Einsatz der Beamten und Ruhestandsbeamten während des Krieges," *Die Reichsbahn* 16 (16 October 1940): 430-33; Bruckauf, "Personalwesen," p. 64, BA R5 Anh I/13.

118. Kleinmann to divisions, etc., "Fürsorge für die Gefolgschaft während des Krieges," 57.568 Usv (K), Berlin, 30 January 1940, BA R5 Anh II/47; Wehner, "Verelendung," 284.

119. Kroener, Müller, and Umbreit, *Das Deutsche Reich und der Zweite Weltkrieg*, 5.1:800; Boelcke, *Deutschlands Rüstung*, 439.

120. Telegrammbrief, Kleinmann, "Bereitstellung von Personal für die besetzten westlichen Gebieten," 50.510 Pwhp (Westen), Berlin, 12 June 1940, BAC R005/546alt.

121. Meyer, "Deutsche Eisenbahner im besetzten Frankreich," p. 4, BA R5 Anh I/109; Kausche, "Eisenbahnen," p. 3, BA R5 Anh I/171.

122. Bruckauf, "Personalwesen," p. 71.

123. Kleinmann, "Abordnung von Reichsbahnpersonal in das besetzte Gebiet," 50.510 Pwhp, Berlin, 17 September 1939, BAC R005/564alt.

124. Kleinmann, "Versetzung von Gefolgschaftsmitgliedern der Deutschen Reichsbahn aus dem Altreich in die eingegliederten Ostgebiete," 52.502 Par (Ostgebiete), Berlin, 19 September 1940, BAC R005/126 Ha.

125. RVD Minsk, *Amtsblatt*, Nr. 27, 7 June 1943, p. 4; USHMA, RG-53.022M. 370/5/44; Telegrammbrief, Kleinmann to divisions, etc., "Auswahl der nach dem Osten abzordnenden Kräfte," 50.510 Pwhp (UdSSR), 2 January 1942, BAC R005/023133; RBD Nuremberg, "Merkblatt für die Anschluß an die Abruftelegramme, 50.511 Pwhp (R).- nach dem Osten abzustellenden Bediensteten," (1941), BA R5 Anh II/47; Petry, "Beitrag über den Einsatz der deutschen Eisenbahner im Osten (Mittelabschnitt) von 1941-1944," 1952, p. 1, BA R5 Anh I/144; Kausche, "Die Organisation der militärischen Transportdienststellen und der Einsatz der Eisenbahner im Kriege," 1952, pp. 12, 14, BA R5 Anh I/171.

126. Osthoff, 50.510 Pwhp (UdSSR), Berlin, 2 December 1941, p. 3, BA R2/23499; Bruckauf, "Personalwesen," pp. 68, 70.

127. Ref 38/34, July 1941, BAC R005/2845.

128. Osthoff, 50.510 Pwhp (UdSSR), Berlin, 2 December 1941, pp. 4-5, BA R2/23491; Bruckauf, "Personalwesen," p. 67.

129. RBD Berlin, "521. Arbeitseinsatz; hier: Sicherung des Gefolgschaftsstands," *Amtsblatt*, Nr. 76, 14 July 1942, p. 270, Archiv Rbd Berlin.

130. Ganzenmüller to Speer, "Deckung des Kräftebedarf der Deutschen Reichsbahn durch die Zentrale Planung," 51.561 Pwhk 76, Berlin, 23 June 1943, BAC R005/149 Ha; Stets, "Gefolgschaftsmitglieder der Reichsbahn," Vid 5103.1/116, Berlin, 7 July 1943, BAC R005/52 Ha; Sauckel, "Kräftebedarf der Deutschen Reichsbahn im zweiten Halbjahr 1943," Via 5241/6180/43g, Berlin, 17 September 1943, BAC R005/52 Ha; Lammers, Rk. 3595B, Führerhauptquartier, 3 May 1944, BA R43 II/187, ff. 151-52.

131. Boelcke, *Deutschlands Rüstung*, 439.

132. Osthoff to divisions, etc., "Heranziehung von Reichsbahnbediensteten zur Waffen-SS," 51.561 Pwhk, Berlin, 5 October 1940, BAC R005/023133.

133. RBD Berlin, "932. Beamtenlaufbahnen der Deutschen Reichsbahn und Abweichung von den Befähigungsvorschriften," *Amtsblatt*, Nr. 110, 17 November 1939, p. 443, Archiv Rbd

Berlin; "Rückblick auf das Jahr 1939," *ZVME* 80 (22 February 1940): 94; Hassenpflug, 54.508 Pol 10, Berlin, 26 July 1943, BAC R005/149 Ha; DRB, "Bereitstellung von Lokomotivpersonal für Notfälle," 34 Pa (Betr) 133, Berlin, 3 October 1944, BA R5/2782; Rief, "Die Deutsche Reichsbahn im Zweiten Weltkrieg Abschnitt Personalwesen," p. 33, BA R5 Anh I/13.

134. Osthoff, "Einsatzmöglichkeiten für ausländische Arbeitskräfte im Eigenbetrieb der Deutschen Reichsbahn," 51.561 Pwhk (Zeitarb) Berlin, 30 May 1940, BAC R005/126 Ha.

135. Osthoff to divisions, etc., "Ersatz ausländischer Arbeiter; hier: Unterkünfte," 51.561 Pwhk (Zeitarb), Berlin, 20 February 1941, BAC R005/023133.

136. RBD Berlin, "165. Kosten für Verpflegung und Unterhaltung bei Beschäftigung von Kriegsgefangenen (KG)," *Amtsblatt*, Nr. 18, 28 February 1941, p. 75, Archiv Rbd Berlin.

137. Schnellbrief, RAM to Landesarbeitämter, "Einsatz sowjetischer Kriegsgefangener bei der Deutschen Reichsbahn," Va 5135/1643, Berlin, 30 October 1941, BAC R005/023133.

138. DRB to divisions, etc., "Pünktliche Ent- und Beladung von Güterwagen," 11 Vgba 170, Berlin, 13 May 1941, USHMA, RG-53.002M, R 1 378/1/275; Göring to DRB, Sauckel, Reich agencies, VP 9712/2, Berlin, 31 May 1942, p. 1, BA R5 Anh II/44.

139. Telegrammbrief, Osthoff to divisions, "Personalverhältnisse im besetzten Gebiet," 50.510 Pwhp, Berlin, 8 September 1939, BA R2/23810.

140. RBD Berlin, "50. Kennzeichnung von Polen," *Amtsblatt*, Nr. 11, 23 January 1942, p. 31, Archiv Rbd Berlin.

141. RBD Berlin, "77. Umgang mit Angehörigen polnischen Volkstums, im Nachfolgenden kurz Polen genannt," *Amtsblatt*, Nr. 15, 3 February 1942, p. 47, Archiv Rbd Berlin.

142. RBD Posed to RVM, "Einführung der Befähigungsvorschriften in den eingegliederten Ostgebieten," 3 P1 Pop, Posen, 27 July 1942, BA R5/2780.

143. DAF to Erdmann, Tgb. Nr. E 1179/A 1009/41, Berlin, 3 June 1941, BAC R005/023058.

144. Telegrammbrief, Osthoff to divisions, 51.561 Pwhk (Zeitarb), Berlin, 11 March 1941, BAC R005/023133; Telegrammbrief, Hassenpflug, "Zuweisung von 15 000 italienischen Kriegsgefangen," 51.561 Pwhk (Zeitarb) 61, Berlin, 23 September 1943, BAC R005/52 Ha.

145. Telegramm, Reeder to Wagner, "Abwerbung der belgischen Eisenbahner," 1230, 26 March 1942, BAMA H12/150.

146. Rief, "Personalwesen," p. 30; Bruckauf, "Personalwesen," p. 65; Kirste, "Der Krankenstand bei der Deutschen Reichsbahn," Nur für den Dienstgebrauch, 1943, p.7, BAC R005/52 Ha.

147. Rief, "Personalwesen," p. 32, BA R5 Anh I/13.

148. RBD Berlin, "Beschäftigung von Frauen im Dienst eines Eisenbahn- Betriebs- und Polizeibeamtin," Nr. 98, 10 October 1939, p. 383, Archiv Rbd Berlin.

149. Abt. II to Abt. V, 23 Bzp, Berlin, 10 November 1939, BA R5/2781.

150. Osthoff to Abt. II, "Beschäftigung von Frauen im Zugbegleitdienst," 50.510 Pwhp, Berlin, 9 December 1939, BA R5/2781.

151. Osthoff to divisions, "Personalwirtschaft; hier: vermehrter Einsatz von Frauen . . . ," 51.510 Pwhp, Sofort, Berlin, 26 April 1940, BA R5/2781.

152. RBD Berlin, "Werbung von Frauen für eine Einstellung in den Reichsbahndienst," *Amtsblatt*, Nr. 48, 17 May 1940, p. 199, Archiv Rbd Berlin.

153. Telegrammbrief, Kleinmann to divisions, "Personalwirtschaft; hier: vermehrter Einsatz von Fraucn," 50.510 Pwhp, Bcrlin, 15 June 1940, BA R5/2781.

154. Abt. E II to Abt. E V, 24 Bzp 128, Berlin, 21 November 1940, BA R5/2781.

155. Telegrammbrief, Hassenpflug to divisions, "Personalwirtschaft; hier: vermehrter Einsatz von Frauen," 50.510 Berlin, 9 April 1941, BA R5/2781.

156. Osthoff to divisions, "Personalwirtschaft; hier: vermehrter Einsatz von Frauen," 50/51.510 Pwhp, Berlin, 1 December 1941, BA R5/2780.

157. Wolfgang Schrag, "Arbeitseinsatzmaßnahmen der Deutschen Reichsbahn im Kriege," *ZVME* 82 (26 March 1942): 169.

158. Hassenpflug to divisions, etc., "Beschäftigung von deutschen Frauen bei der Deutschen Reichsbahn. Zusammenfassung der darüber ergangenen Erlasse und Verfügungen," 51.533 Plt, Berlin, 13 January 1943, BA R5/2781. On the temporary nature of the employment of women with the Reichsbahn, see DRB, "Niederschrift 30. Betriebsleiterbesprechung, 18.–19. August 1943," 26 Babh 37, Berlin, p. 30, BA R5 Anh I/63, also in BA R5/2782.

159. Kirste, "Der Krankenstand bei der Deutschen Reichsbahn," Nur für den Dienstgebrauch, 1943, p. 7, BAC R005/52 Ha.

160. Emrich, ZVL, Minutes, 16 March 1943, Vertraulich, Berlin, 23 March 1943, p. 8, BA R5 Anh II/38.

161. Wehner, "Verelendung," 281.

162. RBD Berlin, "856. Allgemeine Beamtenpflichten," *Amtsblatt*, Nr. 92, 4 October 1940, p. 362, Archiv Rbd Berlin.

163. Bruckauf, "Personalwesen," p. 62.

164. Ibid., p. 61.

165. Hassenpflug, "Politische Beurteilung der Beamten," 52.502 Par, Berlin, 3 June 1943, p. 1, BA R005/149 Ha.

166. Anklageschrift Ganzenmüller, 8 Js 430/67, p. 188, ZSL VI (420) 107 AR-Z 80/61.

167. Ibid., pp. 242-43.

168. Wehner, "Verelendung," 286.

169. Anton Gude, "Finanzwesen der Deutschen Reichsbahn und zweiter Weltkrieg," p. 1, BA R5 Anh I/47.

170. RBD Berlin, "Übernahme von etatsmäßigen Bediensteten der ehemaligen polnischen Staatsbahnen, die in Abt 3 der Deutschen Volksblatt aufgenommen werden als Aushilfsangestellte," *Amtsblatt*, Nr. 114, 23 October 1942, p. 483, Archiv Rbd Berlin.

171. RBD Berlin, "933. Belohnung und Prämien an ausländische Arbeiter," *Amtsblatt*, Nr. 123, 20 November 1942, p. 463, Archiv Rbd Berlin; Hassenpflug, "Entlohnung ausländischer Arbeitskräfte," 56.535 Pldaa, Berlin, 2 March 1944, BAC R005/13 Ha; DRB, "Lohnabzugstaffel für sozialausgleichsabgabepflichtige Arbeitnehmer gültig vom 1. April 1944 an," BAC R005/12646./1.

172. Kirste, "Der Krankenstand bei der Deutschen Reichsbahn," Nur für den Dienstgebrauch, 1943, pp. 4, 8, BAC R005/52 Ha.

173. Fritz Busch, "Wandlungen im Finanzwesen der Deutschen Reichsbahn," *ZVME* 82 (1 October 1942): 512.

174. Kleinmann to RWM, "Kapitalmarkt," 41 Kfr 38, Berlin, 24 January 1939, pp. 1-2, BA R2/3881, ff. 168-69.

175. RFM, "Kapitalbedarf der Deutschen Reichsbahn für Neuinvestitionen in den Jahren 1939-1943 unter Zugrundelegung der für die Führerbauten vorgesehenen Fertigungstellungsfristen," Su 3602 - 191V, Berlin, 11 February 1939, BA R2/3881, f. 120.

176. Prang, "Aktenvermerk," Berlin, 17 February 1939, BA R2/3881, f. 163.

177. Prang to Lange, "Vermerk," Vertraulich, 3 March 1939, BA R2/3881, ff. 160-62.

178. "Kapitalbedarf der Deutschen Reichsbahn für 1939," Anlage zu 41 Kfl 47, Vertraulich, Berlin, 4 March 1939, BA R5/2541.

179. Lange to RVM, IV Kred. 25978/39, Berlin, 15 March 1939, BA R2/3881, ff. 165-67.

180. RWM to DRB, IV Kred. 31 508/39, Berlin, 15 June 1939, BA R5/2499.

181. DRB, BR, Minutes, 3 July 1939, p. 4, BA R2/31652.

182. Kleinmann to RFM, "Ausgabe einer neuen Reichsbahn-Anleihe," 40 Kfb 43/2, Berlin,

23 October 1939, BA R2/3881, f. 228; DRB, "Vermerk," 40 Kfb 43.1, Berlin, 21 September 1939, BA R5/2499.

183. Kleinmann to RFM, 40 Kfb 43/3, Berlin, 24 October 1939, BA R2/3881, f. 233; RFM, "Reichsbahn-Anleihe," Su 3602-224-Gen B, Berlin, 26 October 1939, p. 2, BA R2/3881, f. 235; RFM, "Vermerk," Su 3602-217-Gen. B., Berlin, 26 October 1939, BA R2/3881, f. 234; Reichsbankdirektorium to RVM, Nr. II 10591, Berlin, 27 October 1939, BA R5/2499; Reichsbank, *Verwaltungsbericht der Deutschen Reichsbank für das Jahr 1939* (Berlin, 10 April 1940), p. 7, BA RD51/3-1939.

184. RVM, "7% Reichsbahnvorzugsaktien," 40 Kfa, Berlin, 1 October 1938, BA R2/3882, ff. 52-54.

185. RFM, "Verzinsung der Reichsbahnvorzugsaktien," Berlin, 10 August 1940, pp. 1, 4, 5, BA R2/3882, ff. 43, 45, 47; RFM, "Umgestaltung der Reichsbahnvorzugsaktien (RVA)," Ve 6023-53V, Berlin, August 1940, BA R2/3882, ff. 48-49.

186. Funk to RVM, "Vorsugsaktien der Deutschen Reichsbahn," IV Kred. 36181/40, Berlin, 11 September 1940, p. 1, BA R2/3882, ff. 25-26; Kittel, "Das neue Reichsbahngesetz," *Die Reichsbahn* 15 (12 July 1939): 702.

187. "Einlösung der Reichsbahnvorzugsaktien und Ausgabe einer neuen 4%igen Anleihe der Deutschen Reichsbahn von 1940," *Die Reichsbahn* 16 (18-25 September 1940): 398; Funk to RVM, "Vorzugsaktien der Deutschen Reichsbahn," IV Kred. 36181/40, Berlin, 11 September 1940, p. 1, BA R2/3882, ff. 25-26.

188. Kleinmann to Lammers, 4 Ogbg, Berlin, 28 December 1940, BA R43 II/187a, f. 87; RFM, "Zusammenstellung der vom Reiche übernommenen und noch laufenden Bürgschaften und Garantien nach dem Stande vom 1. Januar 1941," zu F 3414c-5I, Vertraulich, Berlin, 28 July 1941, p. 14, BAP 21.01/9943; Reichsbank, *Verwaltungsbericht der Deutschen Reichsbank für das Jahr 1940* (Berlin, 4 March 1941), p. 7, BA RD51/3-1940; "Die Reichsbahn konvertiert," *Frankfurter Zeitung*, Nr. 480-81, 20 September 1940, BHSA, Rep. MWi 8633; Reichsschuldverwaltung, "4%ige Anleihe der Deutschen Reichsbahn von 1940," 5911-1, Berlin, 21 March 1945, BA R2/3882, f. 244.

189. Reichsbank, *Verwaltungsbericht der Deutschen Reichsbank für das Jahr 1941* (Berlin, 10 April 1940), p. 7, BA RD51/3-1941.

190. Dorpmüller to RFM, "Einlösung 4½%igen Schatzanweisungen der Deutschen Reichsbahn vom Jahre 1936, Reihe I, fällig am 2.1.1944," 40 Kfb XXXIV, Berlin, 28 June 1943, p. 1, BA R2/3882, f. 178.

191. Dorpmüller to RFM, "Verlängerung und Umwandlung der am 2.1.1944 fällig werdenden 4½% Reichsbahnschatzanweisungen von 1936, Reihe I," 40 Kfb 46/1, Berlin, 27 August 1943, BA R2/3882, f. 180; RFM to RVM, "Umtausch der 4½% Schatzanweisungen der Deutschen Reichsbahn von 1936, Reihe I," Su 3602-295-Gen B., Berlin, 19 July 1943, BA R2/3882, f. 179.

192. DRB, "Schuldenstand der DRB seit 1924," BA R5/2589.

193. Kiefer, "Darlehen des Reiches von der Deutschen Reichsbahn," Ve 1410^{43}-10 V 4 V, Berlin, 25 January 1943, BAP 21.01/B9504; Hartenau to Reichsschuldenverwaltung, Su 3560-978 Gen B. 2 Ang, Berlin, 22 October 1940, BA R2/3882, f. 72; DVKB, "Geschäftsbericht über das Geschäftsjahr vom 1. Januar bis 31. Dezember 1942," GStA, Rep. 151 I c/11165.

194. Prang, "Aufzeichnung," 41 Kmb (1944)3, Berlin, 15 November 1943, BAP 21.01/B 9503; Hartenau, Su 3560-489 Gen B, Berlin, 16 December 1943, BAP 21.01/B 9503.

195. Funk, IV Kred. 30248/44, Berlin, 20 February 1944, BA R2/3882, ff. 221-24; RFM to RWM, Schreiben vom 20. Februar 1944 - IV Kred. 30248/44, Berlin, 6 March 1944, BA R2/3882, f. 225; Bayerhofer, "Besprechung bei Herrn Reichsverkehrsminister Dorpmüller am 14. Juni 1944 über die Auflegung einer Reichsbahnanleihe," Su 3602-316-Gen B, Berlin, 14 June 1944,

pp. 1, 3, BA R2/3882, ff. 236, 238; Dorpmüller to RFM, "Niederschrift zur Chefbesprechung über Aufnahme einer langfristigen Reichsanleihe für allgemeine Reichszwecke," IV Kfb 710, Berlin, 14 June 1944, BA R2/3882, ff. 227-30.

196. Schnellbrief, Meilicke to GB f. d. Regelung der Bauwirtschaft, "Unterhaltung und Erneuerung der Gleise und der Brücken der Reichsbahn," 69 Nal 744, Berlin, 24 April 1940, pp. 1-2, BAMA H12/114.1; Ebeling to Transchef, "Lieferung von Oberbaustoffen," L 3 Bmsto 41, Berlin, 16 August 1940, BAMA H12/114.6, f. 43; DRB, "Vermerk," 61 Iou 387, Berlin, 30 May 1940, BA R005/021000; RZA to DRB, "Eisenbezugsrechte a) Oberbau," Berlin, 17 February 1944, BAC R005/021498; DRB to divisions, "Ausbau entbehrlicher Gleise und Weichen," 61 Sto 277, Berlin, 9 April 1940, BA R5 Anh II/46; DRB, "Unterhaltung und Erneuerung des Oberbaues im Geschäftsjahr 1942," 74 Iop 1900, Berlin, 10 January 1942, pp. 1-2, BAC 43.04/246; Rudolphi to Abt II, "Bereitstellung von Oberbaustoffen für den Osten," 74 Sto 485, Eilt, Berlin, 22 May 1942, BA R5/2085; "Stenographische Niederschrift der 56. Sitzung der Zentralen Planung betreffend Baukontingente am 5 April 1944," Geheim, p. 27, NA RG 243, 4(e)6; Becker, "The Basis of the German War Economy under Albert Speer, 1942-1944," 402.

197. Ganzenmüller to divisions, etc., Sofort, 41 Kmbp (1943)1, Berlin, 18 December 1942, p. 1, BAC R005/022871.

198. DRB, *Statistische Angaben 1942*, 136, n. 1; DRB, *Statistische Angaben 1943*, 114, n. 1.

199. Weirauch, "Bericht des Hauptprüfungsamts der Deutschen Reichsbahn über die Prüfung der Wirtschafts- und Rechnungsführung sowie des Jahresabschlusses der Deutschen Reichsbahn für das Geschäftsjahr 1941," p. 10, BA NL171/184, f. 102.

E. *The End of the Third Reich, 1944–1945*

1. For a comprehensive analysis of the events discussed in this section, see Mierzejewski, *Collapse*. See also Boelcke, *Deutschlands Rüstung*, 444; Webster and Frankland, *The Strategic Air Offensive against Germany*, 4: appendix 35, p. 350; RVM/E-Abt. (L4), "Die Einwirkung des Luftkrieges auf den Eisenbahnbetrieb in der Zeit vom 1.-8. November 1944," Berlin, 9 November 1944, p. 3, BA R5/3699; RVM/E-Abt. (L4), "Die Einwirkung des Luftkrieges auf den Eisenbahnbetrieb in der Zeit vom 1.-12. November 1944," Berlin, 13 November 1944, p. 5, BA R5/3699; Ganzenmüller, "Verkehrslage im Ruhrgebiet," 9 December 1944, p. 6, BA R5/3699, translation available in NA RG 243 200 (a) 137; USSBS, "Interrogation of Eckhard Burger," p. 2, NA RG 243, 200(a)127.

2. See the minutes of the ZVL meeting on 21 June, 5 July, and 27 July 1944 in BA R5 Anh II/38. For the meetings on 12 August, 29 August, 6 September, 21 September, 5 October, and 19 October 1944, see BA R5/37. For the minutes of the meeting of 11 November 1944, see NA RG 243 200(a)41. Reports on the meetings of 1 December, 18 December, and 29 December 1944 are available in NA T-77, R-13, FR723682-723964. An English translation of the minutes of the meeting of 11 November 1944 is available in NA RG 243 200(a)41. Pape, *Bombing to Win*, 254-313, disputes this assessment of the effects of transportation bombing. However, Pape's work is poorly researched, relies on artificial analytical criteria, suffers from a complete misunderstanding of Tedder's and Zuckerman's goals, confuses the sequence of events, and is hobbled by inadequate economic analysis.

3. Oppeln to Mineis, etc., Fernspruch Nr. 156, 20 January 1945, BA R5 Anh I/76; Arbeitsgemeinschaft, "Die wesentlichen Aufgaben der Reichsbahndirektion Posen 1939-1945, Betrieb," p. 5, BA R5 Anh I/78; Schmeisse, "Wichtiges aus dem Reisezugfahrplandezernat," Stuttgart, 8 October 1953, p. 4, BA R5 Anh I/75.

4. Telegrammbrief, RBD Cologne Dez 3 to Dez 5, 35 A6a Ogde, Bergish-Gladbach, 4 March

1945, BA R5 Anh I/67; Fernschreiben, RBD Cologne to RBD Hanover, 3S A6a Ogde, Cologne, 4 March 1945, BA R5 Anh I/67.

    5. Based on data in Mierzejewski, *Collapse*, appendix table A.7, p. 195, and RZA Blatt 92, 1943, 1944, 1945, NA RG 243, 200(a)96. See also Emrich, "Wochenberichte der Generalbetriebsleitung Ost," BA R5 Anh II/41.

    6. Based on raw data in RZA, Blatt 92, 1944, 1945, NA RG 243, 200(a)96.

    7. Based on raw data in RZA, Blatt 90 for 1944–45, NA RG 243, 200(a)94, 95, 96, 116, 117. See also Otto Wehde-Textor, "Dokumentarische Darstellung der deutschen Eisenbahnen im Zweiten Weltkrieg. Teil IV. Der Verkehr," p. 38, BA R5 Anh II/11.

    8. Schramm, *Kriegstagebuch des Oberkommandos der Wehrmacht*, 4.1:306; Wehde-Textor, "Dokumentarische Darstellung," p. 45; RMfRuK, "Die Verkehrslage in Großdeutschland (Stichtag 18.1.1945)," Geheim, p. 1, BA R3/1957, f. 727; Ganzenmüller, "Verkehrslage im Ruhrgebiet," 9 December 1944, p. 4, BA R5/3699, translation available in NA RG 243, 200(a)137; Abt. L, "Lagebericht Reichsbahn," Geheime Reichssache, Berlin, p. 3, BA R5/3699.

    9. OKW, Fwi Amt, Fachabt. TuV, "Aktennotiz über die 51. ZVL Sitzung am 29.12.44," Nr. 3210/45 geh, Geheim, Berlin, 2 January 1945, p. 2, NA T-77, R-13, FR 723683; Wissenschaftliche Beratungsstelle, "Verkehrszahlen für die Besprechung . . . ," PLA 080/20-382/45g, Geheim, Berlin, 12 March 1945, BA R5/3699; Kreidler, *Eisenbahnen im Machtbereich*, 279. USSBS, *German Transportation*, 74–75, gives much higher figures.

    10. Abt. 2f to Schmidt, 8 February 1945, BBA 33/1040; RMfRuK, Planungsamt, "Wochenmeldung Nr. 2/45," PlA 210/09/13.1, Geheim, Berlin, 13 January 1945, BA R3/1854a; Kreidler, *Eisenbahnen im Machtbereich*, 264–65.

    11. Zahn, "Der Betrieb," p. 28, BA R5 Anh I/9.

    12. Lammers, "Reichsverkehrsminister," Rk. 5609B, Berlin, 8 July 1944, BA R43 II/1146, ff. 40–41.

    13. Kehrl, *Krisenmanager*, 413.

    14. Fernschreiben, Ganzenmüller to Lamertz, Berlin, 7 November 1944, BA R5/3173; Speer to Hitler, "Situation in the Ruhr Area," 11 November 1944, p. 1, reprinted in Webster and Frankland, *The Strategic Air Offensive against Germany*, 4: appendix 35, p. 349. Also in NA T-73, R-182, FR 3394854.

    15. Dorpmüller to divisions, HWA, "Bestellung von Bevollmächtigten für Wirtschaftstransporte," 10 Val 209, Berlin, 4 January 1945, BA R5/95; Kreidler, *Eisenbahnen im Machtbereich*, 197.

    16. Mierzejewski, *Collapse*, 173.

Bibliography

Archival Collections

American University, Washington, D.C.
  Ludwig Homberger personnel files.
Archiv Rankeberg, Pulheim.
  Nachlaß Paul Freiherr von Eltz-Rübenach.
Auswärtiges Amt, Bonn.
Bayerisches Hauptstaatsarchiv, Munich.
  Rep. MA: Bayerisches Ministerium des Äussern.
  Rep. MWi: Bayerisches Wirtschafts- und Verkehrsministerium.
Bergbau-Archiv, Bochum.
  13: Bergbaugruppe Ruhr.
  15: Wirtschaftsvereinigung Bergbau e. V.
  33: Rheinisch-Westfälisches Kohlen-Syndikat.
Berlin Document Center.
Bundesarchiv, Koblenz.
  Kl. Erw. 409: Restnachlaß Carl Stieler.
  Kl. Erw. 491: Geschichte des Internierungslagers Darmstadt von Februar bis Oktober 1946, zusammengestellt vom Counter Intelligence Staff der amerikanischen Militärregierung, 1947.
  Kl. Erw. 496: Verkehrs- und Transportwesen im 2. Weltkrieg.
  Kl. Erw. 750: Nachlaß Julius Dorpmüller.
  Kl. Erw. 798: Gästebuch des Hauses Funks.
  NL13: Nachlaß Paul Silverberg.
  NL171: Nachlaß Friedrich Ernst Moritz Saemisch.
  NL FA 64: Nachlaß Paul Freiherr von Eltz-Rübenach.
  NS4: NSDAP Partei-Kanzlei.
  NS10: Persönliche Adjutantur des Führers und Reichskanzlers.
  NS19: Persönlicher Stab, Reichsführer SS.
  NS19neu: Persönlicher Stab, Reichsführer SS.
  R2: Reichsfinanzministerium.
  R3: Reichsministerium für Rüstungs- und Kriegsproduktion.

R5: Reichsverkehrsministerium (R005).
R5 Anhang I: Sammlung Sarter.
R5 Anhang II: Sammlung Kreidler.
R6: Reichsministerium für die besetzten Ostgebieten.
R7: Reichswirtschaftsministerium.
R11: Reichswirtschaftskammer.
R28: Dienststellen der Deutschen Reichsbank.
R41: Reichsarbeitsministerium.
R43 I, II: Reichskanzlei.
R52 II: Kanzlei des Generalgouverneurs.
R53: Stellvertreter des Reichskanzlers.
R124: Eisenbahnverwaltung in den besetzten Gebieten.
RD5: *Reichsgesetzblatt.*
RD51/3: *Verwaltungsberichte der Reichsbank, 1923-38.*
RD97/5: *Verhandlungen des Reichseisenbahnrats.*
RD98/10: *Wirtschaftsführung und Finanzwesen bei der Deutschen Reichsbahn.*
RD98/12: *Geschäftsberichte der Deutschen Reichsbahn für Geschäftsjahre, 1920-43.* Weißbücher.
RD98/13: *Die Deutsche Reichsbahn im Geschäftsjahr.* . . . Blaubücher, 1926-31.
RD98/14: *Voranschlag/Wirtschaftspläne der Deutschen Reichsbahn*, 1925-27, 1929, 1936-45.
RD98/16: *Statistische Übersicht wichtiger Ergebnisse der Geschäftsjahre*, 1926-43.
RD98/17: *Statistische Angaben über die Deutsche Reichsbahn im Geschäftsjahr*, 1932-42. Successor to *Die Deutsche Reichsbahn im Geschäftsjahr.* . . . Blaubuch.
RD98/19: *Verzeichnis der oberen Reichsbahnbeamten*, 1935-44/45.
RD98/25: *Lochkartenstellen*, 1935, VBB.
RD98/26: Lochkartenverfahren, 1933.
RD98/27: Bestimmungen für die Beförderung der SA, SS und NSKK auf Eisenbahnen (Besa).
RD98/30: Anweisung- Behandlung- Eisenbahn- Wehrmacht-Angelegenheiten, 1941, 1942, 1943.
RD98/33: Amtliches Bahnhofsverzeichnis 1933 mit Nachträge.
RD98/54: *Die deutschen Eisenbahnen in ihrer Entwicklung 1835-1935.*
RD98/57: DRG, Gruppenverwaltung Bayern, *Eisenbahn-Nachrichtenblatt*, 1920-33. 14 vols.
RD98/64-1944: Entfernungstaffeln.
RD98/72: DR, *Statistische Monatsberichte*, 1928, 1930-44. 14 vols.
ZSg. 101: Sammlung Brammer.
Bundesarchiv, Abteilungen Potsdam.
21.01: Reichsfinanzministerium.
25.01: Deutsche Reichsbank.
46.01: Reichsministerium Speer.
Bundesarchiv, Abteilungen Potsdam, Aussenstelle Coswig (Anhalt).
R005: Reichsverkehrsministerium (formerly 43.01).
43.04: Reichsbahnzentralamt-Berlin.
43.06: HVD Brüssel.
43.16: GBL Ost.
43.17: GVD Osten Warschau.
43.18: RVD Riga.
Bundesarchiv-Militärarchiv, Freiburg-im-Breisgau.
N29: Nachlaß Hans Doerr.

RH2: OKH, Generalstab des Heeres, Organisationsabteilung.
RH4: Chef des Transportwesens and predecessors.
RH66: General der Eisenbahntruppen.
RW5: Oberkommando der Wehrmacht.

Deutsches Museum, Munich.
Linke-Hofmann-Busch.
Maybach.
Plansammlung, Abteilung Photos, Gruppe 16, von Reimer-Archiv.
Plansammlung 715, Triebwagen.
Wumag.

Geheimes Staatsarchiv Preußischer Kulturbesitz, Abteilung Merseburg.
Rep. 93E: Ministerium der öffentlichen Arbeiten, Abteilungen Eisenbahnangelegenheiten.
Rep. 151 I c: Finanzministerium.

Institut für Zeitgeschichte, Munich.
ED93: Nachlaß Hans Schaefer.
Eichmann-Prozess.
MA-120: Frank Tagebücher.
Reichsverkehrsministerium.

National Archives, Washington, D.C.
Record Group 242: Collection of Foreign Records Seized, 1941-. Captured German Documents Microfilmed at Alexandria, Virginia.
T-73: Records of the Reich Ministry of Armaments and War Production.
T-77: Records of the Headquarters of the German Armed Forces High Command.
T-83: Records of Private Austrian, Dutch, and German Enterprises.
T-84: Miscellaneous German Records Collection.
T-175: Records of the Reich Leader of the SS and Chief of the German Police.
T-178: Fragmentary Records of Miscellaneous Reich Ministries and Offices, 1919-45.
Record Group 243: United States Strategic Bombing Survey.

Reichsbahndirektion Berlin, Berlin.
Amtsblatt RBD Berlin, 1920-44.

Reichsbahndirektion Halle (Saale), Halle (S).
Registratur A.

Siemens-Archiv, Munich.
Carl Friedrich von Siemens Nachlaß.

Staatsanwaltschaft, Düsseldorf.
810/8 Ks 1/71: Ganzenmüller Verfahren.

United States Holocaust Museum Archives, Washington, D.C.
RG-02: Survivor Testimonies.
RG-09: Liberation of Camps.
RG-10: Small Collections.
RG-11: Selected Records from the Osobyi Archive, Moscow.
RG-53.002M: Selected Records from the Belorus Central State Archives, Minsk.

Zentrale Stelle der Landesjustizverwaltungen, Ludwigsburg.
Bischoff Prozess. V 203 AR-Z 26/1972.
Fitzke Prozess. V 203 AR-Z 148/1971.
Franz Prozess. 208 AR-Z 230/29.
Ganzenmüller Prozess. VI (420) 107 AR-Z 80/1961.
Geitmann, Wiens, Stier, Fehling Prozesse. II 206 AR-Z 15/1963.

Published Documents

Akten zur deutschen auswärtigen Politik. Series B. 21 vols. Göttingen, 1966–83.
Boelcke, Willi A., ed. *Deutschlands Rüstung im zweiten Weltkrieg. Hitlers Konferenzen mit Albert Speer 1942–1945.* Frankfurt am Main, 1969.
Domarus, Max. *Hitler Reden und Proklamationen.* 2 vols. Würzburg, 1962–63.
Erdmann, Karl Dietrich, and Hans Booms. *Akten der Reichskanzlei.* Boppard, 1968–89.
Germany. *Eisenbahn-Verkehrsordnung (EVO) vom 8. September 1938.* Leipzig, 1943.
Germany. Deutsche Bundesbahn, Hauptverwaltung. *1835–1960. 125 Jahre Deutsche Eisenbahnen.* Darmstadt, 1960. Also appeared in *Die Bundesbahn* 34, nos. 21–22 (1960).
———. *Was geschah wann? Zahlen aus der Geschichte der Eisenbahn.* Frankfurt am Main.
Germany. Deutsche Reichsbahn. *Deutsches Kursbuch. Jahresfahrplan 1944/45.* Berlin, 3 July 1944.
———. *Die Dienststellen der Deutschen Reichsbahn einschliesslich der ehemaligen Österreichische Bundesbahnen . . . Stand 1944.* Edited by Hubert Bernsee. Krefeld-Bochum, 1974.
———. *Die Netzkarten und Bezirkskarten der Deutschen Reichsbahn. Stand 1. September 1939.* Berlin, 1939.
———. *100 Jahre Deutsche Eisenbahnen, 1835–1935.* Berlin, 1935.
———. *100 Jahre Deutsche Eisenbahnen. Die Deutsche Reichsbahn im Jahre 1935. Sonderausgabe des amtlichen Nachrichtenblattes "Die Reichsbahn."* Berlin, 14 July 1935.
———. *Verzeichnis der Maschinenämter, Bahnbetriebswerke, Bahnbetriebswagenwerke, Lokomotivbahnhöfe, Bahnhofsschlossereien und Hilfszüge.* Vienna, 1941. Reprint, Freiburg-im-Breisgau, 1976.
———. *Verzeichnis der Maschinenämter, Bahnbetriebswerke, Bahnbetriebswagenwerke, Lokomotivbahnhöfe, Bahnhofsschlossereien und Hilfszüge für den Bereich der Hauptverwaltung der Eisenbahnen des amerikanischen und britischen Besatzungsgebiets und der Generaldirektion der Betriebsvereinigung der südwestdeutschen Eisenbahnen.* Krefeld, 1949. Reprint, Krefeld, 1978.
Germany. Deutsche Reichsbahn-Gesellschaft. *Bestimmungen für die Beförderung der SA, SS und des NSKK auf Eisenbahnen (Besa).* Munich, 1936.
———. *Die Deutsche Eisenbahnen in ihrer Entwicklung 1835–1935.* Berlin, 1935.
———. *Entwicklungszahlen aus der deutschen Eisenbahnstatistik seit 1900.* Berlin, 1930.
———. *Hundert Jahre Deutsche Eisenbahnen.* Berlin, 1935. Reprint, Munich, 1985.
———. *Reichsbahn-Handbuch.* Berlin, 1937.
———. *Wirtschaftsführung und Finanzwesen der Deutschen Reichsbahn.* Berlin, 1934.
Germany. Reichsbahn-Zentralamt. *Amtliches Bahnhofsverzeichnis der Deutschen Reichsbahn 1938.* Berlin, 1938.
Germany. Reichsbahn-Zentralamt für Rechnungswesen. *Amtliches Bahnhofsverzeichnis, Nachtrag 1. Stand 1 Dezember 1934.* Berlin, 1935.
Germany. Reichsverkehrsministerium. *Deutsche Verkehrsgeschichte. Band I/1–2.* Leipzig, 1939.
———. *Dienst- und Lohnordnung für die Arbeiter der Deutschen Reichsbahn (Dilo) gültig 1. April 1938 an (Fassung vom 1. Juli 1941).* Breslau, 1941.
———. *Die Personalpolitik der Deutschen Reichsbahn seit 1933.* Berlin, 1939.
Germany. Reichsverkehrsministerium. Organisationsausschuss im RVM. *Besoldungsvorschriften für die Reichsbahnbeamten vom 31. März in der Fassung vom 1. November 1943.* Reichenberg, 1944.
Germany. Sicherheitsdienst. *Meldungen aus dem Reich.* 17 vols. Edited by Heinz Boberach. Herrsching, 1984.
Great Britain. Inter-Service Topographical Department. *Plans and Photographs of German Railway Facilities.* London, 1944.

Holborn, Louise, Gwendolyn Carter, and John Herz. *German Constitutional Documents since 1789*. New York, 1970.

International Military Tribunal. *Trial of the Major War Criminals before the International Military Tribunal: Proceedings and Documents*. 42 vols. Nuremberg, 1947–49.

Office of United States Chief Counsel for the Prosecution of Axis Criminality. *Nazi Conspiracy and Aggression*. 9 vols., suppl. vol. A. Washington, D.C., 1946–48.

Picker, Henry. *Hitlers Tischgespräche im Führerhauptquartier*. Wiesbaden, 1983.

Schramm, Percy E., ed. *Kriegstagebuch des Oberkommandos der Wehrmacht*. 4 vols. Herrsching, 1982.

United Restitution Organization. *Dokumente über Methoden der Judenverfolgung im Ausland*. Frankfurt am Main, 1959.

United States. United States Strategic Bombing Survey. *Aircraft Division Industry Report*. Washington, D.C., 1947.

———. *The Effects of Strategic Bombing on German Morale*. Washington, D.C., 1947.

———. *The Effects of Strategic Bombing on German Transportation*. Washington, D.C., 1947.

———. *The Effects of Strategic Bombing on the German War Economy*. Washington, D.C., 1947.

Verband deutscher Eisenbahn-Fachschulen. *Finanz- und Rechnungswesen der Deutschen Reichsbahn*. Berlin, 1943.

Verein Mitteleuropäischer Eisenbahnverwaltungen. *Achsdruckverzeichnis (Vachs V)*. Berlin, 1937.

Diary and Memoir

Brüning, Heinrich. *Memoiren 1918–1934*. Stuttgart, 1970.

Frank, Hans. *Das Diensttagebuch des deutschen Generalgouverneurs in Polen 1939–1945*. Edited by Werner Präg and Wolfgang Jacobmeyer. Stuttgart, 1975.

Books and Selected Articles

Adler, Gerhard, et al. *Lexikon der Eisenbahn*. 6th ed. Berlin, 1981.

Adolph, Ernst. *Eisenbahn-Gütertarifwesen*. Berlin, 1933.

Allen, Geoffrey Freeman. *Railways of the Twentieth Century*. New York, 1983.

Ambrosius, Gerold. *Staat und Wirtschaft im 20. Jahrhundert*. Munich, 1990.

Aubin, Hermann, and Wolfgang Zorn. *Handbuch der deutschen Wirtschafts- und Sozialgeschichte*. 2 vols. Stuttgart, 1971, 1976.

Austin, M. "Die Spurweite der Eisenbahn." *Wissen und Wehr* (1943): 420–24.

Bagel-Bohlan, Anja. *Hitlers industrielle Kriegsvorbereitungen, 1936–1939*. Koblenz, 1975.

Barkai, Avraham. *Das Wirtschaftssystem des Nationalsozialismus*. Cologne, 1977. English edition, *Nazi Economics: Ideology, Theory and Policy*, translated by Ruth Hadass-Vashitz. New Haven, Conn., 1990.

Baum, Rainer C. "Holocaust: Moral Indifference as the Form of Modern Evil." In *Echoes from the Holocaust: Philosophical Reflections on a Dark Time*, edited by Alan Rosenberg and Gerald E. Myers, 53–90. Philadelphia, 1988.

———. *The Holocaust and the German Elite: Genocide and National Suicide in Germany, 1871–1945*. Totowa, N.J., 1981.

Baumann, Hans. *Deutsches Verkehrsbuch*. Berlin, 1931.

Baumgart, Winfried. "Eisenbahnen und Kriegführung in der Geschichte." *Technikgeschichte* 38 (1971): 191–219.

Bäzold, Dieter, and Günter Fiebig. *Elektrische Lokomotiven deutscher Eisenbahnen.* 2nd ed. Düsseldorf, 1986.

Beck, Earl R. *Under the Bombs: The German Home Front, 1942-1945.* Lexington, Ky., 1986.

Becker, Peter W. "The Basis of the German War Economy under Albert Speer, 1942-1944." Ph.D. diss., Stanford University, 1971.

Behrends, H., W. Hensel, and G. Wiedau. *Güterwagenarchiv 1.* Berlin, 1989.

Behrendt, Artur, Uwe Blank, et al. *100 Jahre Eisenbahn Direktion Hamburg 1884-1984.* Hamburg-Altona, 1984.

Berben, Paul. *Dachau, 1933-1945.* London, 1975. French edition, 1968.

Berger, Manfred. *Historische Bahnhofsbauten, Band I, Sachsen, Preußen, Mecklenburg, Thüringen.* 3rd ed. Berlin, 1991.

———. *Historische Bahnhofsbauten, Band II, Braunschweig, Hannover, Preußen, Bremen, Hamburg, Oldenburg und Schleswig-Holstein.* Berlin, 1988.

———. *Historische Bahnhofsbauten, Band III, Bayern, Baden, Württemberg, Pfalz, Nassau, Hessen.* Berlin, 1988.

Bezirksverband der Eisenbahnvereine Wuppertal. *100 Jahre westdeutsche Eisenbahnen 1838-1938.* Wuppertal, 1935.

Bley, Peter. *Berliner S-Bahn.* 5th ed. Düsseldorf, 1991.

Blieding, Fritz, and Willi Hoffmann. *100 Jahre Güterbahnhof Koblenz-Lützel. 1858-1958.* Koblenz-Mülheim, 1958.

Boberach, Heinz, ed. *Meldungen aus dem Reich.* See Germany, Sicherheitsdienst.

Bock, Hans, and Franz Garrecht. *Julius Dorpmüller — Ein Leben für die Eisenbahn.* Pürgen, 1996.

Boelcke, Willi A. *Die Deutsche Wirtschaft 1930-1938.* Düsseldorf, 1983.

———. *Die Kosten von Hitlers Krieg.* Paderborn, 1985.

Born, Erhard. *Lokomotiven und Wagen der deutschen Eisenbahnen.* Mainz, 1967.

Borscheid, Peter. "Lkw contra Bahn — Die Modernisierung des Transports durch den Lastkraftwagen in Deutschland bis 1939." In *Die Entwicklung der Motorisierung im Deutschen Reich und den Nachfolgestaaten,* edited by Harry Niemann and Arnim Hermann, 23-38. Stuttgart, 1995.

Bowen, Ralph H. *German Theories of the Corporative State.* New York, 1947.

Browning, Christopher R. *The Final Solution and the Foreign Office: A Study of Referat DIII of Abteilung Deutschland, 1940-43.* New York, 1978.

———. "One Day in Jozefow: Initiation to Mass Murder." In *Nazism and German Society, 1933-1945,* edited by David F. Crew, 300-315. London, 1994. Also in *Lessons and Legacies: The Meaning of the Holocaust in a Changing World,* edited by Peter Hayes, 196-209. Evanston, Ill., 1991.

———. *Ordinary Men: Reserve Police Battalion 101 and the Final Solution in Poland.* New York, 1992.

Carroll, Berenice A. *Design for Total War.* The Hague, 1968.

Craig, Gordon A. *Germany, 1866-1945.* New York, 1978.

Deist, Wilhelm. *The Wehrmacht and German Rearmament.* Toronto, 1981.

———, ed. *Das Deutsche Reich und der Zweite Weltkrieg.* Vol. 1. Stuttgart, 1979.

Deutsche Gesellschaft für Eisenbahn Geschichte. *Katalog der Bibliothek der Deutschen Gesellschaft für Eisenbahngeschichte.* Dortmund, 1974. Reprint, 1982.

———. *Katalog der Bibliothek der Deutschen Gesellschaft für Eisenbahngeschichte. Supplement 1: Zugänge 1974-1977.* 2 vols. Dortmund, 1977.

———. *Katalog der Bibliothek der Deutschen Gesellschaft für Eisenbahngeschichte. Supplement 2: Zugänge 1978-1983.* 3 vols. Dortmund, 1983.

———. *Katalog der Bibliothek der Deutschen Gesellschaft für Eisenbahngeschichte. Supplement 3: Zugänge 1984–1993.* 4 vols. Dortmund, 1993.

Deutsches Führer Lexikon. Berlin, 1934.

Döbert, Rudolf, and Alfred B. Gottwaldt, eds. *Eisenbahnen und Eisenbahner zwischen 1941 und 1945.* Frankfurt am Main, 1973. [See also Strößenreuther.]

Dombrowski, Erich. *Die Wirkungen der Reparationsverpflichtungen auf die Wirtschaftsführung der Deutschen Reichsbahn-Gesellschaft.* Berlin, 1930.

Dorpmüller, Julius. *Rationalisierung bei der Deutschen Reichsbahn.* Berlin, 1927.

Droege, John A. *Freight Terminals and Trains.* New York, 1912.

Durand, Paul. *La SNCF pendant la guerre: Sa résistance à l'occupant.* Paris, 1968.

Düring, Theodor. *Die deutschen Schnellzug-Dampflokomotiven der Einheitsbauart.* Stuttgart, 1979.

Ebel, Jürgen U., and Hansjürgen Wenzel. *Die Baureihe 50. Band 1: Deutsche Reichsbahn.* Freiburg-im-Breisgau, 1988.

Eisenbahn-Kurier. *Eisenbahn-Werkstätten. EK-Special 5.* Freiburg-im-Breisgau, 1986.

Ellwanger, Gunther, ed. *Die Bahn in Wirtschaft und Gesellschaft.* Darmstadt, 1985.

Ernst, Friedhelm. *Rheingold.* 4th ed. Düsseldorf, 1988.

Ewald, Kurt. *20 000 Schriftquellen zur Eisenbahnkunde.* Kassel, 1941. Reprint, Mainz, 1978.

Fischer, Conan. *Stormtroopers.* London, 1983.

Friedrich, Jörg. *Die kalte Amnestie-NS-Täter in der Bundesrepublik.* Frankfurt am Main, 1984.

Friedrich, Kurt. "Triebwagen. Innovative Dieselfahrzeugtechnik bei der Deutschen Reichsbahn und der Deutschen Bundesbahn." *Kultur & Technik* 11 (1987): 246–50.

Fromm, Günter. *Das Schicksal der Deutschen Reichsbahn und der Reichswasserstrassenverwaltung nach dem Zusammenbruch in der amerikanischen Besatzungszone bis zum Jahre 1948.* Frankfurt am Main, 1950.

———. "Die Unternehmensverfassung der Eisenbahnen im Wandel der Zeiten." *Die Bundesbahn* 62 (1986): 195–99.

Gall, Lothar, and Manfred Pohl. *Die Eisenbahn in Deutschland. Von den Anfängen bis zur Gegenwart.* Munich, 1999.

Gerlach, Klaus. *Dampflok-Archiv.* Berlin, 1969.

Gillingham, John R. *Industry and Politics in the Third Reich.* New York, 1985.

Goetzler, Herbert, and Lothar Schoen. *Wilhelm und Carl Friedrich von Siemens. Die zweite Unternehmergeneration.* Stuttgart, 1986.

Goldhagen, Daniel Jonah. *Hitler's Willing Executioners: Ordinary Germans and the Holocaust.* New York, 1996.

Gottwaldt, Alfred B. *Deutsche Eisenbahnen im Zweiten Weltkrieg. Rüstung, Krieg und Eisenbahn (1939–1945).* Stuttgart, 1983.

———. *Deutsche Kriegslokomotiven 1939–1945.* Stuttgart, 1973.

———. *Deutsche Reichsbahn. Kulturgeschichte und Technik.* Berlin, 1994.

———. *Deutsche Reichsbahn 1935.* Stuttgart, 1976.

———. *Eisenbahn-Brennpunkt Berlin. Die Deutsche Reichsbahn 1920–1939.* Stuttgart, 1976.

———. *Eisenbahn technische Ausstellung Seddin 1924.* Stuttgart, 1985.

———. "Erinnerung an Julius Dorpmüller." *Lok-Magazin* 193 (August 1995): 337–42.

———. "Fahren für Deutschlands Sieg!" In *Ich diente nur der Technik*, edited by Alfred B. Gottwaldt and Silke Klewin, 153–84. Berlin, 1995.

———. *50 Jahre Einheitslokomotiven. Die Dampflokomotiven der Reichsbahn und ihre Schöpfer.* Stuttgart, [1975].

———. *Geschichte der deutschen Einheitslokomotiven.* Stuttgart, 1978.

———. *Julius Dorpmüller, Die Reichsbahn und die Autobahn*. Berlin, 1995.
———. *Reichsbahn-Album*. 3rd ed. Stuttgart, 1978.
———. *Schienenzeppelin*. Augsburg, 1972.
Gottwaldt, Alfred B., and Eduard Bündigen. *Der Rheingoldexpress*. 2nd ed. Stuttgart, 1981.
Grothe, Jüthe. *Verkehr in Berlin. Von den Anfangen bis zur Gegenwart. Band 2. Fernverkehr*. Berlin, 1988.
Gutman, Yisrael, and Michael Berenbaum, eds. *Anatomy of the Auschwitz Death Camp*. Bloomington, Ind., 1994.
Hager, Bernhard. *150 Jahre Taunus-Eisenbahn*. Karlsruhe, 1991.
Hahn, Karl Eugen. *Eisenbahner in Krieg und Frieden*. Frankfurt am Main, 1954.
Hamm, Manfred, Rolf Steinberg, and Axel Föhl. *Bahnhöfe*. Berlin, 1984.
Hammer, Gustav. *Die Deutsche Reichsbahn als Auftraggeberin der deutschen Wirtschaft*. Berlin, 1933.
Hampe, Erich. *Der Zivile Luftschutz im Zweiten Weltkrieg*. Frankfurt am Main, 1963.
Harrer, Kurt. *Eisenbahnen an der Saar*. Düsseldorf, 1984.
Hauptverkehrsdirektion Brüssel. *Wissenswerte über den Bezirk der Hauptverkehrsdirektion Brüssel*. 3rd ed. Brussels, July 1942. Nur zum Dienstgebrauch. In BA R5 Anh I/93.
Heimatverein Porz e. V. "Reichsminister Paul Freiherr von Eltz-Rübenach. Sein Leben und Wirken 1875–1943." In *Unser Porz. Beiträge zur Geschichte von Amt und Stadt Porz*, vol. 2. Porz, 1961.
Heinrich, Peter, and Hans Schülke. *Bahnknotenpunkt Würzburg. Daß große Bahnbetriebswerk in Unterfranken*. Freiburg-im-Breisgau, 1990.
Heintze, Ernst, Roland Hertwig, Otto-Ernst Tilger, and Gerd Wolff. *Eisenbahn-Werkstätten. Special Eisenbahn-Kurier 5*. Freiburg-im-Breisgau, March 1986.
Heisterbergk, Erwin. "Die Erfolgsrechnung der Eisenbahnbetriebe." In *Die Erfolgsrechnung der Handels- und Verkehrsbetriebe*, edited by Carl Lüer and Reinhold Hanzler, 162–78. Frankfurt am Main, 1936.
Helander, Sven. *Nationale Verkehrsplanung*. Jena, 1937.
Hellauer, Josef. *Güterverkehr. Ein Lehr- und Handbuch für Studierende und für die Wirtschaftspraxis*. Jena, 1938.
Hennch, Hans. *Ein Jahrhundert Deutsche Eisenbahnen*. Leipzig, 1935.
Henning, Friedrich-Wilhelm. *Das industrialisierte Deutschland 1914 bis 1978*. Paderborn, 1974.
Herbert, Ulrich. *Fremdarbeiter: Politik und Praxis des "Ausländereinsatzes" in der Kriegswirtschaft des Dritten Reichs.* Berlin and Bonn, 1985.
———. *A History of Foreign Labor in Germany, 1880–1980*. Ann Arbor, Mich., 1990.
Herbst, Ludolf. *Der Totaler Krieg und die Ordnung der Wirtschaft: Die Kriegswirtschaft im Spannungsfeld von Politik, Ideologie und Propaganda 1939–1945*. Stuttgart, 1982.
Hermsen, Stephan. "Die strategische Rolle der Deutschen Reichsbahn im Zweiten Weltkrieg." Master's thesis, Ruhr University, Bochum, 1994.
Hickethier, Knut, et al. *Die Berliner S-Bahn. Gesellschaftsgeschichte eines industriellen Verkehrsmittels*. 2nd ed. Berlin, 1984.
Hilberg, Raul. *The Destruction of the European Jews*. 3 vols. New York, 1985.
———. "German Railroads/Jewish Souls." *Society* 14 (November–December 1976): 60–74.
———. *Sonderzüge nach Auschwitz*. Mainz, 1981.
Hildebrand, Klaus. "Die Deutsche Reichsbahn 1933–1945." In *Unternehmen im Nationalsozialismus*, edited by Lothar Gall and Manfred Pohl, 73–90. Munich, 1998.
Historische Kommission bei der Bayerischen Akademie der Wissenschaften. *Neue Deutsche Biographie*. 15 vols. Berlin, 1953–87.

Hoffmann, Walther G. *Das Wachstum der deutschen Wirtschaft seit der Mitte des 19. Jahrhunderts.* Berlin, Heidelberg, and New York, 1965.
Holzborn, Klaus-Detlev. *Dampflokomotiven.* Düsseldorf, 1968.
Homberger, Ludwig. "Wirkungen des hohen Zinsniveaus auf die Finanzwirtschaft und Wirtschaftsführung der Deutschen Reichsbahn-Gesellschaft." In *Wirkungen und Ursachen des hohen Zinsfußes in Deutschland,* edited by Karl Diel, 297–314. Jena, 1932.
Homze, Edward L. *Foreign Labor in Nazi Germany.* Princeton, 1967.
Horn, Alfred. *Reichsbahndirektion Wien.* Vienna, 1986.
Hubatsch, Walter, ed. *Grundriß zur Deutschen Verwaltungsgeschichte 1815–1945. Band 22: Bundes- und Reichsbehörden.* Marburg/Lahn, 1983.
150 Jahre Eisenbahnen in Halle (S.) 100 Jahre Hauptbahnhof Halle (S.). Halle/Salle, 1990.
Iklé, Fred Charles. "The Effect of War Destruction upon the Ecology of Cities." *Social Forces* 29 (May 1951): 383–91.
———. *The Social Impact of Bomb Destruction.* Norman, Okla., 1958.
Janikowski, Andreas. *Die Entwicklung der S-Bahn-Netze in Deutschland.* Karlsruhe, 1990.
Janis, Irving L. *The Psychological Impact of Air Attacks: A Survey and Analysis of Observation of Civilian Reaction during World War II.* Santa Monica, Calif., 1949.
Jänsch, Eberhard, and Reinhold Rump. *Schienenschnellverkehr I. 150 Jahre Wettlauf mit der Zeit.* Edited by Peter Münschwander. Heidelberg, 1989.
Joachim, Ernst. *Elektrische Lokomotiven: DRG, DB, DR. Daten, Fotos, Zeichnungen.* Düsseldorf, 1973.
Joachimsthaler, Anton. *Die Breitspurbahn Hitlers.* Freiburg-im-Breisgau, 1981. 3rd ed., Munich, 1985.
Jones, Elliot. *Principles of Railway Transportation.* New York, 1925.
Kaissling, Karl. *Eisenbahn-Ausbesserungswerke im besetzten Gebiet.* Cracow, 1944.
Kaldor, Nicholas. "The German War Economy." *Review of Economic Studies* 13, no. 1 (1944–46): 33–52.
Kandler, Udo. *Eisenbahnen im Moseltal. Eisenbahn Journal Sonderausgabe II/91.* Fürstenfeldbrück, 1991.
Kehrl, Hans. *Krisenmanager im Dritten Reich.* Düsseldorf, 1973.
Keller, Hans-Jörg. *100 Jahre Bahnbetriebswerk Frankfurt am Main 1.* Frankfurt am Main, 1989.
Kershaw, Ian. *Popular Opinion and Political Dissent in the Third Reich.* Oxford, 1984.
Klein, Burton. *Germany's Economic Preparations for War.* Cambridge, 1959.
Klein, Erich. *Das Beschaffungswesen der Deutschen Reichsbahn.* Gelnhausen, 1938.
Kleinmann, Wilhelm. *Wir Eisenbahner. 55 preisgekrönte Schilderungen deutschen Eisenbahner.* Berlin, 1937.
Knipping, Andreas. *Die Baureihe 86.* Freiburg-im-Breisgau, 1987.
Koch, Hansjoachim W. *A Constitutional History of Germany.* London, 1984.
Koehler, Peter, and Wolfgang List. *Das Bahnbetriebswerk zur Dampflokzeit.* Düsseldorf, 1989.
Köhler, Günter H., and Andreas Christopher. *Eisenbahnen im Rhein-Main-Gebiet.* Freiburg-im-Breisgau, 1983.
Kopper, Christopher. "Modernität oder Scheinmodernität nationalsozialistischer Herrschaft—Das Beispiel der Verkehrspolitik." In *Von der Aufgabe der Freiheit. Festschrift für Hans Mommsen zum 5. November 1995,* edited by Christian Jansen, Lutz Niethammer, and Bernd Weisbrod, 399–411. Berlin, 1995.
Kraus, August. *Die Deutsche Reichsbahn als Verkehrsunternehmen und als Glied der deutschen Wirtschaft.* Mannheim, 1939.
Krauskopf, Bernd, and Reinhard Vogelbusch. *Das Bahnbetriebswerk Dillenburg.* 3rd ed. Freiburg-im-Breisgau, 1984.

Kreh, Ulrich. *Verzeichnis der höheren Führungskräfte der Deutschen Bundesbahn.* Munich, 1988.

Kreidler, Eugen. *Die Eisenbahnen im Machtbereich der Achsenmächte während des Zweiten Weltkrieges.* Göttingen, 1975.

Kreuser, Helmut. *75 Jahre Kameradschaftlicher Eisenbahner-Verein Rübenach. Festschrift.* Rübenach, 1982.

Krienitz, Gerhard, ed. *Daten, Bilder, Ereignisse aus der Geschichte der deutschen Eisenbahnen.* Berlin, 1986.

Kroener, Bernhard R., Rolf-Dieter Müller, and Hans Umbreit. *Das Deutsche Reich und der Zweite Weltkrieg.* Vol. 5.1. Stuttgart, 1988.

Kruckenberg, Franz. *Fernschnellbahn und Verkehrshaus.* Heidelberg, 1958.

Krüger, Kurt. *Das Finanzwesen bei der Deutschen Reichsbahn.* Berlin, [c. 1939].

Kubinsky, Mihaly. *Architektur am Schienenstrang. Hallen, Schuppen, Stellwerke. Architekturgeschichte der Eisenbahn-Zweckbauten.* Stuttgart, 1990.

———. *Bahnhöfe Europas.* Stuttgart, 1969.

Kurz, Heinz. *Fliegende Züge. Vom "Fliegenden Hamburger" zum "Fliegenden Kölner."* Freiburg-im-Breisgau, 1986.

———. *Die Triebwagen der Reichsbahn-Bauarten.* Freiburg-im-Breisgau, 1988.

Langner, Ulrich, et al. *Zug der Zeit—Zeit der Züge. Deutsche Eisenbahnen 1835–1985.* 2 vols. Berlin, 1985.

Lanzmann, Claude. *Shoah.* Düsseldorf, 1986.

Lauerwald, Paul. *Die Halle-Kasseler Eisenbahn.* Berlin, 1993.

Lawrenz, Dierk, Rüdiger Block, Matthias Maier, Gerd Wolff, Michael Hanssen, Richard Holtz, Per Refsnes, Ingo Seifert, T. Maesato, and George Drury. *Hochgeschwindigkeitsverkehr, EK-Special 21.* Freiburg-im-Breisgau, 1991.

Lehmann, Thomas. "Die 'Vernachlässigung' der Deutschen Reichsbahn im Dritten Reich." Master's thesis, Universität Mannheim, 1997.

Leibbrand, Max. *Die Entwicklung des Reichsbahnbetriebes in neuer Zeit.* Frankfurt am Main, 1937.

Leibbrand, Max, and Hermann Domsch. *Organisation und Durchführung des Betriebsdienstes und Verkehrsdienstes bei der Deutschen Reichsbahn.* Berlin, 1934.

Lichtenstein, Heiner. *In Namen des Volkes: Eine persönliche Bilanz der NS Prozesse.* Cologne, 1984.

———. *Mit der Reichsbahn in der Tod: Massentransporte in den Holocaust.* Cologne, 1985.

———. " 'Pünktlich an der Rampe,' der Horizont des deutschen Eisenbahners." In *"Niemand war dabei und keiner hat's gewusst." Die deutsche Öffentlichkeit und die Judenverfolgung 1933–1945,* edited by Jörg Wollenberg, 204–44. Munich, 1989.

———. "Räder Rollen für den Mord. Die Deutsche Reichsbahn und der Holocaust." *Tribune* 21 (1982): 86–99.

Liebl, Toni, et al. *Offizieller Jubiläumsband der Deutschen Bundesbahn. 150 Jahre Deutsche Eisenbahnen.* Munich, 1985.

Linden, Walter, ed. *Dr. Gablers Verkehrs-Lexikon.* Wiesbaden, 1966.

Locklin, D. Philip. *Economics of Transportation.* 3rd ed. Chicago, 1949.

Logemann, Wilhelm. "Die Generalbetriebsleitungen." *Die Bundesbahn* 27 (August 1953): 684–706.

Ludwig, Karl-Heinz. *Technik und Ingenieure im Dritten Reich.* Düsseldorf, 1979.

MacMahon, Arthur W., and W. R. Dittmar. "Autonomous Public Enterprise—The German Railways." *Political Science Quarterly* 54 (December 1939): 481–513; 55 (March 1940): 25–52; 55 (June 1940): 176–98.

Maey, Hermann. *Die Fahrzeuge der Deutschen Reichsbahn und der Berliner Stadtbahn im Bild.* Moers, 1982.
Mankiw, N. Gregory. *Principles of Economics.* Fort Worth, Tex., 1998.
Matis, Herbert, and Dieter Stiefel. *Das Haus Schenker. Die Geschichte der internationalen Spedition, 1872–1931.* Vienna, 1995.
Mellor, Roy E. H. *German Railways: A Study in Historical Geography of Transport.* Aberdeen, 1979.
Messerschmidt, Wolfgang. *Taschenbuch deutsche Lokomotivfabriken.* Stuttgart, 1977.
Mierzejewski, Alfred C. *The Collapse of the German War Economy, 1944–1945.* Chapel Hill, N.C., 1988.
———. "The Deutsche Reichsbahn and Germany's Supply of Coal, 1939–1945." *Journal of Transport History* 8 (September 1987): 111–25.
———. "The German National Railway between the World Wars: Modernization or Preparation for War?" *Journal of Transport History* 11 (March 1990): 40–60.
———. "The German National Railway Confronts Its Competitors, 1920–1939." *Business and Economic History* 25 (Winter 1996): 89–102.
———. "High Speed Motor Trains of the German National Railway, 1920–1945." *Railroad History* 175 (Autumn 1996): 57–68.
———. "Hochgeschwindigkeitszüge in den Planungen der Reichsbahn, 1920–1945." In *Geschichte der Zukunft des Verkehrs,* edited by Hans-Liudiger Dienel and Helmuth Trischler, 208–22. Frankfurt am Main, 1997.
———. "Irrationality and the Dismal Science: Nazi Economic Preparations for War." In *Proceedings of the Fourth Siena Conference on World War II,* edited by Robert W. Hoeffner, 35–48. Sienna, 1992.
———. "Ludwig Homberger: An Exceptional Man." *Railroad History* 179 (Autumn 1998): 117–34.
———. *The Most Valuable Asset of the Reich: A History of the German National Railway.* Vol. 1, *1920–1932.* Chapel Hill, N.C., 1999.
Milward, Alan S. *The German Economy at War.* London, 1965.
———. *The New Order and the French Economy.* London, 1970.
———. *War, Economy and Society, 1939–1945.* Berkeley, Calif., 1979.
Ministerium für Verkehrswesen der Deutschen Demokratischen Republik. *Uns gehören die Schienenwege.* Berlin, 1960.
Mitchell, Brian R. *European Historical Statistics, 1750–1970.* New York, 1978.
Möllers, Alfons. *Die Entwicklung der Eisenbahn im Rheinisch-Westfälischen Industriegebiet.* 2nd ed. Bühl, 1989.
Mollin, Gerhard. *Montankonzerne und "Drittes Reich."* Göttingen, 1988.
Most, Otto. *Die Tarifpolitik der Deutschen Reichsbahn.* Mannheim, 1948.
Mühl, Albert. *75 Jahre Mitropa. Die Geschichte der Mitteleuropäischen Schlafwagen- und Speisewagen-Aktiengesellschaft.* Freiburg-im-Breisgau, 1992.
Naasner, Walter. *Neue Machtzentren in der deutschen Kriegswirtschaft.* Boppard, 1994.
Noakes, Jeremy. *The Nazi Party in Lower Saxony, 1921–1933.* London, 1971.
Orlow, Dietrich. *History of the Nazi Party, 1919–1933.* Pittsburgh, 1969.
———. *History of the Nazi Party, 1933–1945.* New Abbott, 1973.
Ostendorf, Rolf. *Eisenbahnknotenpunkt Ruhrgebiet.* Stuttgart, 1979.
———. *Die Geschichte der Eisenbahndirektion Essen.* Stuttgart, 1983.
Ottmann, Karl. "Ein Beitrag zur Geschichte der deutschen Eisenbahnen." *Internationales Archiv für Verkehrswesen* 6 (1954): 97–106.

———. "Die Verkehrslage beim Jahreswechsel 1944/45." *Archiv für Eisenbahnwesen* 71 (1961): 41.
Ottmann, Karl, and Hans Joachim Ritzau. *Deutsche Eisenbahn-Geschichte*. Landsberg, 1975.
Overy, Richard J. "'Blitzkriegswirtschaft?,' Finanzpolitik, Lebensstandard und Arbeitseinsatz in Deutschland 1939-1942." *Vierteljahrshefte für Zeitgeschichte* 36 (1988): 379-435.
———. "Cars, Roads, and Economic Recovery in Germany, 1932-8." *Economic History Review*, ser. 2, 28 (1975): 466-83.
———. "Germany, 'Domestic Crisis' and War in 1939." *Past and Present* 116 (1987): 138-68.
———. *Goering: The Iron Man*. London, 1984.
———. "Heavy Industry and the State in Nazi Germany: The Reichswerke Crisis." *European History Quarterly* 15 (1985): 313-40.
———. "Hitler's War and the German Economy: A Reinterpretation." *Economic History Review* 35 (1982): 272-91.
———. "Mobilization for Total War in Germany." *English Historical Review* 103 (July 1988): 613-39.
———. *The Nazi Economic Recovery, 1932-1938*. London, 1982. 2nd ed., Cambridge, 1996.
———. "Transportation and Rearmament in the Third Reich." *Historical Journal* 16 (1973): 389-409.
———. *War, Economy and the Third Reich*. Oxford, 1994.
Overy, Richard J., David Kaiser, and Tim Mason. "Debate: Germany, 'Domestic Crisis' and War in 1939." *Past and Present* 122 (1989): 200-240.
Pape, Robert A. *Bombing to Win: Air Power and Coercion in War*. Ithaca, N.Y., 1996.
Pätzold, Kurt, and Erika Schwarz. *"Auschwitz war für mich nur ein Bahnhof."* Berlin, 1994.
Peters, Wolfgang. *Grossdeutschlands Eisenbahner*. Feldausgabe. Berlin, 1944.
Piekalkiewicz, Janusz. *Die Deutsche Reichsbahn im Zweiten Weltkrieg*. Stuttgart, 1979.
Pinson, Koppel S. *Modern Germany*. New York, 1966.
Pischel, Werner. "Die Generaldirektion der Ostbahn in Krakau 1939-1945." *Archiv für Eisenbahnwesen* 74 (1964): 1-81.
Pottgiesser, Hans. *Die Deutsche Reichsbahn im Ostfeldzug: 1939-1944*. 2nd ed. Neckargemünd, 1975.
Predöhl, Andreas. *Verkehrspolitik*. Göttingen, 1958.
Reed, Robert C. *The Streamline Era*. San Marino, Calif., 1975.
Rees, E. A. *Stalinism and Soviet Rail Transport*. New York, 1995.
Rehbein, Elfriede, Joachim Lindow, Kurt Wegner, and Heinz Wehner. *Deutsche Eisenbahnen 1835-1985*. Berlin, 1985.
Robbins, Michael. "The Third Reich and Its Railways." *Journal of Transport History* 5 (1979): 83-90.
Roessler, Thomas. "Der Staat und die Eisenbahn. Zur Einflussnahme des Staates auf die Wirtschaft beispielhaft dargestellt anhand der Entwicklungsgeschichte der Lokomotivindustrie von 1838 bis 1945." Ph.D. diss., Universität Hamburg, 1993.
Rohde, Horst. *Das deutsche Wehrmachttransportwesen im Zweiten Weltkrieg*. Stuttgart, 1971.
———. "Das Eisenbahnverkehrswesen in der deutschen Kriegswirtschaft 1939-1945." In *Kriegswirtschaft und Rüstung 1939-1945*, edited by Friedrich Forstmeier and Erich Volkmann, 134-63. Düsseldorf, 1977.
Rudolf, Ulrike. "Die wirtschaftliche und militärische Bedeutung der Deutschen Reichsbahn (DR) für die deutschen Ostgebiete und die Bewältigung ihrer Transportaufgaben in Polen und der UdSSR während des Zweiten Weltkrieges." *Jahrbuch für Eisenbahngeschichte* 18 (1986): 71-109.
Sarter, Adolf. *Landesverteidigung und Eisenbahn*. Bad Hersfeld, 1955.

———. *Was Jeder von der Deutschen Reichsbahn wissen muss.* Leipzig, 1938, 1939, 1943.

Schadendorf, Wulf. *Das Jahrhundert der Eisenbahn.* Munich, 1965.

Scharf, Hans-Wolfgang. *Eisenbahnen zwischen Oder und Weichsel. Die Reichsbahn im Osten bis 1945.* Freiburg-im-Breisgau, 1981.

Scharf, Hans-Wolfgang, and Friedhelm Ernst. *Vom Fernschnellzug zum Intercity.* Freiburg-im-Breisgau, 1983.

Scharf, Hans-Wolfgang, and Hansjürgen Wenzel. *Lokomotiven für die Reichsbahn.* 2 vols. Freiburg-im-Breisgau, 1996, 1997.

Schletzbaum, Ludwig. *Eisenbahn.* Munich, 1990.

Schmidt, Karl. *Krauss-Maffei: 150 Years of Progress through Technology, 1838–1988.* Munich, 1988.

"Der Schnelltriebwagen der Deutschen Reichsbahngesellschaft." *Siemens-Zeitschrift* 13 (1933): 57-64.

Schönhoven, Klaus. *Die deutschen Gewerkschaften.* Frankfurt am Main, 1987.

Schote, Lothar, ed. *Die Bahn. Was sie ist und wie sie funktioniert.* Heidelberg, 1988.

Schüler, Klaus A. Friedrich. *Logistik im Rußlandfeldzug.* Frankfurt am Main and Bern, 1987.

Schulz, Gerhard. *Deutschland am Vorabend der grossen Krise. Band III, Von Brüning zu Hitler.* Berlin, 1992.

Schwanck, Ulrich. "Friedrich Witte (Eine Betrachtung zu seinem Übertritt in den Ruhestand)." *Lok-Magazin* 16 (February 1966): 50-55. Reprinted in *Jahrbuch für Eisenbahn Geschichte* 25 (1993): 29-36.

Schymanietz, Peter A. *Die Organisation der deutschen Eisenbahnen, 1835–1975.* Freiburg-im-Breisgau, 1977.

Siemens, Georg. *Carl Friedrich von Siemens—Ein großer Unternehmer.* 2nd ed. Freiburg, 1962.

Simon, Gerhard. "Verkehrsausweitung, Verkehrslenkung und Transportentflechtung in der deutschen Kriegswirtschaft des Zweiten Weltkrieges." *Jahrbuch für Sozialwissenschaft* 20 (1969): 419-41.

Speer, Albert. *Inside the Third Reich.* Translated by Richard Winston and Clara Winston. New York, 1970.

Spoerer, Mark. *Von Scheingewinnen zum Rüstungsboom.* Stuttgart, 1996.

Steinert, Marlis G. *Hitler's War and the Germans.* Translated by Thomas E. J. De Witt. Athens, Ohio, 1977.

Stieler, Karl. *Aus meinem Leben. Ein Stück deutscher Eisenbahngeschichte.* Cologne, 1950.

Stockhorst, Erich. *Wer war was im 3. Reich.* Wiesbaden, n.d.

Stroebe, Hermann. "Fast Railcars of the German State Railways." *Bulletin of the International Railway Congress Association* (July 1937): 1612-31.

Strößenreuther, Hugo. *Eisenbahnen und Eisenbahner zwischen 1925 und 1930.* Vol. 2. Frankfurt am Main, 1970.

———. *Eisenbahnen und Eisenbahner zwischen 1931 und 1935.* Vol. 3. Frankfurt am Main, 1971.

———. *Eisenbahnen und Eisenbahner zwischen 1936 und 1940.* Vol. 4. Frankfurt am Main, 1972.

———. *Eisenbahnen und Eisenbahner zwischen 1941 und 1945.* Vol. 5. Frankfurt am Main, 1973.

Stumpf, Berthold. *Kleine Geschichte der deutschen Eisenbahnen.* 3rd ed. Mainz, 1960.

Teske, Hermann. "Die Eisenbahn als operatives Führungmittel." *Wehrkunde* 2 (1953): 9-11.

———. *Die silbernen Spiegel.* Heidelberg, 1952.

———. "Der Wert von Eisenbahnen im Zweiten Weltkrieg." *Wehrwissenschaftliche Rundschau* 5 (1956): 514-23.

Thomas, Georg. *Geschichte der deutschen Wehr- und Rüstungswirtschaft (1918–1943/45).* Boppard, 1966.

Turner, Henry Ashby. *Hitler: Memoirs of a Confidant.* Translated by Ruth Hein. New Haven, Conn., 1985.

United States Holocaust Memorial Museum. *Historical Atlas of the Holocaust*. New York, 1996.
Vogel, Theodor, ed. *125 Jahre deutsche Eisenbahnen*. Darmstadt, 1960.
Vogelsang, Harald. *Das Bw Bochum-Dahlhausen und die Eisenbahn im mittleren Ruhrtal*. Freiburg-im-Breisgau, 1988.
Vogt, Johannes. *Grundfragen der heutigen Verkehrs- und Tarifpolitik in Deutschland*. Berlin, 1937.
Vogt, Karl. *Deutscher Beamten-Kalender 1936*. Berlin, 1935.
Walz, Werner. *Deutschlands Eisenbahnen 1835–1985*. 2nd ed. Stuttgart, 1985.
Weber, Hans-Adolf. *Betriebsdienst der Deutschen Reichsbahn*. Berlin, 1944.
Webster, Charles, and Noble Frankland. *The Strategic Air Offensive against Germany*. 4 vols. London, 1961.
Wedgwood, Sir Ralph L., and J. E. Wheeler. *International Rail Transport*. New York, 1946.
Wehde-Textor, Otto. "Die Leistungen der Deutschen Reichsbahn im Zweiten Weltkrieg." *Archiv für Eisenbahnwesen* 71 (1961): 1–47.
Wehner, Heinz. "Der Einsatz der Eisenbahnen für die verbrecherischen Ziele des faschistischen deutschen Imperialismus im 2. Weltkrieg." Ph.D. diss., Hochschule für Verkehrswesen, Dresden, 1961.
———. "Räder mussten rollen für den Krieg." In *Deutsche Eisenbahnen 1835–1985*, by Elfriede Rehbein, Joachim Lindow, Kurt Wegner, and Heinz Wehner. Berlin, 1985.
———. "Die Verelendung und Entrechtung der deutschen Eisenbahner in den Jahren des Zweiten Weltkrieges (1939–1945)." *Wissenschaftliche Zeitschrift der Hochschule für Verkehrswesen "Friedrich List" Dresden* 11 (1964): 281–90.
Weigelt, Horst. *Epochen der Eisenbahngeschichte*. Darmstadt, 1985.
Weinberg, Gerhard L. *A World at Arms*. New York, 1994.
Weirauch, Wilhelm. *Eisenbahn-Verkehrsordnung. Vom 8. September 1938*. Berlin, 1939.
Weisbrod, Manfred, and Wolfgang Brozeit. *Baureihe 44. Ihr Weg durch 6 Jahrzehnte*. Berlin, 1983.
Weisbrod, Manfred, Hans Müller, and Wolfgang Petznick. *Dampflokomotiven deutscher Eisenbahnen. Baureihe 01–39*. 4th ed. Düsseldorf, 1987.
———. *Dampflokomotiven deutscher Eisenbahnen. Baureihe 41–59*. 4th ed. Düsseldorf, 1988.
———. *Dampflokomotiven deutscher Eisenbahnen. Baureihe 60–96*. 4th ed. Düsseldorf, 1988.
Weisbrod, Manfred, and Wolfgang Petznick. *Baureihe 01: Geschichte, Bau und Bewährung einer Schnellzuglokomotive*. Berlin, 1981.
Witte, Friedrich. "Zehn Jahre Reichsbahn-Zentralamt und die Kriegslokomotiven 1935–1945." *Lok-Magazin* 40 (1970): 4–20.
Wittland, Kim. *100 Jahre Hauptbahnhof Frankfurt 1888–1988*. Karlsruhe, 1988.
Wohlschläger, Philipp. *Bericht über den Einsatz der Wehrmacht-Verkehrsdirektion Brüssel Abt. Eisenbahn vom 18. Mai bis 31. Oktober 1940*. Brussels, 12 November 1940.
Wolf, Gerd, and Stephan Pauly. *90 Jahre Brohltal-Eisenbahn. Ein geschichtlicher Rückblick*. 2nd ed. Freiburg, 1991.
Wulf, Sigrun, ed. *Nur Gott der Herr kennt ihre Namen. KZ-Züge auf der Heidebahn*. Schneverdingen, 1991.
Wyss, Peter. "Räder müssen rollen für den Sieg." Master's thesis, Bern, 1991.
Yahil, Leni. *The Holocaust*. Translated by Ina Friedman and Hya Galai. New York, 1990.
Zimmermann, Michael. *Verfolgt, Vertrieben, Vernichtet*. Essen, 1989.
Zorn, Wolfgang. *Bayerns Geschichte im 20. Jahrhundert: Von der Monarchie zum Bundesland*. Munich, 1986.
Zschech, Rainer. *Triebwagen deutscher Eisenbahnen. Band 1: ETA und ET*. 3rd ed. Düsseldorf, 1989.
———. *Triebwagen deutscher Eisenbahnen. Band 2: VT und DT*. 3rd ed. Düsseldorf, 1989.

Periodicals

Archiv für Eisenbahnwesen, 1920-65.
Die Bundesbahn, 1949-95.
Degener, Hermann A. L. *Wer ist's?*, 1935.
Deutsche Gesellschaft für Eisenbahngeschichte. *Jahrbuch für Eisenbahngeschichte*, 1968-97.
Deutsche Reichsbahn. *Amtliches Bahnhofsverzeichnis*, Berlin, various years.
DR, DRB, DRG. *Statistische Monatsberichte*, 1920-44.
———. *Die Deutsche Reichsbahn im Geschäftsjahr. . . .* Berlin, 1926-31.
———. *Geschäftsberichte der Deutschen Reichsbahn*, Berlin, 1922-24.
———. *Kursbuch*, various years.
———. *Statistische Angaben über die Deutsche Reichsbahn im Geschäftsjahr . . .* , Berlin, 1932-44.
———. *Statistische Übersicht wichtiger Ergebnisse des Geschäftsjahres . . .* , Berlin, 1926-43.
———. *Statistische Übersicht wichtiger Ergebnisse des Geschäftsjahres 1937 im Vergleich zu 1934, 1935, 1936*, Berlin, 1938.
DRG. *Hausnachrichten der Hauptverwaltung der Deutschen Reichsbahn-Gesellschaft*, 1924-45.
Germany. *Reichsgesetzblatt*, 1919-44.
Glasers Annalen, 1920-44.
Gruppenverwaltung Bayern. *Eisenbahn-Nachrichtenblatt der Deutschen Reichsbahn-Gesellschaft*, Munich, 1920-33.
Die Reichsbahn, 1922-45.
Reichsbahndirektion Augsburg. *Amtsblatt*.
Reichsbahndirektion Berlin. *Amtsblatt*, 1920-44.
Reichsbahndirektion Regensburg. *Amtsblatt*.
Reichsbank. *Verwaltungsbericht der Reichsbank für das Jahr . . .* , 1925-43.
Reichs-Eisenbahn-Amt, later DR. *Statistik der im Betriebe befindlichen Eisenbahnen Deutschlands*, 1905-40.
RVD Minsk. *Amtsblatt*, 1941-43.
Verkehrstechnische Woche, 1920-40, *Großdeutscher Verkehr*, 1940-44.
Voraus, 1920-38.
Zeitschrift des Vereins Deutscher Eisenbahnverwaltungen, 1920-32.
Zeitschrift des Vereins Mitteleuropäischer Eisenbahnverwaltungen, 1933-44.

Index

Accidents, 135-36, 142
Accounting, xii, xv, 21-22
Account W, 126
Advisory board (Beirat), 23, 24, 54
Air, attacks from, 141, 145, 158-61
Aktion Reinhard, 127
Alsace, 83
Anger, Richard, 31, 32
Armed Forces Transportation Division (WVD), 101; in Brussels, 83; in Paris, 83
Army Group Center, 95, 97, 121, 122
Army Group North, 95
Army Group South, 95, 100, 119
Army Transport Commission, 57-58
Association of Central European Railway Administrations, 55
Auschwitz, 115, 116, 120-21, 123, 124, 125, 126, 127
Austria, 48-49, 61
Autobahnen, 40-42, 62, 154

Baden, 7
Bahnschutz, 2, 4, 5, 171 (n. 7)
Bahnspedition, 43
Batocki, Adolf von, 1
Bauer, Colmar, 136
Baumann, Hans, 5, 11, 107
Bavaria, xi, 19
Beck, Emil, 79
Beko (Operating Cost Account), 22
Bell, Johannes, 57
Belzec, 117, 121, 124, 127
Bergmann, Carl, 5, 9

Bergmann, Hermann, 16, 67-71, 90
Berlin, 27, 32, 121; Zoological Garden Station in, 120; Moabit station in, 120, 123
Berlin S-Bahn, 36, 62
Beyer, Alfred, 5
Bialystok, 121, 123, 125
Blackout, 86
Board of Directors (Verwaltungsrat), 7, 24, 25, 45
Bock, Hans, 171 (n. 5)
Booty, trains loaded with, 98
Bormann, Martin, 13
Brandenburg, Ernst, 43
Brauchitsch, Walther von, 94, 99
Breslau-East, 120
Brest-Litovsk, 121, 123, 131
Breuer, Max, 32
Brown, Boveri (BBC), 32
Browning, Christopher, 126
Bruckauf, Franz, 4
Brugmann, Walter, 105
Brüning, Heinrich, xii, 13
Bürckel, Josef, 19
Busch, Fritz, 21, 22, 152

Capacity, excess, xii, 66
Capital, expansion of, xii, 61-64, 71-72, 156-57
Cars
—freight: serviceability ratio of, 53; turn-around time for, 53, 90-91, 141-42, 160-61; placings of, 53-54, 55, 91-92, 99-100, 144,

159, 160; priorities for placing, 56, 89–90, 138–39, 158; excess of, 66; acquisitions of, 66–71, 110; capacity of, 71; number of, 71, 140; overloading of, 90, 141; from France, 137; from Belgium, 137–38; unloading of, 141
—passenger: acqusition of, 66–71; capacity of, 70; for Holocaust, 117
Central Transportation Directorate (ZVL), 109, 138–40, 142, 143, 158, 161
Chelmno, 127
Coal: priority of transporting, 56, 90, 143; placings of cars carrying, 92–93, 143, 160, 200 (n. 78); traffic of, 93, 140, 142–43, 159
Coal Magistrale, 92
Cologne-Kalk, 120
Communists, 2, 5
Construction, 61, 64, 71–72, 133–34
Crakow, 79, 129, 130
Czechoslovakia, 49, 54
Czestochowa, 121

Darmstadt, 120
Degenkolb, Gerhard, 111
Demurrage, charges for, 141
Denmark, 110
Deutsche Bundesbahn, 4
Deutsche Reichsbahn (1920–24), 57–58
Deutsche Reichsbahn (DRB, 1937–45), relationship with Nazi Party of, xii–xiv, 12–13, 151; and WWII, xiii–xiv, 162, 163; and Autobahnen, xiv; and Holocaust, xiv, xv, 162; and Jews, xiv, 114; and price mechanism, xiv, 55, 61, 187 (n. 83); relationship with Reich of, 22–23, 57, 155; and traffic with the USSR, 89, 131, 134–35; and traffic situation, 40–41, 85, 87, 138–45; capacity limit of, 54–56; and military, 59–61; finances of, 65, 152–57; debt of, 65, 154–55, 162, 192 (n. 72); and attack on Poland, 77–78; and Ostbahn, 81–82, 129–30; and May 1940 military operations, 82–83; and rolling stock from SNCF, 84, 137–38; air raid protection by, 85; and war on USSR, 94–96, 99; Winter Crisis of, 99–110; and railways in occupied areas, 101–2, 132; relationship with Hitler of, 102; resettlement of ethnic Germans by, 115; Jewish deportations by, 116–23, 127,

211 (n. 70); finances in east of, 135; and rolling stock from SNCB, 138; loans to Reich by, 155; military revenues of, 157; and Ardennes offensive, 160; and Nazis, 162–63
Deutsche Reichsbahn-Gesellschaft (1924–37), xi, xii, xv; created, xii; organization of, xiii; and Nazi Party, 1–2, 4, and Nuremberg Laws, 14–15; and state treaty, 19–20; symbol of, 20; relationship to Reich of, 22–23; name of, 23; and modal competition, 42–44; buses of, 44; trucks of, 44–45; finances of, 50–53, 62–65; and mobilization schedule, 58, 59, 60; and military, 58–59; and job creation, 60, 62; debt of, 62; bonds issued by, 63; contribution to the Reich of, 65; discrimination against Jews by, 114, 164; stock of, 153–54, 163
Deutsche Verkehrs-Kredit Bank (DVKB), 5, 11
Diegelmann, Oskar, 124
Dilli, Gustav, 108, 126
Dispersal, 140–41
Divisions. See Reichsbahn Divisions
Dnjepropetrovsk, 132
Doerr, Hans, 78, 85
Dorpmüller, Julius, xii, 6, 10, 11, 12, 18, 19, 57, 161; and Holocaust, xiv, 124, 162; and Nazis, xv, 2, 7, 13, 14, 15; personality of, 13–14, 164; and tariffs, 21, 29; succeeds Eltz, 24, and Fliegender Hamburger, 33, 35; and truck competition, 39, 40, 42–44; and Autobahnen, 40–42, 154; and cabinet meeting of 23 June 1935, 41; meets with Hitler 26 November 1935, 51, 66; and capacity limit, 54, 67, 76; and finances, 63, 153, 155; and track, 73–74; and Ostbahn, 79–81, 129–30; and war on USSR, 95, 100–101, 102, 104–6, 132
Dorpmüller Fund, 60

Ebeling, Friedrich, 57, 58, 59, 134
Economic Group Mining, 92
Economy, commonweal, 20–21, 25, 28
Eichmann, Adolf, 115, 116–17, 123–24
Eifel Mountains, 49
Electrification, 60, 64
Eltz-Rübenach, Peter Paul Freiherr von, 7, 8, 13, 18, 23, 51, 67; resignation of, 24; and

242 Index

passenger fares, 29; and truck competition, 39, 40, 42–43; and Autobahnen, 41; and DRG credit, 63
Embargoes, 87, 89, 123
Emmelius, Curt, 16, 19, 33
Emrich, Ernst, 87, 88, 139
Emrich, Wilhelm, 16, 108
Esser, Hermann, 9, 18
Eupen, 83
EVA, 31
Evacuations, 136, 145, 159

Fachgruppe Reichsbahn, 4
Fachschaft Reichsbahn, 4, 5, 6, 9, 11, 12, 13, 14
Fähnrich, Fritz, 117
Fares, 29, discounts on, 29, 38
Feder, Gottfried, 9
Federal Military Archive, 202 (n. 20)
Fehling, Wilhelm, 125
Finance Section, Main Administration, 63
Fliegender Hamburger, xv, 32–34, 36, 37
Forwarders, 39, 40, 42–44
IVB4, 115
Four Year Plan, 52, 54, 60, 65, 67, 89, 92, 110
Frank, Hans, 79, 107, 129, 130
Frankfurt am Main, 42, 44
Freight. See Cars—freight; Tariffs; Traffic—freight; Trains—freight
Frick, Wilhelm, 18
Fuchs, Friedrich, 32
Führerstab Reichsbahn, 6, 8, 13
Funk, Walter, 153

Galicia, 121
Ganzenmüller, Albert, 103, 109, 148, 161; appointed as state secretary in RVM, 105; biography of, 106–8; correspondence with Wolff of, 122; correspondence with Himmler of, 123; and Holocaust, 124, 162; and Ostbahn, 129; and occupied east, 132; and SNCF, 137; and SNCB, 138; and finances, 155, 157
Garbolzum, 2
Garrecht, Franz, 171 (n. 5)
Gedob, 79
General Operating Offices (GBL): East, 80, 85, 82, 117, 122, 139; creation of, 85, 87; West, 85, 89, 92, 100; South, 108, 161

General Transportation Directorate East, 132
Gercke, Rudolf, 59, 61, 69, 78, 80, 96, 110, 140; and Otto Program, 94, 95; and Winter Crisis, 100–101
German Company for Public Works (Öffa), 60, 64
German Labor Front (DAF), 4, 16, 18
German Transportation Credit Bank (DVKB), 5, 11
Gerteis, Adolf, 79, 130, 131
Gesellschaft für Verkehrstechnik, 36
Gibrat, Robert, 137
Glas, Alfons, 125–26
Globocnik, Odilo, 127
Goebbels, Josef, 11
Gollwitzer, Albert, 16, 19, 106
Göring, Hermann, 24, 48, 57, 60, 67, 92, 99, 101, 115
Göttingen, 2
Gottwaldt, Alfred, 171 (n. 5)
Goudefroy, Erich, 15
Gray Railroaders, 60, 96
Grodno, 123
Groener, Wilhelm, xi, 57
Group L, 59, 68, 69, 78, 134
Grunewald, 33
Günther, Rolf, 117

Hafraba, 40
Hamburg, 27, 32, 34, 145
Hanover, 44
Hassenpflug, Werner, 15, 110, 150
Heidelberg, 42, 44
Heiges, Karl, 5
Herrmann, Matthäus, 2, 5, 7
Hertel, Vitus von, 5, 8
Hess, Rudolf, 6, 13, 23, 43, 57
Heydrich, Reinhard, 114, 115, 119
Higher Operating Offices, xiii, 6, 50, 85
Hilse, Willy, 125
Himmler, Heinrich, 114, 116, 123, 127
Hitler, Adolf, 8, 23, 35, 57, 148, 161; and passenger fares, 29; and Kruckenberg, 36; and truck competition, 39, 42–43; and Autobahnen, 40–42
Hitler Youth, 5
Holzer, Marcell, 5, 11
Homberger, Ludwig, xii, xv, 5, 7, 10, 11, 15
Honold, Franz, 5, 7

Höß, Rudolf, 125
Hungary: railways in, 95; Jews in, 123-24, 127

IG Farben, 124
Italian State Railways, 143
Izbica, 120

Jacobi, Karl, 117
Jews: Reichsbahn discrimination against, 5-6, 10; expelled from ÖBB, 48; as labor on railways, 95; from Croatia, 119; from Warsaw Ghetto, 119; from Belgium, 119, 123; from Netherlands, 119, 123, 127; from Austria, 120; from Germany, 120; from Bulgaria, 123; from Greece, 123; from France, 123, 127; from Hungary, 123-24, 127; from Salonika, 126; materials taken from, 127
Joachimsthaler, Anton, 4
Jobs, programs creating, xii, 25

Kaiser, Ernst, 5
Karlsruhe, 44, 120
Kassel, 120
Kattowitz, 124
Kausche, Günter, 4
Keitel, Wilhelm, 23, 94
Keller, Karl, 16
Keppler, Wilhelm, 11, 42-43
Kittel, Theodor, 19, 79
Kleinmann, Wilhelm: biography of, 6; and nazification of Reichsbahn, 6, 8, 9-10, 12, 18, 20, 22; and Nuremberg Laws, 14, 15; and layoffs, 17; and RBD Saarbrücken, 19; and accounting, 22; as Eltz's successor, 23; and tariffs, 29; and technology, 30; and motor trains, 35; and truck competition, 42; and buses, 44; and absorption of ÖBB, 48; and finances, 51, 152; and 26 July 1939 meeting, 56, 76; and rolling stock acquisitions, 67-69, 110-11; and Ostbahn, 79; and freight car priorities, 89, 92; and coal traffic, 93; and railways in east, 98, 99, 104; meetings with Hitler of, 102-3; dismissed, 103, 205 (n. 73); and prisoner deportations, 122
Klemm, Bruno, 117

Klöckner, Peter, 8
Koblenz, 48
Koenigs, Gustav, 7, 8, 9, 51, 67
Kohl, Otto, 83
Köhler, Erich, 8
Körner, Georg, 8, 17, 18
Kreidler, Eugen, 171 (n. 2), 202 (n. 20)
Kruckenberg, Franz, 36-37
Krupp, 33
Krupp von Bohlen und Halbach, Gustav, 8
Kryschak, Eduard, 125
Kühne, Peter, 106

Lamertz, Maximillian, 15, 161
Lammers, Hans, 5, 7, 22, 129, 148
Laval, Pierre, 137
Law for the Ordering of Work in the National Administrations and Enterprises, 16
Law for the Reconstruction of the Professional Civil Service, 5
Law for the Simplification and Cheapening of the Administration, 20
Le Creusot, 110
Leibbrand, Max, 16, 54, 60, 91, 92, 104, 140; and high-speed trains, 34-36; and rolling stock acquisitions, 66-71; relieved, 106, 205 (n. 73)
Leipzig, 18, 115
Liaison Staff, 6
Liebel, Willi, 106
Lithuania, 115
Locomotives, 70; reserves of, 60; acquistion of, 62-71, 110-13; excess of, 66; electric, 68; to west, 83; to east, 102; maintenance of, 103, 141; Class 44, 110; Class 50, 111; Class 52, 111; Class 41, 131; sheds for, 132, 158; coal supplies for, 161. *See also* Motor trains
Lodz, 115, 116, 127
Lorraine, 83
Lübbecke, Günther, 124-25
Lublin, 115, 121, 129
Luxemburg, 83

Main Administration, xiii, 10, 15, 18; and Nazis, 2, 7; reorganized, 20; absorbed into RVM, 23; and Fliegender Hamburger, 33, 34; and modal competition, 44,

244   *Index*

45; Finance Section of, 63; rolling stock acquisitions by, 67; and Jews, 114
Main Auditing Office, 11, 157
Main Car Office, 54, 81, 132, 137
Main Committee for Railway Vehicles, 111-12
Main Railway Divisions (HBD), 98, 101, 108
Main Transportation Divisions (HVD), 136, 158
Majdanek, 123, 127
Malkinia, 121, 125, 131
Malmédy, 83
MAN, 31
Mannheim, 42
Mannl, Walter, 124
Maquis, 137
Marshaling yards, 53, 86, 99, 158-61, 163
Maybach, 31, 32, 33, 34
Mechanical Section (Main Administration/RVM), 20, 32, 35, 68, 69, 110, 148
Merck, Fink, 64
Milch, Erhard, 105, 109
Minsk, 116, 120, 121, 127
Mitropa, 126, 205 (n. 73)
Modal competition, xiii, 39-40, 42-46
Möller, Helga, 126
Moresnet, 83
Motor trains, 30-37, 70
Müller, Josef, 98, 132
Münchmeyer, Hermann, 9
Munich, 44
Münzer, Hans, 83, 136

National Federation of German Officials, 4
National Socialist Factory Cell Organization, 2
Nazi salute, 20
Netherlands, 110
Netherlands National Railways (NS), 101
Neurath, Konstantin von, 80
Neuser, Richard, 125
Novak, Franz, 117, 124
Nuremberg, 120; Nazi Party rally in, 27, 55, 64

Officials, 2, 9, 11-12, 152
OKH, 49
OKW, 23, 69, 94, 98
Operating Office East, 98, 100, 101

Operating Section (Main Administration/RVM), 35, 90, 150
Operation Citadel, 135
Oppermann, Otto, 57, 58
Oranczyce, 123
Organization Todt, 49, 133
Ostbahn, xiv, 78-82, 99, 147, 148; racial policies of, 80-81, 131, rolling stock of, 81, 130-31; traffic on, 82, 131; and Otto Program, 95; and war on USSR, 97-98, 129-31; and Holocaust, 115, 117, 121, 123, 127; reorganization of, 130; finances of, 131
Ostbau (ÖBB), 132-33, 134
Österreichische Bundesbahnen, 48-49
Osthilfe, 191 (n. 59)
Osthoff, Hermann, 16, 18, 74, 110, 148, 149, 150
Otto Program, 89, 94-96, 121, 132-33, 134
Overy, Richard J., 190 (n. 38)

Panszew, 120
Pape, Robert A., 223 (n. 2)
Partisans, attacks by, 135-36, 137
Passengers. *See* Cars—passenger; Fares; Traffic—passenger; Trains—passenger
Peppmüller, Friedrich, 14
Personnel, 74-75, 146-52; excess, xii; pay cuts for, xiii; training of, 18; requirements of, 74; female, 74, 150-55; standards for, 74-75; morale problems of, 75, 152; shortage of, 75-75, 148; to Ostbahn, 80, 147; retired, 146; workweek of, 146; deferments for, 147; to east, 147; to occupied west, 147; to military, 148; and SS, 148; foreigners as, 149-50, 152; standard of living of, 151-52
Personnel Committee, 10, 15
Personnel Section, 15, 16, 110, 148, 150; and Nazis, 2
Piecework, 17-18
Pietzsch, Albert, 7, 10
Pischel, Werner, 202 (n. 20)
Pleiger, Paul, 57
Pohl, Oswald, 127
Polish Corridor, 58
Pomerania, 60, 61
Posen, 93
Prague, 121

Index 245

Prang, Alfred, 7, 11, 15, 16, 68, 79, 153, 155
Prause, Hans, 125
Prisoners, 116, 122
Protectorate of Bohemia and Moravia, 61
Prussia, 4
Purchasing Section (Main Administration), 20

Raasiku, 120
Radom, 121, 129
Railway Transportation Office West, 83
Rail Zeppelin (Schienen Zeppelin), 36
Regauging, 99
Reich Air Ministry, 35
Reich Air Protection Association, 85
Reich Association of German Technology, 9
Reich Chancellory, 7, 8, 22
Reich Coal Association, 143
Reich Defense Council, 69
Reich Economics Ministry, 85, 89, 152
Reich Finance Ministry, 29, 58, 60, 63, 134, 135, 152, 154, 155
Reich Interior Ministry, 114
Reich Labor Ministry, 95
Reich Office for German Travel, 11
Reichsautobahn-Gesellschaft, 42, 63, 154
Reichsbahn Central Office, 10, 16
Reichsbahn Central Office for Accounting (RZR), 62
Reichsbahn Central Office (RZA) for Mechanical Engineering (RZM), 32, 34
Reichsbahn Central Office (RZA) Berlin, 19, 32
Reichsbahn Central Office (RZA) Munich, 19
Reichsbahn Divisions (RBD), 2, 85; Altona, xiii, 108; Magdeburg, 2; Essen, 4, 6, 16, 87, 100, 160; Kattowitz, 6; Mainz, 15, 99, 108; Erfurt, 16; Nuremberg, 16; Saarbrücken, 16, 48, 49, 83, 158; Ludwigshafen, 18; Oldenburg, 18; Halle (Saale), 18, 100, 160; clearing of accounts of, 22; Trier, 48; Wuppertal, 48; Königsberg, 58, 94, 95, 108, 122; Karlsruhe, 83, 99, 158; Cologne, 83, 100, 126; Hamburg, 87, 108; Münster, 87, 150; Danzig, 94; Osten, 94; Posen, 94, 150, 159; Oppeln, 95, 100, 115, 123, 129, 134, 159, 160; Berlin, 100, 150, 160; Munich, 106, 161; Vienna, 122; Kassel, 150; Stuttgart, 150, 161

Reichsbahn Repair Works, 142
Reichsbank, 23, 62, 63, 64, 153
Reich Security Main Office, 114, 115
Reichs-Kraftwagen-Betriebsverband (RKB), 43, 45-46
Reichswehr, 11, 58
Reichswerke Hermann Göring, 72
Reich Transportation Divisions (RVD), 132, 134, 135
Reich Transportation Ministry, xi, 4, 5; responsibility for Reichsbahn of, 22-23; and military, 57; and Ostbahn, 81-82, 129; reorganization of, 109-10; and occupied east, 131-32
Reich War Ministry, 68
Reiner, Rolf, 8
Renninger, Karl, 7, 10, 15
Reparations, xii; Dawes Plan for, xii
Reval, 116
Rhenish Westfalian Coal Syndicate (RWKS), 92
Rhineland, xi, 48, 60
Riga, 116, 120, 127
Röbe, Ludwig, 48
Rolling stock: maintenance of, xiii; purchases of, 32, 34-35, 65-71, 110-13; from France, 84, 112, 137-38; from Belgium, 84, 112, 138. *See also specific types of rolling stock*
Rückel, Rolf, 126
Rudorf, Fritz, 161
Ruhr, 56, 92
Rumania, 110

SA, 5
Saar, 48
Saar Railways, 48
Sabotage, 135-36, 137, 152
Salzburg, 44
Sarter, Adolf, 16, 28, 89
Sauckel, Fritz, 122, 148
Schacht, Hjalmar, 5, 35, 51, 63, 153
Scheffler, Wolfgang, 127
Schelp, Fritz, 107, 108, 141
Schenker, 5, 11, 39, 43
Schmitz, Hermann, 8
Schnell, Paul, 117, 126
Schröder, Kurt Freiherr von, 7, 10, 13
Schultz, Johannes, 54

Schultze-Fielitz, Günther, 105
Schwerin von Krosigk, Lutz, Count, 51, 62, 153
Scientific management, 17
Seddin, exhibition at, 31
Seeckt, Hans von, 57
Seyss-Inquart, Artur, 101
Siebert, Ludwig, 19
Siemens, Carl Friedrich, xii, 7, 8, 9, 11, 24; and Nazis, 8-9; and passenger tariff cut, 29; and electrification, 35; and Autobahnen, 42
Siemens-Schuckert-Werke (SSW), 32
Silverberg, Paul, 5, 8
Slovakia, 61
Sobibor, 117, 119, 121, 127
Social Democratic Party, 2, 4
Société Nationale des Chemins de Fer Belges (SNCB), 83-84, 110, 136-38, 141, 164
Société Nationale des Chemins de Fer Franßais (SNCF), 83-84, 110, 136-37, 141, 164
Sommer, Gerhard, 6
Sommerlatte, Paul, 54
Speer, Albert, 102-6, 109, 161, 111
Spieß, Walter, 21-22, 162
Spiro, Ernst, 10
SS Economic-Administrative Main Office, 127
Stange, Otto, 117
State Railways (Länderbahnen), 65
State Treaty (Staatsvertrag), 19-20, 65, 192 (n. 72)
Stenger, Herbert, 14
Stettin, 93
Stieler, Carl, 1, 10, 11
Stroebe, Hermann, 35
Stuttgart, 44
Sudetenland, 49, 61

Tariffs, xii, xiii, 29, 38
—freight: increase in, 51; discounts on, 51-52; and demurrage charges, 88
Tax, transportation, 29, 60
Tecklenburg, Kurt, xii, 16, 21, 22, 108, 162
Telecommunications, 158
Teske, Hermann, 202 (n. 20)
Theresienstadt, 120, 123
Tilsit, 120

Todt, Fritz, 8, 41, 42-43, 57
Track: strengthening, 26; renewal of, 26, 62, 72-74, 156-57; removal to east of, 137, 156-57
Traffic: in Germany, 40-41, 85, 87, 99, 138-45; Ostbahn, 82, 131; with USSR, 89; in occupied west, 89, 138, 158; in occupied east, 134-35
—freight, 47-48, 50-53, 88-89, 138-44; less-than-carload (LCL), 39, 45, 47, 56, 89, 140; and occupation of Sudetenland, 49; economics of, 52; average haul of, 141
—passenger, 26-29, 37-38, 88, 144-45; market share of, 28-29; economics of, 29, 38
Traffic Section (Main Administration/RVM), 50, 51, 54, 117
Trains
—freight: speed of, 46-47; light, 47; backlog of, 53, 90, 142, 160
—passenger, 27; speed of, 26-27, 144; to Nuremberg rally, 27, 55; to Olympics, 28; added, 27; diesel, 36
Transchef. *See* Gercke, Rudolf
Treblinka, 116, 117, 121, 122, 123, 125
Treibe, Paul, 54, 139
T7, 58, 59

Union of German Locomotive Engineers, 9
Upper Silesia, 92, 159

Versailles, Treaty of, 57
Vienna, 121, 122
Vogt, Johannes, 40
Völkischer Beobachter, 16
Volkswagen, 29

Wagner, Robert Paul, 108
Wannsee, 31, 119
Warsaw, 115, 121, 127, 159
Waterways, inland, 89
Wechmann, Wilhelm, 16
Wehrmacht, 69; command staff of, 78
Weimar, 120
Weirauch, Wilhelm, 6, 11, 157
Welker, Johannes W., 7
Werkverkehr, 43, 46
Westwaggon, 36
Westwall, 49-50, 55

Wifo, 110
Willuhn, Franz, 7
Wilmowsky, Tilo Freiherr von, 9
Winter Crisis, 99–110, 113
Wittenberge, 34
Wolf, Paul, 4, 5
Wolkowysk, 117, 120, 122

Workers, 2, 10, 16–17, 152
Works Councils (Vertrauensräte), 17
Wumag, 32

Young Plan, xii, 59

ZVL. *See* Central Transportation Directorate